TABLE OF CO

BOOK 1
CANNING AND PRESERVING FOR PREPPERS

INTRODUCTION

Canning is a method of preserving foods by processing them in an airtight container. Canning foods goes back to the early 1800s when a French confectioner and brewer noticed that his foods did not spoil when cooked inside a sealed jar. From there, canning took off and became the most popular and effective way to preserve and store foods.

When foods are canned, their shelf life increases, making a perishable food safe to consume for about one to five years, depending on the food. It is a perfect way to preserve food if you have an abundance and do not want it to spoil. It is also a great method of storing food and preparing foods in advance.

Welcome to the world of home canning! Weather you have recently become interested in canning or have always wanted to learn how to can foods, this book is for you. You will learn about all the tools needed to can, the step-by-step process of how to can a wide variety of foods, and the safety guidelines to help you produce delicious and protected foods. By the end of this book, you will be able to can everything!

CHAPTER 1

UNDERSTANDING CANNING AND PRESERVING

HISTORY OF CANNING

Since longer prehistoric times, humans have tried to develop a new technique to keep their food last longer. At that time, they develop various methods like pickling, drying, salting, and smoking food to keep their food lasts for a long time. Canning is one of the most popular methods that help to preserve food for a long time. The food is processed and packed into airtight containers which help to increase the shelf life typically from 1 to 5 years and in some circumstances, it is preserved for a very long time. For example, canned dried lentils are found in the edible state after 30 years of a long time.

During the period of Napoleonic war (1803) Napoleon Bonaparte realizes that his soldiers were starving due to lack of fresh food because fresh foods are decaying during the war period. To find the permanent solution on food preservation Napoleon Bonaparte offered a reward of 12000-franc to those who find the cheap and continent way to preserve a large amount of food for his army and navy soldiers.

Nicolas Appert is young chief accepted this challenge and doing long research over food preservation and finally, in 1809 he found that the food cooked inside the sealed jar did not spoil for a very long period of time unless the jar seal was leaked, and food is exposed with oxygen. In Nicolas Appert method of a jar, sealing allows preserving soups, vegetables, dairy products, fruits, juices, syrup, and jellies. In 1810 French minister awarded Nicolas Appert for his experiment. Before 50 years Louis Pasteur explains the science behind sealing. When the food is heated in bottles or jar the microorganism in the food is vanished and the sealing protects food to enter any microorganism enter into food.

In 1810 instead of bottles and jar tin-coated irons are used and patented by Peter Durand. He also supplies a large quantity of canned food to Navy and army soldiers. In the 19th century, double stem technology is used to manufacture most of the modern can. Today the advanced water bath canning and pressure canning technology are used to preserve the food long-lasting.

BENEFITS OF CANNING

Canning food at home is a safe and satisfying procedure that is regaining popularity as food costs rise and people recognize the importance of safeguarding their food supplies. Home canning is a great way to improve your intake of local foods by preserving food. Eating locally necessitates eating foods in season, and canning allows you to capture the bounty of any particular crop in season and increase its availability year-round.

You can do home canning as a hobbyist or as a full-time enthusiast who preserves a significant portion of his or her food supply. You will reap many personal benefits, while being a better steward of the environment and supporting your local economy, whether you want to enjoy a couple of fun weekend chores putting up jam or significantly supplement your diet. In addition, given the state of the global food market, you'll save money as well, especially as time passes. Unlike grocery store food, which comes in disposable packaging, your home-preserved meals will be stored in jars that you may reuse time after time.

Excellent taste and quality

When you utilize high-quality food and follow the canning process correctly, you'll be able to make items that are superior to those found in the supermarket. Many recipes for home-canned food are delectable, and the quality is unrivaled.

You'll have complete control over the ingredients because you'll be able to see where your food comes from when you can it at home. Your own garden and fruit trees, as well as local organic farms and any local farm, are excellent sources of fruits and vegetables. You can hand-pick your food at the peak of ripeness from any of these sources. You will also decrease your exposure to Bisphenol A, which is used to line the cans of many mass-produced foods. Bisphenol A is an endocrine disruptor, and its potential danger to humans is becoming more widely recognized.

Local economic support

When you buy directly from local growers, you are putting money into the hands of locals. Local growers prefer selling from their own farms or market stands since they are not bound by the pricing established by large commodities buyers. This also permits local growers, particularly small ones, to maintain profitability, which is beneficial to the local economy.

Reduce your carbon impact

The food we eat requires a significant amount of energy to produce and transport. Pesticides, herbicides, and petrochemical fertilizers are also used in highly industrialized agriculture. All of these variables affect the ecosystem and limit the soil's future ability to produce food, resulting in increased scarcity, lower quality, and higher asset prices. When you buy local food products and can it at home, you are avoiding a large portion of the transportation costs connected with moving food across continents due to spent fuel. Yes, home canning consumes energy, but this pales in comparison to transporting food halfway across the country to supply a shop shelf. Lowering the amount of food, you consume which comes from distant locations reduces the amount of gasoline consumed. Also, while purchasing local produce, look for growers who employ environmentally friendly, sustainable producing practices.

Feeling of accomplishment

Once you start canning food, you will feel very satisfied. You'll feel as if you've accomplished something significant in your life, because you have! For most of human history, individuals have spent a large amount of time and effort ensuring their food supplies. I'm not saying that we all go back to digging for roots in the field, but most people have a strong desire to help with food harvesting and preparation. Sitting in an SUV for fast food from a drive-through window does not satisfy. It just encourages excessive energy usage for low-quality goods.

TOOLS FOR CANNING AND PRESERVING

There are several tools that are necessary to canning. Many of them are unique to this form of cooking so you may need to invest in a few new kitchen supplies. However, almost everything in canning is reusable. From the pot you cook the jars in to the jars themselves, so much can be used time and time again, making your investment well worth the money. Choose quality products to ensure that they last you a lifetime of canning.

Jars

There are many sizes and brands of glass canning jars out there. From those with a smaller opening to wide mouth jars, quarts to pints, you can find them all! You always want to start your canning project with clean jars; however, glass jars can be reused again and again so save them after you use the contents. Make sure each jar is free of cracks or chips as this can interfere with the canning process.

Lids and Rings

Canning lids are one of the few things that you cannot reuse; they should only be used one time and then discarded. The metal lid has a rubber ring on it that is responsible for making an airtight seal, keeping the food safely preserved. Using the lid more than once can damage the rubber and make the seal more penetrable, making the food more susceptible to bacteria.

Metal rings, however, can be used time and time again until they become rusty. If you see any rust on your jar rings, dispose of them and use new rings. Be sure the rings and lids you choose fit the jars you have on hand. Different brands of lids and jars may not work together so it is best to stick with one brand for all your canning needs.

Headspace Measuring Tool and Air Bubble Remover

This is one of those tools that is not essential to canning but works fantastically. The tool has a small ruler on one end and a tip on the other end to help remove air bubbles. Headspace is the amount of room left from the top of the food to the top of the jar. It is essential to have the right amount of headspace to allow for the food to expand during cooking but not so much space that there is too much air in the jar, potentially giving bacteria space to grow.

Removing air bubbles from the food is also essential for preventing bacterial growth. The less air, the less chance bacteria have to grow. This tool helps you manage the air in each jar easily. However, you can always opt to use a simple ruler and a butter knife to remove air.

Jar Funnel

Using a funnel to pour the food into the jars is the cleanest way to fill your jars. It also prevents waste as you will spill less food. Many canning funnels can also act as a headspace measurer.

Magnetic Lid Grabber

Lids and metal rings are often sterilized before being placed on top of the jars by being simmered in water. The magnet on the lid grabber will pick the lids up right out of the hot water and help you place them onto the jars without ever having to touch the hot metal.

Jar Grabber

A jar grabber will help you take the jars out of the canner easily. The jars will be extremely hot after the canning process is complete and they will also be wet (meaning a simple dish towel won't help hold them!). Jar grabbers will lift the jar out of the canner, holding onto the lip under the metal ring.

Ladle

You will need a ladle or large spoon to scoop the food into the jars. A slotted spoon can be good to use as well as it can help balance the ratio of solids to liquids in each jar.

Dishtowel

When you take the jars out of the canner, you want to put them onto a dish towel rather than directly on your countertop. The extremely hot jars can damage your countertop if you are not careful, causing granite to crack or stoneware to split. You can also opt to place the hot jars on a cutting board, raising them up off the countertop as well.

Clean Paper Towels or Washcloths

After the food is scooped into the jars, the rims of the jars need to be completely wiped clean. This will help seal the jars and ensure there are no exposed food particles. Clean paper towels or terry washcloths work perfectly for this.

Distilled White Vinegar

Vinegar naturally kills bacteria—canning's number one enemy! Wiping the rim of your jars with vinegar before placing the lids on will prevent bacteria growth. Adding a splash of vinegar to your canning water will also prevent mineral deposits on your jars and keep your canner clean.

Timer

Canning is all about proper timing as jars need to be processed for a certain amount of time to ensure the safety of the food. You will need an accurate timer to help guide you.

Permanent Marker

After your canning is complete and your jars are ready to be put in your pantry, you will want to label and date each jar. You want to remember what is in each jar and how long it will be good for. You can also use jar labels, but a regular old marker will work just fine.

SAFETY CRITERIA FOR EACH PRESERVATION SYSTEM

There are a few safety tips that you should follow when you start canning and preserving foods from home. Canning is a great way to store and preserve foods, but it can be risky if not done correctly. Nonetheless, if you follow these tips, you will be able to can foods in a safe manner.

Choose the Right Canner

The first step to safe home canning is choosing the right canner. First off, know when to use a pressure canner or a water bath canner.

Use a pressure canner that is designed for canning and preserving foods. There are several types of canner out there and some are just for cooking food, not for preserving food and processing jars. Be sure that you have the right type of equipment. Make sure your pressure canner is the right size. If your canner is too small, the jars may be undercooked. Always opt for a larger canner as the pressure on the bigger pots tends to be more accurate, and you will be able to take advantage of the larger size and can more foods at once!

Before you begin canning, check that your pressure canner is in good condition. If your canner has a rubber gasket, it should be flexible and soft. If the rubber is dry or cracked, it should be replaced before you start canning. Be sure your canner is clean and the small vents in the lid are free of debris. Adjust your canner for high altitude processing if needed.

Once you are sure your canner is ready to go and meets all these guidelines, it is time to start canning!

Opt for a Screw Top Lid System

There are many kinds of canning jars that you can choose to purchase. However, the only type of jar that is approved by the USDA is a mason jar with a screw-top lid. These are designated "preserving jars" and are considered the safest and most effective option for home preserving uses.

Some jars are not thought to be safe for home preservation despite being marketed as canning jars. Bail Jars, for example, have a two-part wire clasp lid with a rubber ring in between the lid and jar. While these were popular in the past, it is now thought that the thick rubber and tightly closed lid does not provide a sufficient seal, leading to a higher potential for botulism. Lightening Jars should not be used for canning as they are simply glass jars with glass lids, with no rubber at all. That will not create a good seal!

Reusing jars from store-bought products is another poor idea. They may look like they're in good condition, but they are typically designed to be processed in a commercial facility. Most store-bought products do not have the two-part band and lid system which is best for home canning. Also, the rubber seal on a store-bought product is likely not reusable once you open the original jar. You can reuse store-bought jars at home for storage but not for canning and preserving.

Check Your Jars, Lids, and Bands

As you wash your jars with soapy water, check for any imperfections. Even new jars may have a small chip or crack and need to be discarded. You can reuse jars again and again as long as they are in good condition.

The metal jar rings are also reusable; however, you should only reuse them if they are rust free and undented. If your bands begin to show signs of wear, consider investing in some new ones.

Jar lids need to be new as the sealing compound on the lid can disintegrate over time. When you store your jars in damp places (like in a basement or canning cellar) the lids are even more likely to disintegrate. Always use new lids to ensure that your canning is successful.

Check for Recent Canning Updates

Canning equipment has changed over the years, becoming more high tech and therefore more efficient at processing foods. In addition to the equipment becoming more advanced, there have also been many scientific improvements, making canning safer when the proper steps are taken. For example, many people used to sterilize their jars before pressure canning. While this is still okay to do, it is not necessary as science has shown that any bacteria in the jars will die when heated to such a high temperature in a pressure canner. Sterilization is an extra step that you just don't need!

Make sure that your food preservation information is all up to date and uses current canning guidelines. Avoid outdated cookbooks and reassess "trusted family methods" to make sure they fit into the most recent criteria for safe canning. When in doubt, check with the US Department of Agriculture's Complete Guide to Home Canning which contains the most recent, up-to-date canning tips.

Pick the Best Ingredients

When choosing food to can, always get the best food possible. You want to use high quality, perfectly ripe produce for canning. You will never end up with a jar of food better than the product itself, so picking good ingredients is important to the taste of your final product. Also, products that past its prime can affect the ability to can it. If strawberries are overripe, your jam may come out too runny. If your tomatoes are past their prime, they may not have a high enough pH level to be processed in a water bath. Pick your ingredients well and you will make successful preserved foods.

Clean Everything

While you may know that your jars and lids need to be washed and sanitized, don't forget about the rest of your tools. Cleaning out your canner before using it is essential, even if you put it away clean. Make sure to wipe your countertop well, making sure there are no crumbs or residue. Wash your produce with clean, cold water and don't forget to wash your hands! The cleaner everything is, the less likely you are to spread bacteria onto your jarred foods

Follow Your Recipe

Use recipes from trusted sources and be sure to follow them to the letter. Changing the amount of one or two ingredients may alter the balance of acidity and could result in unsafe canning (especially when using a water bath canner). Use the ingredients as directed and make very few changes—none if possible.

Adhere to the processing times specified by your recipe. Sometimes the times may seem a little long, but the long processing time is what makes these products safe to store on the shelf. The processing time is the correct amount of time needed to destroy spoilage organisms, mold spores, yeast and pathogens in the jar. So, as you may have guessed, it is extremely important to use the times that are written in your recipe as a hard rule.

Cool the Jars

Be sure that you give your jars 12 hours to cool before testing the seal. If you test the seal too early, it may break as the jar is still warm, making the rubber pliable. Be sure to cool the jars away from a window or fan as even a slight breeze may cause the hot jars to crack. Once cool, remove the metal band, clean it and save it for your next canning project.

Don't Risk It

If you suspect that the food you have canned is bad, don't try to eat it, just toss it! Each time you open a jar of canned food, inspect it and check for the following:

- Is the lid bulging, swollen, or leaking at all?
- If the jar cracked or damaged?
- Does the jar foam when opened?
- Is the food inside discolored or moldy?

Does the food smell bad?

If you observe any of these warning signs in a food that you have canned, throw it away. Do not taste it to check if it is good. It is not worth risking your health to try the food after seeing one of the above signs.

Luckily, it is fairly easy to spot a jar of food that has gone bad. Home-canned food can spoil for many reasons. A dent in the lid, a small crack in the jar, an improper seal, or not enough processing time are all common errors that may cause canned foods to go bad. Follow the exact canning directions and hopefully, you will never get a bad jar of food!

CHAPTER 2

FAQ'S ON CANNING & PRESERVING FOODS

This book has tried to cover all areas that a beginner or newbie in canning and preserving food would want to know. Nevertheless, there may still be some questions that are hanging in your mind. Here are the most frequently asked questions and their answers regarding canning and preserving foods.

As an interested beginner who would like to take this skill into a higher level, is there a canning class or course that one can take?

Anybody can preserve or can foods without formal education. For those who would like to have advanced canning skills, canning classes are oftentimes offered in some grocery stores, kitchen stores, cooking schools, community centers, and sometimes, even in libraries. You could also search online for correspondence that offers this course. Be careful with blogs or articles that teach canning techniques. Some of these articles may contain ideas or suggestions that go contrary to the recommendations of USDA. If in doubt, refer to the USDA manual or contact an authorized person.

What is the shelf life of canned food?

Properly sealed canned and preserved foods placed in a cool, dry place, with no signs of spoilage inside and out, are considered safe to consume for at least a year. However, canned foods stored near a furnace, in indirect sunlight, a range or anywhere warm can decrease shelf life. It would be safe to consume within a few weeks until a couple of months only. Placing the jars or cans in damp areas may corrode cans and this can cause leakage, causing the food to be contaminated and unsafe to eat.

Can you process two layers of jars at one time?

Yes, this can be done. The jars at the upper layer would enjoy the same benefits as those in the bottom. The temperature is equally distributed making it safe for all jars, whether in the upper and lower layer. Just make sure that you place a wire rack between the layers to allow the circulation of water and steam around the jars. Also, when using bath-water canning method, make sure that the water is up to one inch above the tops of the jars in the upper layer. If you are using a pressure canner, the water should be 2 to 3 inches from the bottom. As always, comply with the processing time and required temperature.

During processing, some liquid of the contents were lost. What should be done about it?

If the liquid loss is minimal, there is nothing to worry about. The food will not spoil and the seal will not be affected. It may cause slight discoloration of the food, however, but that's about it. However, if the liquid loss is at least half of the original amount, then the most that you can do is to refrigerate it and consume within 2 to 3 days.

What is kettle canning and is this safe to use?

In this method, the foods to be preserved are cooked in an ordinary household kettle. After that, the foods are placed into hot jars, covered, and sealed. You would notice that no processing is done in this method. In addition, the temperature when using the kettle canning method is not high enough to eliminate the harmful bacteria that may be in the food. Also, during the transfer of food from the kettle to the jars, microorganisms can enter the food and cause spoilage and worse, food poisoning, later on. Therefore, the safety of food is not guaranteed. The kettle canning method is not included in the recommendation of USDA with regards to canning.

Why do some jars break during canning?

There are many reasons breakage occurs during the process of canning. Here are five reasons:

The glass of the jar is not tempered. A tempered or toughened glass underwent a process that increased its strength and ability to withstand heat compared to normal glass. Before buying commercial food jars, make sure that they are manufactured for home canning.

Another reason is using jars with hairline cracks. These cracks are so thin that they can be missed or overlooked. Such jars would not be able to stand the extreme heat during processing time.

Not placing a wire rack on the bottom of the pot or canner could also cause the jars to break.

Putting newly cooked food into cold jars. The difference in the temperature between the food and the jars could lead to breakage. That is why it is advised that the jars should be maintained on a hot temperature before filling them with hot food.

Jars with unheated or raw food placed directly into boiling water can also break because of the sudden change in temperature. It is better to use hot water first and let it achieve boiling point after several minutes.

An article said that a jam or jelly with molds could still be used. Simply remove or scoop out the parts with molds. The rest would still be okay for consumption. Is this true?

Molds can cause an increase in the pH of the food. For instance, if the canned food is high acid, then because of the raised pH, it could become low acid. This places the preserved food into the risk of having botulism and other bacterial growth. Therefore, all canned foods with molds should be disposed of properly. Follow the proper waste disposal for spoiled canned food.

Can canning be done for those people with special diets?

Some people, because of their medical conditions, would not be allowed to consume some of the canned foods because of some ingredients like sugar and salt. Sugar is discouraged among Diabetic people due to the effect of increased blood sugar with the intake of simple sugar.

On the other hand, salts are always restricted among people with cardiovascular disorders as this can cause increased high blood pressure as more body water is retained because of salts. Still, canning foods can be done for these people even in the absence of salt or sugar. However, the color, texture, flavor of these canned foods will differ from those with sugar or salt in them, as expected. Other people find these special diet canned foods to be less acceptable and less appealing.

To can vegetables, meats, seafood, or tomatoes without salt, proceed with the regular canning minus the salt. This method is allowed, as salts are not considered as preservatives, hence the safety of food is still guaranteed even in the absence of salt. Salt substitutes can be offered upon serving to make the preserved food taste better.

What is the future of canning and preserving foods?

The trend all over the world right now is towards healthy food and lifestyle. You can see everything "organic" from cosmetics, hair products, food, baby products, and even processed foods. People prefer "fresh" than canned or commercially prepared processed foods.

This is where home canning and preserving fresh fruits, meats, poultry, salsa, vegetables, sauces, and what-have-you enter the picture. This is a combination of being healthy and modern, rolled into one. It meets the requirements of being healthy and at the same time, lasting longer on the shelf or pantry. It is ready to eat, answering the need for convenience and saving precious time.

More and more people are going into canning and preserving food. The threat of not having enough good food to eat in the future due to excessive wasting and unnecessary throwing of food today has found its solution in canning.

CHAPTER 3

WHY GO THROUGH THE EFFORT OF CANNING?

To get the benefits of canning, you don't need a vast garden or a large-scale business. Even if your garden produces a few jars of your favorite vegetables, canning will reduce waste and preserve your crop, primarily if your garden produces more summer vegetables than you can consume right away. It can help you save your money on groceries while also giving you a sense of pride and self-sufficiency in food storage. You also control the components, including additives and preservatives, because you can find your vegetables. It can be pretty beneficial for both mindful eating and unique dietary requirements. Regardless of why you choose to can, you must understand when and how to can summer vegetables properly.

HOW TO PREVENT DARKENING FOOD

Preventing darkening food in the jars is one of the most accessible can problems to fix. Here's what you need to do. Check the recommended processing time for the recipe that you're using because you need to know it. Water or syrup should completely cover anything you're canning. Before closing the jars, be sure to remove any air bubbles and utilize the required headspace depending on the recipe.

FLOATING FLUID

Do you have any jars with floating fruits in them? Fruits and tomatoes that have been over-processed might lose their natural pectin. Fruit may also float if the fruit is lighter weight than the sugar syrups or if it has been inappropriately packed.

What to Do If Your Fruit Is Floating

It's a simple repair if you detect floating fruit. The essential thing is to follow the instructions for processing periods to prevent over-processing the delicate fruits. Also, make sure the fruit is firm and ripe. Before packaging the fruit, warm it up. Fruits, unlike vegetables, should not be packed uncooked. Use a light or medium syrup, and compress the fruit carefully to prevent crushing it.

Canning, like gardening, is a skill that takes time to master. Making errors is an integral part of learning a new skill, so don't give up if you commit one of the most frequent canning blunders. Learn how to correct and avoid these blunders so that your canned foods endure for years in your cupboard.

CONCLUSION

Canning is also a great way to save money. You can preserve foods in bulk when they are at their cheapest (typically at the peak of the season when in abundance). Then, you will have the food on hand for whenever you like. You can pay the discount price up front and enjoy the canned food later, when the prices may have risen. Also, purchasing in bulk typically will reduce the cost of any food.

All canning is essentially the same; food is placed inside a clean jar and then sealed with a lid. The jars are then placed inside a water bath cooker or pressure cooker and processed (cooked) until the food reaches a high enough temperature to kill any micro bacteria. The jars are then cooled, at which time the lid will seal completely, and the canning process will be complete! Of course, this process will be covered in much greater detail throughout the book, but the general concept is this easy.

By now, you are likely ready to dive right into canning and get your first satisfying batch of canned foods made and on your shelf. So, let's begin! It is time to learn all about canning foods right in your own kitchen.

Canning and preserving foods at home is an amazing hobby that is beneficial and fun. It can help you save money on food, capture foods when they are at their peak ripeness and help you fill your pantry with foods that you love. Canning is completely safe to do at home when you follow all the necessary guidelines and it is also just a fun, satisfying pastime. There is nothing quite as pleasing as a cupboard full of newly canned foods!

If you have been wanted to try canning foods, now is the time to do it. Think of what food you would like to preserve and then dive right in! Start with basic water bath canning and then work your way up to using a pressure canner. Or, dive right in and start pressure canning like a seasoned canner! No matter what you choose to create first, you are bound to be successful when you follow the steps in this guide. One key to canning that you always should follow is to have fun!

Hello, my fellow prepping enthusiast! :)

<u>Thank you for your purchase!</u>

Scan this QR-CODE to get your
FREE BONUS GUIDE
to enhance your food preservation skills
and boost your self-reliance journey.

Best wishes on your prepping adventures!

Tyler

BOOK 2

DEHYDRATOR COOKBOOK FOR PREPPERS

1000 Days of Delicious Homemade Recipes forFruit,
Vegetables, Jerky, Mushrooms and More

INTRODUCTION

Dehydrated food retains many of the nutrients of fresh food far better than other methods of food preservation. Fresh food can lose up to 50 percent of its nutritional value sitting in the refrigerator. But dried food retains all the antioxidants and minerals of fresh food, and most of the vitamins. Dehydrated food weighs less and takes up less space in the pantry, making it ideal for road trips, hiking, emergency preparedness, and weekday meal prep. Let's dive in!

Dried food is typically brittle and can be snapped in half when bent. If food is still moist and pliable after drying, it should be returned to the dryer.

The easiest way to preserve food is by dehydrating or drying it. This method has been used for several years to help food last without being refrigerated. It is one of the least expensive and fastest ways to store your harvest for later use. Drying will also lighten the weight of foods prepared for backpacking and camping.

Dehydrating spectacularly lessens your food's moisture contents, making it last longer and still maintain its delicious taste. This is because it lessens the moisture contents of your food to between five to twenty percent, and the bacterium causing food decay cannot survive within that range. When you remove moisture from the foods you love to eat, you have also automatically extended their shelf-life.

As moisture leaves food, it often shrivels up and takes on a leathery, tough texture. The skin will wrinkle as the food inside shrinks. Compare a raisin to a grape taken straight off the vine and you get the picture. Grapes lose a lot of volume as the moisture inside them evaporates and they become raisins.

The health benefits of dehydrating are undeniable; this method retains up to 90 percent of the vitamins, minerals, and antioxidants in food. Preserving food by freezing retains about the same nutrition as dehydrating, but frozen food has a shorter shelf life. Dehydrated food is nutritionally superior to canned food; the high temperatures of the canning process deplete vitamin C, vitamin A, and many of the B vitamins.

Dehydrating allows you to control the ingredients in your food. You can choose how much sugar to put in the fruit leather or how much salt to put in your beef jerky. I especially like that you can also control cross-contamination with such common allergens as wheat, peanuts, or soy.

Drying food allows me to be creative both when preserving and using the ingredients in meals and snacks. It also bolsters my confidence, knowing my family is prepared for emergencies with safely stored healthy food, even if the power goes out.

This book is divided into three parts. In the first section, you'll find the basics to help you get started, even if you've never used a dehydrator. You'll learn about the equipment you need, some important techniques to ensure that your food is safe and free of bad bacteria, and how to pretreat food to ensure that the nutrients, texture, flavor, and color are preserved both in drying and in storage.

CHAPTER 1

UNDERSTANDING DEHYDRATING

Dehydration which is popularly known as 'drying' is a long-practiced method for preserving foods. It can also be referred as the process of removing water through evaporation from a solid or liquid food. The aim of this is to arrive at a solid material that has been sufficiently water-reduced. This process consists of reducing the level of food moisture into smaller levels in order to extend the lifespan of the food. It requires adding different forms of energy to the food.

Note that dehydration does not include mechanical pressing of liquid foods. In most cases, Hot-air is used to add heat to the food and to reduce its moisture.

It is very easy for pathogenic bacteria to survive comfortably in the unfavorable environment of dried foods. This means that once your dried food is rehydrated and eaten, it could cause you food poisoning. Of course, you would not want to suffer food poisoning, all in the name of preserving your foods for later use.

What should you do then to prevent this when drying your food? Make use of high-quality materials with low contaminants when drying your foods. High-quality materials with low contaminants are materials and tools specifically made for dehydrating foods. Also, ensure proper sanitation of all tools and surfaces and ensure that the storage condition of the dried food is one that prevents contact with dust, rodents, insects and other house insects.

When you decide to dehydrate your food to make it last longer, then you have numerous options available for you. You could dry your food by air, vacuum, inert gas, steaming, or by directly applying heat to the food. Usually, the most popular and acceptable means of drying is by air. This is okay for obvious reasons. Using this method allows your food to dry gradually, plus it is very convenient. And, yes, air is very plentiful, and free! Allowing your food to dry gradually by using air prevents scorching and discoloration of your food, which is popular with other drying systems.

Dehydrating foods started as far back as times when early men spread their harvests or hunts out in the sun for sun drying. It is one of the oldest methods of preservation, as the prehistoric men were fond of drying some seeds before planting.

Fish, meats and food plants have been preserved over the years by drying them in the sun or naturally spreading them in the desert heat, across different desert areas.

In more recent times, American Indians stored their meats by laying them under the sun. The people of China also dried their eggs from the sunshine and the Japanese dried rice and fish under the sun's rays as well. During the Second World War, there was a great need to move food in bulk from place to place and this challenge ignited the developments of modern strategies on preserving foods, hence dehydration. In the year 1975 however, the French made a major breakthrough in the development of hot-air dehydration, which is the drying of foods through the method of blowing hot air over them.

Browning reactions are one of the most common chemical reactions that occur in dried foods. They occur when chemical compounds in the food being dried react with compounds in the air. Browning is usually considered undesirable because it can change the taste of the food as it changes its appearance. A little known fact about browning is it can sometimes damage the nutritional value of the food as the color changes.

Many fruits and vegetables undergo enzymatic browning when they're cut open and their flesh is exposed to the air. This sort of browning also occurs when produce is dropped, hit with something or otherwise damaged. It's a stress response brought on by the rapid conversion of chemical compounds in the flesh into brown melanin. The enzymes that cause browning can be deactivated through careful use of heat, acids or chemicals like sulphites. Blanching foods and/or exposing them to citric acids before setting them out to dry can inhibit browning enough to where it isn't much of a problem.

THE WONDER OF DEHYDRATING

A centuries-old technology, dehydrating removes moisture from fresh food so bacteria cannot grow. Dehydrating preserves your food for a year or more, without refrigeration. With 90 percent of the moisture removed, the food intensifies in flavor, concentrates its nutritional value, and takes up less room in your pantry.

In areas where the relative humidity is 30 percent or less, fruit naturally dries on the tree or vine, right in the garden. Airflow and heat are both essential to the dehydrating process. When left to nature, grapes turn into raisins slowly, dependent on local weather conditions. But in many areas the humidity is too high for this natural process to be successful. A food dehydrator controls the variables of temperature and humidity, speeding up the drying process and ensuring an end product that is safely preserved.

The first food-drying machine was invented in France in 1795 to aid Napoleon's war efforts. It used circulating airflow and temperature control to speed up the dehydration process. Dried food was useful for traveling armies because it was lightweight, retained its nutritional value, and took up less space than its fresh counterpart.

During the two world wars, dehydrated food was essential to provisioning the troops, leading to an increased demand and further innovation on an industrial scale. In fact, instant mashed potatoes were born from the war effort with the technology gained from dehydrating food for the troops.

Interest in home dehydrating was slower to take hold until the mid 1970s, when the back-to-the-land movement increased interest in home-scale food preservation. In response to this increased demand, several electric dehydrators for home use were patented that offered both airflow and heat.

When a recipe calls for blanching fruit or vegetables, it's usually done to stop or slow enzymatic action on the produce. Foods that need blanching should be processed quickly after cutting into them. The enzymatic action will initiate as soon as the flesh of the fruit or vegetable is exposed to oxygen. If you're planning on drying large amounts of produce, it's best to do so in smaller batches. Trying to do it all in one batch might result in the produce you cut in the beginning degrading to the point it can't be used by the time you get around to blanching it.

Color loss can also come about as a result of drying. This effect is especially pronounced when high heat or sunlight is used to dry leafy greens and brightly-colored vegetables that get their color from carotenoids, which are fat-soluble pigments. Pigments will often fade during drying and can further fade during storage.

Dried foods change texture when the moisture is removed. This is due to a number of factors, including the loss of moisture, changes to the cellulose material and degradation of some of the compounds found in the food. When foods are dried at too high a temperature, the outside of the food can dry before all the moisture leaves the inside, creating what's known as case-hardened foods. They appear dry on the outside, but there's still too much moisture inside the hard outer shell.

While it may sound like food drying is an invasive process that drastically changes food, it actually isn't that bad once you get past the physical changes. It's the least damaging food preservation technique and foods that are dried retain most of their nutritional value. Other preservation techniques involve the use of extreme heat or extreme cold, which is even more damaging to the structure and chemical composition of foods subjected to them.

From a technical standpoint, most food starts degrading as soon as it is harvested. Once a plant or animal is no longer alive, it starts to lose nutritional value. This loss is slow at first, but quickly accelerates into rapid degeneration once the food begins to spoil. Anything done to prepare the food like heating it, washing it, slicing it or otherwise processing it further damages the food.

Dehydrators for home use offer continuous circulating airflow, temperature control, food-safe tray materials, and special aftermarket add-ons like silicone sheets to make it easier to make leathers and snacks. The latest digital models allow for temperature control between sections of the dehydrator, as well as programmable temperature and time variations for different foods. With electronic precision, you can put the food in, set the cycle, and go about your day.

WHAT SHOULD (AND SHOULDN'T) BE DEHYDRATED

Fruits and vegetables are the easiest and most forgiving foods to process. Dried fruit can be eaten without rehydrating. It's a nutrient-dense food that makes an ideal snack. It can be added to oatmeal, muffins, and hot cereal to improve the nutritional quality of simple meals.

Dried vegetables are convenient for soups, stews, sauces, and dips where they can be rehydrated in the cooking process. Aromatic vegetables such as onions, garlic, carrots, celery, and peppers can be used as ingredients in meals on their own or combined into spice blends to add flavor to other dishes.

Lean meat, poultry, and fish can also be dehydrated, provided a few precautions are taken with these high-protein foods. When dehydrating, temperatures should reach 165°F (74°C) to kill any spoilage organisms. If your dehydrator doesn't go this high, place the food in the dehydrator at 145°F for at least 4 hours, until it is done. Then put it in a preheated oven at 275°F for 10 minutes so that it reaches an internal temperature of 165°F (74°C).

Cured ham can be successfully dehydrated, but pork should never be dehydrated at home or used for jerky. The temperatures used in a home dehydrator cannot destroy the trichinella parasite nor other harmful bacteria that are commonly found in pork.

Raw eggs and milk products do not dehydrate well. They are prone to bacterial contamination at dehydrating temperatures.

Fatty and oily foods cannot be dried adequately in a home dehydrator. The fat won't dry properly and as a result, the food spoils quickly. This includes high-fat foods such as avocados and olives.

When dehydrating meat, you should remove all visible fat. Only lean meat, poultry, or fish should be used for dehydrating. Ground meat should be no more than 10 percent fat. Fish like salmon and mackerel have too high a fat content to make them good candidates for dehydrating; they can be dried for short-term storage, but they should not be used for long-term storage due to the increased risk of spoilage.

Foods high in sugar or alcohol won't dry properly. Foods like alcohol-soaked fruit, honey, or candy tend to absorb moisture from the air and resist dehydration.

BENEFITS OF DEHYDRATING

Everyone comes to dehydrating for different reasons. Some like the convenience and portability of dried food. Others use their dehydrator to preserve their garden veggies. Still others use their dehydrator to make food for hiking or camping trips. I use my dehydrator to preserve produce in season, when it is at the peak of freshness and nutrition. But regardless of your reason for dehydrating food, there are several benefits to dehydrating food that are universal.

Reduction of Spoilage

Dehydrating helps reduce unnecessary food waste. You can stop putting leftovers in the refrigerator and then tossing them in the garbage or compost pile a week or two later when they grow green fuzz. Both leftover vegetables and main dishes can be dehydrated, preserving your investment in healthy food, plus you'll have future meals for busy days. Dehydrating also allows you to stock up on produce discounts like overripe bananas or onions past their prime. Many grocery stores and produce stands have discount bins where "seconds," like citrus fruit, apples, sweet peppers, and tomatoes are offered at significant savings. Dehydrating these foods helps you stock your pantry while saving money.

A church in my community collects excess produce from local grocery stores, dehydrates it, and turns it into dried soup mixes and dried fruit for food banks in several nearby towns. Using a commercial dehydrator with 20 trays, they divert 9,000 pounds of produce from the local landfill each month and convert it into nourishing food for hundreds of families.

Extended Lifespan

When foods are dehydrated, they last longer because the moisture is reduced and the dry food does not encourage the survival of bacteria. The absence of bacteria keeps food in good shape and this can last for as long as three months. When food items are dehydrated, they are sometimes converted into substances that can last a lifetime. Examples are spices such as cinnamon and curry powder which is derived from the dehydration and grinding of curry leaves. In most cases, spices like this can last for several years without getting spoiled.

Waste Reduction

When foods spoil, they reduce the amount of food available for consumption. Some food preservative methods usually give a very short extension before the spoilage of food. In many cases when we buy raw materials in the markets, the ability and knowledge to store them in good conditions help us keep the foods for a long time.

Improvement in Food Taste

The application of heat to reduce the water tastes in foods brings out the original taste of the other constituents of the food. The process of dehydration greatly improves the taste of food. When foods are water-filled, they are sometimes tasteless or acrid. When fruits are dried, the real taste is felt. In most cases, food tastes better when they are dehydrated.

Easy Storage

The fact that dehydrating foods make them easy to be stored is a great advantage of the process. When large bulks of foods are preserved in smaller packages, like the case of milk dehydrated into powder, it aids transportation and storekeeping. Through dehydration, storage is easier as it takes up lesser spaces.

Taste (and nutrition)

Dehydrated foods often taste better than when they're fresh, because their flavors are intensified. Moisture literally "waters down" flavor, so dried fruits taste much sweeter, even without added sugar. Dehydrated mushrooms are so flavorful that many chefs use them as a spice, not a vegetable, while a small handful of sun-dried tomato flavors an entire pasta dish. The icing on the cake is that dehydrated food also maintains their nutritional value. Removing the moisture doesn't destroy healthy vitamins, minerals, or calories.

Clean-eating

You can buy dried fruits, vegetables, and other snacks at the store, but more often than not, they're full of sugar and artificial ingredients. Even though dried foods last longer than fresh ones, packaged versions usually contain preservatives to make them last even longer. This is especially true for dried meats, which are not only highly-processed, they're usually extremely salty. Processed meat has also been classified as carcinogenic, which means it contains chemicals that might cause certain types of cancer! For all of this, you also pay a pretty penny. Making your own dehydrated snacks at home means you have total control over what goes in and what stays out.

Easy to carry around

There aren't a lot of truly portable snacks and the ones that are, like fruits and vegetables, got easily squished and bruised. When they're dry, they're hardened and much more durable. They also don't take up much space in a bag and they don't squirt juice everywhere when you're trying to eat them. Dehydrated food is the way to go if you're always on the run.

Dehydrating food at home saves money and space, makes clean and tasty snacks, and reduces food waste.

Preservation of Nutrients

Dehydrating food maintains the nutrients in the food before they are dehydrated. Nutrients such as minerals, vitamins and enzymes are absolutely preserved during dehydration. Dehydration is the only method that can ascertain the preservation of nutrients in food particles. Cooking and other preservative methods often lead to loss of nutrients. The entire essence of consuming food is to get benefits from the nutrients, if these nutrients are reduced; the essence of consuming the food has been lost.

Absence of Chemicals

The only substance needed to dehydrate food is the heat added to the food material. Unlike some other preservative methods, it does not involve the addition of chemicals. Dehydrating food therefore makes it safe from the fear of consuming poisonous substances because nothing but heat is added. The dehydrated food will only maintain its initial nutrients and that makes it perfect for consumption.

Economic and Financial Advantages

Dehydrating food makes food last longer. As such, people may buy food in bulk or harvest large quantity of produce and dehydrate it in batches, making it a very convenient method.

Reliability for Emergency Situations

Dehydrating keeps a person prepared for any emergency that requires immediate need for dehydrated food. Dehydrated food can be very useful for individuals traveling in extreme conditions, such as for mountain climbers and cross-country bike riders.

More Control over Food Contents

When you prepare your snacks and staple foods at home using your dehydrator, you control every step of the process—especially the ingredients. Healthy snack foods that are low in sugar and salt, or food without allergens, can be made easily in your dehydrator. You can adapt recipes to ensure there is no cross-contamination of food, making dehydrating ideal for families who deal with food allergies.

One member of my family has a serious wheat allergy. Almost all commercially dried or freeze-dried food has an ingredient warning "may contain wheat." But by drying our own produce and using our dehydrator for snacks and travel food, I have confidence that the food he eats is safe from cross-contamination, even when we are away from home.

Peanut, soy, milk, wheat, and other common allergens are easier to exclude when you provision your pantry with ingredients that you dehydrate yourself. When you make your own meals and snacks from scratch, you'll no longer need a magnifying glass to read ingredient labels!

You can also control the amount of sugar, starch, artificial colors and flavoring, and other chemical additives when you dry your own food at home. If you have dietary restrictions or preferences, using your dehydrator to make meals or pantry items can help you reach your personal goals.

Raw foodies can control the temperature at which the food is dried, ensuring high availability of enzymes, vitamins, and minerals for their special dietary needs.

Time, Space & Savings

Investing in a dehydrator ultimately saves you money. Buying produce in bulk—and in season—offers considerable savings over grocery-store prices. Fruit, vegetables, and nuts can be purchased in bulk directly from local farms, and then dehydrated while at their peak of flavor and nutrition, at significant savings over buying fresh or even frozen vegetables.

Last fall, I picked up a 20-pound bag of Walla Walla onions for $20 and a 25-pound bag of sweet peppers for $10 from the bargain bin at a farm stand. Walla Walla onions are $3 per pound at my grocery store, and sweet peppers are $4 to $5 per pound. That's a savings of almost $200! In just a few days, I dried all the onions in my dehydrator. I divided the peppers by color and dried the red ones first while waiting for the green ones to ripen.

The dried onions and peppers took up significantly less space in my pantry than the big bags of onions and peppers I brought home. Those two huge bags were reduced to four 1-quart jars and a pint jar that are much easier to store in my modest pantry.

Filling your dehydrator takes a little time, but it saves you time in the long run. Your dehydrated foods become convenience items once they are stored in jars in your pantry. It's so much faster to grab dried onions when you need them than to cut up a raw onion while making dinner. Think of the time it takes to prepare food for your dehydrator, and package it when it's done, as an investment in future convenience.

Emergency Preparedness

Dehydrated food is ideal for emergency food storage. Whether you are preparing for a weather event, a period of unemployment, or a natural disaster, having a 30-day supply of nutritious food on hand is wise.

Dehydrating food your family already eats ensures that you have as little disruption as possible in a real emergency. By stocking your pantry with dehydrated food that you've prepared from wholesome ingredients, you can be assured that your family's nutritional needs are met, even if you can't get to the grocery store.

Dehydrated food, when properly prepared and packaged for long-term storage, can form the foundation of a robust preparedness plan. Taking the extra step to package your dehydrated food in Mylar bags or glass jars with oxygen absorbers ensures that your dehydrated food will still be fresh and retain its nutrients in storage.

But even minor disruptions can be helped by having the convenience of dehydrated food in your pantry. An extra dinner guest, sickness in the house, or an unexpected bill doesn't have to shake your confidence. Having dehydrated ingredients to make your favorite comfort foods already in your pantry can help you move through even minor inconveniences with grace.

High Nutritional Value

When food is dehydrated, the water is removed, but the nutrition in the food remains stable. The flavor and nutrients become more concentrated, and the caloric value remains the same. Dehydrated food has the same calories, protein, fiber, and carbohydrates as fresh food. It also retains the same minerals, fatty acids, and antioxidants as fresh food, as well as most of the vitamins. Dehydrated food retains many of these nutrients in storage, even over several months and years.

There is some loss of vitamin C and some B vitamins during blanching, because some of these water-soluble vitamins are lost in the blanching water. Vegetables that are blanched before dehydrating have the same vitamins as frozen food, but dehydrated food has a longer shelf life. This vitamin loss can be minimized by blanching with steam before dehydrating, rather than immersing vegetables in boiling water prior to dehydrating.

Hikers and athletes benefit from the concentration of nutrients provided by dehydrated foods, allowing them to eat less while maintaining their energy levels.

To ensure that your dehydrated food retains the most nutrition, it should be dehydrated at its peak of ripeness, when the flavor, color, and texture are best. Vegetables that are past their prime and are fading in color, scent, or flavor will not make quality dried vegetables. Skip over the fading-green kale in the refrigerator vegetable bin. Choose the most vibrant-colored vegetables to get the most nutrition from your dehydrated food.

HOW TO DEHYDRATE

Preparing Fruits for Dehydration

Most dehydrating machines, no matter which brand or model you choose, are user-friendly. The first step in preparing fruits for the dehydration machine is selecting high-quality fruits.

Fruit should be fresh and at the peak of ripeness. Once you pick or purchase your produce, thoroughly wash it and discard any bruised or damaged pieces. Fruits may need to be peeled, cored or pitted, depending on the particular fruit you are handling.

After fruit has been peeled and sliced, it is advisable to apply a pre-treatment to maintain the color and freshness of the produce. Once certain fruits, such as apples, pears and peaches are sliced, their exposure to air initiates a chemical process called oxidation that results in discolored flesh. Using an antioxidant will temporarily halt the enzyme action and prevent further damage to the texture, flavor and appearance of the fruit. To make this solution, combine a small amount of ascorbic acid (1-2 tsp.) with one cup of water and coat the fruit evenly with the liquid.

Preparing Vegetables for Dehydration

When preparing your vegetables for dehydration, be sure to select high-quality, unblemished vegetables.

Particularly for certain vegetables such as root vegetables and potatoes, make sure they are thoroughly scrubbed and cleaned prior to dehydration. Similar to fruits, vegetables should be sliced thinly and uniformly for the best results.

Nearly all vegetables should be blanched first. Blanching vegetables halts enzyme action and thereby preserves the color and flavor of the food over time. Because some nutrients may be lost during the blanching process, place the vegetables in boiling water only for the required length of time.

After the vegetables are submerged in ice cold water, carefully dry the foods prior to placing them on trays. Note that a small number of vegetables, like mushrooms and onions, do not need to be blanched prior to dehydration.

Preparing Meat for Dehydration

Dehydrated meats are delicious and simple to prepare, but do warrant special handling instructions. Only lean meats in excellent condition should be utilized for making jerky. When using ground meat for jerky, it should be at least 93% lean.

All other meat should have its fat thoroughly trimmed prior to slicing.

You might consider applying a marinade beforehand to flavor the meat. If so, keep marinated meats in the refrigerator or freezer before placing them in the dehydrator. After removing the meat from the refrigerator, blot its surface thoroughly to remove excess moisture and place on dehydrator trays. As always, raw meat should be kept away from other foods, and all surfaces and utensils that come into contact with raw meat should be thoroughly cleaned.

After using the dehydrator, experts recommend heating dried meat strips for ten minutes in a 275° F oven or for a longer time at a lower temperature. This additional step reduces any residual chance of contamination by eliminating pathogens, and also produces the most traditional style of jerky with respect to taste and texture.

Preparing Grains, Nuts, Beans and Seeds for Dehydration

Nuts, seeds, beans and grains can all be dehydrated using a similar two-step process. First, these foods must be soaked in a water solution. Soaking deactivates anti-nutrients, stimulates nutrients such as iron, potassium and magnesium, and is beneficial to your digestive system. Soak nuts or seeds in a salt brine solution for 12-18 hours. Add ½ tsp. high-quality sea salt for every cup of water. Since wet nuts and seeds are not appealing to most people, you can place the nuts in the dehydrator to create a delicious, crunchy, ready to eat snack. After soaking for the recommended time, drain the water and proceed with instructions for your dehydrating machine.

Using Your Dehydrator Machine

Once the fruits, vegetables, herbs, meat, nuts or grains have been prepped, spread them in thin layers without overlapping on the drying trays. Turn on the dehydrating machine and set the temperature. Drying times vary depending on the dehydrator model you own and the food you are dehydrating. Most dehydrators contain guides that provide recommended temperatures and times for dehydrating specific foods.

In general, it is recommended that fruits and vegetables be dried at 130°-140° F. Meats and fish should be dehydrated at the highest temperature setting on your machine, which is typically between 145°-155° F. When dehydrating meats, it is necessary to use dehydrator models with adjustable temperature controls to ensure a product that is safe for consumption. Dried herbs require a temperature not exceeding 90° F, as aromatic oils in herbs are sensitive to high heat. Nuts, seeds and grains, which also have a high oil content, dry optimally at 90°-100° F.

Determining Food Readiness

Foods should always be tested for adequate dehydration before removal. Many factors determine the length of time necessary to dehydrate foods, such as the temperature, humidity, type of food, amount of food on the tray, size of the food pieces, and total quantity of food in the machine.

In general, meats should be dehydrated to 20% moisture content, fruits to 10% and vegetables to about 5%. You can analyze the appearance and texture of foods for signs of readiness. It is important to test only a few pieces at a time and allow them to cool before determining whether they are ready.

Checking food for readiness is largely a matter of assessing its structure. Fruits should be pliable, but not totally brittle. Test fruits by cutting them in half; if you cannot squeeze out any moisture, then the fruit are fully dehydrated. Vegetables, however, should be brittle when they are done. Test vegetables by hitting them with a hammer to see if they shatter.

Most fully dehydrated vegetables should break into pieces. Certain vegetables, however, will retain a pliable and leathery texture upon complete dehydration. These include mushrooms, green peppers and squash. To test jerky, bend one piece and see how pliable it is. The meat should bend, but not snap completely like a dry stick. The jerky should present as dark brown to black in color once it is fully dehydrated. Herbs are considered dried when they crumble easily. The stems of the herb should bend and break with little effort.

RECOGNIZING DONENESS

Food is done when it is dry enough to prevent bacteria from growing and spoiling the food. Different foods have different moisture requirements for safe food storage. The amount of moisture left in dehydrated food affects its flexibility. The more moisture, the more flexible your dehydrated food will be. You'll find specific guidelines in each produce entry and in each recipe to test for doneness so you won't be guessing. But here are some general guidelines for vegetables, fruit, herbs, and meat to get you started.

- Allow a sample to cool completely before testing for doneness. Most dehydrated food is flexible when warm but will firm up when cooled. If you are in doubt, dehydrate the food for a few more hours. It's better to dry longer than to stop drying too soon.
- Vegetables are usually done when they are leathery and brittle. When pressed between the thumb and forefinger, they should snap cleanly in half, without bending.
- Fruit is done when it is leathery but still flexible, and no soft pockets remain in the fruit. If you find soft, squishy sections, give the fruit more time. When the fruit is done, there will be no soft spots.
- Herbs are done when the leaves crumble when crushed. Stems should be hard and brittle. If the stems bend, they need more time.
- Meat should be dry and leathery with little flexibility when done, but specific meats vary in the test for doneness.

Storage

Once your food is properly dehydrated, your job isn't finished. It's important to package the food and store it to protect it from spoilage. Moisture, oxygen, and light can degrade your stored food, shortening the shelf life and allowing bacteria to ruin the food.

When stored properly and protected from moisture, heat, and light, dehydrated food can last for up to 10 years. The actual shelf life varies depending on the food, with fruit lasting longer than vegetables because the natural sugar in fruit helps extend its shelf life. (Consult the recipes for specifics on storage needs and the shelf life of individual foods.)
If you see any signs of spoilage, such as off-odors or mold, discard the contents of the package. It is not safe to eat.

REHYDRATING

Rehydrating restores the moisture to dried food, returning it to its original size, form, and appearance. Rehydrated food retains its aroma, flavor, and texture as well as its nutritional content. There are several methods for rehydrating dried food, but in their simplest form, they all add moisture back into the food using either cold or hot liquids.

As a general rule, 1 cup of liquid reconstitutes 1 cup of dehydrated food. If the food hasn't softened enough after an hour, add more liquid. The liquid can be plain water, broth, juice, or milk. Fruit can also be reconstituted in liqueur or brandy.

Most fruit and vegetables reconstitute in one to two hours. However, larger pieces of food may take longer to reconstitute than powders or finely diced pieces. Generally, food that took longer to dehydrate also takes longer to rehydrate. Use only enough liquid as the food will absorb. Using too much liquid makes the food soggy and unappetizing.

Soaking does not take the place of cooking. Food still needs to be cooked after it is reconstituted by soaking.

Save the soaking liquid to add to soups, stews, or cereals. It contains the water-soluble vitamins and minerals leached from the dehydrated food.

Methods

There are two main methods of rehydrating: cold soaking and hot soaking.
Cold soaking should be used for foods that are commonly eaten raw, like fruit. It is a slower process that allows the tissues of the food to relax and absorb the liquid. Food that is reconstituted in room-temperature or cooler water retains its shape and texture better than food rehydrated using hot water.

The soaking liquid, like juice or yogurt, adds additional flavor as it rehydrates the food, but don't add additional salt or sugar to the soaking water, as they hinder the rehydration process. These can be added once the food is fully hydrated.

Use hot soaking when the food being rehydrated will be served cooked or added to a hot dish. Hot soaking breaks some of the plant cells as it rehydrates the food, causing the food to become softer. Hot soaking rehydrates food quicker than cold soaking.

Rehydrating the food while cooking it is fast and easy. Place dried vegetables in soups, stews, or sauces and rehydrate as the sauce cooks on the stovetop. Add dried fruit to sauces, puddings, and warm cereals during the cooking process and rehydrate it while the rest of the mixture cooks.

THE OBJECTIVES OF FOOD DEHYDRATION

Impacting a peculiar feature, such as a different crispiness and flavor, to a food product: An example is the transformation of maize to cereal.

Shrinking the food material into smaller and more portable sizes to change their forms: Food materials, when the water has been reduced, become more portable and are easily packaged for transportation. Examples are the draining and grinding of curry leaves, thymes seeds etc. into spices.

Reducing the volume and the weight of the food: The volume of water poses a substantial addition to the volume and weight of the food, by reducing the water content, the weight and volume of the food particle is also reduced.

The conversion of food meals to a different form that is more convenient for storage, packaging and easy transportation: A great example is the conversion of milk or dairies to dry powder. When these products get to the places of consumption, they are reconverted to the previous forms through the addition of water. The effect of water depression which leads to preservation and longevity of the nutrients.

DISADVANTAGES OF DEHYDRATION

Time Consumption: Dehydrating food requires a lot of time in order to achieve perfect results. Some foods have a large amount of water content and to reduce the water will require a lot of time and meticulous observation. Taking so much time may be inconvenient for some individuals.

Unwanted Weight Gain: Dehydrated food might be rich in calories. Since it has shrunken in size, it may appear small; a little quantity consumed may seems insufficient while a large quantity consumed implies large nutrient consumption. The excess calories in the dehydrated food may lead to weight gain. People should be aware of it when consuming dried food.

Loss of Nutrients: Although when done correctly, dehydrating food can preserve nutrients, when done incorrectly it may lead to loss of nutrients in the food. Some nutrients can't stand high levels of heat. The degree of heat applied therefore determines the survival of the nutrients in food. If the dehydrated food is not stored properly too, nutrient can be lost due to excessive heat and poor storage condition.

Change in Taste and Look: With high heat, the appetizing appearances of common meals change. In most cases, people are easily turned off when foods don't wear the expected looks. When foods are dehydrated, the loss of water makes it shrink and the looks drastically change.

Technical Knowledge: Since not all foods are dehydrated in the same way or following the same pattern, dehydration requires technical knowledge in order to be carried out well. There is also the place of experience which gradually makes a person perfect in the art.

WHY IS DEHYDRATION HEALTHY?

Dehydration is healthy for consumption because of the following reasons:
Retains Nutrients: As mentioned earlier, when we dehydrate foods, the nutrients in the food is one of our primary concerns. Unlike other methods of preservation, dehydration saves the nutrients in the dehydrated food, when it is carried out effectively.

Bacteria Free: Dehydrated foods are germ-free. When we keep these foods for a long period of time, they still maintain their healthy state.

No Addition of External Chemicals: The heat used to dehydrate food is the only external requirement for the process. This heat contains no chemicals or acids that may be dangerous for the food. Unlike some preservative methods which engage the addition of preservative chemicals, dehydration is a healthy choice for storing food.

Safe Handling: Since dehydration has nothing to do with handling dangerous chemicals or intense equipment, it is safe for the user to easily dehydrate. Dehydration can be done with the simplest household mechanical devices like oven, microwave or a dehydrator. The smoke or steam that escapes from dehydrating food is not unhealthy to the environment, unlike regular burning of waste products. This makes the process healthy.

CHAPTER 2

DEHYDRATING METHODS

You can get started drying using items you probably already have in your kitchen.

The following items are essential to the drying process:

- Food.
- A source of heat.
- Trays or racks to dry the food on.

The trays should be slotted wood or mesh trays. Avoid using solid trays because they block air from circulating all the way around the food. In a pinch, you can cover a wood frame with cheesecloth and use it as a drying rack.

CONTAINERS TO STORE THE FOOD IN:

That's it. That's all you need to get started drying. There are other items you can use to make life easier on yourself, but the above items are the only absolute necessities.

You want to avoid trays made from the following materials because they can add harmful substances to your food during the drying process:

- Fiberglass.
- Vinyl.
- Aluminum.
- Copper.
- Plastic.
- Galvanized metal.
- The following items aren't required, but will make life easier on you:
- A commercial food dehydrator.

- A fan.
- A blancher.
- A sulfur box.
- A scale.
- A thermometer.

Now that we've established the items you need and the items you can buy to make life easier, let's take a look at the various methods used to dehydrate food.

Use a fan to circulate fresh air into the area where the food is drying.

USING YOUR OVEN

If you have an oven (and who doesn't?), you have a tool you can use to dry foods.

It isn't the best choice when it comes to drying, but it'll work in a pinch. The upside to using this method is it's one of the fastest methods of drying food. The downside is you can easily burn or scorch the food you're drying because it's difficult to keep the heat as low as you need it.

You can only dry small amounts of food in a normal kitchen oven. If you're planning on drying large amounts of food, buy a dehydrator and save yourself a lot of work.

You need to keep your oven temperature somewhere between 140 and 160 degrees F. To check oven temps, place an oven thermometer on the top rack and leave it there so you can monitor it. The temperature needs to be checked every 15 minutes to make sure it isn't getting too hot.

Place the food in a single layer on the drying trays. You can usually fit a couple pounds of food on each tray. Since most ovens have two racks, you're only going to be able to dry around 4 pounds of food at a time.

Here's a little trick you can use to fit more food in the oven: Place a couple 1 1/2-inch tall wood blocks on the bottom tray and set the next drying tray on the blocks. Then add a couple more blocks to the second tray and place another tray on it. You can fit up to four racks in your oven using this method, which will effectively double the amount of food you're able to dry at once. Since you're not heating the oven up too hot, you don't have to worry about scorching or burning the wood.

You need to prop the door open so there's a gap of 2 to 6 inches during the drying process. If you have a fan, set it up so it's blowing air into the oven through this gap. You need to keep the air inside moving so the oven doesn't fill full of humid air.

SET YOUR OVEN AT ITS LOWEST TEMPERATURE

If you have a gas oven, you may be able to get away with just using the heat from the pilot light. Monitor the temperature to ensure it stays above 140 degrees F and below 160 degrees F.

The top rack is going to be a little cooler than the bottom rack. Additionally, the air isn't going to be the same temperature in the front of the oven as it is in the back, especially if you're using a fan to circulate air. For this reason, it's important to rotate the trays every 20 to 30 minutes. Rotate the top trays to the bottom and flip the trays around so the food that was in the front is now in the back. You're also going to want to periodically flip your food over or stir it on the tray because the side of the food that's facing down will dry at a slower rate than the side that's facing up.

The process used to dry foods in a toaster oven is same as with a conventional oven. Place the food on a tray and put it in your toaster oven. Set the oven on its lowest setting and prop open the door. If you have a fan, use it to circulate new air into the oven.

Since this sort of oven is smaller than a conventional oven, it's going to dehydrate the food you're drying faster than the larger oven. Make sure you watch it closely and soon you'll have a small batch of dried foods.

Here's a quick tip you won't see in too many other books about drying: Open the door of your oven every few hours to let out all the damp air trapped inside. Sure, it will cause the temperature to drop inside, but it will let all the moist air inside escape, replacing it with dry air. The hit you take in temperature is temporary and it's worth it to fill the oven with fresh air.

If you only dry occasionally, your oven will do the trick nicely.

SUN-DRYING

A Sun-drying food is the oldest method used to dehydrate foods, predating ovens by thousands of years. This method is all-natural and doesn't require use of electricity or gas (to preserve the food or store it).

All you need is a nice, sunny day or two (or 5) in a row and you can use the power of the sun to dry your food.

In warmer climates, you can dry food using this method year-round. In cooler places or in areas where there's typically a lot of cloud cover, there may only be a handful of days a year this method can be used.

You need dry, clear weather with temperatures of at least 90 to 100 degrees F to sun-dry food.

If you live in an area where it's typically cloudy or there's a lot of moisture in the air, you're probably better off using one of the other methods of dehydrating. It's OK to move foods you've started sun-drying in and finishing the process in the oven or a dehydrator if it looks like inclement weather is on its way.

To sun-dry your foods, spread a layer out on a wood frame covered in cheesecloth. If you're worried about bugs or other animals getting to your food, you can place a layer of cheesecloth over the top of your food as well. Turn your foods regularly to assure even drying or the side left exposed to the sun will dry at a faster clip.

Alternatively, you can run a piece of string through your food items and hang them out to dry. Items like meat can be hung from hooks.

Spread food out in a single layer with at least a couple millimeters space between each piece so air can flow around it. Set the tray out in an area that gets sun for most of the day and has good circulation. Now, all you have to do is leave it there until the food is dry.

Leave the food out during the heat of the day, and then move it inside during the evening and night hours.

This accomplishes two things. It prevents the food from rehydrating due to condensation and it keeps the critters away. Animals enjoy dehydrated foods as much as you do and have been known to raid backyards at night. You don't want all of your hard work to be wasted at the hands of a marauding deer or raccoon.

Flip the food partway through each day. The bottom side gets less air and sun and will lose less moisture. Flip the food you're cooking over regularly so both side get equal amounts of sun.

There's no set time you need to leave food out to dry. All times shown in books and on the Internet are approximations of what it takes under "normal" conditions.

What exactly constitutes normal conditions is anyone's guess. What's normal in one place would be out of the ordinary somewhere else. That's probably why there's such variation in the dry times in different literature. I've tried to provide ranges in this book, but even the ranges can be off. The only way to make sure you dry your food correctly is to keep a close eye on it. When it gets close to the bottom end of the range, check it periodically.

The drying time varies based on the heat applied to the food, the humidity and the circulation of air in the area you're doing the drying. The hotter it is the faster food is going to lose moisture. The more humidity there is the slower moisture is going to be absorbed.

If you live in an area with a lot of vehicle traffic or high pollution levels, you shouldn't air-dry your food outside. Pollution particles can land on your food and contaminate it. Over time, the particulates you're eating can build up in your system and make you sick.

DEHYDRATING EQUIPMENT

Dehydration is mostly about prep work, so having the appropriate tools will make your job easier. Make sure you have the following tools on hand.

Baking sheet: If you don't already have one, a good-quality baking sheet that disperses heat properly and doesn't buckle under high heat is a great addition to your kitchen. Use it for roasting vegetables and fish.

Blender: Blenders are great for making purées for sauces, soups, and fruit leather. A food processor or immersion blender also works for this purpose.

Four-cup measuring pitcher: These pitchers are good for measuring liquids and for measuring the yield of dehydrated foods (if you don't have a kitchen scale).

Kitchen knife: Aside from the dehydrator itself, a kitchen knife is the most important tool for dehydrating. A good knife will make your prep work much easier. Perhaps you already have a favorite knife one that keeps a good edge, has a straight blade, and is comfortable to hold for extended periods. Good knives don't need to be expensive. In our kitchen we use the same knives many culinary schools offer; they are inexpensive but great tools for the job.

Kitchen scale: An inexpensive digital scale is very useful for measuring ingredients with precision and is also helpful for measuring and portioning the completed and dehydrated meals.

Parchment paper: Line baking sheets with parchment paper to prevent food from sticking to the pan. It also makes for easy cleanup.

HOW TO DEHYDRATE

Preparing Fruits for Dehydration

Most dehydrating machines, no matter which brand or model you choose, are user-friendly. The first step in preparing fruits for the dehydration machine is selecting high-quality fruits.

Fruit should be fresh and at the peak of ripeness. Once you pick or purchase your produce, thoroughly wash it and discard any bruised or damaged pieces. Fruits may need to be peeled, cored or pitted, depending on the particular fruit you are handling.

After fruit has been peeled and sliced, it is advisable to apply a pre-treatment to maintain the color and freshness of the produce. Once certain fruits, such as apples, pears and peaches are sliced, their exposure to air initiates a chemical process called oxidation that results in discolored flesh. Using an antioxidant will temporarily halt the enzyme action and prevent further damage to the texture, flavor and appearance of the fruit. To make this solution, combine a small amount of ascorbic acid (1-2 tsp.) with one cup of water and coat the fruit evenly with the liquid.

Preparing Vegetables for Dehydration

When preparing your vegetables for dehydration, be sure to select high-quality, unblemished vegetables.

Particularly for certain vegetables such as root vegetables and potatoes, make sure they are thoroughly scrubbed and cleaned prior to dehydration. Similar to fruits, vegetables should be sliced thinly and uniformly for the best results.

Nearly all vegetables should be blanched first. Blanching vegetables halts enzyme action and thereby preserves the color and flavor of the food over time some nutrients may be lost during the blanching process, place the vegetables in boiling water only for the required length of time.

After the vegetables are submerged in ice cold water, carefully dry the foods prior to placing them on trays. Note that a small number of vegetables, like mushrooms and onions, do not need to be blanched prior to dehydration.

Preparing Meat for Dehydration

Dehydrated meats are delicious and simple to prepare, but do warrant special handling instructions. Only lean meats in excellent condition should be utilized for making jerky. When using ground meat for jerky, it should be at least 93% lean.

All other meat should have its fat thoroughly trimmed prior to slicing.

You might consider applying a marinade beforehand to flavor the meat. If so, keep marinated meats in the refrigerator or freezer before placing them in the dehydrator. After removing the meat from the refrigerator, blot its surface thoroughly to remove excess moisture and place on dehydrator trays. As always, raw meat should be kept away from other foods, and all surfaces and utensils that come into contact with raw meat should be thoroughly cleaned.

After using the dehydrator, experts recommend heating dried meat strips for ten minutes in a 275° F oven or for a longer time at a lower temperature. This additional step reduces any residual chance of contamination by eliminating pathogens, and also produces the most traditional style of jerky with respect to taste and texture.

Preparing Grains, Nuts, Beans and Seeds for Dehydration

Nuts, seeds, beans and grains can all be dehydrated using a similar two-step process. First, these foods must be soaked in a water solution. Soaking deactivates anti-nutrients, stimulates nutrients such as iron, potassium and magnesium, and is beneficial to your digestive system. Soak nuts or seeds in a salt brine solution for 12-18 hours. Add ½ tsp. high-quality sea salt for every cup of water. Since wet nuts and seeds are not appealing to most people, you can place the nuts in the dehydrator to create a delicious, crunchy, ready to eat snack. After soaking for the recommended time, drain the water and proceed with instructions for your dehydrating machine.

Using Your Dehydrator Machine

Once the fruits, vegetables, herbs, meat, nuts or grains have been prepped, spread them in thin layers without overlapping on the drying trays. Turn on the dehydrating machine and set the temperature. Drying times vary depending on the dehydrator model you own and the food you are dehydrating. Most dehydrators contain guides that provide recommended temperatures and times for dehydrating specific foods.

In general, it is recommended that fruits and vegetables be dried at 130°-140° F. Meats and fish should be dehydrated at the highest temperature setting on your machine, which is typically between 145°-155° F. When dehydrating meats, it is necessary to use dehydrator models with adjustable temperature controls to ensure a product that is safe for consumption. Dried herbs require a temperature not exceeding 90° F, as aromatic oils in herbs are sensitive to high heat. Nuts, seeds and grains, which also have a high oil content, dry optimally at 90°-100° F.

VEGETABLES

Dehydrating fresh produce entails a little more work. These need to be rinsed, peeled, and sliced into thin layers. Some may need blanching, boiling, coring and/or de-seeding.

Always dehydrate fresh produce in a conventional oven, with temperature set between 49° / 120° and 54° / 130° only. This allows gradual loss of moisture and prevents smaller pieces from burning.

When using the dehydrator, set the machine at lowest heat for delicate vegetables (e.g. leafy vegetables, onions, etc.); and at highest heat for hardier produce (e.g. legumes, root crops, etc.) or those that have thicker cuts.

Use approximately 1½ to 2 pounds per rotation.

Artichoke hearts, green peas, freshly shelled, etc.

Blanch with hot water and then dunk into an ice bath immediately to preserve color.

Drain well. Pat-dry using paper towels, if needed.

Follow recommended steps for oven drying or dehydrating. See: Oven drying: on page 28 and Dehydrating: on page 29. These may take between five to fourteen hours. These are done when these become brittle and wrinkled.

Beets, carrots, cassava, daikon (Asian radish,) potatoes, purple carrots, purple yam, sweet potatoes, yam, zucchini.

Scrub skins well.

Except for the zucchini, parboil (partially boil) veggies until slightly fork-tender (or when you can pierce outer layer with a fork.)

Remove from water and dunk into an ice bath immediately.

When veggies are cool enough to touch, peel, and slice into ⅛-inch thick disks. Drain well. Pat-dry using paper towels, if needed.

Follow recommended steps for oven drying or dehydrating. See: Oven drying: on page 28 and Dehydrating: on page 29. Beets may need three to ten hours of drying. These are done when individual disks feel dry and leathery to the touch. (Important: wear food-safe gloves to prevent beet juice from staining your hands.)

Carrots, potatoes, purple yam, sweet potatoes, and yam may need six to twelve hours. While the zucchini may need five to ten hours of drying. These are done when chips become crispy. Some pieces may have air pockets or browned edges, but these are normal.

DRYING HERBS AND SPICES

Most herbs and spices are easy to grow at home, and many can be grown in small containers on your balcony, porch or any area of your house or yard that gets regular sunlight. In addition to being a considerable way to flavor foods, herbs and spices have a number of health benefits associated with them.

Drying is the convenient way to preserve herbs and spices because all you usually have to do is lay out the leaves, flowers or seeds and let them dry and then grind or crush them as you see fit. Herbs and spices should be dried in a dehydrator because drying them in the sun can bring them to lose some of their potency.

The following herbs and spices are good candidates for drying:

- Bay.
- Celery leaves.
- Chervil.
- Chicory.
- Chives.
- Cilantro.
- Cinnamon sticks.
- Cloves.
- Dill.
- Laurel.

- Marjoram.
- Mint.
- Oregano.
- Parsley.
- Peppercorns.
- Rosemary.
- Sage.
- Summer savory.
- Tarragon.
- Thyme.

Harvest herbs and spices by removing them from the plant in the early morning. Harvest them before the flowers open and be careful not to damage them during the harvest. Do not attempt to dry damaged pieces. The drying process isn't going to make damaged herbs and spices any better.

Lay the herbs or spices out in a single layer on the dehydrator tray and spread them out so there's a bit of space between them for air circulation. Most herbs and spices should be dried at temperatures between 115 and 125 degrees F, but be assured to check the documentation that came with your dehydrator to see what the recommended temperature for drying herbs and spices is.

The drying time for herbs and spices should be short. Most herbs and spices should be done drying in less than 4 hours. Herbs and spices are done when they feel crispy and are brittle to the touch. You should be able to crumble leaves, stems and flowers between your fingers.

Some herbs and spices can be hung out to air dry. Rosemary, thyme, sage and parsley can all be hung inside the house and left to dry. Basil, oregano and mint leaves need to be placed inside a paper bag before being hung out to dry. Air-drying can be done indoors or out, but be sure to hang the herbs and spices in a shaded area if drying them outside. Air-drying herbs by hanging them can take a week or two to properly dry the herbs.

Herbs and some spices can be dried in the microwave if you're in a hurry. Microwave them on high for 2 minutes and check them. If they're still wet, microwave them for 30 seconds and check them again. Continue microwaving the herbs in 30-second increments until they're done drying.

STORING HERBS AND SPICES

Here's the dilemma. Herbs and spices will last a lot longer when they're left whole, but they're usually ground or crushed when they're used in recipes. It's kind of a hassle to grind or crush your herbs every time you want to use them, especially when you're looking to make a quick meal.

What I do is dry a large batch of herbs and spices. I crush up half of it and store it that way, so I always have crushed or ground herbs and spices on hand. I then store the rest of it in the freezer whole. When I start to run low, I crush or grind the herbs I have in the freezer and I'm ready to go. I know when I pull a batch out of the freezer, I'm going to need to dry more soon or I'm going to run out.

ARE NUTRIENTS LOST DURING DRYING?

There are some nutrients lost during pretreatment and drying. Any time the food is exposed to heat, light or oxygen, there will be some degradation of nutritional value. The longer the exposure, the greater the damage. Most fruits start degrading as soon as they're harvested. This degradation is sped up by cutting into them or otherwise exposing the flesh to oxygen.

Many fruits contain enzymes that react to the air and cause browning and nutrient loss to begin as soon as they're cut into. If you've ever left an apple or a banana out for a while and seen it turn brown, you've seen these enzymes in action. This reaction to the oxygen in the air can be slowed to a crawl by pretreating or blanching the fruit after it's been cut.

The following vitamins can be damaged by too much heat, light or air exposure:

- Folate (heat).
- Riboflavin (heat).
- Thiamine (heat, light).
- Vitamin A (air, light).
- Vitamin B12 (heat, light).

Commercial foods that undergo intense treatment lose a lot more nutrients than fruit dried at home. While commercially dried foods can lose up to 80% of certain vitamins, foods dried at home usually don't come anywhere near that magnitude.

Take the following precautions to reduce the amount of vitamins lost while treating and drying produce:

Work on small batches of food at a time.

When you work on large batches and try to get a lot of fruit done at once, the pieces you cut into first are left to sit out while you process the rest of the produce. This can result in the earlier pieces degrading a lot faster than those cut later on.

Move food into pretreatment shortly after it's been cut.

Time is of essence when treating fruit that's prone to discoloration. It's important to slow down enzymatic reactions as early as possible to avoid nutrient loss.

Carefully regulate heat.

High heat can accelerate nutrient loss, so its important heat is monitored closely. Using a dehydrator allows you the most control over the amount of heat drying food is exposed to. Blanching also exposes food to heat and can damage nutrients, but may be critical to ensuring food can be properly stored. Blanching isn't as critical of a process with fruit as it is with vegetables.

Store dried food in an airtight container.

This will minimize the amount of air the food comes in contact with. If air is allowed into the container, the food can take up moisture from the air, drastically shortening how long the food will last.

Drying food in the sun exposes it to UV rays that can damage light-sensitive vitamins.

When vitamin retention is of concern, a dehydrator may be the better choice for drying.

Store food in small, single-serving containers.

Every time you open a container, more air is let in. Using single serving containers only exposes the food you plan on eating to new air.

No minerals are lost during the drying process, but pretreatment can cause some mineral loss. Boiling or otherwise exposing fruit to water may cause some of the minerals to leach out into the water. This can happen during blanching and again during rehydration. The drying process itself doesn't affect minerals.

Calories and sugar are largely unaffected by the drying process, but they will be concentrated into a smaller package. A raisin has the same caloric content and amount of sugar as it did when it was a grape, but it's now packed into the smaller raisin. Dried produce has more calories and more sugar than regular produce when compared by volume. For example, 100 grams of grapes have 15 grams of sugar and 70 calories. 100 grams of raisins have 60 grams of sugar and 300 calories. Raisins have 3 times the sugar and more than 4 times the calories than grapes when compared by volume.

For this reason, it's important not to overeat when it comes to dried fruit and vegetables. They can be a healthy part of most diets, but only if consumed in moderation.

THE BEST TECHNIQUES TO PRESERVE DRIED FOODS

Over drying the dried food is just impossibility. So, when you are unsure if the food is completely dry or not, keeps drying it until you are entirely sure.

Never use granulated sugar in fruit leathers as the sugar will get crystallize over time. You can opt for honey or corn syrup if you need.

To be considered "dehydrated," foods must be at least 95% moisture-free. If they aren't and you try to store them, they'll quickly rot. How can you tell? If the food is soft, spongy, and sticky, it's back in the dehydrator they go. You can't really "over dry" food, so the harder and crunchier, the better. If you don't want certain foods to be that dry, you'll have to plan on eating them pretty much right away before bacteria has a chance to get at that moisture.

STORE FOOD PROPERLY

The last step you need to remember in the dehydration process is safe storage. All food should be stored in clean and dry containers, with airtight lids that can keep out moisture and bugs. If you're a prepper and don't plan on snacking frequently on your dehydrated foods just yet, vacuum-sealing is a great option.

Safe storage also means knowing how long a food is going to last, because even the most dehydrated food doesn't last forever. The only exception is freeze-dried foods, which can last decades, but most people don't have a special freeze-drier machine. Bear in mind that store-bought dehydrated foods last longer than homemade ones, because of the added preservatives. As an example, jerky you buy at the store lasts about a year, while home-dehydrated will only last 1-2 months when properly stored.

Health food stores usually stock bulk items such as rice, flour, pasta, millet, etc. Ask if you can buy them in bulk. Many stores will usually give a discount for whole case or whole bag purchases.

You will still have to store them in a bucket or some other container. You can use whatever food containers you have. Just make sure they were not used for toxic or hazardous materials. You don't want toxic residues to contaminate your food.

If you want, you can store your bulk items in plastic food storage bags available in any grocery store. The one-gallon and two-gallon sizes work well for this purpose. Squeeze the air out of the bag before sealing it. You can also add oxygen absorber packets before

After sealing the plastic bag, you can add an extra layer of protection by wrapping it with aluminum foil. This will act as a light bather. Then put this in another larger plastic bag, squeeze the air out and seal.

Mylar Bags (Metalized Liners)

To seal these bags, you can use foil tape. One brand is Refectix and should be available in hardware stores. If not, check with plumbing supply stores. A 30-foot roll costs around $4. If there is still air in the bag after you seal it, prick a little hole in it and push the air out. Then seal up the hole. Or you can use a portable heat sealer which can cost over 100 dollars.

If you don't want to use food buckets, you can store these packages in cardboard boxes – just make sure you have no mice. Or you can use the 18 gallon and 22 gallon storage tote containers sold just about anywhere (Wal-Mart, Kmart, Pamida, Gibson, hardware stores). Rubbermaid makes them as well as other companies. They cost around $5 to $7 each.

If there is a food service (restaurant) supplies store near you, go and see what is available that you can use.

The dryer the food is, the longer it can be stored for, so you'll want as much moisture in the food to be removed as possible. Airtight plastic bags and/or containers are great options for holding the food and resisting spoilage. Most of the nutritional value in dehydrated foods will be preserved, although it won't be as nutritious as it would be otherwise.

Remember that when storing any food for the long term, the food needs to be stored in a cool and dry location at room temperature. Any location that's humid or excessively hot should be automatically rejected for storing food because the food will be more likely to mold, even if it's been preserved.

HOW TO STORE JERKY

The best way to store jerky is to treat it like a fresh food item.

Limit the jerky's exposure to air.

Retain the quality of your jerky by placing it in an airtight container. Vacuum packing, sealable bags and plastic wrap can be used to wrap your jerky and are effective at keeping air out. The option that would allow the jerky to be most easily accessible is to place it in a storage container or jar that has a lid.

Label the container with the date at the beginning of the storage life so you know the age of the jerky and how long it has been stored.

Separate your jerky by type. Place different types of jerky in different containers to keep the flavors separate, ensuring top quality.

Eradicate any source of moisture.

Use a paper towel to dry your jerky. If you notice moisture or oil on your jerky, noted by wetness or a sheen on the surface, gently pat the surfaces of the meat with a paper towel.

Keep moisture at bay while the jerky is in storage by placing the jerky between layers of paper towel in the container. The towels will absorb any moisture from the jerky or container. Replace the towels when you notice any presence of moisture.

Know the shelf life of your jerky.

Time will take a toll on the quality of your jerky. With proper storage techniques, jerky can safely be stored for varying lengths of time depending on where you choose to store it.

Leave your jerky in a cool, dry place. When placed properly in an airtight container, you can leave your jerky on the counter top or another cool, dry place for no longer than 1 month.

Put your jerky in the refrigerator. Jerky can be stored in the refrigerator to be used within 6 months.

Store homemade jerky in the freezer. Jerky lasts up to 1-year when kept in your freezer

HOW TO STORE HERBS?

When completely dry, separate the leaves from the stems, and store the leaves (either whole or gently crumbled) in light-proof containers.

In terms of oven-drying, allow the dried herbs to cool, and gently crush the leaves. Store the dried herbs in light-proof containers.

Store all your dried herbs in a cool dark place, in airtight containers.

Never store your herb vinegars in the sun or on a lighted counter if you intend to use them, no matter how pretty they look. They should always be stored in the refrigerator.

FAQS

How long will dehydrated food last?

If prepared and stored properly, dehydrated food is can last 5 to 10 years. But it is advisable to use your own within four to six months.

Does dehydrating food remove (or preserve) nutrients?

Yes, some nutrients may be removed when food is dehydrated but no more than other methods of preservation. Heat and light are responsible for the breakdown of vitamins. By implication, the canning method of preservation tears down more nutrients than the low heat, low moisture dehydrating method. The amount of thiamin and vitamin A & C that diminishes from your vegetables can be reduced through blanching.

Does dehydrating food kill bacteria?

Provided that you dehydrate your vegetables and fruits until their moisture levels are anywhere between five and twenty percent, you have removed the bacteria that can cause food to decay. If you are concern about bacteria on meat, it is recommended by the USDA that you first heat your raw meat to 160°F temperature and then dehydrate at a steady temperature of 145°F.

Does Dehydrate Food Increase Sugar

In most cases, yes, because when you dehydrate food at a higher temperate, it will cause the death of enzymes. More dense foods may withstand higher temperatures without the enzymes being killed. But most enzymes will ultimately become dormant when the temperature rises between 140° to 160°F.

Can Cooked Food Be Dehydrated?

Yes. Meals can even be dehydrated, but some cooked food dehydrates better than others. If you are drying food for long-term storage, camping, or backpacking, you can prepare rice dishes, stews, and desserts and dry them by using nonstick sheets on the trays of dehydrator. And then remove the nonstick sheet when they have reached a moist, crumbly consistency.

How can I store dried food?

Dehydrated vegetables can last up to ten years and fruit up to five if properly stored. The best way to preserve your dried food for the long term is to vacuum seal using an oxygen absorber and keep it in a cool, dark place. If you are going to eat non-meat dried food within 12 months, store them in reusable storage bags or freezer bags with the air squeezed out.

If you will consume seafood and meat within a month, you can store in freezer bags and keep them in a cool, dark place; otherwise, the best thing is to vacuum seal and freeze them. Meat can last for up to a year if properly stored in the freezer.

THE BEST WAYS, TEMPERATURE AND COOKING TIMES TO DRY FOODS WAYS AT HOME

Pre-treating food

For best results, most of the food items need to be pre-treated before dehydration. Following are the commonly used pre-treatments:

Ascorbic acid or Vitamin C bath

By soaking fruits or soft vegetables in an ascorbic acid solution (one-part of ascorbic acid in 1 gallon of water) immediately after cutting will stop discoloring and browning. An exception is leafy greens, herbs, and broccoli as the acid will discolor them severely. For this, soak the cut fruits immediately in the solution for 8 to 10 minutes. Drain for dehydration.

Skin cracking

Fruits with tougher skins such as plums, cherries, grapes, figs, or berries may need their skins to be cracked before dehydration to pull moisture out from the fruit properly. For this, boil a pot of water and dip the fruit in it for 15 seconds. Remove and dip them in ice-cold water immediately. Drain water entirely before drying them.

Blanching

It is a process used for scalding vegetables in boiling water or steam, to stop the enzymatic action within the vegetables. Be cautious about the timing, as over blanching results in loss of nutrients and under blanching can cause food spoilage during or after the dehydration. For blanching, usually, two methods are used: boiling vegetables in water for some time, and scalding vegetables above the boiling water level, also known as steam blanching — steam from the boiling water scalds the vegetables.

Citric Acid bath

Citric Acid kills bacteria and stops food discolouration. For this, mix a teaspoon of citric acid in 2.5 cups of water, or you can mix equal parts of water and lemon juice. Soak the food for 8 to 10 minutes and drain entirely before dehydration.

Storage

Dehydrated foods can last for years if stored properly. To ensure maximum shelf life, you need to prevent dried food from moisture, heat, microorganism, light and oxygen. Essential steps of storage are:

Cooling

When the fruit is dry enough, remove it from the dehydrator and cool the fruit completely in a cool and dry place for half an hour; storing warm food will reintroduce moisture due to condensation. Make sure not to leave the dried food for too long as it will also result in moisture to come back into the food.

Conditioning

To ensure even distribution of moisture within the food, place the dried food in loose packaging and seal it for 2 to 4 days.

Packaging

As a final step of storage, you need to pack your dehydrated food in air-tight jars or cans. Store your jars or containers in a cool, dark, and dry place to maximise the shelf-life.

TYPES OF DEHYDRATORS

Although there are many methods to dehydrate food such as sun drying and oven drying, the most convenient method is by using an electric dehydrator. Why?

Because it is an easy and hassle-free way to dehydrate your food.

You can get commercial electrical dehydrators from the market that matches your needs, or you can go for DIY dehydrator at home.

DIY home dehydrator

You can construct your dehydrator, if you need to produce large batches of dried foods, from a wooden framed box. All you need is constant heat (gas burner) and airflow (a fan) and few shelves or trays to put food on. However, it becomes difficult to control the temperature levels if you are a beginner, and sometimes it results in a complete mess due to a complicated cleaning process. You need a lot of experimentation and testing to achieve the optimum temperature levels in DIY dehydrators.

Electric dehydrators

If you plan to dry your food regularly, then investing in a commercial electrical dehydrator is the best option. They can handle large quantities of food, and the best part is, you can control the temperature and air circulation without putting much effort. In a useful and well-made electric dehydrator, the temperature remains constant throughout the drying process with the help of a thermostatically-controlled heating system, and proper airflow is achieved through a built-in fan to ensure complete evaporation.

You can get a small unit with 4 or 5 trays under a hundred dollars if you want to dry small batches in one go. However, if you intend to dry a lot of food at once, you can get a commercial dehydrator with ten trays or more.

DEHYDRATION TOOL KIT

You have bought a good and suitable dehydrator, but there are still some other tools and products you may need to increase the productivity and the quality of your dried food. But remember to keep them simple and easy to use. You would need:

- Apple peeler and cherry pitter for quick and efficient work
- You will need a deep container with a tight lid for blanching
- A colander to fit into the container to hold food items for blanching
- Stainless steel knives for cutting food and meat
- Ascorbic acid or lemon juice to give Vitamin C bath to fruits
- Large pot or tub to hold Ascorbic Acid or lemon juice solution
- A blender to make fruit leathers, or to powder your dehydrated food
- Disposable latex or vinyl gloves to handle dried foods to prevent spoilage as handling dried foods with hands transform moisture and heat from your hands to the food.
- Nylon mesh to place on trays or shelves
- Air-tight containers for storing dehydrated foods such as mason jars or cans with air-tight lids, or zip lock bags that can be vacuum-sealed.
- A food processor for grating and slicing vegetables evenly
- A meat slicer to cut the meat evenly in desired thickness quickly and efficiently, and for slicing the fruits and vegetables evenly for making chips and crackers.
- .Sometimes you need to soak and spray the food with vitamin C or lemon juice before dehydrating to avoid browning. For this, a spray bottle is a mess-free option and do the work quickly.
- For making leathers, a squeeze bottle is quite useful. You can squeeze the puree out straight onto drying sheets, or you can even mix different colored purees to form a multi-colored design.

Using a dehydrator is the most effective way to remove moisture from food and extend its shelf-life.

DEHYDRATOR-DRYING

Dehydrating with a food dehydrator is the best method these days. You have control over temperature, time, and air flow. You place food on a tray, close the lid, and heat at the appropriate temperature with an electrical heating element for the given time. Times vary depending on what you're drying and how much. A fan circulates heat around the food, while vents allow the moist air to escape.

QUALITY

Any appliance that touches food should meet certain standards. Add heat, and the possibility of food becoming contaminated with chemicals, and the quality of materials becomes a big issue. Dehydrator trays are made of plastic, so you want to check if they're BPA-free if it's a concern for you. With better materials comes a higher price tag, but that isn't the primary driver of cost. You can still find affordable dehydrators made from relatively chemical-free parts.

CHAPTER 3

CRACKERS BREAD AND CHIPS

CARROT CRACKERS

Preparation time: 20 minutes
Dehydration time: 6 hours
Servings: 10

Ingredients:

- 1 cup almonds, soaked overnight, rinsed, and drained
- 2 cups carrot pulp
- 1 tablespoon ground chia seeds
- 2 tablespoons ground flax seed
- 1 teaspoon italian seasoning
- 1 tablespoon coconut aminos
- ½ teaspoon smoked paprika
- 1 tablespoon dried onion
- ½ teaspoon red pepper flakes
- 2 cups water

Direction:

- ❖ Add the almonds to a food processor or blender.
- ❖ Pulse until crumbly.
- ❖ Stir in the rest of the ingredients.
- ❖ Pulse until fully combined.
- ❖ Spread a thin layer of the dough in the cosori premium food dehydrator.
- ❖ Dry at 125 degrees f for 2 hours.
- ❖ Score the dough to form the crackers.
- ❖ Dry at 115 degrees for 8 hours.
- ❖ Storage suggestions: store in an airtight food container for up to 5 days.

Tip: soak the almonds overnight the day before processing.

Nutrition Calories:: 122 fat: 7.4 g, carbs: 10.8 g protein: 3.9 g.

SWEET POTATO CHIPS

Preparation time: 15 minutes
Dehydration time: 4 hours
Servings: 2

Ingredients:

- 2 sweet potatoes, scrubbed and sliced thinly
- Salt to taste
- 2 teaspoons onion powder

Direction:

- ❖ Arrange the sweet potatoes in the cosori premium food dehydrator.
- ❖ Process at 155 degrees f for 2 hours.
- ❖ Flip and dry for another 2 hours.
- ❖ Sprinkle with salt and onion powder.
- ❖ Storage suggestions: store in a sealable plastic bag.

Tip: use homemade onion powder.

Nutrition: calories 195, fat 3, fiber 1, carbs 20, protein 4

TOMATO & FLAXSEED CRACKERS

Preparation time: 20 minutes
Dehydration time: 8 hours
Servings: 24

Ingredients:

- 1 cup flaxseed
- 8sun-dried tomatoes
- 1 bell pepper, chopped
- 1tablespoon olive oil
- Salt to taste
- 2 tomatoes, chopped
- 1 onion, chopped
- 1 clove garlic, crushed through garlic press
- ¼ cup dried oregano leaves, crushed
- Salt and pepper to taste

Direction:

- ❖ Place the flaxseed in a bowl.
- ❖ In another bowl, combine the remaining ingredients.
- ❖ Stir in the flaxseeds.
- ❖ Combine all the ingredients in the food processor.
- ❖ Pulse until fully combined.
- ❖ Spread the mixture in the cosori premium food dehydrator.
- ❖ Process at 110 degrees f for 12 hours.
- ❖ Storage suggestions: store in an airtight jar for up to 9 days.

Tip: soak the flaxseeds in water for 2 hours before processing.

Nutrition: Calories: 178, Fat: 13.3g, Carbs: 10.7g, Protein: 4.4g

SEED CRACKERS

Preparation time: x hours
Dehydration time: x hours
Servings: 10

Ingredients:

- ¼ cup chia seeds
- ¾ cup flax seeds
- 1 cup water
- ¼ cup hemp seeds
- 1/3 cup sunflower seeds
- 2 tablespoons pumpkin seeds
- 1 tablespoon italian seasoning
- Salt and pepper to taste

Direction:

- ❖ Soak the chia seeds and flax seeds in water for 1 hour.
- ❖ Drain.
- ❖ Transfer to a bowl.
- ❖ Stir in the rest of the ingredients.
- ❖ Process at 115 degrees f for 90 minutes.

- ❖ Flip and break into smaller pieces.
- ❖ Dry at 105 degrees f for 8 hours.
- ❖ Storage suggestions: store in an airtight container for up to 7 days.

Tip: serve with hummus.

Nutrition: Calories: 178, Fat: 13.3g, Carbs: 10.7g, Protein: 4.4g

APPLE CHIPS WITH CINNAMON

Preparation time: 15 minutes
Dehydration time: 8 hours
Servings: 4

Ingredients:

- 4 apples, sliced thinly
- ¼ cup sugar
- 1 tablespoon ground cinnamon

Direction:

- ❖ Mix the cinnamon and sugar.
- ❖ Coat the apple slices with this mixture.
- ❖ Place the apple slices in the cosori premium food dehydrator.
- ❖ Process at 135 degrees f for 12 hours.
- ❖ Storage suggestions: store in an airtight food container.

Tip: use a mandoliner slicer to slice the apples thinly.

Nutrition: calories 195, fat 3, fiber 1, carbs 20, protein 4

VEGAN BREAD

Preparation time: 30 minutes
Dehydration time: 6 hours
Servings: 4

Ingredients:

- 1 head cauliflower
- 1 teaspoon turmeric
- 2 tablespoons flax seed
- 1/2 cup psyllium hust
- 1/2 cup brewer's yeast
- 4 large zucchini
- Salt and black pepper

Directions:

- ❖ Place cauliflower and zucchini in a food processor and pulse until they form a paste. Add the turmeric, flax seeds, psyllium, yeast, and a pinch of salt and black pepper. Pulse again until all ingredients are thoroughly combined.
- ❖ Place paraflexx screens on the racks of your excalibur food dehydrator. Form the mixture into slices about 1/2-inch-thick, and place on the screens.

- ❖ Set your excalibur to 150f and dehydrate for 6 hours. The bread should not be completely dry. One side should be slightly soft.

Nutrition Calories: 219 fat: 1.9 g, carbs: 61.6 g protein: 10.1 g.

FLUFFY DINNER ROLLS

Preparation time: 15 minutes
Dehydration time: 7 hours
Servings: 4

Ingredients:

- 2 cups almond flour
- 1 cup psyllium
- 3 tablespoons ground flax seeds
- 1 tablespoon onion powder
- 2 teaspoons garlic powder
- 1 tablespoon lemon juice
- 1 teaspoon salt
- 1/3 cup water

Directions:

- ❖ In a large bowl, combine the flour, psyllium, flax seeds, onion powder, garlic powder, lemon juice, salt, and water. Mix well until combined.
- ❖ Form the mixture into 6 round rolls.
- ❖ Place paraflexx screens on the racks of your excalibur. Place the rolls on the screens so they are not touching. Dehydrate at 145f for one hour, and then lower the temperature to 110f for the remaining 6 hours. Remove from the screens and serve warm or allow cooling before storing.

Nutrition Calories: 319 fat: 7.1 g,carbs: 95.2 g protein: 3.5 g.

HERB AND ALMOND CRACKERS

Preparation time: 10 minutes
Dehydration time: 12 hours
Servings: 4

Ingredients:

- 2 cups almonds
- 1/2 cup ground flax seeds
- 1/4 cup brewer's yeast
- 3/4 cups water
- 2 tablespoons fresh rosemary, finely chopped
- 1 teaspoon salt
- 1/2 teaspoon black pepper

Directions:

- ❖ In a food processor, combine the almonds, flax seed, yeast, salt, and pepper. Pulse until well combined.
- ❖ Slowly add the water while continuing to pulse until a paste forms.

- Place paraflexx screens on the racks of your excalibur and spread a thin layer of the paste onto each screen. Set your excalibur to 115f and dehydrate for 12 hours or until the crackers are crispy. Remove from the screens and break into small pieces to serve.

Nutrition Calories: 260 fat: 19.3 g, carbs: 13.3 g protein: 11.6 g.

CARROT CRACKERS

Preparation time: 20 minutes
Dehydration time: 12 hours
Servings: 12

Ingredients:

- 6 large carrots, peeled
- 1/2 cup ground flax seeds
- 1 tomato, diced
- Juice from 1 lemon
- 1/2 cup sesame seeds
- 1/2 cup chia seeds
- 3/4 cups water

Directions:

- In a food processor, combine the carrots, flax seeds, tomato, lemon juice, and water, and pulse until a paste forms. Add the chia seeds and sesame seeds and stir to combine.
- Place paraflexx screens on the racks of your excalibur food dehydrator. Spread the paste evenly on the screens about 1/4 inch thick.
- Set your excalibur to 105f and dehydrate for 12 hours. Remove the crackers from the excalibur and allow cooling completely. The crackers will become crispy as they cool.

Nutrition Calories: 122 fat: 7.4 g, carbs: 10.8 g protein: 3.9 g.

SWEET POTATO CHIPS

Preparation time: 10 minutes
Dehydration time: 14 hours
Servings: 4

Ingredients:

- 2 large sweet potatoes
- 2 teaspoons coconut oil, melted
- 2 teaspoons salt

Directions:

- Using a mandolin, slice the potatoes into thin rounds. In a large bowl, combine the potato slices, salt, and coconut oil and toss to coat.
- Place paraflexx screens on the racks of your excalibur food dehydrator and place the potato slices on the screens in a single layer.

- Set your excalibur to 125f and dehydrate for 12 to 14 hours or until the potato slices are crisp. Remove from the screens and store in a cool dry place if not using immediately.

Nutrition Calories: 13 fat: 1.5 g carbs: 0.1 g protein: 0 g.

MEXICAN CRACKERS

Preparation time: 30 minutes
Dehydration time: 6 hours
Servings: 15

Ingredients:

- ½ cup chia seeds
- 1 cup golden flaxseeds
- ½ cup pumpkin seeds
- ½ cup sunflower seeds
- 1 red bell pepper, chopped
- ¼ onion, chopped
- 1 cup carrot pulp
- 1 ½ teaspoons chipotle powder
- 1 teaspoon garlic powder
- Salt to taste
- ½ teaspoon cayenne pepper

Direction:

- in a blender process all the seeds until powdery.
- Stir in the bell pepper and onion.
- Pulse until smooth.
- Stir in the rest of the ingredients.
- Pulse until fully combined.
- Spread the mixture in the cosori premium food dehydrator.
- Score the crackers.
- Dry at 115 degrees f for 6 hours.
- Storage suggestions: store in a sealed food container for up to 5 days.

Tip: soak the seeds in separate bowls of water for 6 hours before processing.

Nutrition Calories: 122 fat: 7.4 g, carbs: 10.8 g protein: 3.9 g.

FLAX CRACKERS

Preparation time: 4 hours and 10 minutes
Dehydration time: 24 hours
Servings: 12 crackers

Ingredients:

- 1 ½ cups water
- 1 clove garlic, minced
- ¾ cup golden flax seeds
- ¼ cup flax seeds
- 3 teaspoons sesame seeds, crushed
- 3 teaspoons poppy seeds, crushed
- 3 teaspoons garlic flakes

- 3 teaspoons onion flakes
- 3 teaspoons salt

Direction:

- ❖ Add the water and garlic in a blender.
- ❖ Blend until smooth.
- ❖ Pour the mixture in a bowl with the flaxseeds.
- ❖ Soak for 4 hours.
- ❖ Spread the gelatin mixture in the cosori premium food dehydrator.
- ❖ Score the crackers with a knife.
- ❖ Combine the remaining ingredients in a bowl.
- ❖ Sprinkle the mixture on top of the crackers.
- ❖ Process at 110 degrees f for 24 hours.
- ❖ Storage suggestions: store in a glass jar with lid for up to 5 days.

Tip: make your own garlic and onion flakes.

Nutrition Calories: 122 fat: 7.4 g, carbs: 10.8 g protein: 3.9 g.

GREEN CRACKERS

Preparation time: 20 minutes
Dehydration time: 8 hours
Servings: 4

Ingredients:

- 1 cup green juice pulp
- ¼ cup ground flax seeds
- ¼ cup chia seeds
- ¼ cup nutritional yeast
- 2 tablespoons sesame seeds
- 1 tablespoon tamari
- ½ teaspoon salt
- ¼ cup water

Direction:

- ❖ Combine all the ingredients in a bowl.
- ❖ Transfer to a food processor.
- ❖ Pulse until fully combined.
- ❖ Spread a thin layer of the mixture in the cosori premium food dehydrator.
- ❖ Score the crackers.
- ❖ Process at 115 degrees f for 5 hours.
- ❖ Flip the crackers.
- ❖ Dry for another 3 hours.
- ❖ Storage suggestions: store in a sealable plastic bag for up to 7 days.

Tip: the mixture layer should be 1/8 inch thick only.

Nutrition Calories: 122 fat: 7.4 g, carbs: 10.8 g

protein: 3.9 g.

SEAWEED & TAMARI CRACKERS

Preparation time: 15 minutes
Dehydration time: 24 hours
Servings: 15

Ingredients:

- 1 cup flax seeds
- 2 nori sheets, broken
- 2 tablespoons tamari
- 1 ½ cups water

Direction:

- ❖ Mix all the ingredients in a bowl.
- ❖ Spread a layer in the cosori premium food dehydrator.
- ❖ Set it at 110 degrees f.
- ❖ Process for 24 hours.
- ❖ Break into crackers.
- ❖ Storage suggestions: store in a glass jar with lid for up to 5 days.

Tip: soak flaxseeds in water for 1 hour before processing.

Nutrition Calories: 122 fat: 7.4 g, carbs: 10.8 g protein: 3.9 g.

GARLIC ZUCCHINI CHIPS

Preparation time: 15 minutes
Dehydration time: 4 hours
Servings: 4

Ingredients:

- 3 zucchinis, sliced into thin rounds
- 2 tablespoons olive oil
- 2 tablespoons sesame seeds
- 2 tablespoons dried thyme, crushed
- 2 cloves garlic, grated
- Salt to taste

Direction:

- ❖ Coat the zucchini with olive oil.
- ❖ Sprinkle with the sesame seeds, thyme, garlic and salt.
- ❖ Add these to the cosori premium food dehydrator.
- ❖ Dehydrate at 158 degrees f for 2 hours.
- ❖ Flip and dry for another 2 hours.
- ❖ Storage suggestions: store in a sealable plastic bag.
- ❖ **Tip:** before dehydrating, press the zucchini rounds with paper towel to remove excess moisture.

Nutrition: calories 70, fat 4, fiber 4, carbs 30, protein 2

PEAR CHIPS

Preparation time: 10 minutes
Dehydration time: 6 hours
Servings: 10

Ingredients:

- 10 pears, cored and sliced thinly

Direction:

- ❖ Arrange the pear slices in the cosori premium food dehydrator.
- ❖ Dehydrate at 145 degrees f for 8 hours.
- ❖ Storage suggestions: store in a sealed food container for up to 7 days.

Tip: make sure the pear slices do not overlap to ensure even crisp.

Nutrition: calories 70, fat 4, fiber 4, carbs 30, protein 2

BANANA CHIPS

Preparation time: 15 minutes
Dehydration time: 12 hours
Servings: 4

Ingredients:

- 4 bananas, sliced thinly
- 1 teaspoon lemon juice

Direction:

- ❖ Drizzle the banana slices with lemon juice.
- ❖ Add these to the cosori premium food dehydrator.
- ❖ Process at 135 degrees f for 12 hours.
- ❖ Storage suggestions: store in a vacuum sealed plastic for up to 3 months.

Tip: drizzling bananas with lemon juice prevents browning.

Nutrition: calories 70, fat 4, fiber 4, carbs 30, protein 2

SESAME & CARROT CRACKERS

Preparation time: 45 minutes
Dehydration time: 24 hours
Servings: 15

Ingredients:

- 1 ½ cups of golden flaxseeds
- ¼ cup sesame seeds
- 2 cups carrot pulp
- 1 teaspoon of garlic powder
- ½ teaspoon of ground coriander
- 3 tablespoons tamari
- 1 cup water

Direction:

- ❖ Grind the flaxseeds in the spice grinder.
- ❖ Add to a bowl along with the remaining ingredients.
- ❖ Mix well.
- ❖ Let sit for 30 minutes.
- ❖ Spread the mixture in the cosori premium food dehydrator.
- ❖ Process at 110 degrees f for 24 hours.
- ❖ Storage suggestions: store in an airtight jar for up to 7 days.

Tip: make your own garlic powder.

Nutrition Calories: 122 fat: 7.4 g, carbs: 10.8 g protein: 3.9 g.

PEANUT BUTTER & BANANA CRACKERS

Preparation time: 4 hours and 20 minutes
Dehydration time: 6 hours
Servings: 12

Ingredients:

- 3 bananas, sliced
- ½ cup peanut butter
- ½ teaspoon cinnamon powder
- 1 cup ground peanuts
- 3 cups graham cracker crumbs

Direction:

- ❖ Mash the bananas and peanut butter in a bowl.
- ❖ Stir in the rest of the ingredients.
- ❖ Roll the dough into a large ball.
- ❖ Flatten the ball to form a long rectangle.
- ❖ Wrap the dough with wax paper and refrigerate for 4 hours.
- ❖ Roll out the dough and slice.
- ❖ Add the slices to the cosori premium food dehydrator.
- ❖ Process at 145 degrees f for 6 hours.
- ❖ Storage suggestions: store in a glass jar with lid for up to 5 days.

Tip: do not skip refrigerating the dough before the dehydration process.

Nutrition: Calories: 178, Fat: 13.3g, Carbs: 10.7g, Protein: 4.4g

CHAPTER 4

VEGETABLES

MAPLE CARROT STRAWS

Preparation time: 15 minutes
Dehydration time: 6 hours
Servings: 4

Ingredients:

- 1 lb. Carrots, sliced into long strips
- 1 tablespoon maple syrup
- 1 tablespoon olive oil
- Salt to taste

Direction:

- ❖ Combine all the ingredients in a bowl.
- ❖ Arrange the strips in the cosori premium food dehydrator.
- ❖ Process at 135 degrees f for 6 hours.
- ❖ Storage suggestions: store in a food container.

Tip: use a peeler to slice the carrots.
Nutrition Calories: 214 Fat 3 g Carbs 41.4 g Protein 4.3 g

DEHYDRATED ASPARAGUS

Preparation time: 10 minutes
Dehydration time: 6 hours
Servings: 2

Ingredients:

- 4 cups asparagus, trimmed and sliced

Direction:

- ❖ Arrange the asparagus in the cosori premium food dehydrator.
- ❖ Process at 125 degrees f for 6 hours.
- ❖ Storage suggestions: store in a sealable plastic bag.

Tip: you can also season the asparagus with salt or garlic powder.

Nutrition Calories: 434 Fat 39.4 g Carbs 20.9 g Protein 5.8 g

FALL CARROT CHIPS

Preparation time: 15 minutes
Dehydration time: 6 hours
Servings: 4

Ingredients:

- 1 pound of carrots, peeled
- 3 tbsp. Melted coconut oil
- ¾ tsp. Salt
- 2 tsp. Allspice (or combination of cinnamon, allspice or nutmeg)

Direction:

- ❖ Wash, dry and slice carrots into uniform disks.
- ❖ Mix together carrots, oil, salt and allspice.

- ❖ Place carrots onto dehydrator trays and dry for 6-6 hours at 125 degrees or until crisp.

Nutrition Calories:: 11, sodium: 337 mg, dietary fiber: 0.7 g, total fat: 0 g, total carbs: 2.7 g, protein: 0.2 g.

HERBED SWEET POTATO CHIPS

Preparation time: 15 minutes
Dehydration time: 6 hours
Servings: 4

Ingredients:

- 3 medium to large sweet potatoes
- 4 tbsp. Olive oil
- 2 tbsp. Fresh lemon juice
- 2 tsp. Dried thyme
- 1 ½ tsp. Salt
- ¼ tsp. Pepper

Direction:

- ❖ Slice sweet potatoes into thin, uniform slices.
- ❖ In a bowl combine sweet potato slices, oil, lemon juice, thyme, salt and pepper. Toss until well coated.
- ❖ Place slices on dehydrator trays.
- ❖ Set the temperature to 140 degrees. Dehydrate for 6-6 hours, or until crisp to touch.

Nutrition Calories: 35, sodium: 721 mg, dietary fiber: 1.9 g, total fat: 0.2 g, total carbs: 8.3 g, protein: 0.6 g.

DRIED CAULIFLOWER POPCORN

Preparation time: 15 minutes
Dehydration time: 8 hours

Serving: 1

Ingredients:

- 2 cups cauliflower florets
- 4 tablespoons hot sauce
- 3 tablespoons coconut oil
- 1 teaspoon smoked cayenne
- ½ teaspoon ground cumin
- 1 tablespoons paprika

Direction:

- ❖ Toss the cauliflower florets in hot sauce and coconut oil.
- ❖ Sprinkle with the smoked cayenne, cumin and paprika.
- ❖ Add the seasoned cauliflower to the cosori premium food dehydrator.
- ❖ Dry at 130 degrees f for 8 hours.
- ❖ Storage suggestions: store in an airtight plastic bag.

Tip: add more cayenne pepper for spicier cauliflower popcorn.

Nutrition Calories:: 9, sodium: 0 mg, dietary fiber: 0 g, total fat: 0 g, total carbs: 2.1 g, protein: 0.2 g.

ZUCCHINI SNACKS

Preparation time: 45 minutes
Dehydration time: 12 hours
Servings: 4

Ingredients:

- 8 zucchinis, sliced into rounds and seeds removed
- 1 cup grape juice concentrate
- 1 cup water

Direction:

- ❖ Add all the ingredients to a pot over medium heat.
- ❖ Bring to a boil.
- ❖ Reduce heat and simmer for 30 minutes.
- ❖ Drain the zucchini and let cool.
- ❖ Add the zucchinis to the cosori premium food dehydrator.
- ❖ Process at 135 degrees f for 12 hours.
- ❖ Storage suggestions: store in the refrigerator for up to 1 week.

Tip: do not overcook the zucchinis.

Nutrition Calories:: 9, sodium: 0 mg, dietary fiber: 0 g, total fat: 0 g, total carbs: 2.1 g, protein: 0.2 g.

CUCUMBER CHIPS

Preparation time: 15 minutes
Dehydration time: 6 hours
Servings: 4

Ingredients:

- 3 cucumber, sliced into rounds
- 1 tablespoon avocado oil
- 2 teaspoons apple cider vinegar
- Salt to taste

Direction:

- ❖ Toss the cucumber slices in avocado oil and vinegar.
- ❖ Season with the salt.
- ❖ Add the cucumber slices to the cosori premium food dehydrator.
- ❖ Dehydrate at 135 degrees f for 6 hours.
- ❖ Storage suggestions: store in an airtight container.
- ❖ **Tip:** you can use a mandoline slicer to slice the cucumbers thinly. Dry the cucumber slices with a paper towel before processing.

Nutrition Calories:: 9, sodium: 0 mg, dietary fiber: 0 g, total fat: 0 g, total carbs: 2.1 g, protein: 0.2 g.

DEHYDRATED OKRA

Preparation time: 15 minutes
Dehydration time: 12 hours
Servings: 4

Ingredients:

- 12 okra, sliced

Direction:

- ❖ Add the okra to the cosori premium food dehydrator.
- ❖ Dry at 130 degrees f for 12 hours.
- ❖ Storage suggestions: store in an airtight container.

Tip: sprinkle with powdered herb or spice for added flavor.

Nutrition: calories 70, fat 4, fiber 4, carbs 30, protein 2

DRIED SWEET POTATO

Preparation time: 10 minutes
Dehydration time: 12 hours
Servings: 4

Ingredients:

- 2 sweet potatoes
- 1 teaspoon onion powder

Direction:

- ❖ Season the sweet potato slices with onion powder.
- ❖ Arrange in a single layer in the cosori premium food dehydrator.
- ❖ Set at 115 degrees f.
- ❖ Process for 12 hours.
- ❖ Storage suggestions: store in a sealable plastic bag.

Tip: use a mandolin slicer to prepare the sweet potatoes.

Nutrition: calories 70, fat 4, fiber 4, carbs 30, protein 2

DEHYDRATED BEETS

Preparation time: 20 minutes
Dehydration time: 12 hours
Servings: 4

Ingredients:

- 3 beets, sliced thinly
- ¼ cup water
- ¼ cup vinegar
- 1 tablespoon olive oil
- Salt to taste

Direction:

- ❖ Combine all the ingredients in a bowl.
- ❖ Marinate for 10 minutes.
- ❖ Arrange the beet slices in the cosori premium food dehydrator.

- ❖ Dehydrate at 135 degrees f for 12 hours.
- ❖ Storage suggestions: store in a sealable plastic bag.

Tip: use a mandoliner slicer to slice the beets thinly.

Nutrition: calories 70, fat 4, fiber 4, carbs 30, protein 2

DEHYDRATED TOMATOES

Preparation time: 20 minutes
Dehydration time: 8 hours
Servings: 2

Ingredients:

- 2 tomatoes, sliced into quarters
- Salt to taste

Direction:

- ❖ Add the tomatoes to the cosori premium food dehydrator.
- ❖ Sprinkle with salt.
- ❖ Set to 135 degrees f.
- ❖ Process for 8 hours.
- ❖ Storage suggestions: store in a sealable plastic bag. Squeeze out the air. Store for up to 2 months in a cool dry place.
- ❖ Freeze and store for up to 6 months.

Tip: don't forget to scrape the seeds before drying.

Nutrition Calories: 250 Fat 7.6 g Carbs 41.8 g Protein 4.5 g

SPICED CUCUMBERS

Preparation time: 20 hours
Dehydration time: 4 hours
Servings: 2

Ingredients:

- 2 cucumbers, sliced into rounds
- 2 teaspoons olive oil
- 2 teaspoons vinegar
- 1 tablespoon paprika
- 2 teaspoons onion powder
- 2 teaspoons garlic powder
- 2 teaspoons sugar
- Pinch chili powder

Direction:

- ❖ Toss the cucumbers in oil and vinegar.
- ❖ Sprinkle with the sugar and spices.
- ❖ Put the cucumber slices in the cosori premium food dehydrator.
- ❖ Process at 135 degrees f for 6 hours.
- ❖ Storage suggestions: store in an airtight container.

Tip: dehydrate longer if you want your cucumber crispier.

Nutrition Calories: 250 Fat 7.6 g Carbs 41.8 g Protein 4.5 g

DEHYDRATED CORN

Preparation time: 10 minutes
Dehydration time: 12 hours
Servings: 4

Ingredients:

- 8 cups corn kernels

Direction:

- ❖ Spread the corn kernels in the cosori premium food dehydrator.
- ❖ Process at 125 degrees f for 12 hours.
- ❖ Storage suggestions: store in a glass jar with lid.

Tip: you can also drizzle the corn kernels in olive oil before dehydrating.

Nutrition Calories: 214 Fat 3 g Carbs 41.4 g Protein 4.3 g

HOT & SPICY POTATO STICKS

Preparation time: 15 minutes
Dehydration time: 6 hours
Servings: 4

Ingredients:

- 2 large idaho potatoes, peeled and cut like french fries
- 3-4 tsp. Olive oil
- ½ tsp. Cumin
- ¼ tsp. Black pepper
- ¼ tsp. Cayenne pepper (or more for increased spiciness)
- Dash of hot pepper sauce
- Salt to taste

Direction:

- ❖ Blanch potatoes in a pot of boiling water for 4-6 minutes.
- ❖ Transfer potatoes to a bowl of ice water.
- ❖ Combine potatoes, olive oil, cumin, both peppers and hot pepper sauce.
- ❖ Lay potatoes onto dehydrator trays.
- ❖ Set the dehydrator to 135 degrees and dehydrate for 8-6 hours.

Nutrition Calories:: 5, sodium: 1 mg, dietary fiber: 0 g, total fat: 0.1 g, total carbs: 1 g, protein: 0.1 g.

INDIAN CAULIFLOWER

Preparation time: 15 minutes
Dehydration time: 6 hours
Servings: 4

Ingredients:

- 2 heads cauliflower, cut into bite size pieces
- ¼ cup low sodium soy sauce

- 1/8 cup honey
- 1 tsp. Curry powder
- 1 tsp. Turmeric

Direction:

- ❖ Blend all ingredients in a bowl except cauliflower. Whisk to ensure honey is incorporated. Add cauliflower and mix well so vegetables are well coated.
- ❖ Place cauliflower pieces onto dehydrator sheets and dehydrate at 140 degrees for one hour. Lower the temperature and dehydrate at 110 degrees for another 6 hours or until crispy.

Nutrition Calories:: 20, sodium: 8 mg, dietary fiber: 0.9 g, total fat: 0.2 g, total carbs: 4.7 g, protein: 0.6 g.

LEMON PEPPER YELLOW SQUASH ROUNDS

Preparation time: 15 minutes
Dehydration time: 6 hours
Servings: 4

Ingredients:

- 2 large yellow squash, cut into 1/8" thick rounds
- 3-4 tsp. Olive oil
- 1 tbsp. Lemon juice
- ½ tsp. Lemon pepper seasoning
- Salt to taste

Direction:

- ❖ Toss squash slices with olive oil until well coated. Add lemon juice, lemon pepper seasoning and salt and combine all ingredients thoroughly.
- ❖ Spread squash onto dehydrator trays.
- ❖ Set the dehydrator to 135 degrees and dehydrate for 10-12 hours. Halfway through, flip each chip over to prevent sticking.

Nutrition Calories:: 5, sodium: 3 mg, dietary fiber: 0 g, total fat: 0.1 g, total carbs: 0.9 g, protein: 0.3 g.

SMOKED COLLARD GREEN CHIPS

Preparation time: 15 minutes
Dehydration time: 6 hours
Servings: 4

Ingredients:

- 1 bunch collard greens, washed and leaves roughly torn
- 3 tbsp. Olive oil
- ½ tsp. Smoked paprika
- ½ tsp. Sea salt
- ¼ tsp. Pepper

Direction:

- ❖ Toss collard greens, olive oil and spices in a bowl.
- ❖ Place collard greens onto a dehydrator tray.
- ❖ Set the temperature to 140 degrees. Dehydrate for 2-4 hours, or until crispy.

Nutrition Calories:: 16, sodium: 262 mg, dietary fiber: 0.7 g, total fat: 0.1 g, total carbs: 3.4 g, protein: 0.9 g.

SMOKY SWEET POTATO CHIPS

Preparation time: 15 minutes
Dehydration time: 6 hours
Servings: 4

Ingredients:

- 3 large sweet potatoes, washed and sliced into very thin slices
- 2 tsp. Olive oil
- 1 ½ tsp. Smoked paprika
- Sea salt to taste

Direction:

- ❖ Blanch potatoes in a pot of boiling water for 4-6 minutes.
- ❖ Transfer potatoes to a bowl of ice water.
- ❖ Combine sliced potatoes, olive oil, smoked paprika and salt.
- ❖ Lay potatoes onto dehydrator trays.
- ❖ Set the dehydrator to 135 degrees and dehydrate for 8-6 hours, or until crispy.

Nutrition Calories:: 37, sodium: 3 mg, dietary fiber: 1.8 g, total fat: 0.3 g, total carbs: 8.5 g, protein: 0.7 g.

SPINACH BALLS

Preparation time: 15 minutes
Dehydration time: 6 hours
Servings: 4

Ingredients:

- 3 cups cashews
- 3 cups blanched spinach
- 4 tbsp. Olive oil
- ¼ cup dehydrated onion flakes
- 3 cloves of garlic
- ¼ tsp. Nutmeg
- Pinch of cayenne pepper

Direction:

- ❖ Process the cashews until they are finely ground. Add all the remaining ingredients and pulse several times until well combined and paste-like in consistency.
- ❖ Pour mixture into a bowl and form into small, bite-size balls.

- ❖ Place spinach balls on dehydrator sheets and dehydrate at 120 degrees for 5 hours.

Nutrition Calories:: 137, sodium: 7 mg, dietary fiber: 0.9 g, total fat: 10.5 g, total carbs: 9.2 g, protein: 3.7 g.

SOUR CREAM AND ONION POTATO CHIPS

Preparation time: 15 minutes
Dehydration time: 6 hours
Servings: 4

Ingredients:

- 2 large russet potatoes, washed, peeled and sliced into chunks
- ½ cup sour cream
- 1 ½ cups water
- 1 tbsp. Onion powder
- 1 tbsp. Minced onion
- 1 tbsp. Dried parsley
- 1 ½ tsp. Salt
- ½ tsp. Black pepper

Direction:

- ❖ Cook potatoes in a pot of boiling water until soft.
- ❖ Drain potatoes when done and place in a bowl with the remaining ingredients.
- ❖ Use an immersion blender to create a soft paste.
- ❖ Use a spatula to smooth the paste onto the dehydrator sheets in a fairly thin layer.
- ❖ Set the dehydrator to 145 degrees. Place trays in dehydrator for 4-6 hours. Flip and return to the dehydrator for several hours, for a total of 9-6 hours.
- ❖ Once cooled, break into smaller pieces.

Nutrition Calories: 40, sodium: 505 mg, dietary fiber: 0.6 g, total fat: 2.2 g, total carbs: 4.7 g, protein: 0.9 g.

SOUTHWESTERN STYLE CAULIFLOWER POPCORN

Preparation time: 15 minutes
Dehydration time: 6 hours
Servings: 4

Ingredients:

- 1 head cauliflower, cut into bite sized pieces
- 1 tsp. Paprika
- 1 tsp. Oregano
- 1 tsp. Coriander
- 1 tsp. Cumin
- ¼ tsp. Onion powder
- ¼ tsp. Garlic powder
- 1/8 – ¼ tsp. Cayenne pepper
- ½ tsp. Salt
- 3 tbsp. Olive oil

Direction:

- ❖ Blend all the seasonings and olive oil in a bowl. Add cauliflower and combine to coat all the florets.
- ❖ Place cauliflower pieces onto dehydrator sheets and dehydrate at 140 degrees for one hour. Lower the temperature and dehydrate at 110 degrees for another 6 hours or until crispy.

Nutrition Calories: 17, sodium: 212 mg, dietary fiber: 1.6 g, total fat: 0.5 g, total carbs: 3.1 g, protein: 1 g.

MARINATED EGGPLANT

Preparation time: 15 minutes
Dehydration time: 6 hours
Servings: 4

Ingredients:

- 1 eggplant, peeled or unpeeled
- ¼ cup olive oil
- 4 tbsp. Balsamic vinegar
- 2 tbsp. Maple syrup
- ½ tsp. Sriracha sauce
- Salt and pepper to taste

Direction:

- ❖ Slice eggplant into long, uniform strips.
- ❖ Combine oil, vinegar, maple syrup and srircaha sauce with eggplant in a bowl. Sprinkle on salt and pepper to taste. Refrigerate for a minimum of 2 hours.
- ❖ Place eggplant on dehydrator trays and dehydrate for 12-18 hours at 115 degrees.

Nutrition Calories:: 17, sodium: 7 mg, dietary fiber: 0.8 g, total fat: 0.1 g, total carbs: 4.3 g, protein: 0.2 g.

MEDITERRANEAN STYLE "SUN-DRIED" TOMATOES

Preparation time: 15 minutes
Dehydration time: 6 hours
Servings: 4

Ingredients:

- 4 large firm, ripe tomatoes
- 1 ½ tsp. Mixed dried herbs, such as oregano, thyme and basil
- ½ tsp. Sea salt

Direction:

- ❖ Wash tomatoes and cut off tops. Tomatoes do not need to peeled and seeded. Slice tomatoes into ¼ inch thick slices.
- ❖ Sprinkle tomatoes with herbs and salt and place on dehydrator trays.

❖ Set the dehydrator to 145 degrees and dehydrate for 8-6 hours, or until leathery.

Nutrition Calories:: 5, sodium: 325 mg, dietary fiber: 0 g, total fat: 0.1 g, total carbs: 1.1 g, protein: 0.2 g.

MOROCCAN CARROT CRUNCH

Preparation time: 15 minutes
Dehydration time: 6 hours
Servings: 4

Ingredients:

- 1 pound of carrots, peeled
- 4 tbsp. Olive oil
- 1 tbsp. Honey
- 1/8 tsp. Cayenne pepper
- 2 tsp. Cumin
- 1 tsp. Dried parsley flakes
- ½ tsp. Salt

Direction:

❖ Wash, dry and thinly slice carrots.
❖ Mix together oil, honey, and seasonings.
❖ Place carrots onto dehydrator trays. Using a pastry brush, dab the mixture onto the carrot rounds.
❖ Dehydrate for 6-6 hours at 125 degrees or until crisp.

Nutrition Calories:: 26, sodium: 262 mg, dietary fiber: 0.7 g, total fat: 0.3 g, total carbs: 6 g, protein: 0.5 g

PARMESAN CUCUMBER CHIPS

Preparation time: 15 minutes
Dehydration time: 6 hours
Servings: 4

Ingredients:

- 5 cups cucumber slices, thinly sliced with a mandolin
- 2 tbsp. Olive oil
- ½ tsp. Salt
- ¼ tsp. Black pepper
- ½ tsp. Dried parsley flakes
- ½ cup freshly grated parmesan cheese

Direction:

❖ Mix the salt, pepper, parsley flakes and parmesan cheese in a bowl. Toss sliced cucumbers with olive oil and combine with seasoning and cheese mixture. Coat the slices well.
❖ Place slices on dehydrator sheets and dehydrate for 8-6 hours at 135 degrees.

Nutrition Calories:: 39, sodium: 220 mg, dietary fiber: 0 g, total fat: 2.4 g, total carbs: 1.1 g, protein: 3.7 g.

RANCH BRUSSELS SPROUT SKINS

Preparation time: 15 minutes
Dehydration time: 6 hours
Servings: 4

Ingredients:

- 4 cups brussels sprouts, coarsely chopped, tough centers discarded
- 1 cup buttermilk
- 1 tsp. Mustard
- 3 tbsp. Oil
- ½ tsp. Salt
- 1 tsp. Onion powder
- 1 tsp. Minced garlic flakes
- 1 tsp. Dried dill
- 1 tsp. Dried parsley
- 1 tsp. Celery salt

Direction:

❖ Place sliced brussels sprouts in a bowl. Blend the seasonings in another small bowl.
❖ Whisk together buttermilk, mustard and oil. Pour over brussels sprouts.
❖ Spray dehydrator tray with nonstick spray and place brussels sprouts on tray. Sprinkle with seasonings. Set the dehydrator to 110 degrees and dehydrate for 8-6 hours.

Nutrition Calories:: 16, sodium: 104 mg, dietary fiber: 0.8 g, total fat: 0.2 g, total carbs: 3 g, protein: 1.1 g.

ROOT VEGETABLE MEDLEY

Preparation time: 15 minutes
Dehydration time: 6 hours
Servings: 4

Ingredients:

- 2 medium beets
- 1 sweet potato
- 2 medium parsnips
- 1 medium celery root
- 3 tbsp. Olive oil
- 1 ½ tsp. Salt
- 1 tsp. Garlic powder
- ½ tsp. Oregano
- Pinch of black pepper

Direction:

❖ Wash, peel and slice vegetables as thinly as possible, preferably with a mandolin.
❖ Place vegetables in a bowl. Mix olive oil with seasonings and pour over vegetables. Toss to coat.
❖ Lay vegetables on trays using different trays for different vegetables. Dehydrate at 105 degrees for at least 8 hours.

Nutrition Calories:: 48, sodium: 737 mg, dietary fiber: 2.1 g, total fat: 0.2 g, total carbs: 11 g, protein: 1.3 g.

SALT & PEPPER VINEGAR ZUCCHINI CHIPS

Preparation time: 15 minutes
Dehydration time: 6 hours
Servings: 4

Ingredients:

- 2 large green zucchini, cut into 1/8" thick rounds
- 3-4 tsp. Olive oil
- 1 tbsp. + 1 tsp. Apple cider vinegar
- Salt & pepper to taste

Direction:

- ❖ Toss zucchini slices with olive oil until well coated. Add vinegar, salt and pepper and combine.
- ❖ Spread zucchini onto a dehydrator tray.
- ❖ Set the dehydrator to 135 degrees and dehydrate for 10-12 hours. Halfway through, flip each chip over to prevent sticking.

Nutrition Calories:: 7, sodium: 338 mg, dietary fiber: 0 g, total fat: 0 g, total carbs: 1.8 g, protein: 0.2 g.

SALT AND VINEGAR CUCUMBER CHIPS

Preparation time: 15 minutes
Dehydration time: 6 hours
Servings: 4

Ingredients:

- 2 large cucumbers, peeled and sliced thins
- 2 tsp. Apple cider vinegar
- 1 tsp. Fresh lemon juice
- ½ tsp. Kosher salt
- ½ tsp. Sugar

Direction:

- ❖ In a bowl, whisk together vinegar, lemon juice, salt and sugar. Add cucumbers and toss in dressing.
- ❖ Place cucumber slices on dehydrator tray and dehydrate for 4-6 hours at 135 degrees.

Nutrition Calories:: 6, sodium: 0 mg, dietary fiber: 0.6 g, total fat: 0 g, total carbs: 1.2 g, protein: 0.3 g.

SWEET KALE CHIPS

Preparation time: 15 minutes
Dehydration time: 6 hours
Servings: 4

Ingredients:

- 1 bunch curly kale, washed, tough stems removed and leaves roughly torn
- ½ cup pine nuts
- 1/8-1/4 cup white sugar
- ½ tbsp. Cinnamon
- 1/3 cup water
- 1/8 cup apple cider vinegar

Direction:

- ❖ Place pine nuts, sugar and cinnamon in a food processor.
- ❖ Blend water and vinegar and add slowly to food processor.
- ❖ Pour mixture over kale and mix until coated.
- ❖ Place on dehydrating trays for 2-4 hours at 140 degrees.

Nutrition Calories:: 108, sodium: 5 mg, dietary fiber: 1.3 g, total fat: 7.9 g, total carbs: 9.4 g, protein: 1.9 g.

SWEET AND SAVORY BEET ROUNDS

Preparation time: 15 minutes
Dehydration time: 6 hours
Servings: 4

Ingredients:

- 4 large beets, washed
- 2 tbsp. Olive oil
- 1 tsp. Fresh rosemary, finely chopped
- ½ tsp. Sea salt
- ¼ tsp. Pepper

Direction:

- ❖ Cut tops of beets. Slice beets about 1/8-1/4 inch wide. Use a mandolin if possible.
- ❖ Toss beets, olive oil, rosemary, salt and pepper in a bowl until evenly coated.
- ❖ Set the dehydrator to 145 degrees. Place trays in dehydrator for 10-12 hours.

Nutrition Calories:: 21, sodium: 539 mg, dietary fiber: 1.9 g, total fat: 0.5 g, total carbs: 4.6 g, protein: 0.6 g.

TEX-MEX GREEN BEANS

Preparation time: 15 minutes
Dehydration time: 6 hours
Servings: 4

Ingredients:
- 5 pounds green beans
- 1/3 cup melted coconut oil
- 1 tsp. Chili powder
- 1 tsp. Cumin
- ½ tsp. Each paprika, onion powder, garlic powder, salt and pepper

Direction:
- ❖ Blanch green beans in boiling water for several minutes. Dry beans.
- ❖ Melt coconut oil in microwave. Mix oil and seasonings in a bowl.
- ❖ Coast green beans in oil mixture.
- ❖ Place green beans onto dehydrator and dry for 8-6 hours at 125 degrees.

Nutrition Calories:: 12, sodium: 7 mg, dietary fiber: 1.1 g, total fat: 0.2 g, total carbs: 2.4 g, protein: 0.6 g.

VEGAN BROCCOLI CRISPS

Preparation time: 15 minutes
Dehydration time: 6 hours
Servings: 4

Ingredients:
- 2 heads broccoli, washed and cut into bite size florets
- ½ cup cashews, soaked for at least 1 hour and drained
- 4 tbsp. Nutritional yeast
- 1 tsp. Curry powder
- ½ tsp. Red pepper flakes

Direction:
- ❖ Blend the cashews, nutritional yeast and spices in a food processor. Add water to achieve a smooth texture. Nuts should be fully blended.
- ❖ Pour dressing into a bowl and add broccoli. Coat the florets evenly.
- ❖ Place florets onto dehydrator sheets and dehydrate at 110 degrees for 18 hours.

Nutrition Calories:: 104, sodium: 8 mg, dietary fiber: 2.3 g, total fat: 6.8 g, total carbs: 8 g, protein: 5.1 g

CHAPTER 5

SIDE DISHES

ZUCCHINI CHIPS

Preparation time: 15 minutes
Dehydration time: 12 hours
Servings: 8

Ingredients:

- 4 cups zucchini, sliced thinly
- 2 tbsp. Balsamic vinegar
- 2 tbsp. Olive oil
- 2 tsp. Sea salt

Direction:

- ❖ Add olive oil, balsamic vinegar, and sea salt to the large bowl and stir well.
- ❖ Add sliced zucchini to the bowl and toss well.
- ❖ Arrange zucchini slices on dehydrator trays and dehydrate at 135 f/ 58 c for 8-12 hours.
- ❖ Store in air-tight container.

Nutrition Calories: 40 fat: 3.6g protein: 0.7g carbs: 1.9g

EGGPLANT SLICES

Preparation time: 10 minutes
Dehydration time: 4 hours
Servings: 4

Ingredients:

- 1 medium eggplant, cut into ¼ inch thick slices
- ¼ tsp. Onion powder
- ¼ tsp. Garlic powder
- 1 ½ tsp. Paprika

Directions:

- ❖ Add all ingredients into the mixing bowl and toss well.
- ❖ Arrange eggplant slices on dehydrator trays and dehydrate at 145 f/ 63 c for 4 hours or until crispy.
- ❖ Store in air-tight container.

Nutrition Calories: 32 fat: 0.3g protein: 1.3g carbs: 7.4g

TASTY ZUCCHINI CHIPS

Preparation time: 15 minutes
Dehydration time: 8 hours
Servings: 4

Ingredients:

- 2 medium zucchini wash and cut into ¼ inch slices
- 1/8 tsp. Cayenne pepper
- ½ tsp. Garlic powder
- 1 tsp. Olive oil
- 1/8 tsp. Sea salt

Direction:

- ❖ Add all ingredients into the mixing bowl and toss well to coat.

- ❖ Arrange zucchini slices on dehydrator trays and dehydrate at 135 f/ 58 c for 6-8 hours.
- ❖ Store in air-tight container.

Nutrition Calories: 27 fat: 1.4g protein: 1.3g carbs: 3.6g

BRUSSELS SPROUT CHIPS

Preparation time: 15 minutes
Dehydration time: 6 hours
Servings: 4

Ingredients:

- 2 lbs. Brussels sprouts, wash, dry, cut the root and separate leaves
- 2 fresh lemon juice
- ½ cup water
- ¼ cup nutritional yeast
- 1 jalapeno pepper halved and remove seeds
- 1 cup cashews
- 2 bell peppers
- 1 tsp. Sea salt

Directions:

- ❖ Add brussels sprouts leaves to the large bowl and set aside.
- ❖ Add bell peppers, water, lemon juice, nutritional yeast, jalapeno, cashews, and salt to the blender and blend until smooth.
- ❖ Pour blended mixture over brussels sprouts leaves and toss until well coated.
- ❖ Arrange brussels sprouts on dehydrator trays and dehydrate at 125 f/ 52 c for 6 hours.
- ❖ Allow to cool completely then store in air-tight container.

Nutrition Calories: 237 fat: 11.7g protein: 12.3g carbs: 27.7g

BBQ JERKY STRIPS

Preparation time: 15 minutes
Dehydration time: 6 hours
Servings: 4

Ingredients:

- 2 ½ pounds lean ground beef
- 2 tsp. Salt
- ½ tsp. Garlic powder
- ½ tsp. Onion powder
- 1 ½ tbsp. Brown sugar
- ¼ cup worcestershire sauce
- ½ cup barbecue sauce, slightly diluted with water

Direction:

- ❖ Mix ground beef with dry ingredients until incorporated.
- ❖ Combine liquids and coat beef strips with sauce.

- ❖ Press strips into jerky gun. Squeeze onto dehydrator trays and dry at 145-155 degrees for 6-12 hours.

Nutrition Calories:: 54, sodium: 329 mg, dietary fiber: 0 g, total fat: 1.2 g, total carbs: 4.6 g, protein: 5.8 g.

BOLD BEEF JERKY

Preparation time: 15 minutes
Dehydration time: 6 hours
Servings: 4

Ingredients:

- 2 pounds sliced lean meat
- ¼ cup soy sauce
- 1 tbsp. Worcestershire sauce
- 1 tsp. Hot sauce
- ¼ tsp. Pepper
- ¼ tsp. Garlic powder
- ¼ tsp. Onion powder
- ¼ tsp. Paprika
- 1 tsp. Liquid smoke

Direction:

- ❖ Cut strips into ¼ inch thick slices.
- ❖ Mix all ingredients and coat meat strips.
- ❖ Cover and refrigerate overnight.
- ❖ Place meat slices on dehydrator trays and dry at 145-155 degrees for 6-6 hours.

Nutrition Calories:: 51, sodium: 27 mg, dietary fiber: 0 g, total fat: 1.7 g, total carbs: 0 g, protein: 8.3 g.

ORANGE FLAVORED BEEF JERKY

Preparation time: 15 minutes
Dehydration time: 6 hours
Servings: 4

Ingredients:

- 3 pounds lean beef, trimmed of all fat and sliced into strips 1/8 inches -3/8 inches thick
- 3 oranges, (2 peeled and juiced, and 1 zested)
- 3 tbsp. Soy sauce
- 3 tbsp. Rice vinegar
- 2 tbsp. Sugar
- 3 tbsp. Sesame oil
- 1 ½ tbsp. Toasted sesame oil
- 1 tsp. Asian chili-garlic paste
- 2 tbsp. Fresh ginger, grated

Direction:

- ❖ Place all the ingredients, except for the beef, into a blender and process until smooth.
- ❖ Pour marinade over meat and mix.
- ❖ Keep marinated meat in refrigerator overnight.
- ❖ Remove from refrigerator and let meat come to room temperature.

- ❖ Lay meat on dehydrator sheets in a single layer.
- ❖ Dehydrate at 145-160 degrees for 6-6 hours.

Nutrition Calories:: 61, sodium: 16 mg, dietary fiber: 0 g, total fat: 1.6 g, total carbs: 4.3 g, protein: 7.3 g.

PASTRAMI JERKY

Ingredients:

- 3 pounds lean beef, such as flank
- ½ cup soy sauce
- ¼ cup brown sugar
- ½ cup worcestershire sauce
- 1 tbsp. Lemon juice
- ½ tsp. Cayenne pepper
- 2 tbsp. Coarse pepper seeds
- 2 tbsp. Coriander seeds
- 1 tbsp. Mustard seeds

Direction:

- ❖ Cut each slice of beef into ¼ inch thick strips.
- ❖ Combine all ingredients except seeds. Pour ingredients over sliced meat and refrigerate overnight.
- ❖ Remove from refrigerator and let meat come to room temperature.
- ❖ Lay meat on dehydrator sheets and sprinkle with seeds.
- ❖ Dehydrate at 145-155 degrees for 6-6 hours.

Nutrition Calories:: 56, sodium: 50 mg, dietary fiber: 0 g, total fat: 1.4 g, total carbs: 4.2 g, protein: 6.1 g.

SALMON JERKY

Preparation time: 15 minutes
Dehydration time: 6 hours
Servings: 4

Ingredients:

- 1 ½ pounds salmon, bones removed
- ¼ cup soy sauce
- ¼ cup teriyaki sauce
- 1 tbsp. Dijon mustard
- 1 tbsp. Maple syrup
- 1 freshly squeezed lime
- ½ tsp. Black pepper

Directions:

- ❖ Freeze salmon for 45 minutes to 1 hour prior to slicing.
- ❖ Place remaining ingredients in a bowl and whisk together.
- ❖ Slice salmon into thin strips and add them to the liquid. Marinate for 3 hours.
- ❖ Remove salmon strips, pat dry and place on dehydrator sheets.
- ❖ Dehydrate for 10-12 hours at 155 degrees.

Nutrition Calories:: 36, sodium: 166 mg, dietary fiber: 0 g, total fat: 1.4 g, total carbs: 1.3 g, protein: 4.7 g.

"SMOKED" TURKEY

Preparation time: 15 minutes
Dehydration time: 6 hours
Servings: 4

Ingredients:

- 1 pound, skinless, boneless turkey
- ¼ cup brown sugar
- ¾ cup soy sauce
- 2 tbsp. Liquid smoke
- 1 tbsp. Smoked paprika
- ½ tbsp. Paprika

Direction:

- ❖ Slice turkey into ¼ inch thick strips.
- ❖ Combine all ingredients and pour over turkey strips. Cover turkey and refrigerate 4-6 hours.
- ❖ Place turkey slices on dehydrator trays and dry at 155 degrees for 12-16 hours. Rotate trays occasionally to ensure consistent dehydration.

Nutrition Calories:: 72, sodium: 14 mg, dietary fiber: 1.2 g, total fat: 1.5 g, total carbs: 10 g, protein: 5.6 g.

SMOKEY MEXICAN JERKY

Preparation time: 15 minutes
Dehydration time: 6 hours
Servings: 4

Ingredients:

- 2 pounds beef top round or bottom round, fat trimmed, sliced into ¼ inch thick slices
- ½ cup soy sauce
- 1 cup fresh lime juice
- 1-2 canned chipotle peppers in adobo sauce
- 1 tsp. Chili powder
- 1 cup mexican beer

Direction:

- ❖ Place all the ingredients, except for the beef, into a blender and process until smooth.
- ❖ Pour marinade over meat and refrigerate for 6-8 hours.
- ❖ Remove from refrigerator and place meat on dehydrator sheets in a single layer.
- ❖ Dehydrate at 145-160 degrees for 6-6 hours.

Nutrition Calories:: 59, sodium: 24 mg, dietary fiber: 0.6 g, total fat: 1.7 g, total carbs: 2.7 g, protein: 8.2 g.

SPICED "HAMBURGER" JERKY

Preparation time: 15 minutes
Dehydration time: 6 hours

Servings: 4

Ingredients:

- 2 ½ pounds lean ground beef
- 1 tsp. Adobo seasoning
- 2 tsp. Salt
- ½ tsp. Garlic powder
- ½ tsp. Onion powder
- 1 tbsp. Meat tenderizer
- ½ tsp. Cayenne pepper
- ¼ cup tomato sauce
- 1 ½ tbsp. Brown sugar
- ¼ cup worcestershire sauce
- ¼ cup liquid smoke

Direction:

- ❖ Mix ground beef with dry ingredients until seasonings are well distributed.
- ❖ Combine liquids and coat beef strips with sauce.
- ❖ Press strips into jerky gun. Squeeze onto dehydrator trays and dry at 145-155 degrees for 6-12 hours.

Nutrition Calories:: 52, sodium: 319 mg, dietary fiber: 0 g, total fat: 1.3 g, total carbs: 3.5 g, protein: 6.2 g.

SPICED TURKEY JERKY

Preparation time: 15 minutes
Dehydration time: 6 hours
Servings: 4

Ingredients:

- 2 pounds skinless, boneless turkey
- ¾ cup soy sauce
- 3 tbsp. Brown sugar
- 2 tsp. Chopped garlic
- 2 tsp. Red chili flakes

Direction:

- ❖ Freeze turkey prior to slicing. Cut into ¼ inch thick strips.
- ❖ Combine all ingredients and dip turkey strips into mixture.
- ❖ Cover turkey strips and refrigerate overnight.
- ❖ Place turkey slices on dehydrator trays and dry at 155 degrees for 8-6 hours.

Nutrition Calories:: 62, sodium: 17 mg, dietary fiber: 0 g, total fat: 1.4 g, total carbs: 5.1 g, protein: 6.9 g.

SPICY HARISSA FLAVORED JERKY

Preparation time: 15 minutes
Dehydration time: 6 hours
Servings: 4

Ingredients:

- 3 pounds lean beef, such as bottom round or eye of round
- 2 tbsp. Salt
- 1 tbsp. Brown sugar
- 1 tbsp. Chili powder
- 1 tbsp. Smoked paprika
- 1 tbsp. Cumin
- 1 tbsp. Coriander
- 1 tbsp. Garlic powder
- 1 tbsp. Onion powder
- ¼ tsp. Cayenne pepper

Direction:

- ❖ Cut each slice of beef into ¼ inch thick strips.
- ❖ Combine ingredients and pour into ziplock bag. Add the meat strips and and refrigerate overnight.
- ❖ Remove from refrigerator and let meat come to room temperature.
- ❖ Lay meat on dehydrator sheets and dehydrate at 145-155 degrees for 6-6 hours.

Nutrition Calories:: 56, sodium: 692 mg, dietary fiber: 0.9 g, total fat: 1.8 g, total carbs: 3.5 g, protein: 6.9 g.

SWEET AND SPICY VENISON OR BEEF JERKY

Preparation time: 15 minutes
Dehydration time: 6 hours
Servings: 4

Ingredients:

- 2 pounds venison or beef
- ½ cup brown sugar
- ¼ cup pineapple juice
- 1 tbsp. Black pepper
- 1 tbsp. Lemon juice
- 1 tbsp. Minced garlic
- 1 tbsp. Paprika
- ¼ cup worcestershire sauce
- ½ cup soy sauce
- 1 tsp. Sriracha sauce

Direction:

- ❖ Cut pre-frozen venison or beef into ¼ inch thick slices.
- ❖ Mix all ingredients and coat strips in the sauce.
- ❖ Cover and refrigerate overnight.
- ❖ Place beef or venison slices on dehydrator trays and dry at 145-155 degrees about 6-6 hours.

Nutrition Calories:: 53, sodium: 22 mg, dietary fiber: 1.1 g, total fat: 0.4 g, total carbs: 9.5 g, protein: 3.5 g.

TERIYAKI JERKY

Preparation time: 15 minutes
Dehydration time: 6 hours
Servings: 4

Ingredients:

- 2 ½ pounds sliced lean beef
- 1 cup teriyaki sauce
- 1 cup worcestershire sauce
- ½ cup soy sauce
- 2 tsp. Onion powder
- 2 tsp. Garlic powder
- 1 tsp. Paprika
- 1 tsp. Ground ginger
- 1 tbsp. Red pepper flakes
- 3 tbsp. Honey
- 1 tsp. Lemon juice

Direction:

- ❖ Cut strips into ¼ inch thick slices.
- ❖ Mix ingredients together and marinate meat in sauce mixture.
- ❖ Cover and refrigerate overnight.
- ❖ Place meat slices on dehydrator trays and dry at 145-155 degrees for 6-6 hours.

Nutrition Calories:: 48, sodium: 276 mg, dietary fiber: 0 g, total fat: 1 g, total carbs: 5 g, protein: 4.7 g.

THAI SWEET CHILI JERKY

Preparation time: 15 minutes
Dehydration time: 6 hours
Servings: 4

Ingredients:

- 2 pounds beef top or bottom round, trimmed, cut into ¼ inch slices
- 3 tbsp. Soy sauce
- 1 tbsp. Worcestershire sauce
- 1 tbsp. Teriyaki sauce
- ½ cup water
- 1 cup sweet chili sauce
- 1 tsp. Ground ginger

Direction:

- ❖ Combine the marinade ingredients in a large bowl. Place meat in a ziplock bag and pour marinade over meat.
- ❖ Marinate meat in refrigerator overnight.
- ❖ Place meat on dehydrator sheets in a single layer.
- ❖ Dehydrate at 155 degrees for 6-8 hours.

Nutrition Calories:: 59, sodium: 131 mg, dietary fiber: 0.6 g, total fat: 1.1 g, total carbs: 5 g, protein: 5.6 g.

BOOZY JERKY

Preparation time: 15 minutes
Dehydration time: 6 hours
Servings: 4

Ingredients:

- 2 pounds lean steak, trimmed and frozen up to 2 hours prior to slicing
- 16 ounces dark belgian beer
- 2 tbsp. Teriyaki sauce
- ¼ cup soy sauce
- 2 tbsp. Dark brown sugar
- ½ tsp. Seasoned salt
- 2 cloves of garlic, minced
- ½ tsp. Cayenne pepper

Direction:

- ❖ Mix the marinade ingredients in a large bowl. Place meat in a ziplock bag and pour marinade over meat.
- ❖ Keep meat in refrigerator overnight.
- ❖ Remove from refrigerator and let meat come to room temperature.
- ❖ Lay meat on dehydrator sheets in a single layer.
- ❖ Dehydrate at 160 degrees for 6-8 hours.

Nutrition Calories:: 60, sodium: 76 mg, dietary fiber: 0 g, total fat: 1.6 g, total carbs: 3.5 g, protein: 7.6 g.

KALE CHIPS

Preparation time: 10 minutes
Dehydration time: 4 hours
Servings: 4

Ingredients:

- 2 kale heads
- 1 tsp. Garlic powder
- 1 tsp. Sea salt
- 1 tbsp. Fresh lemon juice
- 3 tbsp. Nutritional yeast
- 2 tbsp. Olive oil

Directions:

- ❖ Wash kale and cut into bits.
- ❖ Add remaining ingredients into the bowl and mix well.
- ❖ Add kale bits to the bowl and mix until well coated.
- ❖ Arrange kale bits on dehydrator trays and dehydrate at 145 f/ 63 c for 3-4 hours or until crispy.

Nutrition Calories: 111 fat: 7.5g protein: 4.9g carbs: 8.5g

DRIED BELL PEPPERS

Preparation time: 10 minutes
Dehydration time: 24 hours
Servings: 4

Ingredients:

- 4 bell peppers cut in half and de-seed

Directions:

- ❖ Cut bell peppers in strips then cut each strip in ½ inch pieces.
- ❖ Arrange bell peppers strips on dehydrator racks and dehydrate at 135 f/ 58 c for 12-24 hours or until crisp.
- ❖ Store in air-tight container.

Nutrition Calories: 38 fat: 0.3g protein: 1.2g carbs: 9g

AVOCADO CHIPS

Preparation time: 15 minutes
Dehydration time: 6 hours
Servings: 4

Ingredients:

- 4 avocados, halved and pitted
- ¼ tsp. Sea salt
- ¼ tsp. Cayenne pepper
- ¼ cup fresh cilantro, chopped
- ½ lemon juice

Directions:

- ❖ Cut avocado into the slices.
- ❖ Drizzle lemon juice over avocado slices.
- ❖ Arrange avocado slices on dehydrator trays and sprinkle with cayenne pepper, salt and cilantro dehydrate at 160 f/ 71 c for 6 hours.

Nutrition Calories: 62 fat: 5.1g protein: 1.1g carbs: 3.2g

SWEET POTATO CHIPS

Preparation time: 10 minutes
Dehydration time: 12 hours
Servings: 2

Ingredients:

- 2 sweet potatoes peel and sliced thinly
- 1/8 tsp. Ground cinnamon
- 1 tsp. Coconut oil, melted
- Seal salt

Directions:

- ❖ Add sweet potato slices in a bowl. Add cinnamon, coconut oil, and salt and toss well.
- ❖ Arrange sweet potato slices on dehydrator trays and dehydrate at 125 f/ 52 c for 12 hours.
- ❖ Store in air-tight container.

Nutrition Calories: 132 fat: 2.3g protein: 2.1g carbs: 26.3g

HEALTHY SQUASH CHIPS

Preparation time: 10 minutes
Dehydration time: 12 hours
Servings: 8

Ingredients:

- 1 yellow squash, cut into 1/8 inch thick slices
- 2 tbsp. Apple cider vinegar
- 2 tsp. Olive oil
- Salt

Directions:

- ❖ Add all ingredients into the bowl and toss well.
- ❖ Arrange squash slices on dehydrator trays and dehydrate at 115 f/ 46 c for 12 hours or until crispy.
- ❖ Store in air-tight container.

Nutrition Calories: 15 fat: 1.2g protein: 0.3g carbs: 0.9g

BROCCOLI CHIPS

Preparation time: 15 minutes
Dehydration time: 12 hours
Servings: 4

Ingredients:

- 1 lb. Broccoli, cut into florets
- 1 tsp. Onion powder
- 1 garlic clove
- ½ cup vegetable broth
- ¼ cup hemp seeds
- 2 tbsp. Nutritional yeast

Directions:

- ❖ Add broccoli florets in a large mixing bowl and set aside.
- ❖ Add remaining ingredients into the blender and blend until smooth.
- ❖ Pour blended mixture over broccoli florets and toss well.
- ❖ Arrange broccoli florets on dehydrator trays and dehydrate at 115 f/ 46 c for 10-12 hours.

Nutrition Calories: 106 fat: 4.3g protein: 8.7g carbs: 11.2g

ASIAN JERKY

Preparation time: 15 minutes
Dehydration time: 6 hours
Servings: 4

Ingredients:

- 1 pound sliced lean beef
- 4 tbsp. Soy sauce
- 4 tbsp. Worcestershire sauce
- 1 tsp. Ground ginger
- ½ tsp. Pepper
- 3 cloves garlic
- 1 tsp. Toasted sesame oil
- 1 tsp. Honey

Direction:

- ❖ Cut strips into ¼ inch thick slices.
- ❖ Blend ingredients and coat meat strips in sauce.
- ❖ Cover and refrigerate overnight.
- ❖ Place meat slices on dehydrator trays and dry at 145-155 degrees for 6-6 hours.

Nutrition Calories: 129 Fat 3.6 g Carbohydrates 23 g Protein 2.3 g

GARLICKY BEEF JERKY

Preparation time: 15 minutes
Dehydration time: 6 hours
Servings: 4

Ingredients:

- 2 pounds thinly sliced beef
- 1 can of coke
- 7 cloves crushed garlic
- ½ cup soy sauce
- 3 tbsp. Worcestershire sauce
- 2 tbsp. Ketchup
- 2 tsp. Red hot sauce
- 1 tsp. Fresh lime juice

Direction:

- ❖ Combine the marinade ingredients in a large bowl. Place meat in a ziplock bag and pour marinade over meat.
- ❖ Marinate meat in refrigerator for 4-8 hours.
- ❖ Lay meat on dehydrator sheets in a single layer.
- ❖ Dehydrate at 155 degrees for 6-8 hours.

Nutrition Calories:: 52, sodium: 60 mg, dietary fiber: 0 g, total fat: 1.6 g, total carbs: 1.1 g, protein: 7.7 g.

MARINATED JERKY

Preparation time: 15 minutes
Dehydration time: 6 hours
Servings: 4

Ingredients:

- 2 pounds sliced lean meat
- ½ gallon water
- ¼ cup plus 1 tbsp. Salt
- ¼ cup sugar
- 2 tbsp. Liquid smoke
- ½ tsp. Black pepper
- ½ tsp. Smoked paprika

Direction:

- ❖ Cut strips into ¼ inch thick slices. Prepare the brine by mixing all the ingredients.
- ❖ Soak meat strips in the brine overnight.
- ❖ Pour off brine. Rinse and pat meat dry.
- ❖ Place meat slices on dehydrator trays and dry at 145-155 degrees for 6-6 hours.

Nutrition Calories:: 54, sodium: 1,842 mg, dietary fiber: 0 g, total fat: 1.2 g, total carbs: 5 g, protein: 5.8 g.

CHAPTER 6

MEAT

PORK JERKY IN CHIPOTLE SAUCE

Preparation time: 12 hours and 10 minutes
Dehydration time: 6 hours
Servings: 2

Ingredients:

- 1 tablespoon tomato paste
- 7 oz. Chipotle adobo sauce
- 1 teaspoon salt
- 1 teaspoon sugar
- 1 teaspoon garlic powder
- 1 lb. Pork tenderloin, sliced

Direction:

- ❖ Mix the tomato paste, chipotle adobo sauce, salt, sugar and garlic powder in a bowl.
- ❖ Transfer to a sealable plastic bag along with the pork tenderloin slices.
- ❖ Seal and refrigerate for 12 hours.
- ❖ Drain the marinade.
- ❖ Add the pork slices to the cosori premium food dehydrator.
- ❖ Process at 158 degrees f for 6 hours.
- ❖ Storage suggestions: place in a glass jar with lid. Store in a cool dry place, away from sunlight.

Tip: pork tenderloin should be sliced at least 5 mm thick.

Nutrition Calories: 54 Fat 0.3 g Carbohydrates 11.3 g Protein 2.5 g

PAPRIKA PORK JERKY

Preparation time: 12 hours and 10 minutes
Dehydration time: 6 hours
Servings: 2

Ingredients:

- 1 lb. Pork tenderloin, sliced
- ½ cup ketchup
- 1 teaspoon onion powder
- 1 teaspoon garlic powder
- 1 teaspoon smoked paprika
- 1 teaspoon ground mustard
- 1 teaspoon chili powder
- Salt and pepper to taste

Direction:

- ❖ Add the ketchup to a bowl.
- ❖ Stir in the onion powder, garlic powder, paprika, mustard, chili powder, salt and pepper.
- ❖ Mix well.
- ❖ Transfer the mixture to a sealable plastic bag.
- ❖ Add the pork to the plastic bag.
- ❖ Seal and refrigerate for 12 hours.
- ❖ Remove the pork from the marinade.
- ❖ Add to the cosori premium food dehydrator.
- ❖ Dry at 158 degrees f for 6 hours.

- ❖ Storage suggestions: store the pork jerky in a glass jar with lid. Store in a cool dry place for up to 2 weeks.

Tip: you can also use garlic salt in place of garlic powder and salt.

Nutrition Calories: 382 Fat 1.2 g Carbs 67.1 g Protein 26.1 g

BEEF BULGOGI JERKY

Preparation time: 12 hours and 10 minutes
Dehydration time: 6 hours
Servings: 4

Ingredients:

- 2 lb. Beef round, sliced
- 4 tablespoons brown sugar
- 4 tablespoons soy sauce
- 1 tablespoon garlic powder
- 1 tablespoon sesame oil
- Sal to taste

Direction:

- ❖ Place the beef inside a sealable plastic bag.
- ❖ In a bowl, mix the remaining ingredients.
- ❖ Add the mixture to the plastic bag.
- ❖ Place the beef in the refrigerator for 12 hours.
- ❖ Drain the marinade.
- ❖ Add the beef to the cosori premium food dehydrator.
- ❖ Set at 165 degrees f.
- ❖ Process for 6 hours.
- ❖ Storage suggestions: place in a glass jar with lid and store in a cool, dry place.

Tip: slice the beef across the grain. Each slice should be at least 5 mm thick.

Nutrition Calories: 382 Fat 1.2 g Carbs 67.1 g Protein 26.1 g

MUSTARD BEEF JERKY WITH BALSAMIC VINEGAR

Preparation time: 12 hours and 10 minutes
Dehydration time: 6 hours
Servings: 4

Ingredients:

- 2 lb. Beef round, sliced
- 2 tablespoons olive oil
- 1 tablespoon dijon mustard
- 1 cup balsamic vinegar
- 2 garlic cloves, crushed
- 1 teaspoon salt

Direction:

- ❖ Add the beef to a sealable plastic bag.
- ❖ Combine the rest of the ingredients in a bowl.
- ❖ Mix well.
- ❖ Pour the mixture into the plastic bag.
- ❖ Place in the refrigerator for 12 hours.
- ❖ Drain the marinade.
- ❖ Add the beef slices to the cosori premium food dehydrator.
- ❖ Set the dehydrator to 165 degrees f.
- ❖ Dry for 6 hours.
- ❖ Storage suggestions: keep the beef jerky slices in a glass container with lid. Store in an area away from sunlight.

Tip: you can dehydrate longer for up to 8 hours.

Nutrition Calories: 372 Fat 27.5 g Carbohydrates 9.6 g Protein 24 g

BUFFALO JERKY

Preparation time: 15 hours and 10 minutes
Dehydration time: 6 hours
Servings: 4

Ingredients:

- 2 lb. Beef round, sliced
- 1 teaspoon salt
- 1 cup buffalo sauce

Direction:

- ❖ Season the beef slices with the salt.
- ❖ Add the buffalo sauce to a bowl.
- ❖ Stir in the seasoned beef.
- ❖ Cover the bowl.
- ❖ Refrigerate for 15 hours.
- ❖ Drain the marinade.
- ❖ Add the beef slices to the cosori premium food dehydrator.
- ❖ Process at 165 degrees f for 6 hours.
- ❖ Storage suggestions: place the beef jerky in a sealable glass container. Store for up to 2 weeks.

Tip: you can also add hot sauce to the marinade for extra zing.

Nutrition Calories: 372 Fat 27.5 g Carbohydrates 9.6 g Protein 24 g

BARBECUE BEEF JERKY

Preparation time: 12 hours and 10 minutes
Dehydration time: 6 hours
Servings: 4

Ingredients:

- 2 lb. Beef round, sliced
- Salt and pepper to taste
- 2 teaspoons dried oregano

- 2 teaspoons ground cumin
- 1 teaspoon onion powder
- 1 teaspoon ground coriander
- 4 cloves garlic, grated
- ½ cup olive oil
- ½ cup lime juice
- 1 teaspoon red pepper flakes

Direction:

- ❖ Add the beef slices to a sealable plastic bag.
- ❖ In a bowl, mix the salt, pepper, herbs, spices, garlic, olive oil, lime juice and red pepper flakes.
- ❖ Pour mixture into the plastic bag.
- ❖ Turn to coat beef slices evenly with the mixture.
- ❖ Seal and marinate for 12 hours.
- ❖ Drain the marinade.
- ❖ Place the beef slices to the cosori food dehydrator dehydrator.
- ❖ Set it to 165 degrees f and process for 6 hours.
- ❖ Storage suggestions: keep the beef jerky in a vacuum sealed plastic bag.

Tip: you can also use lemon juice instead of lime juice.

Nutrition Calories: 372 Fat 27.5 g Carbohydrates 9.6 g Protein 24 g

SWEET & SOUR PORK

Preparation time: 12 hours and 10 minutes
Dehydration time: 6 hours
Servings: 4

Ingredients:

- 1 lb. Pork tenderloin, sliced
- 2 tablespoons fish sauce
- ¼ cup lime juice
- ¼ cup brown sugar
- 1 shallot, grated
- 2 garlic cloves, grated
- Salt and pepper to taste

Direction:

- ❖ Combine all the ingredients in a bowl.
- ❖ Mix well.
- ❖ Transfer to a sealable plastic bag.
- ❖ Chill in the refrigerator for 12 hours.
- ❖ Remove from the marinade.
- ❖ Transfer the pork slices to the cosori premium food dehydrator.
- ❖ Process at 158 degrees f for 6 hours.
- ❖ Storage suggestions: store in a glass jar with lid, away from direct sunlight.

Tip: see to it that the slices are at least 5 mm thick.

Nutrition Calories: 372 Fat 27.5 g Carbohydrates 9.6 g Protein 24 g

LAMB JERKY

Preparation time: 13 hours
Dehydration time: 6 hours
Servings: 4

Ingredients:

- 3 lb. Leg of lamb, sliced
- ¼ cup soy sauce
- 3 tablespoons worcestershire sauce
- 1 tablespoon oregano
- 1 teaspoon garlic powder
- 1 1/2 teaspoons onion powder
- Pepper to taste

Direction:

- ❖ Add the lamb slices to a sealable plastic bag.
- ❖ Combine the remaining ingredients in a bowl.
- ❖ Mix well.
- ❖ Pour the mixture into a sealable plastic bag.
- ❖ Marinate in the refrigerator for 13 hours.
- ❖ Place the lamb slices to the cosori premium food dehydrator.
- ❖ Process at 145 degrees f for 6 hours.
- ❖ Storage suggestions: store the lamb jerky in a glass jar with lid for up to 2 weeks.

Tip: freeze the lamb for 1 hour first so it will be easier to slice into strips.

Nutrition Calories: 183 Fat 5 g Carbs 28 g Protein 7.3 g

BEEF JERKY

Preparation time: 10 minutes
Dehydration time: 6 hours
Servings: 4

Ingredients:

- 2 lb. Beef eye of round
- ½ cup soy sauce
- ½ cup worcestershire sauce
- 1 teaspoon salt
- 1 tablespoon honey

Direction:

- ❖ Slice the beef eye of round across the grain.
- ❖ Add the soy sauce, worcestershire sauce, salt and honey in a sealable plastic bag.
- ❖ Add the beef to the plastic bag.
- ❖ Turn to coat.
- ❖ Place inside the refrigerator for 12 hours.
- ❖ Drain the marinade.
- ❖ Add the beef to the cosori premium food dehydrator.
- ❖ Process at 165 degrees f for 6 hours.
- ❖ Storage tips: store in a cool dry place. Store in a glass jar with lid for up to 2 weeks.

Tip: slices should be about 5 mm thick.

Nutrition Calories:: 59, sodium: 131 mg, dietary fiber: 0.6 g, total fat: 1.1 g, total carbs: 5 g, protein: 5.6 g.

CANDIED BACON

Preparation time: 12 hours and 10 minutes
Dehydration time: 6 hours
Servings: 4

Ingredients:

- 10 slices bacon
- 3 tablespoons brown sugar
- 3 tablespoons soy sauce
- 2 teaspoons mirin
- 2 teaspoons sesame oil
- 2 tablespoons chili garlic sauce

Direction:

- ❖ Slice each bacon strip into 3 portions.
- ❖ Add the rest of the ingredients in a bowl.
- ❖ Mix well.
- ❖ Add the bacon slices in the mixture.
- ❖ Cover and refrigerate for 12 hours.
- ❖ Add the bacon to the cosori premium food dehydrator.
- ❖ Dehydrate at 165 degrees f for 6 hours.
- ❖ Storage tips: store candied bacon in a glass jar with lid for up to 2 weeks.

Tip: add chili powder to the marinade if you want your candied bacon extra spicy.

Nutrition Calories:: 59, sodium: 131 mg, dietary fiber: 0.6 g, total fat: 1.1 g, total carbs: 5 g, protein: 5.6 g.

BEEF TERIYAKI JERKY

Preparation time: 12 hours and 10 minutes
Dehydration time: 6 hours
Servings: 4

Ingredients:

- 2 lb. Beef round, sliced
- ¼ cup brown sugar
- ½ cup soy sauce
- ¼ cup pineapple juice
- 1 clove garlic, crushed
- ¼ teaspoon ginger, grated

Direction:

- ❖ Add all the ingredients in a bowl.
- ❖ Mix well.
- ❖ Transfer to a sealable plastic bag.
- ❖ Add the beef to the plastic bag.
- ❖ Marinate in the refrigerator for 12 hours.
- ❖ Discard the marinade before dehydrating.
- ❖ Add to the cosori premium food dehydrator.
- ❖ Process at 165 degrees f for 6 hours.

- ❖ Storage suggestions: keep in a glass jar with lid or vacuum sealed bag.

Tip: beef should be sliced at least 5 mm thick.

Nutrition Calories: 129 Fat 3.6 g Carbohydrates 23 g Protein 2.3 g

VIETNAMESE BEEF JERKY

Preparation time: 12 hours and 10 minutes
Dehydration time: 6 hours
Servings: 4

Ingredients:
- 2 lb. Beef round
- 3 tablespoons fish sauce
- 1 tablespoon soy sauce
- 2 tablespoons lime juice
- ¼ cup brown sugar

Direction:
- ❖ Combine all the ingredients in a bowl.
- ❖ Transfer to a sealable plastic bag.
- ❖ Turn to coat the beef strips evenly with the marinade.
- ❖ Place in the refrigerator for 12 hours.
- ❖ Drain the marinade.
- ❖ Add the beef to the cosori premium food dehydrator.
- ❖ Process at 165 degrees f for 6 hours.
- ❖ Storage suggestions: store the jerky in a glass jar with lid for up to 1 week.

Tip: slice the beef across the grain. Make sure beef is at least 5 mm thick.

Nutrition Calories: 129 Fat 3.6 g Carbohydrates 23 g Protein 2.3 g

SMOKED HERBED BACON JERKY

Preparation time: 10 minutes
Dehydration time: 6 hours
Servings: 4

Ingredients:
- 10 slices smoked bacon
- 1 teaspoon ground fennel seeds
- 1/8 teaspoon onion powder
- 1/8 teaspoon garlic powder
- ¼ teaspoon dried sage
- ¼ teaspoon dried thyme
- 1 teaspoon brown sugar
- ¼ teaspoon red pepper flakes
- 1/8 teaspoon black pepper

Direction:
- ❖ Slice the bacon into 3 portions.
- ❖ In a bowl, mix the rest of the ingredients.
- ❖ Sprinkle both sides of the bacon with the seasoning mixture.

- ❖ Add the bacon slices to the cosori premium food dehydrator.
- ❖ Dehydrate at 165 degrees f for 6 hours.
- ❖ Storage suggestions: store the bacon jerky in a glass jar with lid for up to 1 week.

Tip: you can add more red pepper flakes if you want the jerky to be spicier.

Nutrition Calories: 54 Fat 0.3 g Carbohydrates 11.3 g Protein 2.5 g

LEMON FISH JERKY

Preparation time: 4 hours and 10 minutes
Dehydration time: 8 hours
Servings: 2

Ingredients:
- 1 lb. Cod fillet, sliced
- 1 tablespoon lemon juice
- 1 teaspoon lemon zest
- 2 tablespoons olive oil
- 1 teaspoon dill
- 1 clove garlic, grated
- Salt to taste

Direction:
- ❖ Combine the fish slices and the rest of the ingredients in a sealable plastic bag.
- ❖ Turn to coat the fish evenly with the marinade.
- ❖ Place the plastic bag inside the refrigerator for 4 hours.
- ❖ Drain the marinade.
- ❖ Add the fish slices to the cosori premium food dehydrator.
- ❖ Process at 145 degrees f for 8 hours.
- ❖ Storage suggestions: store the fish jerky in a glass jar with lid or vacuum sealed bag for up to 2 weeks.

Tip: you can also use salmon for this recipe.

Nutrition Calories: 183 Fat 5 g Carbs 28 g Protein 7.3 g

SALMON JERKY

Preparation time: 4 hours and 10 minutes
Dehydration time: 8 hours
Servings: 2

Ingredients:
- 1 ¼ lb. Salmon, sliced
- ½ cup soy sauce
- 1 tablespoon molasses
- 1 tablespoon lemon juice
- Pepper to taste

Direction:
- ❖ Place the salmon slices in a sealable plastic bag.
- ❖ Combine the rest of the ingredients in a bowl.
- ❖ Add the mixture to the plastic bag.
- ❖ Marinate inside the refrigerator for 4 hours.

- ❖ Drain the marinade.
- ❖ Add the salmon slices to the cosori premium food dehydrator
- ❖ Process at 145 degrees f for 8 hours.
- ❖ Storage suggestions: place the fish jerky in a food container with lid. Store for up to 2 weeks.

Tip: use freshly squeezed lemon juice. Salmon slices should be ¼ inch thick.

Nutrition Calories: 183 Fat 5 g Carbs 28 g Protein 7.3 g

FISH TERIYAKI JERKY

Preparation time: 4 hours and 10 minutes
Dehydration time: 8 hours
Servings: 2

Ingredients:
- 1 lb. Salmon, sliced
- ¼ teaspoon ginger, grated
- ¼ cup sugar
- ½ cup soy sauce
- ¼ cup orange juice
- 1 clove garlic, minced

Direction:
- ❖ Combine all the ingredients in a bowl.
- ❖ Mix well.
- ❖ Transfer to a sealable plastic bag.
- ❖ Seal and refrigerate for 4 hours.
- ❖ Drain the marinade.
- ❖ Add the salmon to the cosori premium food dehydrator.
- ❖ Process at 145 degrees f for 8 hours.
- ❖ Storage suggestions: store the salmon jerky in a glass jar with lid.

Tip: you can process longer in the dehydrator if you want the fish slices crispier and dryer.

Nutrition Calories: 389 Fat 6.4 g Carbs 22.9 g Protein 49.3 g

CAJUN FISH JERKY

Preparation time: 4 hours and 10 minutes
Dehydration time: 8 hours
Servings: 2

Ingredients:
- 1 teaspoon garlic powder
- 1 teaspoon paprika
- 1 teaspoon onion powder
- ¼ teaspoon cayenne pepper
- 1 tablespoon lemon juice
- Salt and pepper to taste
- 1 lb. Cod fillet, sliced

Direction:
- ❖ Mix the spices, lemon juice, salt and pepper in a bowl.

- ❖ Season the fish with this mixture.
- ❖ Transfer the seasoned fish and marinade in a sealable plastic bag.
- ❖ Marinate in the refrigerator for 4 hours.
- ❖ Drain the marinade.
- ❖ Arrange the salmon slices on the cosori premium food dehydrator.
- ❖ Process at 145 degrees f for 8 hours.
- ❖ Storage suggestions: store in a vacuum sealed plastic bag or glass jar with lid.

Tip: you can use other white fish fillet for this recipe.

Nutrition Calories: 389 Fat 6.4 g Carbs 22.9 g Protein 49.3 g

VENISON JERKY

Preparation time: 1 day and 30 minutes
Dehydration time: 4 hours
Servings: 2

Ingredients:
- 1 lb. Venison roast, silver skin trimmed and sliced thinly
- 4 tablespoons coconut amino
- ¼ teaspoon onion powder
- ¼ teaspoon garlic powder
- ¼ teaspoon red pepper flakes
- 1 tablespoon honey
- 4 tablespoons worcestershire sauce
- Salt and pepper to taste

Direction:
- ❖ Place the venison roast slices in a bowl.
- ❖ In another bowl, combine the rest of the ingredients.
- ❖ Pour this mixture into the first bowl.
- ❖ Stir to coat meat evenly with the mixture.
- ❖ Cover the bowl.
- ❖ Chill in the refrigerator for 1 day, stirring every 3 or 4 hours.
- ❖ Drain the marinade.
- ❖ Place the venison slices in the cosori premium food dehydrator.
- ❖ Process at 160 degrees f for 4 hours.
- ❖ Storage suggestions: store in vacuum sealed bags for up to 3 months or in ziplock bags for up to 2 weeks.

Tip: freeze the venison meat for 1 hour before slicing.

Nutrition Calories: 389 Fat 6.4 g Carbs 22.9 g Protein 49.3 g

HICKORY SMOKED JERKY

Preparation time: 12 hours and 10 minutes
Dehydration time: 4 hours
Servings: 4

Ingredients:
- 1 lb. Beef round, sliced
- ½ cup hickory smoked marinade
- ¼ cup barbecue sauce
- 2 tablespoons brown sugar
- 1 teaspoon onion powder
- Pinch cayenne pepper
- Salt and pepper to taste

Direction:
- ❖ Place the beef slices in a sealable plastic bag.
- ❖ In a bowl, combine the marinade, barbecue sauce, sugar, onion powder, cayenne, salt and pepper.
- ❖ Pour the mixture into the bag.
- ❖ Seal and marinate in the refrigerator for 12 hours.
- ❖ Discard the marinade and add the beef to the cosori premium food dehydrator.
- ❖ Process at 180 degrees f for 4 hours, flipping halfway through.
- ❖ Storage suggestions: store in a glass jar with lid for up to 2 weeks.

Tip: arrange the meat in a single layer without overlapping.

Nutrition Calories: 389 Fat 6.4 g Carbs 22.9 g
Protein 49.3 g

BEER BEEF JERKY

Preparation time: 6 hours and 10 minutes
Dehydration time: 5 hours
Servings: 2

Ingredients:
- 1 lb. Beef round, sliced
- ½ cup soy sauce
- 2 cloves garlic, minced
- 2 cups beer
- 1 tablespoon liquid smoke
- 1 tablespoon honey
- Pepper to taste

Direction:
- ❖ Add the beef to a sealable plastic bag.
- ❖ Combine the rest of the ingredients in a bowl.
- ❖ Pour the mixture into the bag.
- ❖ Seal and refrigerate for 6 hours.
- ❖ Drain the marinade.
- ❖ Place the beef in the cosori premium food dehydrator.
- ❖ Dehydrate at 160 degrees f for 1 hour.
- ❖ Reduce temperature to 150 degrees f and process for additional 4 hours.
- ❖ Storage suggestions: store in a food container with lid for up to 2 weeks.

Tip: make sure beef is trimmed of fat before dehydrating.

Nutrition Calories: 389 Fat 6.4 g Carbs 22.9 g
Protein 49.3 g

CHAPTER 7

FRUIT RECIPES

RAW FIG BALLS

Preparation time: 15 minutes
Dehydration time: 6 hours
Servings: 4

Ingredients:

- 1 cup raw almonds
- 10 dried figs
- ½ cup raisins
- ½ tsp. Almond extract
- ½ tsp. Vanilla extract
- ¾ cup unsweetened coconut flakes

Direction:

- ❖ Place the almonds in a food processor and pulse until they are ground. Add the figs, raisins and extracts and pulse until well combined.
- ❖ Once the mixture is a dough-like consistency, roll into balls. Roll the balls in the coconut flakes.
- ❖ Place balls on dehydrator trays and dry at 135 degrees for 4-6 hours.

Nutrition Calories:: 141, sodium: 4 mg, dietary fiber: 3 g, total fat: 9.7 g, total carbs: 12.3 g, protein: 2.8 g.

SPICED APPLE CHIPS

Preparation time: 15 minutes
Dehydration time: 6 hours
Servings: 4

Ingredients:

- 3-4 ripe apples (any variety)
- 1 tbsp. Ground cinnamon
- 1/8 tsp. Either nutmeg, cloves, allspice, ginger or cardamom
- 1 tbsp. Sugar

Direction:

- ❖ Slice the apple into thin rounds, between 1/8 – 1/4 inch thick. Peels can be removed or left intact. Remove core and seeds.
- ❖ Toss sliced apples with the cinnamon, nutmeg, cloves and sugar.
- ❖ Arrange in a single line in your dehydrator and set temperature to 135. Allow apples to dehydrate for 6-8 hours.

Nutrition Calories:: 36, sodium: 1 mg, dietary fiber: 2.7 g, total fat: 0.1 g, total carbs: 10.3 g, protein: 0.2 g.

SPICY STRAWBERRY FRUIT LEATHER

Preparation time: 15 minutes
Dehydration time: 6 hours
Servings: 4

Ingredients:

- 1 lb strawberries, hulled and chopped

- 1/3 cup granulated sugar
- 1 tbsp. Lemon juice
- 1 jalapeno or serrano pepper, seeds removed

Direction:

- ❖ Puree strawberries, sugar, lemon juice and pepper.
- ❖ Pour mixture onto fruit leather sheet of your dehydrator.
- ❖ Spread puree evenly, about 1/8 inch thick, onto drying tray.
- ❖ Set the temperature to 140 degrees. Dry for 6-8 hours, or touch center of leather to determine dryness.

Nutrition Calories:: 67, sodium: 0 mg, dietary fiber: 0 g, total fat: 0 g, total carbs: 17.9 g, protein: 0.1 g.

BLACKBERRY TUILE

Preparation time: 10 minutes
Dehydration time: 3 hours
Servings: 4

Ingredients:

- 1 ½ lb. Blackberries
- 2 tablespoons white sugar

Direction:

- ❖ Process the blackberries and sugar in a blender.
- ❖ Strain the mixture to remove the seeds.
- ❖ Add the mixture to the blender.
- ❖ Process on high speed.
- ❖ Pour the fruit liquid into a fruit roll sheet.
- ❖ Place these in the cosori premium food dehydrator.
- ❖ Dehydrate at 165 degrees f for 3 hours.
- ❖ Storage suggestions: store in a food container with lid, away from direct sunlight.

Tip: you can also slice the blackberries first and remove the seeds so you only have to blend it once.

FRUIT LEATHER

Preparation time: 30 minutes
Dehydration time: 8 hours
Servings: 4

Ingredients:

- 3 peaches, sliced
- 3 apricots, sliced
- 1 tablespoon sugar

Direction:

- ❖ Put the peaches and apricots in a pot over medium low heat.
- ❖ Sprinkle with sugar.
- ❖ Mix well.
- ❖ Cook for 10 minutes.
- ❖ Let cool.

- ❖ Transfer to a blender.
- ❖ Blend on low speed until pureed.
- ❖ Pour the mixture into a fruit roll sheet.
- ❖ Place the roll sheet in the cosori premium food dehydrator.
- ❖ Dehydrate at 165 degrees f or 8 hours.
- ❖ Storage suggestions: arrange the solidified fruits on a baking tray and let it sit for a few minutes before storing in a food container.

Tip: you can also dehydrate for up to 12 hours to obtain drier results.

VANILLA-APRICOT SLICES

Preparation time: 15 minutes
Dehydration time: 6 hours
Servings: 4

Ingredients:

- • 6-9 medium sized apricots, pitted
- • 1 ½ tsp. Honey
- • 4 tbsp. Warm water
- • Seeds from one vanilla bean, scraped out

Direction:

- ❖ In a bowl, mix honey and vanilla seeds. Add the water and mix well. Combine until vanilla seeds are well separated.
- ❖ Slice apricots into thin slices. Place apricot slices onto dehydrator tray and brush on a thin layer of vanilla mixture. It is not necessary for all the vanilla seeds to stick to the fruit.
- ❖ Dehydrate for 9-12 hours at 135 degrees.

Nutrition Calories:: 17, sodium: 0 mg, dietary fiber: 0.5 g, total fat: 0.2 g, total carbs: 4.1 g, protein: 0.3 g.

WATERMELON CANDY SLICES

Preparation time: 15 minutes
Dehydration time: 6 hours
Servings: 4

Ingredients:

- • 1 watermelon
- • Fleur de sel

Direction:

- ❖ Cut the watermelon into slices and remove the rinds. Slices should be approximately ¼ inch thick.
- ❖ Lay watermelon slices on trays.
- ❖ Sprinkle fleur de sel on top of the watermelon.
- ❖ Place sheets in dehydrator at 135 degrees for 18 hours.

Nutrition Calories:: 9, sodium: 0 mg, dietary fiber: 0 g, total fat: 0 g, total carbs: 2.1 g, protein: 0.2 g.

HONEY PEACHES WITH BOURBON

Preparation time: 4 hours and 10 minutes
Dehydration time: 16 hours
Servings: 1

Ingredients:

- • 1 peach, cored and sliced
- • ¼ cup honey
- • ¼ cup hot water
- • 3 tablespoons bourbon

Direction:

- ❖ Add the slices to a sealable plastic bag.
- ❖ In a glass bowl, mix the honey and hot water.
- ❖ Mix until the honey has been dissolved.
- ❖ Pour in the bourbon.
- ❖ Let cool.
- ❖ Once cool, add this to the plastic bag.
- ❖ Marinate for 4 hours.
- ❖ Drain the marinade.
- ❖ Add these to the cosori premium food dehydrator.
- ❖ Dehydrate at 145 degrees f for 16 hours.
- ❖ Storage suggestions: pack in a sealable plastic bag for up to 10 days.

Tip: you can also skip the bourbon and marinate in honey only.

Nutrition Calories: 389 Fat 6.4 g Carbs 22.9 g Protein 49.3 g

RASPBERRY ROLLS

Preparation time: 10 minutes
Dehydration time: 5 hours
Servings: 4

Ingredients:

- • 1 ½ lb. Raspberries
- • 2 tablespoons sugar

Direction:

- ❖ Add the raspberries and sugars to a blender.
- ❖ Blend until smooth.
- ❖ Strain to remove the seeds.
- ❖ Add the pureed raspberry back to the blender.
- ❖ Blend until the mixture has turned into liquid.
- ❖ Add the liquid to a fruit roll sheet.
- ❖ Place these in the cosori premium food dehydrator.
- ❖ Dehydrate at 165 degrees f for 5 hours.
- ❖ Storage suggestions: store in a glass jar with lid in a cool dry place.

Tip: you can also use strawberries or blueberries to make this recipe.

Nutrition Calories: 389 Fat 6.4 g Carbs 22.9 g Protein 49.3 g

DRIED APPLE CHIPS WITH CINNAMON

Preparation time: 15 hours
Dehydration time: 6 hours
Servings: 2

Ingredients:
- 2 apples, sliced
- 1 tablespoon lemon juice
- 2 teaspoons cinnamon powder

Direction:
- ❖ Drizzle the apple slices with lemon juice.
- ❖ Arrange the apple slices in the cosori premium food dehydrator.
- ❖ Process at 135 degrees f for 6 hours.
- ❖ Sprinkle with the cinnamon before serving.
- ❖ Storage suggestions: store in a glass jar with lid.

Tip: you can also keep the apple peel if you like but scrub the peel first with apple cider vinegar before processing.

Nutrition Calories: 389 Fat 6.4 g Carbs 22.9 g Protein 49.3 g

CANDIED PUMPKIN

Preparation time: 15 minutes
Dehydration time: 8 hours
Servings: 2

Ingredients:
- 1 cup coconut milk
- 2 cups applesauce
- 2 cups pumpkin puree
- ¼ cup honey
- ½ teaspoon ground allspice
- ½ teaspoon ground nutmeg
- 1 teaspoon ground cinnamon
- ¼ cup coconut flakes
- 2 tablespoons dried cranberries, chopped

Direction:
- ❖ Combine all the ingredients in a bowl.
- ❖ Spread the mixture in the fruit leather sheet of your cosori premium food dehydrator.
- ❖ Dehydrate at 135 degrees f for 8 hours.
- ❖ Storage suggestions: slice the fruit leather before storing in a food container with lid.

Tip: grease the fruit leather sheet with a little bit of oil before processing.

Nutrition Calories: 163 Fat 12.3 g Carbs 6.7 g

Protein 6.6 g

ORANGE FRUIT LEATHER

Preparation time: 10 minutes
Dehydration time: 6 hours
Servings: 4

Ingredients:
- 1 cup applesauce
- 1 cup orange juice concentrate
- 32 oz. Vanilla yogurt

Direction:
- ❖ Add all the ingredients in your blender.
- ❖ Pulse until smooth.
- ❖ Spread the mixture onto the roll sheet.
- ❖ Dry at 135 degrees f for 6 hours.
- ❖ Storage suggestions: store in an airtight food container for up to 2 weeks.

Tip: grease the roll sheet with a little olive oil before processing.

Nutrition Calories: 163 Fat 12.3 g Carbs 6.7 g Protein 6.6 g

DRIED LEMON

Preparation time: 5 minutes
Dehydration time: 6 hours
Servings: 2

Ingredients:
- 2 lemons, sliced

Direction:
- ❖ Arrange the lemon slices in the cosori premium food dehydrator.
- ❖ Dry the lemon at 125 degrees f for 6 hours.
- ❖ Storage suggestions: store in an airtight container.

Tip: drizzle with honey before drying if you like them a little sweeter.

DRIED PAPAYA CUBES

Preparation time: 10 minutes
Dehydration time: 12 hours
Servings: 4

Ingredients:
- 2 papaya, diced

Direction:
- ❖ Add the diced papaya to the cosori premium food dehydrator.
- ❖ Process at 135 degrees f for 12 hours.
- ❖ Storage suggestions: store in an airtight jar.

Tip: you can also sprinkle with sugar before dehydrating.

Nutrition Calories: 11 protein: 0.04 g fat: 0.03g carbs: 2.85 g

DRIED KIWI

Preparation time: 15 minutes
Dehydration time: 12 hours
Servings: 2

Ingredients:
- 2 kiwis, peeled and sliced thinly

Direction:
- ❖ Place the kiwi slices in the cosori premium food dehydrator.
- ❖ Dry at 135 degrees f for 12 hours.
- ❖ Storage suggestions: store in a glass jar with lid. Place the jar in a cool dry place.

Tip: kiwi slices should be at least 6mm thick.

Nutrition Calories: 11 protein: 0.04 g fat: 0.03g carbs: 2.85 g

CINNAMON APPLE CHIPS

Preparation time: 10 minutes
Dehydration time: 12 hours
Servings: 4

Ingredients:
- 2 apples, sliced thinly
- 1 tablespoon white sugar
- 1 tablespoon lemon juice
- ¼ teaspoon nutmeg
- ½ teaspoon vanilla extract
- 1 teaspoon ground cinnamon

Direction:
- ❖ Combine all the ingredients in a bowl.
- ❖ Coat the apples slices evenly with the mixture.
- ❖ Arrange the apple slices in the cosori premium food dehydrator.
- ❖ Dehydrate at 145 degrees f for 6 hours.
- ❖ Storage suggestions: store in a glass jar with lid.

Tip: apple slices should be at least ¼ inch thick.

PLUM & GRAPE FRUIT LEATHER

Preparation time: 20 minutes
Dehydration time: 12 hours
Servings: 4

Ingredients:
- 2 cups red grapes (seedless)
- 5 plums, sliced
- 2 tablespoons sugar

Direction:
- ❖ Put all the ingredients in a pot over medium low heat.
- ❖ Cook for 15 minutes.
- ❖ Transfer the mixture to a blender.
- ❖ Blend until smooth.
- ❖ Pour the mixture into a fruit roll sheet.

- ❖ Place in the cosori premium food dehydrator.
- ❖ Process at 165 degrees f for 12 hours.
- ❖ Storage suggestions: dry the fruit leather on a tray after dehydrating and before storing.

Tip: you can also process for 8 hours only.

BERRY FRUIT LEATHER

Preparation time: 10 minutes
Dehydration time: 6 hours
Servings: 4

Ingredients:
- 1 lb. Strawberries
- ½ cup raspberries
- 1 teaspoon vanilla extract

Direction:
- ❖ Process all the ingredients in a blender.
- ❖ Pulse until smooth.
- ❖ Strain to remove seeds.
- ❖ Put the mixture back to the blender.
- ❖ Pulse until liquified.
- ❖ Pour the fruit puree into a fruit roll sheet and place in the cosori premium food dehydrator.
- ❖ Dehydrate at 165 degrees f for 6 hours.
- ❖ Storage suggestions: sprinkle with white sugar before storing in a glass jar.

Tip: you can also use other berries for this recipe.

DRIED STRAWBERRIES

Preparation time: 10 minutes
Dehydration time: 8 hours
Servings: 4

Ingredients:
- 1 lb. Strawberries, sliced

Direction:
- ❖ Place the strawberry slices in the cosori premium food dehydrator.
- ❖ Process at 135 degrees f for 8 hours.
- ❖ Storage suggestions: keep in a glass jar with lid.

Tip: hull and slice the strawberries before dehydrating them. Slices should be 1/8 inch thick.

HAZELNUT BANANA LEATHER

Preparation time: 5 minutes
Dehydration time: 3 hours
Servings: 2

Ingredients:

- 2 bananas, sliced
- Chocolate hazelnut spread

Direction:

- ❖ Combine the bananas and chocolate hazelnut spread in your food processor.
- ❖ Pulse until smooth.
- ❖ Form round shapes of about ¼ inch thick on parchment paper.
- ❖ Transfer to the cosori premium food dehydrator.
- ❖ Process at 125 degrees f for 4 hours.
- ❖ Storage suggestions: store in a glass jar with lid. Place jar in a cool dry place.

Tip: the treats should no longer be sticky when touched.

APPLE FRUIT LEATHER

Preparation time: 10 minutes
Dehydration time: 6 hours
Servings: 2

Ingredients:

- 2 cups applesauce
- 2 cups sweet potatoes, cooked and mashed
- ¼ cup honey
- 1 teaspoon cinnamon
- Salt to taste

Direction:

- ❖ Add all the ingredients to a blender.
- ❖ Pulse until smooth.
- ❖ Add the mixture to fruit roll sheets and place in the cosori premium food dehydrator.
- ❖ Dry at 100 degrees f for 6 hours.
- ❖ Storage suggestions: store apple leather in a sealable plastic bag.

Tip: you can also add a little lemon juice to the mixture to balance the flavor.

PEANUT BUTTER & BANANA LEATHER

Preparation time: 5 minutes
Dehydration time: 4 hours
Servings: 2

Ingredients:

- 2 bananas, sliced
- 2 tablespoons peanut butter

Direction:

- ❖ Process bananas and peanut butter in a food processor for 1 minute.
- ❖ Spread a layer of the mixture onto the dehydrator sheet.
- ❖ Dry at 135 degrees f for 4 hours.
- ❖ Storage suggestions: slice the leather before storing.

Tip: you can also add melted chocolate into the mixture if you like.

SWEET AND SOUR CRANBERRIES

Preparation time: 15 minutes
Dehydration time: 6 hours
Servings: 4

Ingredients:

- 12 oz. Cranberries
- ¼ cup corn syrup (or sugar)
- Zest of one orange and one lime

Direction:

- ❖ Place cranberries in a bowl and pour boiling water over them until the skins crack. Drain.
- ❖ Toss the berries with corn syrup or sugar and zests. Place berries on cooking sheet and freeze for 2 hours to promote faster drying.
- ❖ Assemble berries on a mesh sheet in the dehydrator and dry at 135 degrees for 12-16 hours or until chewy.

Nutrition Calories:: 41, sodium: 0 mg, dietary fiber: 0.6 g, total fat: 0 g, total carbs: 10.2 g, protein: 0 g.

SWEET "CARAMEL APPLES"

Preparation time: 15 minutes
Dehydration time: 6 hours
Servings: 4

Ingredients:

- 3-4 granny smith apples
- ½ cup store-bought caramel sauce

Direction:

- ❖ Slice the apple into thin rounds, between 1/8-1/4 inch thick. Peels can be removed or left intact. Remove core and seeds.
- ❖ Use a pastry brush to spread a small amount of caramel onto each apple round.
- ❖ Arrange in a single line in your dehydrator and set temperature to 135 degrees. Allow apples to dehydrate for 10-12 hours.

Nutrition Calories:: 41, sodium: 45 mg, dietary fiber: 0 g, total fat: 0 g, total carbs: 10.6 g, protein: 0.2 g.

SWEET POTATO- CINNAMON LEATHER

Preparation time: 15 minutes
Dehydration time: 6 hours
Servings: 4

Ingredients:

- 3 medium sweet potatoes
- ½ tsp. Cinnamon
- 1/8 tsp. Ground ginger

Direction:

- ❖ Preheat oven to 400 degrees and place sweet potatoes in a baking dish. Cover and bake 35-45 minutes, or until soft.

- ❖ Peel skins and put potatoes in food processor with cinnamon and ginger. Puree until smooth.
- ❖ Pour mixture onto dehydrator trays and spread to ¼ inch thickness. Dehydrate at 135 degree for 8-6 hours.

Nutrition Calories:: 33, sodium: 3 mg, dietary fiber: 1.2 g, total fat: 0.1 g, total carbs: 7.9 g, protein: 0.4 g

TANGY DRIED MANGOS

Preparation time: 15 minutes
Dehydration time: 6 hours
Servings: 4

Ingredients:
- 4-5 ripe mangoes
- 1 tbsp. Honey
- 1/4 cup lime juice
- Pinch of salt

Direction:
- ❖ Peel and slice mangoes into thin, even strips.
- ❖ Dissolve honey in lemon juice. Mix well and add salt.
- ❖ Dip mango slices into honey mixture. Shake off excess.
- ❖ Arrange in a single line in your dehydrator and set temperature to 135 degrees. Allow mangoes to dehydrate for 8-9 hours.

Nutrition Calories:: 21, sodium: 1 mg, dietary fiber: 0.5 g, total fat: 0.1 g, total carbs: 5.3 g, protein: 0.1 g.

TROPICAL PINEAPPLE CRISPS

Preparation time: 15 minutes
Dehydration time: 6 hours
Servings: 4

Ingredients:
- 1 ripe pineapple
- Coconut oil
- ½ cup sweetened coconut flakes
- Sea salt to taste

Direction:
- ❖ Peel and core the pineapple. Slice into thin, uniform rounds about ½ inch thick.
- ❖ Using a pastry brush, spread a thin layer of coconut oil on each pineapple slice. Sprinkle with coconut flakes and a small amount of sea salt.
- ❖ Arrange in a single line in your dehydrator and set temperature to 135 degrees. Allow pineapple to dehydrate for 12-16 hours, flipping the slices halfway through for even dryness.

Nutrition Calories:: 51, sodium: 21 mg, dietary fiber: 0.8 g, total fat: 2.6 g, total carbs: 6.1 g, protein: 0.7 g.

CHAPTER 8

GRAINS, NUTS AND SEEDS RECIPES

ALMOND CRANBERRY COOKIES

Preparation time: 15 minutes
Dehydration time: 6 hours
Servings: 4

Ingredients:

- Wet pulp from almond milk
- 1 banana
- 2 tbsp. Coconut oil
- ¾ cup shredded coconut flakes
- ½ cup dried cranberries
- 1 tbsp. Honey
- ½ cup almonds, coarsely chopped

Direction:

- ❖ Place almond pulp, banana and coconut oil in food processor.
- ❖ Mix remainder of ingredients and add to the almond pulp mixture.
- ❖ Place a small scoop of dough on dehydrator sheets and flatten into a cookie.
- ❖ Set temperature to 105 degrees and dehydrate for 6 hours or more.
- ❖ Set temperature to 105 degrees and dehydrate for 6 hours or more.

Nutrition Calories:: 91, sodium: 2 mg, dietary fiber: 2.3 g, total fat: 7.6 g, total carbs: 4.8 g, protein: 2 g.

APPLE AND NUT "RAW" CEREAL

Preparation time: 15 minutes
Dehydration time: 6 hours
Servings: 4

Ingredients:

- 1 apple, peeled, cored and diced
- 1 cup sprouted wheat berries
- ½ cup flax seeds, ground
- ½ cup diced raw walnuts
- ½ cup millet flour
- 1 cup sunflower seeds
- 1 tsp. Cinnamon
- ¼ tsp. Salt
- ¼ cup coconut oil, melted
- ¼ cup maple syrup
- 3 tbsp. Apple juice

Direction:

- ❖ Combine apple, wheat berries, flax seeds, walnuts, flour, seeds, cinnamon and salt.
- ❖ Blend coconut oil, maple syrup and apple juice with a whisk.
- ❖ Add dry ingredients to wet ingredients and stir thoroughly.
- ❖ Dehydrate at 115 degrees for 18-24 hours. When crispy, break into large pieces.

Nutrition Calories:: 120, sodium: 19 mg, dietary fiber: 2.5 g, total fat: 7.6 g, total carbs: 9.9 g, protein: 4.2 g.

APPLE CINNAMON GRAHAM COOKIES

Preparation time: 15 minutes
Dehydration time: 6 hours
Servings: 4

Ingredients:

- 1 cup cashews, soaked for 1 hour
- 1 cup pecans, soaked for 1 hour
- 6 cups ground almonds
- 2 apples, peeled, cored and chopped
- 1 pear, peeled, cored and chopped
- 1 cup almond butter
- 1 ½ cups flax seed
- ½ cup honey
- 1 tbsp. Cinnamon
- ½ tsp. Nutmeg
- Pinch of salt

Direction:

- ❖ After nuts have been soaked, drain and rinse them.
- ❖ Pulse cashews and pecans in food processor until small crumbs form. Add the ground almonds and place in a bowl.
- ❖ In the food processor, combine apples, pear, almond butter, flax seed, honey, cinnamon, nutmeg and salt. Add the ground nuts.
- ❖ Spread mixture on dehydrator trays, about ¼ inch thick, to the edges.
- ❖ Dehydrate 6-8 hours at 115 degrees. Flip over and cut into squares. Continue dehydrating for 6-8 hours or until crunchy.

Nutrition Calories:: 160, sodium: 2 mg, dietary fiber: 3.5 g, total fat: 13.3 g, total carbs: 6.8 g, protein: 5.1 g.

ASIAN-INSPIRED NUTS

Preparation time: 15 minutes
Dehydration time: 6 hours
Servings: 4

Ingredients:

- 16 ounce jar of roasted peanuts
- 1/3 cup soy sauce
- ¼ cup water
- 1 ½ tsp. Sesame oil
- ½ tsp. Five spice powder
- ¼ tsp. Ground ginger

Direction:

- ❖ Place nuts in a bowl. Combine all other ingredients and whisk together.
- ❖ Pour over nuts. Marinate nuts at least 8 hours or overnight.
- ❖ Drain liquid and place nuts on dehydrator tray. Dehydrate for 5 hours at 135 degrees.

Nutrition Calories:: 152, sodium: 5 mg, dietary fiber: 2.3 g, total fat: 13.1 g, total carbs: 4.4 g, protein: 6.9 g.

BANANA BREAKFAST CREPES

Preparation time: 15 minutes
Dehydration time: 6 hours
Servings: 4

Ingredients:

- 2 medium size ripe bananas
- 1 tsp. Ground flax seed
- 1 tsp. Almond meal
- 1 tsp. Almond milk
- Dash of cinnamon

Direction:

- ❖ Place all ingredients in a food processor and blend into a liquid.
- ❖ Line 2 dehydrator sheets and pour mixture onto them. Liquid should only be about 1/8 inches in thickness. Spread with a spatula.
- ❖ Dehydrate at 115 degrees for 3 hours. Crepes should be totally smooth. Do not remove crepes early or they will not hold their shape. Cut into crepe-sized circles.

Nutrition Calories:: 48, sodium: 1 mg, dietary fiber: 1.6 g, total fat: 2 g, total carbs: 6.6 g, protein: 1.2 g.

BASIC "SOAKED NUTS"

Preparation time: 15 minutes
Dehydration time: 6 hours
Servings: 4

Ingredients:

- Nuts, in any quantity and variety
- Sea salt, approximately 1 tbsp. Per every 4 cups of nuts
- Filtered water (to cover the nuts)

Direction:

- ❖ Combine nuts, sea salt and water in a glass bowl. Cover with a lid or plate and place in a warm location for 12 hours.
- ❖ Remove lid and rinse nuts in a colander.
- ❖ Spread nuts in a single layer on dehydrator trays for 12-24 hours at 105-150 degrees.

FLAX SEED CRACKERS

Preparation time: 15 minutes
Dehydration time: 6 hours
Servings: 4

Ingredients:

- 2 cups flaxseeds
- 2 cups water
- ¼ cup low sodium soy sauce
- 2 tbsp. Sesame seeds

- Sea salt and black pepper, to taste
- 1 ½ tbsp. Fresh lime juice

Direction:

- ❖ Cover flax seeds with water and soak for 1-2 hours. Mixture should be gooey, but not too thin. Add more water to achieve this texture.
- ❖ Stir in the remainder of the ingredients.
- ❖ Spread the mixture about 1/8 inch thick on dehydrator sheets.
- ❖ Set the temperature to 105-115 degrees and dehydrate 4-6 hours. Flip over mixture and dehydrate another 4-6 hours. Break crackers into large pieces after dehydrating.

Nutrition Calories:: 133, sodium: 7 mg, dietary fiber: 6.5 g, total fat: 8.2 g, total carbs: 7.1 g, protein: 4.6 g.

FRUIT N' NUT BALLS

Preparation time: 15 minutes
Dehydration time: 6 hours
Servings: 4

Ingredients:

- ½ cup dried dates
- ½ cup figs
- ½ cup dried cherries
- ½ cup dried apricots
- ½ cup dried cranberries
- 1 cup crushed pecans
- 1 cup crushed almonds
- 3 tsp. Coconut oil, melted
- 1 cup flaked coconut

Direction:

- ❖ Finely process dates, figs, cherries, apricots and cranberries in a food processor. Mix with nuts and coconut oil in a bowl.
- ❖ Shape into 1" balls and roll balls in coconut.
- ❖ Place in dehydrator at 135 degrees for 6 hours.

Nutrition Calories:: 102, sodium: 2 mg, dietary fiber: 2.3 g, total fat: 8.4 g, total carbs: 6.9 g, protein: 2 g.

FRUIT & NUT CLUSTERS

Preparation time: 15 minutes
Dehydration time: 6 hours
Servings: 4

Ingredients:

- ½ cup cashew butter
- ½ cup maple syrup
- 1 ½ tsp. Cinnamon
- 1 tsp. Salt
- 1 tsp. Vanilla extract
- 8 dates, pitted
- 2 cups cashews

- 1 cup pecans
- 1 cup dried cranberries
- 1 cup dried blueberries
- 1 cup rolled oats, raw

Direction:

- ❖ In a food processor, combine cashew butter, maple syrup, cinnamon, salt, vanilla extract and dates. Pulse until the mixture is smooth.
- ❖ In a bowl, combine cashews, pecans, dried fruits and oats. Pour liquid mixture on top and toss to coat.
- ❖ Pour batter onto dehydrator sheets and dehydrate for 1 hour at 145 degrees. Reduce temperature to 115 degrees and continue dehydrating for up to 24 hours.

Nutrition Calories:: 110, sodium: 37 mg, dietary fiber: 1.6 g, total fat: 7.9 g, total carbs: 9.2 g, protein: 2.8 g.

GRAHAM CRACKERS"

Preparation time: 15 minutes
Dehydration time: 6 hours
Servings: 4

Ingredients:

- 4 cups almond flour
- 1 cup oat flour
- ½ cup flax seeds
- ½ cup almond milk
- 1 cup maple syrup
- 1 tbsp. Vanilla
- 1 tbsp. Cinnamon

Direction:

- ❖ Pulse all ingredients in the food processor.
- ❖ Spread onto dehydrator trays. Make sure graham cracker mixture is about 1/8 inch thick. Dehydrate at 115 degrees for 4 hours.
- ❖ Cut into squares and then flip and dehydrate for 6 more hours.

Nutrition Calories:: 142, sodium: 7 mg, dietary fiber: 3.2 g, total fat: 10.2 g, total carbs: 9.6 g, protein: 5 g.

HAZELNUT LEMON CRACKERS.

Preparation time: 15 minutes
Dehydration time: 7 hours
Servings: 4

Ingredients:

- ½ cup chia seeds
- 1 cup water
- 3 cups hazelnuts, soaked overnight, skins removed
- 1 ½ tbsp. Lemon zest
- 1 tbsp. Maple syrup
- ½ tsp. Sea salt
- Black pepper to taste

Direction:

- ❖ Mix chia seeds in 1 cup water and allow to soften.
- ❖ Remove soaked hazelnuts and drain them. Place hazelnuts in food processor and grind until fine.
- ❖ Pour ground nuts into a bowl and combine with chia seeds, lemon zest, maple syrup, salt and pepper.
- ❖ Spread onto dehydrator trays. Use a spatula to flatten dough to approximately ¼ inch thick. Dehydrate at 145 degrees for 1 hour. Decrease heat to 115 and continue to dehydrate for 8 hours.

Nutrition Calories:: 169, sodium: 31 mg, dietary fiber: 3.7 g, total fat: 15.6 g, total carbs: 5.5 g, protein: 4.4 g.

MACADAMIA-SAGE CRACKERS

Preparation time: 15 minutes
Dehydration time: 6 hours
Servings: 4

Ingredients:

- 2 cups macadamia nuts
- 2 cups chia or flax seeds
- 1 ½ tbsp. Fresh sage, crushed
- Sea salt and white pepper to taste
- 3 cups water
- ½ cup olive oil

Direction:

- ❖ Place macadamia nuts and flax seeds into a food processor and grind into a flour. Add sage, salt and pepper. Process until you have a fine texture.
- ❖ In a large bowl, add water to nut and seed mix and stir until thick. Don't pour all the water at once. Add small amounts until a soft dough forms.
- ❖ Spread onto dehydrator sheets. Drizzle with olive oil and sprinkle additional sea salt.
- ❖ Dehydrate at 110 degrees for 4 hours. Score the crackers, flip them over and dehydrate another 8 hours.

Nutrition Calories:: 176, sodium: 1 mg, dietary fiber: 6.4 g, total fat: 15.1 g, total carbs: 7.2 g, protein: 4.2 g.

MINT-SCENTED CHOCOLATE CHIP COOKIES

Preparation time: 15 minutes
Dehydration time: 6 hours
Servings: 4

Ingredients:

- 1 ½ cups almond meal
- 1 ½ cups ground pecans
- 1 cup cocoa powder
- ¼ cup cacao nibs
- ½ cup maple syrup

- 3 tbsp. Coconut oil
- 1 tsp. Peppermint extract
- 1 tsp. Vanilla extract
- 1 tbsp. Almond milk
- ½ tsp. Salt

Direction:

- ❖ Place all ingredients in food processor and pulse until combined. Ingredients should form a cohesive dough.
- ❖ Roll out dough to about ¼ inch thickness.
- ❖ Cut out circles using a small glass. Alternatively, skip this process, roll dough into balls and flatten into disks.
- ❖ Dehydrate for 24 hours at 115 degrees.

Nutrition Calories:: 140, sodium: 25 mg, dietary fiber: 4.7 g, total fat: 12.1 g, total carbs: 8.8 g, protein: 4.3 g.

ORANGE-SCENTED GRANOLA WITH DRIED BLUEBERRIES

Preparation time: 15 minutes
Dehydration time: 6 hours
Servings: 4

Ingredients:

- 2 cups raw buckwheat or oat groats
- 1 cup dates, pitted
- 1 cup freshly squeezed orange juice
- 1 orange, juiced
- 1 tsp. Almond extract
- 1 tsp. Lemon juice
- ½ cup dried blueberries

Direction:

- ❖ Soak the groats in water and drain after about 1 hour. Rinse well and drain again. Transfer them to a small bowl.
- ❖ In a food processor, pulse all other ingredients except dried blueberries until a paste forms. Blend this mixture with the groats. Mix thoroughly.
- ❖ Spread mixture on dehydrator sheets. Dehydrate for 12 hours at 115 degrees and flip over. Dehydrate for another 12-15 hours until granola is crispy.
- ❖ After dehydrated, crumble granola into bite size pieces and add dried blueberries.

Nutrition Calories:: 85, sodium: 0 mg, dietary fiber: 2 g, total fat: 0.7 g, total carbs: 17.4 g, protein: 2.2 g.

PARMESAN BLACK PEPPER FLAX CRACKERS

Preparation time: 15 minutes
Dehydration time: 6 hours
Servings: 4

Ingredients:

- 1 cup flax seeds
- 1 cup water
- ¼ cup parmesan cheese
- ½ tbsp. Black pepper
- 1 clove garlic
- 1 tsp. Flaky sea salt

Direction:

- ❖ Stir all ingredients in a large bowl until it forms a gelatinous dough.
- ❖ Spread onto dehydrator sheets so that mixture is about ¼ inch thick. Slice the dough into squares.
- ❖ Set temperature to 145 degrees and dehydrate for 30-45 minutes. Reduce temperature to 115 degrees and after 6 hours, flip the crackers.
- ❖ Continue dehydrating for 12-18 hours. Crackers should be crispy when ready.

Nutrition Calories:: 131, sodium: 214 mg, dietary fiber: 6.4 g, total fat: 7.8 g, total carbs: 7.1 g, protein: 5.2 g.

PEPITA CRACKERS

Preparation time: 15 minutes
Dehydration time: 6 hours
Servings: 4

Ingredients:

- 2 ½ cups sprouted quinoa
- ¾ cup chia seeds, finely ground
- ¼ cup low sodium soy sauce
- 2 cloves garlic
- 1 tsp. Onion powder
- ½ tsp. Salt
- ½ cup pepitas

Direction:

- ❖ Process quinoa until finely ground. Add all the other ingredients except pepitas and pulse until well combined.
- ❖ Spread mixture on dehydrator sheets. Sprinkle pepitas on top and press down to adhere to mixture.
- ❖ Cut into squares. Dehydrate for 8-12 hours at 140 degrees or until crunchy.

Nutrition Calories:: 107, sodium: 2 mg, dietary fiber: 3.3 g, total fat: 4.3 g, total carbs: 14.9 g, protein: 4.5 g.

RAW CHEESY THYME CRACKERS

Preparation time: 15 minutes
Dehydration time: 6 hours
Servings: 4

Ingredients:

- 2 cups almonds, soaked overnight and dried

- 4 tbsp. Ground chia seeds
- 4 tbsp. Nutritional yeast
- 2 ½ tbsp. Fresh thyme, chopped
- ½ tsp. Salt

Direction:

- ❖ Soak chia seeds in ½ cup of water for 30 minutes. Drain.
- ❖ Place almonds, chia seeds, nutritional yeast, thyme and salt in a food processor. Pulse several times.
- ❖ Add a few drops of water while motor is running until mixture becomes spreadable.
- ❖ Spread mixture onto dehydrator sheets and set temperature to 115 degrees. Dehydrate for 4-6 hours. Flip over and cut into cracker shapes. Dehydrate another 8 hours.

Nutrition Calories:: 132, sodium: 37 mg, dietary fiber: 4.5 g, total fat: 10.4 g, total carbs: 7.2 g, protein: 5.5 g.

"RAW" GRANOLA

Preparation time: 15 minutes
Dehydration time: 6 hours
Servings: 4

Ingredients:

- 3 cups rolled oats
- ¼ cup oat bran
- 1 cup raw pumpkin seeds
- 1 cup raw sunflower seeds
- 1 cup coconut
- 1 cup walnuts, pecans or almonds
- ½ cup honey
- ½ cup coconut oil, melted
- ½ cup water
- 1 tsp. Cinnamon
- ¼ tsp. Nutmeg

Direction:

- ❖ Mix together honey, oil and water. Add all the remaining ingredients.
- ❖ Spread mixture onto dehydrator sheets and smooth to create a thin layer.
- ❖ Dehydrate for 18 hours at 105-115 degrees.

Nutrition Calories:: 131, sodium: 7 mg, dietary fiber: 2.3 g, total fat: 7.8 g, total carbs: 12.1 g, protein: 4.7 g.

SAVORY ONION AND GARLIC CRISPS

Preparation time: 15 minutes
Dehydration time: 6 hours
Servings: 4

Ingredients:

- 1 vidalia onion, peeled and halved
- 2 cloves garlic, peeled and ground

- 1 cup ground flax seeds
- 1 cup ground chia seeds
- 1 ½ cups ground sunflower seeds
- ½ cup low sodium soy sauce
- ½ cup extra virgin olive oil
- ½ tsp. White pepper

Direction:

- ❖ Place onions and garlic in food processor and process roughly, but do not create a paste.
- ❖ Transfer to a mixing bowl and add all other ingredients. Mix until combined.
- ❖ Spread mixture on dehydrator sheet and dehydrate at 100 degrees for 24-36 hours.
- ❖ After dehydrating, cut into large squares.

Nutrition Calories:: 116, sodium: 4 mg, dietary fiber: 7.7 g, total fat: 8.1 g, total carbs: 8.9 g, protein: 4.9

SAVORY TRAIL MIX

Preparation time: 15 minutes
Dehydration time: 6 hours
Servings: 4

Ingredients:

- 1 cup raw almonds, soaked overnight and dried
- 1 cup raw pumpkin seeds, soaked overnight and dried
- 1 cup raw sunflower seeds, soaked overnight and dried
- 3 tbsp. Low sodium soy sauce
- 3 tbsp. Olive oil
- 1 tsp. Garlic powder
- 2 tsp. Onion powder
- ½ tsp. Celery salt
- Pinch of cayenne pepper

Direction:

- ❖ Combine soy sauce, olive oil and seasonings. Pour onto nuts and seeds and stir until they are well coated.
- ❖ Spread mixture onto dehydrator tray using mesh sheets.
- ❖ Dehydrate for 18 hours at 105-115 degrees.

Nutrition Calories:: 120, sodium: 19 mg, dietary fiber: 2.5 g, total fat: 7.6 g, total carbs: 9.9 g, protein: 4.2 g.

SEASONED SUNFLOWER SEEDS

Preparation time: 15 minutes
Dehydration time: 6 hours
Servings: 4

Ingredients:

- 2 tbsp. Olive oil
- 1 tbsp. Soy sauce
- ½ tsp. Garlic powder

- ½ tsp. Onion powder
- ½ tsp. Celery salt
- ¼ tsp. Crushed red pepper flakes
- 2 cups shelled sunflower seeds, raw

Direction:

- ❖ Soak sunflower seeds overnight. Rinse and dry thoroughly.
- ❖ Mix together the olive oil, soy sauce and seasonings. Toss seeds in the mixture until they are well coated.
- ❖ Place on a dehydrator tray and dehydrate for 12-18 hours at 105-115 degrees.

Nutrition Calories:: 140, sodium: 3 mg, dietary fiber: 2.1 g, total fat: 12.3 g, total carbs: 5 g, protein: 5 g.

SESAME SEED CRISPS

Preparation time: 15 minutes
Dehydration time: 6 hours
Servings: 4

Ingredients:

- ½ cup flax seeds
- 1 cup water
- ½ cup sesame seeds, toasted
- ½ cup black sesame seeds
- ½ tsp. Sea salt
- ½ tsp. Dried thyme
- ½ tsp. Garlic powder

Direction:

- ❖ In a bowl, mix seeds and seasonings with water. Stir until the mixture is well incorporated and leave for 10-15 minutes to allow seeds to become pudding-like.
- ❖ Spread onto dehydrator trays. Batter should be less than ¼ inch thick. Dehydrate at 110 degrees for 8-12 hours. Flip them over and dehydrate for another 8 hours.

Nutrition Calories:: 147, sodium: 71 mg, dietary fiber: 4.5 g, total fat: 11.4 g, total carbs: 6.8 g, protein: 4.8 g.

SPICY CASHEWS

Preparation time: 15 minutes
Dehydration time: 6 hours
Servings: 4

Ingredients:

- 16 ounce jar of roasted cashews
- ½ cup water
- ¼ cup hot sauce
- 1 ½ tbsp. Chili powder
- ¼ cayenne pepper
- 3 tbsp. Fresh lime juice
- 1 lime, zested

Direction:

- ❖ Place nuts in a bowl. Combine all other ingredients and whisk together.
- ❖ Pour over nuts. Marinate nuts at least 8 hours or overnight.
- ❖ Drain liquid and place nuts on dehydrator tray. Dehydrate for 5 hours at 135 degrees.

Nutrition Calories:: 148, sodium: 68 mg, dietary fiber: 1.5 g, total fat: 11.8 g, total carbs: 9.3 g, protein: 4 g

SWEET AND SALTY PUMPKIN SEEDS

Preparation time: 15 minutes
Dehydration time: 6 hours
Servings: 4

Ingredients:

- 2 cups pumpkin seeds
- 2 tbsp. Olive oil
- 1 tbsp. Paprika
- 1 tbsp. Turmeric
- 1 tbsp. Sugar
- 1 tsp. Ground ginger

Direction:

- ❖ Soak pumpkin seeds overnight in enough water to cover the seeds.
- ❖ Dry seeds and mix remaining ingredients. Toss seeds in the mixture until they are well coated.
- ❖ Place on a dehydrator tray.
- ❖ Dehydrate for 12-18 hours at 105-115 degrees.

Nutrition Calories:: 131, sodium: 5 mg, dietary fiber: 1.3 g, total fat: 10.6 g, total carbs: 5.8 g, protein: 5.7 g.

SWEET COCOA CHIA BARS

Preparation time: 15 minutes
Dehydration time: 6 hours
Servings: 4

Ingredients:

- 1 cup chia seeds
- 2 cups water
- ¼ cup cocoa powder
- 6 figs, chopped
- 1 apple, peeled, cored and chopped
- 1 cup walnuts, chopped
- 3 tbsp. Honey
- 3 tbsp. Cacao nibs

Direction:

- ❖ Soak chia seeds in ½ cup of water for 30 minutes. Drain.
- ❖ Blend all remaining ingredients in a blender, except for cacao nibs. Add small amounts of water to achieve the right consistency.
- ❖ Stir together chia seeds, blended mixture and cacao nibs.

- ❖ Allow to rest for 20-25 minutes.
- ❖ Spread the mixture onto dehydrator tray. Dehydrate for 1 hour at 135 degrees. Cut into bars.
- ❖ Lower temperature to 110 degrees and dehydrate another 8 hours. Flip bars and dehydrate another 8 hours.

Nutrition Calories:: 125, sodium: 32 mg, dietary fiber: 6 g, total fat: 9.6 g, total carbs: 5.6 g, protein: 5.2 g.

SUNDRIED TOMATO FLAX CRACKERS

Preparation time: 15 minutes
Dehydration time: 6 hours
Servings: 4

Ingredients:

- 1 cup flax seeds
- 1 cup water
- 1 tbsp. Dried basil
- ½ tbsp. Dried thyme
- 2 tbsp. Sundried tomatoes, ground
- 1 tbsp. Extra-virgin olive oil
- 1 tsp. Flaky sea salt

Direction:

- ❖ Stir all ingredients, except salt, in a large bowl until it forms a gelatinous mass. This should take about an hour.
- ❖ Spread onto dehydrator sheets so that mixture is about 1/8 inch – ¼ inch thick. Sprinkle with sea salt.
- ❖ Set temperature to 105 degrees and dehydrate for 4 hours. Flip and score the mixture.
- ❖ Continue dehydrating for 6-6 hours.

Nutrition Calories:: 120, sodium: 232 mg, dietary fiber: 6.4 g, total fat: 6.7 g, total carbs: 8.2 g, protein: 4.4 g.

CHAPTER 9

HERBS & POWDER

DRIED BASIL POWDER

Preparation time: 10 minutes
Dehydration time: 15 hours

Serving: 5

Ingredients:
- 3 cups basil leaves

Direction:
- ❖ Add the basil leaves to the cosori premium food dehydrator.
- ❖ Dry at 105 degrees for 15 hours.
- ❖ Grind the dried basil in a spice grinder or food processor.
- ❖ Storage suggestions: store in an empty spice jar.

Tip: use only fresh basil leaves.

Nutrition: calories 198, fat12, carbs 16, protein 8

DRIED HERB MIX

Preparation time: 15 minutes
Dehydration time: 8 hours

Serving: 5

Ingredients:
- ½ cup thyme leaves
- ½ cup rosemary leaves
- 2 teaspoons lemon zest
- 6 cloves garlic, peeled

Direction:
- ❖ Combine all the ingredients in a food processor.
- ❖ Pulse until smooth.
- ❖ Spread the mixture in the cosori premium food dehydrator.
- ❖ Dehydrate at 135 degrees f for 8 hours.
- ❖ Storage suggestions: store in an empty spice bottle.

Tip: you can also add other herbs into the mix such as oregano or thyme.

Nutrition: calories 98, fat12, carbs 16 , protein 8

ONION POWDER

Preparation time: 10 minutes
Dehydration time: 8 hours

Serving: 5

Ingredients:
- 5 onions, sliced

Direction:
- ❖ Arrange the onion slices in a single layer in the cosori premium food dehydrator.
- ❖ Dehydrate at 145 degrees f for 8 hours.
- ❖ Transfer the dried onion to a food processor.
- ❖ Pulse until powdery.

- ❖ Storage suggestions: store the onion powder in a mason jar.

Nutrition: calories 76, fat 5 , fiber 3 , carbs 5 , protein 3

TOMATO POWDER

Preparation time: 15 minutes
Dehydration time: 12 hours

Serving: 5

Ingredients:
- Skins from 10 tomatoes

Direction:
- ❖ Add the tomato skins to a cosori premium food dehydrator.
- ❖ Dry at 135 degrees f for 12 hours.
- ❖ Transfer the dried tomatoes to a coffee grinder.
- ❖ Grind until the mixture turns to powder.
- ❖ Storage suggestions: store in a glass jar with lid.

Tip: you can also make tomato flakes from this recipe.

Nutrition: calories 243, fat 14, fiber 3 , carbs25 , protein 14

LEEK POWDER

Preparation time: 5 minutes
Dehydration time: 12 hours

Serving: 5

Ingredients:
- 4 cups leeks, sliced

Direction:
- ❖ Place the leeks in the cosori premium food dehydrator.
- ❖ Dehydrate at 135 degrees f for 4 hours.
- ❖ Put the dried leeks in a spice grinder.
- ❖ Grind until powdery.
- ❖ Storage suggestions: store in a tightly sealed food or spice container.

Tip: do not use any browned parts of leeks.

Nutrition: calories 23, fat 14, fiber 3 , carbs2 , protein 4

DRIED PARSLEY, BASIL & OREGANO POWDER

Preparation time: 15 minutes
Dehydration time: 8 hours
Servings: 5

Ingredients:
- 2 tablespoons parsley leaves
- 2 tablespoons basil leaves
- 2 tablespoons oregano leaves

- 2 tablespoons brown sugar
- 2 tablespoons salt

Direction:

- ❖ Add the herb leaves to the cosori premium food dehydrator.
- ❖ Dehydrate at 135 degrees f for 8 hours.
- ❖ Transfer the dried leaves to a food processor.
- ❖ Stir in the sugar and salt.
- ❖ Storage suggestions: store in a mason jar with lid.

Tip: you can also skip the sugar and salt, and simply mix the dried herbs.

Nutrition: calories 98, fat12, carbs 16 , protein 8

GARLIC POWDER

Preparation time: 15 minutes
Dehydration time: 12 hours
Servings: 2

Ingredients:

- 6 heads garlic, cloves separated, peeled and sliced

Direction:

- ❖ Spread the garlic slices in the cosori premium food dehydrator.
- ❖ Dry at 125 degrees f for 12 hours.
- ❖ Transfer the dried garlic into a blender or spice grinder.
- ❖ Storage suggestions: sift the mixture before storing. Store the garlic powder in an airtight spice jar. Keep it in a cool and dry area.

Tip: you can also use a coffee grinder to grind the dried garlic.

Nutrition: calories 98, fat2, carbs 16 , protein 8

POWDERED GINGER

Preparation time: 15 minutes
Dehydration time: 8 hours

Serving: 5

Ingredients:

- 5 pieces ginger, sliced

Direction:

- ❖ Put the ginger in the cosori premium food dehydrator.
- ❖ Dry at 95 degrees f for 8 hours.
- ❖ Transfer the dried ginger to a food processor or spice grinder.
- ❖ Grind the dried ginger into powder.
- ❖ Storage suggestions: store in a mason jar.

Tip: use a mandoliner slicer to slice the ginger.

Nutrition: calories 75, fat 3, fiber 4, carbs5, protein 10

ONION & GARLIC POWDER MIX

Preparation time: 20 minutes
Dehydration time: 12 hours
Servings:

Ingredients:

- 5 cloves garlic, peeled and sliced
- 1 onion, sliced

Direction:

- ❖ Place the garlic and onion slices in the cosori premium food dehydrator.
- ❖ Dehydrate at 135 degrees f for 12 hours.
- ❖ Transfer to a spice grinder.
- ❖ Grind until powdery.
- ❖ Storage suggestions: store in a mason jar.

Tip: slice the onion and garlic thinly before dehydrating.

Nutrition: calories 75, fat 3, fiber 4, carbs5, protein 10

KIMCHI POWDER

Preparation time: 5 minutes
Dehydration time: 12 hours
Servings: 5

Ingredients:

- 2 cups kimchi

Direction:

- ❖ Add the kimchi to the cosori premium food dehydrator.
- ❖ Dehydrate at 155 degrees f for 12 hours.
- ❖ Add the dried kimchi to a spice grinder, blender or food processor.
- ❖ Process until powdery.
- ❖ Storage suggestions: store the powder in an empty spice jar.

Tip: dehydrate longer if there is still moisture after 12 hours.

Nutrition: calories 76, fat 5 , fiber 3 , carbs 5 , protein 3

THYME, GARLIC, ROSEMARY & LEMON HERB MIX

Preparation time: 15 minutes
Dehydration time: 8 hours
Servings: 5

Ingredients:

- ½ cup thyme leaves
- 6 cloves garlic, peeled
- ½ cup rosemary leaves
- 2 teaspoons lemon zest

Direction:

- ❖ put all the ingredients to a food processor.
- ❖ Pulse until well mixed.
- ❖ Add the mixture to the cosori premium food dehydrator.
- ❖ Dry at 135 degrees f for 8 hours.
- ❖ Storage suggestions: store in a mason jar.

Tip: you can also use garlic powder in lieu of garlic slices with this recipe.

Nutrition: calories 43, fat 14, fiber 3 , carbs5 , protein 14

PARSLEY, OREGANO, BASIL, THYME & RED PEPPER HERB MIX

Preparation time: 15 minutes
Dehydration time: 8 hours
Servings: 5

Ingredients:

- 2 tablespoons fresh oregano leaves
- 2 tablespoons fresh parsley leaves
- 2 tablespoons fresh basil leaves
- 1 tablespoon fresh thyme leaves
- 1 teaspoon lemon zest
- 1 teaspoon red pepper, sliced

Direction:

- ❖ Combine all the ingredients in a bowl.
- ❖ Add to the cosori premium food dehydrator.
- ❖ Dehydrate at 135 degrees f for 8 hours.
- ❖ After dehydrating the herbs and spices, transfer to a food processor.
- ❖ Pulse until powdery.
- ❖ Storage suggestions: store in a glass jar with lid.

Tip: you can also use red pepper flakes for this recipe.

Nutrition: calories15, fat 13, fiber 1, carbs 2, protein 1

LEMON POWDER

Preparation time: 30 minutes
Dehydration time: 12 hours
Servings: 5

Ingredients:

- Peel from 6 lemons

Direction:

- ❖ Add the lemon peels to the cosori premium food dehydrator.
- ❖ Dehydrate at 95 degrees f for 12 hours.
- ❖ Transfer to a food processor.
- ❖ Pulse until powdered.
- ❖ Storage suggestions: store in sealable plastic bags.

Tip: you can stir in garlic powder for lemon garlic mix.

Nutrition: calories85, fat 13, fiber 1, carbs 32, protein 11

CONCLUSION

Dehydrating has the potential to be a great solution for many people who are trying to find a cheaper and healthier way to eat, store, and preserve their foods. After the initial investment that comes in the form of buying Dehaydrating supplies, canning your own food in the comfort of your kitchen can be a rewarding – and economic – experience. For beginners who are just trying to figure out whether they'd like to take Dehaydrating up as for the long-term, you do not have to go all out and buy all the supplies. There are many alternatives to the standard Dehaydrating supplies that you can purchase – they tend to be cheaper and just as effective as the original canning supplies.

You do need to know, though, that there are different methods for different foods. Some methods involve boiling water; other methods involve pressure cookers and other tools. With every method, there are different sets of supplies needed. If you are a beginner, you will struggle with finding the appropriate tools and selecting the right methods for canning and preserving your foods.

When food comes out of the dehydrator, it looks vastly different from its original state. Hummus and soups can look as cracked and parched as a desert floor. Food can come off the trays in thin sheets, which you can break into smaller pieces. Properly dried pieces of fruit bend but don't break, and they do not feel moist when you squeeze them. Other foods—vegetables, grains, and legumes—should be hard and dry.

It is possible to burn food in a dehydrator, so pay attention to both the temperature and timing recommendations given in the recipes. Also, when you're learning how to dehydrate food, be sure to check the food every few hours. You may need to rotate the trays to ensure that the food dries evenly, and if you find that part of your recipe is dry before the rest, remove that part and store it while the rest of the recipe continues to dry. There is often one ingredient in each recipe that takes longer to dry than the rest, and that ingredient will be called out in the recipe as the barometer for when the food is dry. In the **Red Curry Vegetable Stir-Fry**, for example, that ingredient is the red bell pepper, which has a very high-water content.

Storing dried food is a crucial step to ensure the most extended shelf life. If not stored well, moisture, heat and oxygen decreases the shelf life and turn them bad sooner than expected. Store you dehydrated bounties in a cool and dry place, or in zip lock bags in the freezer to ensure longer shelf life. You can increase it by vacuum sealing the bags and then store them in the freezer.

The moral of the book is that before you get too enthusiastic about dehydrating batches upon batches of dried foods and pilling your pantry up with all your favourite foods, you need to look and practice all the rules of dehydration and have an idea for the space you have for storing; it will be of no use if you are drying more than the available space unless you intend to sell or gift them.

Remember, different foods have different timings and pre-treatments, so you must follow each step accordingly. Thoroughly drying the food is the key to successful dehydration. The presence of liquid in the dehydrated food turn it fetid and prone to many harmful bacteria such as E. coli. Also, selecting the best quality food ensures a healthy and perfect dried food. Always prefer farmer's market for selecting fruits and vegetables as they provide the freshest food.

When you start to head off with your creative ideas for dehydration, try to limit it to one or two new ingredients. Occasionally what appears to be a great idea, can muddle the flavours or emphasise the taste of the original fruit, vegetable or meat. Limiting the ingredients to one or two possible suspects will enable you to distinguish the culprit quickly.

BOOK 3

CANNING MEAT FOR PREPPERS

INTRODUCTION

Preserving food is a process that has been around for centuries. Modern technology has been a boon, making life very simple for us. While we can simply head out to the supermarket to pick out what we need, our ancestors had to preserve food to survive the winter. Historical evidence shows that people in the Middle East would preserve food by drying it in the sun. While that process took a lot of time, it saved people from starving in the winter. The practice of drying food, especially fruit, was also a common practice in ancient Rome. In regions where there wasn't enough sunlight available, the Romans built "still houses," making it feasible. In different regions, different were used approaches based on the means available to their inhabitants.

Food preservation at home is still a prominent topic of discussion. When a shortage of canning supplies such as jars, lids, and canners became an actuality in 2020, experts and household food preservers noticed a surge in demand in home food preservation. As more people store food at home, it's worth revisiting the history of food preservation.

Although chemical reactions like oxidation can harm some food, most food is spoiled in-store by living organisms such as bacteria, molds, and yeast. As a result, food preservation methods rely on destroying or preventing the development of these microorganisms.

Many of our most popular methods of food preservation have been around since the dawn of time and can be found in a variety of places. Drying, smoking, pickling, and fermenting have all found their way into the cuisines of different nations worldwide. Although the approaches differ, they all aim to produce a condition that is unfriendly to microorganisms like molds, bacteria, and yeasts.

Canning is the process of preserving foods inside a glass jar. Most foods are stored in either pint—or quart-sized jars, although other sizes are available as well. Canning helps to prevent the growth of harmful microbes in your food, and also protects against countless foodborne illnesses. When done properly, canned foods can last anywhere from a year to a hundred years.

If done correctly, canning is a vital and safe technique of meat preservation that should be used often. The canning procedure is putting foods in jars and heating them to a temperature that kills bacteria that may provide a health risk or cause the food to deteriorate if left untreated. Canning also has the additional benefit of inactivating enzymes that may cause the food to deteriorate. Vacuum seals are created by forcing air from the jar during heating and then allowing it to cool. This keeps the product from being refilled with air, where it might introduce bacteria that could taint the meal once again.

Canning and preserving meta offers numerous benefits. While preserved meat can easily be purchased from the market, commercial products neither offer the same quality nor the satisfaction of preserving food on your own. In addition, they usually are more expensive and often contain artificial preservatives. Whether you grow your food or purchase food in bulk, food preservation can help you stock up, save money, and enjoy your favorite foods all year long.

CHAPTER 1

UNDERSTANDING MEAT CANNING

Canning and preserving meat is an amazing hobby that is beneficial and fun. It can help you save money on food, capture foods when they are at their peak ripeness and help you fill your pantry with foods that you love. Canning is completely safe to do at home when you follow all the necessary guidelines and it is also just a fun, satisfying pastime. There is nothing quite as pleasing as a cupboard full of newly canned foods!

If you have been wanted to try canning foods, now is the time to do it. Think of what food you would like to preserve and then dive right in! Start with basic water bath canning and then work your way up to using a pressure canner. Or, dive right in and start pressure canning like a seasoned canner! No matter what you choose to create first, you are bound to be successful when you follow the steps in this guide. One key to canning that you always should follow is to have fun!

So, grab those canning jars, take out that big canner pot and start cooking some food to preserve! You will have your shelves filled with beautifully preserved foods in no time.

Canning your own meat is a deeply satisfying activity. When you take a look at your canned foods and you realize that you were able to do it on your own, it will fuel the motivation you need to turn this into a regular habit. If you choose to can your own food on a regular basis, you will notice a decline in the amount of money you use to buy produce and other canned foods. Home canning will also influence your eating habits in a positive way. The foods that will be preserved will be far healthier than the preserved foods that are sold in supermarkets.

It's funny how we always crave our favorite fruits and veggies during their off-season. Not being able to satisfy those cravings can be quite frustrating. But it doesn't have to be like that. Canning and preserving your favorite food can give you a way out. Canned and preserved food can taste just as good as when you first preserved them. The best thing about this is that the process is quite straightforward, and a lot of things can be canned and preserved, such as jams and jelly, fresh fruit and vegetables, and meat and pickles. And all this can be done without adding any artificial preservatives.

As time goes by, though, the number of mistakes you make will decrease, and eventually, you won't need this guide to assist you. You will be able to come up with creative recipes of your own! This all has to start with the first steps; the first steps are that you are giving this a chance.

Whether you are new to preserving or an old hand, there is a recipe in this book that will inspire and amaze you. You will have no problem finding a simple method for dishes like spicy apple chutney to spread on your pork chops to delicious mango chutney to spread on a fresh piece of bread. Store these delicacies in the refrigerator in jars or sealable containers in the freezer or eat the batch in one sitting with your favorite people! One thing is for sure; chutney is a delicious preserve.

Don't let your fears stop you from trying out this great method of preserving your own food. It is a highly rewarding experience that is capable of benefitting you for years to come.

HISTORY AND DEVELOPMENT OF CANNING MEAT

The need to preserve food dates as far back as the first years of the Napoleonic Wars. The French government offered the hefty reward of 12,000 francs to the inventor that could produce an effective way of preserving large quantities of food for a prolonged period of time. The requirement resulted from the need to support Napoleon's military campaigns. The winner of the contest was Nicolas Appert in 1809.

He noticed that unless the seals leaked, the food cooked inside a jar did not spoil. Acting on this observation he developed a method to seal food in glass jars. The reason that the food did not spoil, was discovered 50 years later by none other than Louis Pasteur who noticed and recorded how microbes affected the food spoilage.

Glass jars presented a challenge, as there were a lot of problems involved in their transportation. The solution was given by Peter Durand in 1810 who devised the familiar cylindrical wrought-iron canisters (the root of the modern term cans). Durand's cans solved the fragility problem of the glass jars and they were also cheaper and faster to manufacture. However, glass jars still remain as a good option for canning high value products at home.

Durand's cans may have solved the glass jars' inadequacies, but they presented another problem. Not everyone could use a bayonet to open a can up. Sometimes it was necessary to smash the cans with rocks to open them up. This necessitated the development of a can opener which didn't happen until 1840, largely due to the fact that the factory and the know-how of Nicolas Appert were all but destroyed in 1814 by the coalition soldiers invading France.

The next step was the development of the famous tin can. It would seem that the entire canning concept was something that the French could be identified with (in a similar fashion that the Fins were identified with driving and the Brazilians identified with soccer), as another Frenchman, Philippe de Girard was the one who thought of the method and developed it with the assistance of Bryan Donkin and John Hall. The product was dubbed as a tin can because the material used was tinned wrought iron.

Tin cans became a massive success. Initially amongst the military forces of the British Army and the Royal Navy and then commercially. It is indicative of this success that by the mid-19th century, canned food became a status symbol for the middle class.

This success was mitigated heavily after the Franklin expedition disaster in 1845, which vividly demonstrated that canned food may entail serious health hazards. In this case it was the lead solder that was used for sealing the cans and that was proved to be extremely poisonous to humans. The situation was remedied through various improvements and side inventions, and by 1860 the increase in urban populations demanded for increasing quantities of canned food. At that point, the time required to cook food in a sealed can was reduced from six hours to thirty minutes.

The next major advancement in the canning technology occurred during World War I. In the beginning the food contained was cheap and of low quality. The majority of the cans contained the then famous 'Bully Beef' which was actually very cheap corned beef. To improve the morale of their soldiers the British begun purchasing food of higher quality and then created the staple of all military forces even to this date: the complete meals.

As incredible as it may seem, the last major development that occurred around the 1900s remains the same until today. And this is the double seeming technique which completely sealed the cans and made them totally airtight and allowed for the food inside to remain uncompromised for a period of at least five years, even at the worst of storing conditions.

The only change that has happened during the manufacturing stage of a can recently, is the substitution of steel and wrought iron with aluminum compounds, which made the can production faster and cheaper.

While it is possible to manufacture metal cans at home, it is preferable to either purchase readily made ones that have observed the safety precautions, or use glass jars if you want to prepare and can your own canned food and keep it stored to be used in case of an emergency.

BENEFITS OF CANNING AND PRESERVING MEAT

Nutrition

Fresh produce, like fruits and vegetables, are known to start 'dying' and lose their vitamins from the moment they are harvested from the ground. Up to half, or even more of the vitamins may be lost within a few days if the fruits or vegetables are not stored in a cool place or preserved appropriately. It takes up to two weeks for refrigerated produce to lose its vitamins and start deteriorating. If fresh produce is harvested, cleaned, and stored in a good time, the majority of its vitamins will be preserved. Fruits and vegetables that are harvested and canned properly will be able to be of higher nutritional value than fresh produce that is stored in makeshift conditions.

The problem with a lot of products that is sold in commercial facilities these days is that a number of chemicals and substances have been used to improve the appearance of the produce, and its shelf life too. Fresh produce, when exposed for a long amount of time, will become home to microorganisms, regardless of the storage conditions. Some shops are neglectful with their products and this ends up affecting the health of consumers. When you choose to can your own food and even grow your own produce, you can avoid using potentially harmful substances. Canning is simply preserving fresh food in its original state. The preservatives that you will use are also natural; acids such as lemon juice or vinegar are known to have a great number of benefits for the human body.

Economical

As mentioned above, fresh produce is not able to last for long; it isn't cheap, either. Canning can be very useful for a person, especially when it comes to preserving seasonal fruits and vegetables. The price of seasonal produce is usually high and after a certain amount of time, it becomes hard to find these fruits and vegetables again. Canning allows you to preserve fruits, vegetables (and other foods) in bulk, allowing you to keep a steady supply of vegetables for a longer period of time, and for a lesser amount of money. If you are into planting and harvesting your own produce, this will slash your food expenses in half. You will be able to rule out buying produce regularly since you'll be supplying yourself with your own stock. If you have business acumen, you could look into starting a small business of your own. If not, that's okay. At least you will have a ready supply of fruits and vegetables at any time you want. If you are a fan of homemade jams that they sell in stores, you will be pleased to know that you will be able to make your own, with your own canned fruits and vegetables, and at a lower cost. Canning really is a much more economical option in comparison to buying produce on a daily/weekly basis.

Durability

Cans are able to withstand extreme conditions: heat, cold, wet, dry, etc. This means you can store your canned food in almost any kind of environment without worrying about the condition of the can. What you do need to watch out for, though, are signs of rusting, leakage, denting or bulging; these are signs that could mean that the cans have been damaged and the food has been affected.

Increased Shelf Life

The process of canning, which involves the use of high temperatures and very sterile containers, ensures that any organism that can cause spoilage is destroyed. As long as the container remains intact, the food will remain safe. Once a container is compromised, you have to throw the food out in order to avoid anyone from contracting harmful diseases or infections. Canning is able to provide a shelf life that can span anywhere from one to four or five years. The shelf life can be longer than this under certain circumstances; some products are known to have a shelf life of over thirty years.

You won't need your food to last for over one hundred years, but it will definitely last longer than a couple of months. Canning is an effective method for families to incorporate into their lifestyles because it saves mothers and fathers from spending money every day on the produce for daily meals. If you are someone who personally grows and harvests your own produce, canning will be a great way for you to preserve your harvest. Having a long shelf life means you can create a food supply without worrying about the food spoiling or rotting in a short space of time.

Rewarding Experience

Canning your own food is also a very rewarding personal experience. It can easily become a skill or hobby you develop for your spare time. Canning involves mental and physical work, which improves your body in more ways than one. It can also be a good experience for couples and families since it is something that can be done as a group. You will get to educate your children on the origins of the food that they eat, and you will also be teaching them a very useful skill that could be passed down in your family. If you are a sucker for old school, canning is also a great thing for you as it will rouse nostalgia within you. Many canners have spoken of the sentimental connection they have developed with canning, because it reminds them of earlier times in their childhood.

It's Eco-Friendly Too

The problem with the produce that is sold in commercial facilities is that the process of preserving them is not environmentally friendly. The facilities that are used to cool produce run on electricity, which is generated by fossil fuels. We all already know how bad the burning of fossil fuels is for the environment. Produce is also stored in plastic containers which are discarded off after the produce has been consumed. Plastic materials are never good for the environment because they are not biodegradable.

Save room in the freezer.

Most individuals don't have a lot of freezer room, and frozen meat occupies most of it. If we can move those meats out of that valuable area and into a canning jar on the table or shelf, we could use that space for stuff like ice cream. Avoiding the cost of spoiled meat in the event of a power failure is just as crucial. Meat is no longer fit to consume if the freezer level reaches the dangerous level of 41 degrees Fahrenheit for two hours more. Everything in your freezer, including ground beef, pork, chicken, brisket, will have to be thrown out. You don't have to bother about power failures if you can some portion of that meat and keep it at room temperature. The fact is, there are so many benefits to canning meat that it's worthwhile getting over your fear and diving in.

Ability to Purchase in large quantities.

When we come across a great 'can't-miss' price on meat, we can take the opportunity of it by home-canning it. When you buy several types of meat at a discount and can them, you and your household won't have to consume the same meats over and over by getting them out of the freezer before they go bad.

Prevent spoilage in emergencies

We have fuel in our ordinary, non-emergency life. We use it to prepare food, heat, and cool, and we don't give it a second thought. Many folks have a backup plan in case of a power failure, figuring they'll just bring out the camp stove and gas, then prepare or home can all of the meat in the freezer. Everyone has a plan till they get hit in the gut by a power failure- Mike Tyson!

I'm glad to inform you that if you're in the middle of a long term situation, you'll have a lot more to stress about than canning your defrost meats. Why not take charge of it now, while you have the time?

You're aware of the contents of the bottle.

There are no secret additives when you can meat at yourself. You are sure of what goes in and out. Would you like to reduce your sodium intake? Then leave out any salt or sodium-rich condiments. Is there anyone in the family who has a food allergy? When you can meat, you can avoid adding those additives.

Meal preparation during a power outage is painless and straightforward.

With home-canned meats, cooking during a power failure is simple. They're already fully cooked and healthy to consume, so all we have to do now is add them to any recipe we're making and heat it. There are no long cooking durations, which waste valuable alternative fuels. Another alternative is to rinse the meat and utilize it in a simple household meal like chicken salad.

helps you save money

The cost of canned meats at the food shop might be pretty high. A tiny tuna-sized can of chicken (10 ounces) costs roughly $3 where I stay. Getting canned meats for my big household gets expensive, but I can bottle an entire quart (2 lbs.) of chicken for roughly $3.00. I purchase chicken in quantity for under $2 per pound and occasionally even less.

Satisfaction

In a society where practically anything can be outsourced, there is much to be said about the satisfaction of doing things yourself. Whenever you add new talent to your repertoire, your self-reliance grows. Even better, you may now transfer your knowledge and skills to the subsequent generation. Our primary responsibility is to provide for our families, and doing so well is a beautiful thing.

There will be less waste.

Jars for canning exist in a variety of sizes. Use the portion size that your household will consume in a single meal. We use either quarts and pints for chicken and beef at my home since occasionally the supper is for the whole family. On other occasions, the kids are out enjoying kid activities, and its just mommy and daddy and the baby at home.

Protect the environment.

We're not saving the environment, but because canning jars are reusable, we're not adding to the waste by using cans. If you purchase new can and lids when you start house canning meat, it will be an investment, but they may also be acquired through yard sales, thrift stores, or simply asking about your area. You might be able to discover an old friend who is willing to give their jars to those who will need them.

Save time

Thanks to the properly prepared meats from home canning, we've saved a lot of time on dinner prep. Although canning the meats takes time at first, it is a targeted and productive amount of work scheduled for the day. I would open a can of prepared chicken or ground beef at suppertime, which makes meal prep so much simpler and faster.

Since we're on the subject of canning and time saving, one of the simplest products to can is meat. In most situations, you'll place raw meat in a canning jar, add some broth or water (depending on the meat), and pressure can the jars. It doesn't get any easier than this.

WHERE TO PURCHASE CANNING SUPPLIES

Canning supplies are available across the country, in all kinds of stores. The first place to check is your local hardware store. Most hardware stores will carry canning supplies year round and have a good variety of jar sizes and tools. Larger hardware stores like Home Depot and Lowe's also carry canning jars and tools.

You can check your local grocery store; however, grocery stores tend to only stock canning supplies during canning season. The same can be said about home goods stores such as Bed Bath and Beyond and Tractor Supply.

Big box stores like Target and Walmart also carry canning supplies during canning season. If you are lucky, they may also have a few shelves of jars in the off season hidden in the aisles. These stores often have good deals on jars as they can purchase in bulk and pass the savings on to you.

You can also purchase your canning supplies online and have them delivered directly to your door. Amazon has all types of jars available and they will run coupon specials during canning season, giving you a great price on the jars. The companies that make the canning jars, such as Ball, have their own websites where you can purchase jars and accessories. Many of these company-owned sites will have unique canning tools since the product is coming straight from the company.

Many people have had success finding jars at yard sales or thrift stores. People looking to get rid of their canning jars may bring them to a second-hand store in order to make space in their own cabinet. When buying previously used jars, you should always check for chips or cracks before using them for canning.

Be sure that your canning supplies are up to the most current canning safety standards. While you may want to use your grandma's old double hinge jars to preserve foods, it may not be the safest option. Be sure you have a canner that is in good condition and equipped with all the newest safety features.

Website Authorities

There are a few websites that are considered authorities in home canning. It is a good idea to look at these sites periodically to see if any new canning advances have been made.

The first site is freshpreserving.com which is owned by the company who makes Ball and Kerr jars. This site contains tried and true recipes, general information about canning, a store to purchase canning supplies and a forum for home canners to talk and compare recipes and experiences. This is a user-friendly site for anyone, whether they are an experienced canner or a novice.

The National Center for Home Food Preservation is a government-owned website that will give you lots of scientific information about canning at home. If you are interested in the science behind canning and preserving, this is the site for you. There are also many detailed recipes to try. Find it all at nchfp.uga.edu.

METHOD OF MEAT PRESERVATION

Freezing

It's impossible to go wrong with freezing, except you utilize the unsuitable container or fail to turn on the freezer. Whether you buy meat in large, hunt it, or raise it locally, portioning the cuts and wrapping them in a freezer sheet or using freezer-safe bags or containers requires no effort. Based on the cut and fat concentration, meat kept at 0° F will last longer, but the flavor will deteriorate after four months to a year. When stored in vacuum-sealed containers, the storage life can be doubled or tripled. To avoid freezer damage, eliminate as much air as possible when using freezer sheets or plastic bags. To save storage, stack meat before it freezes.

Freezing has drawbacks. And the drawbacks might be terrible because when it fails, everything fails at the same time. When the electricity goes off, or your appliance fails, you may not notice until brown-reddish fluid oozes from the inside and blowflies swarm near the source of the foul stench. Many homesteaders have found out the hard way that relying only on a freezer is dangerous. Examine your appliances regularly to make sure they're fully functional. If the door isn't opened, food in a fully loaded freezer can stay frozen for up to a week, giving you enough time to contact a repair service or rescue the food.

Freeze drying

Freeze-dried foods are one of the greatest survival foods, and they may be organized into single meals that fit within a jar, ready to be hydrated and cooked. The most convenient way to use this meat preservation technique is to get a freeze-drying device that takes care of most of the work for you.

Place fresh or prepared meats on the unit's trays by slicing them. The temperature is then dropped to -30° to -50°F, creating a vacuum around the meat. In this vacuum condition, the meat is slowly heated, and all of the liquid in the meat is converted to water vapor and sucked off.

If you don't want to spend extra cash on a freeze-drying machine, you can freeze-dry using a deep freeze, dry ice, or a vacuum chamber. Some of these procedures can take up to a week and risk freezer damage, resulting in foods that can be dried and kept in pantries.

Dehydrating

Drying meat on smooth rocks in the sun, handcrafted hanging racks, and using electrical equipment is one of the ancient meat preservation techniques. However, a dehydrator can be acquired for less than $40 new or considerably less if bought used. Jerky is dried meat that has been steeped in brine and seasonings before being dehydrated. When mastering how to cook venison, it's common also to learn to create jerky.

Because residual fat can rapidly turn sour and destroy the whole food, dehydrate the thinnest slices of meat and extract it. Slice finely for faster processing; freezing the cuts ahead of time will help you get the thinnest slices possible. If you're making jerky, soak it for up to 24 hours in acid fluids like vinegar, honey, or beer, along with your selected spices.

To maintain safety, University cooperative extensions recommend pre-cooking meat before dehydrating it. Boil for at least 10 minutes in a preheated oven at 275°F or steam/roast to an internal temperature of 160°F. Preheat the oven to 165 degrees Fahrenheit. Place the meat in a straight line on the racks of a food dehydrator and dry at the highest level. Make sure the internal temperature is atleast145 degrees Fahrenheit. Allow four to six hours for drying before storing in sealed containers.

Although frozen meat usually lasts a year, pairing it with dehydration can extend its storage life to several years. It also helps to preserve space. Just dry your meat as directed above, vacuum seals it, and freeze it.

Curing

Nitrates have recently earned a poor rap. This is partly because huge amounts of sodium nitrate are hazardous. It is, nevertheless, required for curing meat because salt does not eradicate the risk of botulism, whereas sodium nitrate does. To apply this meat preservation approach, look for "curing salts." Due to the additional dye, these are referred to as "pink salts," however they are not similar to Himalayan pink salt.

Dry-curing entails mixing the curing salts with table salt and spices, dry-rubbing meat like pig belly to maintain even covering, and storing in the refrigerator for up to a week. The meat is then carefully cleaned, wrapped in cheesecloth to put pests at bay, and stored for up to eight weeks in a cool, dry area such as a walk-in refrigerator.

Combine a brine with water, table salt, curing salt, spices, and optionally brown sugar to wet-cure meat. For every two pounds of meat, the meat is brined for a day. For large hams, this can take up to a week. Strain the meat on a mesh screen for a day after carefully cleaning it, then store it for up to a month. After smoking, a cured ham becomes much tastier.

Hoof

Have you ever pondered why beef, pork, or venison are the most common classical cured or dried meats? Chicken and rabbit sausages do exist, but they are more uncommon. This is because curing and drying were required for bigger animals.

The simplest way of meat preservation is to feed the animal alive till it is consumed. Rabbits, chickens, and geese can sustain a family for one supper and reach butcher size in a matter of months. "Fat calves" were kept for important events when a large group of neighbors or family could share the animal, and hardly anything went to waste. In the parable of the Prodigal Son, the father requested the bigger calf to be butchered to celebrate his son's return.

Families who live off the grid may not have the resources to operate multiple freezers to preserve their animals until they are needed. The difficulty of discovering alternate meat preservation methods for cattle or pigs is avoided by raising smaller, more sustainable animals. Smaller animals also enable homesteaders to grow more meat without requiring much land.

If all grownups have a full-time job, raising animals "on the hoof" may not be possible. It takes effort to butcher, prepare, and brine meat.

If power and appliances are more restricted than food or grass, raising the animals alive for a longer period may solve a storage space challenge.

DRAWBACKS OF THE CANNING METHOD

Although canning has several benefits, it also has some drawbacks. Although the advantages supersede the disadvantages, knowing the weaknesses and risks is important.

Glass jars are prone to breaking.

Seals can be damaged, resulting in food spoilage.

Canning takes a long time.

When jars refuse to seal, spoilage occurs. However, insufficient preparation or poor hygiene can lead to Clostridium botulinum contamination, which can be fatal. It's always a good idea to strictly follow the directions that came with your canner.

The majority of canning is made in the summer, which raises air conditioning expenses.

Canned food does not have the same flavor as fresh food.

Canned food has a lesser nutrient benefit than fresh food. Freshly harvested mature fruits and vegetables have 65 percent higher vitamins and minerals than canned fruits and vegetables.

It also necessitates substantial time and financial effort. Using canning tools only once or twice a season may not be sufficient to cover the equipment's expense.

Canning jars that have been filled are large and weighty. Storage of such jars necessitates the use of heavy-duty shelves. They're also cumbersome to transport from one place to another.

CANNING DO'S AND DON'TS

Canning is relatively simple but when not done properly, it can result in disastrous consequences. For you to truly be a master on this very important skill, let me provide you with some canning dos and don'ts that you'll surely find helpful.

Be Organized

Did you notice that in both water bath and pressure canning methods above studying the recipe is always the first step? This is because knowing what to do keeps you organized. You have to be organized when preserving food since it could help your work go smoothly and canning should be done as quickly as possible.

Spices and seasoning only as specified

Do you know that spices and seasoning are usually high in bacteria? Having too many seasonings and spices on your food beyond what was required in the recipe could be unsafe.

Overripe fruits and vegetables are a no-no

I have mentioned this before but let me just reiterate this for you, canning can increase the life of the food but it certainly couldn't increase its quality. Canning overripe fruits may become worse in storage.

No butter and fat ever

You should not put these two in your home canned products as they do not store well. Adding them to your product will only decrease the food's life. In addition, butter and fat slows heat transfer during the processing time which can result to an unsafe preserve.

You can go smaller but not bigger

When it comes to the size of jar you should use, if you can't stick to the jar size on the recipe, then you should pick up a smaller jar than getting a bigger one since this can result in an unsafe product.

The higher the altitude = longer processing time

In high altitudes, the boiling point is of lower altitude. This is why you have to increase the processing time to compensate for the lower temperatures at an altitude above 1000 feet.

Hot and cold do not go well together

Indeed, hot and cold do not go well together especially when it comes to jars. Abrupt changes in temperature would certainly result in breakage so here are things you should remember: if the food will be hot when placed in the jar, your jar should be preheated and the water in the canner should already be heated to. If the food is cold, do not preheat the jars, just sterilize them. Also, put the jars before turning on the heat on the canner so that the water and the food can be heated together.

Safety first before removing jars

After the processing time, jars will sure to be hot in both the water bath and the pressure canning method so you have to make sure to handle them carefully. You can use a footstool to avoid tiptoeing while removing the jars because that could be dangerous!

Patience on seals

After removing the jars from the rack and putting them on a paper towel, avoid moving them or you will be interrupting its sealing process. Just leave them be or else put the jars in a place where it wouldn't be disturbed the moment you take them out of the canner.

Write the details down meticulously

I'm just talking about the labels on the jars. Remember to always attach a label to each jar and write down the recipe and the production date. This is the best way to keep track of the life span of the food.

To be truly a master of something, you have to work hard on it to. Knowledge of the steps in canning and preserving plus the additional tips I mentioned would not be enough to create a canning master in you. You have to work hard on it too. As always, practice is the key!

CANNING JARS (STANDARD)

Use conventional canning jars, which usually have the company's name or the word MASON written on the side of the jar. Mayonnaise, pickle jars, or Peanut butter, for example, may not be able to sustain the 10-pound pressure (240 F) required to can vegetables. Check the jars for chipping or cracks if you're utilizing conventional canning jars you already have. Examine the jar's mouth with your finger to check whether it has any fractures or cracks. The jar will not seal if this happens. If treated properly and without nicks or fractures, jars may last for years.

To avoid shattering the jars, clean and rinse them by hand shortly before filling them with hot vegetables or other produce. Preheat the jars until you're ready to fill them with hot products. Preheat the pressure canner or the water in it to put the hot jars in it right away. If the water is not heated, this lowers the time required for the canner to get up to pressure.

Add at least three inches of boiling water to a seven-quart pressure canner to get it set for processing. (If you have a larger canner, you'll need additional water; see the manufacturer's directions.) Put the canner on the stove unit to heat and place the rack on the base of the canner.

LIDS FOR CANNING

The 2-piece lid, which consists of a screw band and a thin metal top, is the best option as thin metal tops cannot be used again and again. Before putting the lids into the jars, read the manufacturer's directions on how to handle the lids that came with them. Some conditions need heating, while others do not.

CHAPTER 2

METHOD OF CANNING MEAT

You can choose *raw* or *hot pack*s, but both will result in pressure canned meat. The raw pack is usually misunderstood as a boil, and the hot pack is commonly mistaken as a pressure canned technique, but this is incorrect!

Raw/cold pack

Simply inserting raw meat cut in cubes into a safe and sanitized jar is all it takes to pressure can meat with a raw pack. Many of the air bubbles inside the jar are removed by squeezing the meat down to the appropriate headspace. Apply the lid to the jar after cleaning the rim with vinegar-soaked tissue or paper towels. Now, fill your pressure canner with the jars and the appropriate quantity of water, and begin by letting it vent heat for 10 minutes before adding the jar and getting it up to pressure.

When raw packing meat for pressure canning, you'll notice that no extra water is used. It'll make its broth on its own.

Proteins stick to the edge of the jar when using a raw pack, and they must be thoroughly washed away.

Don't raw pack in pint normal mouth-sized jars if you don't have a nice cleaning brush to get deep in. The raw pack technique works well with wide opening pints and quarts. I put raw meat in 8 oz. jelly jars with straight sides and a narrow opening. It's considerably simpler to wash than the bigger jars with rounded shoulders.

According to researches done, some people have concluded that the raw pack method:

Saves you preparation time;

Because the meat shrinks during preparation, your jars may appear to be 25% empty.

During preparation, the meat may emit more surplus fat. Surplus fat may flow to the surface of jars, causing an unattractive appearance and perhaps turning rotten over time. (However, particularly in extra-lean minced beef, you'd be shocked at how much fat there is.)

Some claim that jars containing raw-packed meat are more difficult to wash afterwards.

According to North and South Dakota Extension Services,

"When loading jars with raw meat, don't pack them too tightly. A loose pack is when you fill the jar with air. Using the palm of your hand, carefully tap the base of the jar after putting raw meat in the jar and gripping it with one hand. Set a folded kitchen cloth or pot pad on your countertop and tap the jar strongly on the cloth or pot pad. Keep adding meat and tapping the jar's base until the appropriate head space is achieved. Do not squeeze the meat into the jar too tight."

Hot pack

When packaging meat in jars, everything must be hot, as well as the jars themselves. You'll also have to fill the jar with hot water or broth. When it comes to pressure canning meat, hot-packed meat will maintain its form more when used in a meal.

Meat is fried till it is partially cooked when it is hot packed. It will then be placed in the jar and filled to the required headspace with boiling water—this aids in the preservation of the meat's shape and appearance in the jars. The jars will be considerably easier to wash because no proteins from the meat will attach to them.

Be certain that you have the pressure canner water hot when you bring the hot packed jars of meat to it.

According to researches done, some people have concluded that the hot pack method:

Since the meat has shrunk during precooking, you can put so much in the jar;

It offers the possibility to burn or brown the meat, generating flavor buttery flavor on the skin of the meat;

Most don't like the mouthfeel of the hot pack with all meats: they say that with more tender meats such as chicken, browning it first can make it stringy.

Note: There is no alternative when it comes to ground meat of any kind: you must do a hot pack by either sautéing the ground meat first or forming it into patties and sautéing those as well. The reason for this is density: raw ground beef would clump together and inhibit even heat transfer through the jar. The ground meat isn't entirely cooked; it's only sautéed until it doesn't form a dense mass in the jar. It's fine to make patties or meatballs (they allow heat to flow around and between them.)

SOME USEFUL TIPS FOR BEGINNERS

Before you begin, gather all of your equipment and supplies. It's awful to learn midway through a process that you're out of some ingredients (has happened to me before) or that you can't locate your jar lifter when the jars are set to be removed.

Give yourself plenty of time! Canning is a delightful pastime, but it is unquestionably time-consuming. When you're in a hurry, the fun fades rapidly, and the situation becomes increasingly unpleasant. I have a basic policy that I don't can on weeknights; I leave it for the weekend when I have more free time.

The first error individuals commit while pressure canning is altering the recipe. This is one case when you should adhere to the recipe as precisely as possible and only apply recommended canning recipes for preservation. Don't tamper with science; there's a huge science behind ensuring adequate acidity in the food to prevent bacteria from ruining it. Ensure you're following food-safe procedures to ensure you're staying within the right pH and consistency standards for the item you're canning.

Do it with a mate! Washing, drying, and cutting meat, as well as boiling and canning it, is a lot of effort. When you have company, time passes more quickly.

Learn from another who has more expertise than you if you have the opportunity. My grandmother showed me how to can, and asking questions when you're a novice to something is quite beneficial.

The next pressure canning blunder is overfilling the canner. Regardless of how many containers you're canning, don't ever load your pressure canner with far higher above two inches of water from the base. Water bath canning, on the other hand, necessitates submerging the jars. When pressure canning, your containers should never be filled with water up to the necks, and worst of all, covering their lids.

Overlooking headspaces requirements: There's a purpose why different types of canning require different amounts of headspace.

The headspace (or open space) guidelines are in place to guarantee that your food is properly sealed. In order for the jar to be properly sealed, many recipes need at minimum one-inch headspace at the top.

Another common error made by beginners is speeding up the procedure by cooling or releasing pressure very soon. It requires a lot of time for the canner to cool down to room pressure when your processing time is over, so you'll have to wait a little while before you can remove your jars.

This is an important step in the canning technique, so don't rush it by pressing the jiggler, bringing out the weight, or submerging the whole canner in ice water.

Placing your pressure canner in water changes the pressure too rapidly, which can damage your seals, shatter your jars, or even destroy your pressure canner.

HOW TO PROPERLY CLEAN & SANITIZE CANNING JARS

There are several safety considerations to follow if you plan on canning your meats. Washing and sterilizing your canning jars thoroughly is an essential step. Improperly conducting these steps or utilizing non-safe cleaning products—can lead to serious health issues. Cleaning products that are free of harsh chemicals are considered safe. Safe detergents will not contaminate your canning jars and food.

MATERIALS FOR CLEANING AND SANITIZING CANNING JARS

You will require the following materials to successfully clean and sanitize your jars. Some of them are almost certainly present in your kitchen.

- Basin or bucket

- Dishwashing liquid
- tongs
- vinegar (white)
- Fresh dish towels
- cloths for cleaning
- Pressure canner

CLEANING

You should properly wash and clean your canning jars before sterilizing them. If they've remained resting on a dusty rack without their lids, you'll need to use a clean cloth to remove any dust and dirt.

Dip your jars in a bucket or basin full of heated water and white vinegar if they have scaling or hard-water film on them. For every gallon of hot water, add one cup of white vinegar. Leave the jars to rest in this solution for a few hours before commencing the cleaning procedure.

You could wash your canning jars manually or put them in the dishwasher. In any case, ensure all soap residue is removed. Any food item you want to can be ruined by leftover soap, causing an unpleasant taste.

STERILIZING

Just like meat you can, the jars and lids may carry bacteria that might thrive and destroy your meat. As a result, all canning tools must be adequately sterilized. According to experts, sterilization is only required for water bath canning less than ten minutes. If your recipe requires a 10-minute or lengthier preparation period, the jars and lids will be disinfected along with your food.

The best technique to sanitize jars and lids for pressure canning is to use the canning method itself. It's necessary, to begin with, to clean jars and lids; however, the extra sterilizing step can be skipped.

If you want to sterilize jars, the National Center for Home Food Preservation recommends doing so as follows:

Set the washed jars right-side-up on a stand in a canner and load the jars and canner with water to one inch over the tops of the jars. Bring the water to a boil and then boil for 10 minutes at altitudes under 1,000 feet elevation. For every 1,000 feet, you gain in elevation, add one minute. Retrieve the jars one by one when you're set to load them, pouring the water back into the canner. This will leave the canner hot enough to process filled jars.

CLEANING YOUR CANNING JARS' LIDS AND SCREW BANDS

Would you also need to sanitize the lids and screw bands on the canning jars? No, but give attention to this crucial caution. The lids, made of metal and rubber, are not reusable, contrary to popular assumptions. Each moment you can food, they should be changed.

Because the screw bands are never in contact with the food, they do not have to be renewed. Instead, hand-wash them with heated water and little droplets of liquid dish soap.

After washing screw bands, the first crucial thing is to ensure they are totally dry. Use a dry cotton kitchen napkin for this, then turn it upside down on an additional clean kitchen napkin for a few hours before using it. This will aid to avoid rusting on the bands.

JARS SHOULD BE TESTED FOR PROPER SEAL.

After cooling for 12 to 24 hours, the jars must be checked for satisfactory sealing before being kept. Loosen the screw bands and inspect the seal using one of the procedures below.

Using a finger or thumb, apply pressure at the middle of the lid. The lid is correctly sealed if it does not shift down or up.

Take the jar by the lid and lift it. The container is correctly closed if the lid stays on without releasing. When verifying the seal, place a hand underneath the jar to hold it if it loosens from the lid, or put it over a table lined with a napkin for padding.

Picking up the jar and looking at the lid at eye level is an alternative to verify the sealing. The jar has correctly sealed if the lid is somewhat bent downwards in the middle.

Test the seal by knocking the middle of the lid with the base of a tablespoon. If it generates a high-pitched ring tone, the jar is fully sealed. If it creates a low bang, the jar may not be well sealed, or there could be stuff at the top of the jar meeting the lid. Pick the jar and inspect the top to see whether there is any food in contact with the lid. If it is, you should use one of the alternative strategies to test for a clean seal.

If any jars are not securely sealed, they can be modified to seal them. Loosen the lid and inspect the rim of the jar for scratches if needed. If the jar has a tear, transfer the substance to a clean jar and make a new lid to sit on top. Reprocess in the same manner as before. Reprocessing will result in an output of lower quality than the initial processed result.

If you don't want to go through the whole procedure for only one or two jars, the unopened jars can be refrigerated and used within two to three days.

CARE AND STORAGE OF THE PRESSURE CANNER

Wash the rack and canner inside and out. Dry completely and lay torn newspaper or paper sheets in the pot's base to retain moisture during storage. Insert the rack into the canner.

While washing the canner lid, take special caution to avoid denting or bending it. To clean the gasket, remove it. Carefully dry the lid and gasket. Look for any evidence of damage to the gasket. Change the gasket if it is cracked or damaged.

Because the dial gauge should never be covered in water, pressure canners with a non-removable cover with a dial gauge must be maintained by cleaning the cover off with a moist towel.

The following season before utilizing the dial gauge, keep a record of getting it examined by the local County Extension Office. Remove safety valves and petcocks if they are detachable to be properly washed and dried. To make sure the vent or petcock is clear of dirt, draw a rope through it.

Turn the cover upside down on the pot and put it in a dry area to store the canner. When storing the canner, do not close the lid. Other canning equipment and tools should be stored in the exact place as the canner so that everything is simple to find when the subsequent canning season commences.

Pressure Canners - How to Use Them Safely

If the pressure canner possesses a dial gauge, it should be examined for reliability once a year before using it. The gauges can be evaluated at most local County Cooperative Extension offices. If the gauge is inaccurate by more than one pound at 5, 10, or 15 pounds of pressure, it should be changed since it may result in inappropriate processing. Before usage, clean all pieces, such as the vent, safety valve, and lid and canner edges.

Time for Proper Processing

The meals must be processed for the appropriate amount of time to confirm that all germs have been effectively killed. Make sure to modify processing timeframes if you're in a high-altitude area.

WHAT ARE THE FACTORS THAT AFFECTS PROCESSING TIME?

- Acid level
- Size of the food cuts
- Jars' original temperature
- Is the meat boneless or has bones?
- Size and structure of the jar
- Viscosity
- how tight is the food is arranged in the jar?
- The temperature the food is being processed

Inspect for Spoilage

Before utilizing canned goods, make sure they are thoroughly inspected for any signs of rotting. Botulism is caused by Clostridium botulinum, found in damaged canned food. It's a great habit to inspect your canned foods for symptoms of spoiling on a routine basis but double-check them before usage. If the food shows indications of spoilage, it should be discarded correctly.

If you're not certain a food is spoilt, do not try to evaluate spoilage by tasting it; instead, toss it in the trash to be safe. The list of indicators of rotting that should be checked before utilizing canned foods is listed below.

Check to ensure that the jar's lid is securely fastened. The jar has an excellent vacuum seal if the middle of the lid is concave.

Check for new leaks or traces of dried food on the jar coming from the top.

Look for discolored areas. It's a sign of rotting if the content is dark in color. If the meal has a mild discoloration, it might be due to mineral elements, in which case the contents are still good.

It is spoilt if the contents are slippery, shriveled, or hazy in appearance.

If the contents of the jar spill out when it is opened, it should be thrown.

Scan for any indications of mold after opening the jar, which might be whitish, blue, greenish, or black in color. Inspect both the bottom of the lid and the contents of the jar for indications of mold.

Sniff the contents; they should be thrown away if they have an off-putting odor.

Getting Rid of Spoiled Food

The jars of food must be appropriately disposed of if it has been confirmed that the canned items have spoiled or are likely to rot. If the jar is still sealed, put it in a disposal bag, securely wrap the bag around the jar, and dispose of it in the ordinary trash. The food should be detoxified before discarding if the jar's seal is damaged, the jar is spilling, or the jar has been unsealed. To detox, follow the instructions outlined below.

Fill a pot with the contents of the jar. If the ingredients are rather thick, add additional water to make it simpler to boil.

Put the lid, jar, screw band (if applicable), and any additional utensil that got into touch with the damaged food in a separate pot. To cover the jar with water, turn it on its side if required. Fill the container with enough water to fill the objects by at least one inch.

Bring the water to a boiling state in both pots—Cook for 30 minutes at a full boil.

Throw the contents of both pots in a thick trash bag and seal it securely when they have finished boiling. Try to get rid of the bag and contents appropriately in the waste.

Scrub the table and any areas connected to the food or jars with warm, soapy water. Any brushes or towels used in the cleaning should be thrown in a thick disposal bag, sealed firmly, and thrown away.

Hands should be washed properly with hot, soapy water.

Canning Storage

After testing for a proper seal, wipe off any residue on the jars and lids.

Label the jars with the contents and the date of processing. Apply a label on the jars to write the data on, or write on a piece of masking tape. On the surface of the lid, a black marker may be employed to write the item and date.

Keep the jar in a dry, cool, and dark area. The lids may rust if the region is moist, weakening the seal. The appearance and taste of food will be affected if it is subjected to many light or warm temperatures.

Temperatures should be kept between 50 and 70 degrees Fahrenheit. Cans of food ought to be kept for roughly a year before losing their quality if preserved properly.

For the finest appearance and taste in canned foods, choose a high-quality food clean of blemishes, at peak maturity, and not infected.

When processing food for canning, it's crucial to avoid exposing some foods to too much air because they can have dark colors.

The number of canned products you will consume within a year should be canned to preserve them fresh year after year.

Canning should not be done in commercial jars, such as mayonnaise jars. They are poorly sturdy and will fracture or shatter more often during preparation.

Wash the jars in the dishwasher if the preparation time is greater than 10 minutes. During the processing, they will be sterilized.

If you're using spices to flavor your meal before canning it, tie them in cheesecloth instead of placing them straight into the food. This allows them to be taken out before the canning process begins, preventing the food from being too flavorful or colored due to the spices.

Because dried herbs are harsher than fresh herbs, reduce the amount by about 1/3 if dried.

If you're at a higher elevation, be sure to adjust the processing duration in accordance with the Processing Temperature and Time tables. Water boils at a reduced temperature at higher elevations, necessitating longer processing time.

Do not fasten screw bands after processing.

CHAPTER 3

FAQS

Is there a canning class or course that you can enroll in as a novice who is interested in taking this ability to the next level? Anyone who wants to can or preserve food does not need a formal degree. If you want to learn more advanced canning techniques, canning courses are often given at various locations such as grocery shops, kitchen supply stores, culinary schools, community centers, and, on occasion, even libraries.

This course is also available through correspondence, so you may wish to check for that option on the internet as well. Pay close attention to websites or publications that educate you how to can food safely. Some of these articles may include thoughts or proposals that are in direct conflict with USDA guidelines and recommendations. Whenever in doubt, consult the USDA handbook or speak with a qualified professional.

How long does canned food have a shelf life?

Foods that have been properly packed, kept in a cool, dry environment, and show no indications of rotting on the interior or outside are deemed safe to eat for at least one year after being opened. Cans of food kept near an oven, in indirect sunlight, in an oven, or in any other heated environment will, nevertheless, have a shorter shelf life.

You should eat it within a few weeks to a couple of months at the most, according to the manufacturer. When jars or cans are exposed to moisture, they corrode, resulting in leaks that can lead to contamination of the food and its ingestion by unqualified people.

One of the recipes called for the use of pectin, which was used to create jam.

Is it possible to remove pectin from a recipe if a person does not want to utilize this ingredient?

It has been emphasized over and over again throughout this book how important it is to follow recipes exactly as written. If you want a flawless outcome, don't make any changes to the recipe, including decreasing, removing, or adding ingredients. There are numerous trustworthy recipes that do not call for the use of pectin that you may discover online. Instead of attempting to alter the recipe, make use of them.

Is it possible to process two layers of jars at the same time?

Yes, it is possible to do this. All of the advantages would apply to the jars in the top layer as well as those in the bottom layer. The temperature is uniformly spread throughout the jars, ensuring that all jars in both the top and bottom levels are safe. All that is required is that you create a grid between the layers in order for water and steam to flow around the jars.

Also, when using the water bath canning technique, be sure that the water level in the top layer of the jars is at least an inch over the tops of the jars. If you are using a pressure canner, the water level should be 2 to 3 inches over the bottom of the can. Maintain strict adherence to the processing time and temperature specifications at all times.

Some of the liquid from the contents is lost during the procedure. What should be done in this situation?

If the amount of liquid lost is small, there is no need to be concerned. The food will not deteriorate, and the seal will not be compromised in any way. However, it is possible that it may produce a little discoloration of the meal, although this will be minimal. The best you can do, however, is refrigerate the liquid and consume it within 2 to 3 days if the liquid loss is more than half of the original quantity.

What exactly is kettle canning, and is it a safe method of preserving food?

In this technique, the meals to be preserved are boiled in a standard home kettle before being placed in the freezer. Once this is completed, the items are placed into heated jars and sealed. In this technique, it can be observed that there is no processing done at all.

Furthermore, while utilizing the kettle technique, the temperature is not high enough to completely destroy any dangerous germs that may be present in the food. In addition, when food is transferred from the kettle to the jars, germs may infiltrate the food and cause spoiling or worse, food poisoning, later on in the cooking process.

Therefore, the food's quality and safety cannot be guaranteed. The USDA does not advocate using the kettle technique for canning since it is very time consuming.

What causes some jars to shatter during the canning process?

There are a variety of factors that contribute to breaking during the canning process. Here are five compelling arguments:

The glass in the jar has not been tempered in any way. Toughened glass, also known as tempered glass or toughened glass, has gone through a procedure that has improved its strength and capacity to withstand heat when compared to normal glass. Make certain that the commercial food jars you purchase are designed for home canning before purchasing them.

Two other reasons are that jars with hairline cracks are being used. These fissures are so little and inconspicuous that they may easily be ignored or disregarded. During the processing period, such jars would not be able to resist the high temperatures.

Failure to place a rack on the bottom of the pot or canner may also result in the jars cracking.

Pack the newly prepared food in ice-cold jars. In certain cases, breaking may be caused by a temperature differential between the food and the jar. Consequently, it is suggested that the jars be kept at a warm temperature before to being filled with hot food.

Jars containing uncooked or raw food that are dropped straight into boiling water may shatter as a result of the rapid shift in temperature. It is preferable to start with hot water and let it to come to a boil after a few minutes of heating.

Is it possible to can food for individuals who follow a particular diet?

Some individuals are unable to eat canned goods because of medical problems that prevent them from consuming specific components such as sugar and salt. Due to the impact of elevated blood sugar levels associated with simple sugar consumption in diabetics, sugar is not advised for them.

When it comes to individuals who have cardiovascular problems, salts are always restricted since they may cause an increase in high blood pressure because more water is retained in the body as a result of the salts' presence in the body. Canned meals, on the other hand, may be prepared for these individuals even in the absence of salt or sugar. However, the color, texture, and flavor of these canned goods will be distinct from those that include sugar or salt, as is to be anticipated in this situation. Other individuals find these canned meals for special diets to be less acceptable and more unappealing than they would like.

You may also preserve and can normal fruit that hasn't been treated with sugar. Choosing firm, fully ripe (but not overripe) fruit of the highest quality is the key to success. You may use unsweetened fruit juice or plain water for the sugar syrup if you want. Another method is to mix some of the same fruit that will be canned. Essentially, this will act as a syrup or juice for the canned food. Fill the container halfway with the blended fruit, then top it up with the solid fruit. Sugar replacements may be added towards the end of the cooking process to make it more appetizing.

If you want to can vegetables, meats, shellfish, or tomatoes without salt, follow the directions for normal canning, but leave out the salt. Because salts are not considered preservatives, this technique is allowed, and food safety is still ensured even when salt is not included in the recipe. Salt replacements may be provided at the time of serving to enhance the flavor of the preserved meal.

What do you think the future of food canning and preservation will be like?

Healthier diet and lifestyle choices are now popular all across the globe, and this is expected to continue. Everything "organic" may be found here, including cosmetics, hair products, food, baby goods, and even processed foods, among other things. People prefer "fresh" meals to canned or pre-prepared processed foods from a commercial kitchen.

In this case, canning and preserving fresh fruits, vegetables, meats, poultry, salsa, sauces, and other foodstuffs come in handy. Being healthy and contemporary are combined in one one package to create something really unique. It satisfies the criteria of being nutritious while being fresher for a longer period of time on the shelf or in the pantry. It is ready to eat, which meets the need for convenience while also saving precious time and effort.

People are becoming more and more interested in canning and preserving food. Because of excessive and needless food waste now, the danger of not having enough excellent food to consume in the future has been alleviated via the use of canning technology.

CONCLUSION

As a result of canning your food on a regular basis, you will notice an overall reduction in the amount of money you spend on vegetables and other canned goods. In addition, canning at home will have a beneficial impact on your eating habits. The foods you can will be much healthier than those available in stores.

You can buy more locally and seasonally when you can your food, and enjoy those items year-round, even after they've gone out of season.

Canning is one of the most effective ways to share delicious food with your family, friends, and neighbors. Once you get started, you are likely to become addicted to it.

Be aware that you will make mistakes the first few times, but that is to be expected! After all, you are a complete beginner.

BOOK 4

WATER BATH CANNING & PRESERVING COOKBOOK FOR PREPPERS

1000 Days of Tasty Homemade Recipes to Store Nutrient
Dense Food and Be Prepared for the Next 3 Years

INTRODUCTION

Since the invention of glass jars with ground glass joints, cooks have preserved food by hermetically sealing it in sterilized jars. Water bath canning was invented independently in other countries around the same time, such as France and Australia. This process has become known as canning. Water bath canning is a method of processing canned foods in which jars are filled with raw fruits or vegetables that have been precooked by blanching or boiling and then immersed in boiling water to cover for some time, such as 15 minutes.

Water bath canning is a technique that is used to preserve high acidic foods. This preservation method involves boiling water that is poured over the top of the food in a jar. Then, the pots are submerged into boiling water for an allotted time before they are removed and allowed to cool down. The food in the jar is sealed with a lid. The food is heated through the boiling water and then cooled through the cold water. This method is used to process foods that have high acidity to prevent harmful bacteria from growing.

Water bath canning has a dual purpose in the canning process. For one, it can preserve high acid foods such as tomatoes, peppers, and berries which would otherwise turn quickly if exposed to light or air for too long. Through the reduction of oxygen, the products can attain a long shelf life. Furthermore, water bath canning allows the food to reach a final storage temperature of 140 degrees Fahrenheit (60 degrees Celsius) to ensure that all microbes are killed. The jars are then cooled in their current state before they are sealed and put into storage. Foods should have a pH of 4 or lower to be preserved through water bath canning. The acidity of food is generally maintained by adding vinegar, wine or other acidic ingredients. Vegetables in water bath canning are typically prepared by blanching them in boiling water for a brief period. The vegetables are then removed from the boiling water and placed into jars that have been previously sterilized with boiling water or hot vinegar. Water bath canning is an ideal method of preserving for many reasons. Still, the most important is

that it allows for the integrity of your food to be maintained and your food to retain its natural taste. The only way water bath canning destroys much of the natural flavors and nutrients that are contained in your food is by reducing a simple sugar or acid such as vinegar.

Water bath canning is a safe and easy way to begin preserving your food simply and effectively. This book will focus on water bath canning fruits, vegetables, jam and jellies, and much more. There are various advantages that you will have when you begin preserving your foods—in addition to saving money. You will be able to prolong the growing season since you can use products that would not be ripe or mature at certain times of the year. You will also customize the recipes to make your food taste exactly how you want it.

CHAPTER 1

JAM AND JELLIES

PEAR AND PINEAPPLE JAM

Preparation time: 15 minutes
Cooking time: 30 minutes
Servings: 6 pint jars

Ingredients:

- 2 pounds pears, peeled, pitted, and chopped
- 1-pound pineapple, peeled, cored and chopped
- 1 tablespoon lemon juice
- 1 cup sugar
- Zest from 1 lemon

Directions:

- ❖ Sterilize the bottles in a water bath canner. Allow the bottles to cool.
- ❖ Set all ingredients in a saucepan and bring to a boil over medium flame.
- ❖ Set the heat to medium low and allow simmering for 15 minutes while stirring constantly.
- ❖ Turn off the heat and allow cooling slightly.
- ❖ Transfer the mixture to sterilized bottles and remove the air bubbles. Close the lid.
- ❖ Bring in a water bath canner and process for 10 minutes.
- ❖ Consume within a year.

Nutrition Calories: 174 Protein: 1.1 g Carbs: 44.8 g Fat: 0.4 Sugar: 37.9 g

GUAVA JAM

Preparation time: 15 minutes
Cooking time: 1 hour 25 minutes
Servings: 8 pint jars

Ingredients:

- 6 ripe guavas (overripe preferred)
- 3 cups water
- Juice from 3 limes, freshly squeezed
- 1 cup sugar
- 2 tablespoons pectin

Directions:

- ❖ Sterilize the bottles in a water bath canner. Allow the bottles to cool.
- ❖ Chop the guavas and place in a saucepan. Spill in water and bring to a boil for 60 minutes,
- ❖ Turn off the heat and strain the juice. Discard the solids.
- ❖ On a clean pot, place the juice and stir in the lime juice and sugar. Set on the heat and bring to a boil over medium flame. Reduce the heat to simmer for another 10 minutes. Add in the pectin stir for 2 more minutes.
- ❖ Turn off the heat and allow cooling slightly.
- ❖ Transfer the mixture to sterilized bottles and remove the air bubbles. Close the lid.

- ❖ Bring in a water bath canner and process for 10 minutes.
- ❖ Consume within a year.

Nutrition Calories: 68 Protein: 0.1g Carbs: 14g Fat: 0.1g Sugar: 10g

MAPLE BLACKBERRY JAM

Preparation time: 15 minutes
Cooking time: 60 minutes
Servings: 6 half pint jars

Ingredients:

- 6 canning bottles
- 6 cups blackberries, crushed
- 1 1/2 cup pure maple syrup
- Zest and juice from one lemon

Directions:

- ❖ Sterilize the bottles in a water bath canner. Allow the bottles to cool.
- ❖ Set all ingredients in a saucepan and bring to a simmer. Cook for 50 minutes while stirring constantly over medium low heat or until the mixture thickens.
- ❖ Dip an old spoon into the jam and tip gently. If it runs off in a sheet and if the liquid does not drip, the jam is ready.
- ❖ Set off the heat and allow the mixture to slightly cool before transferring into the sterilized bottles.
- ❖ Remove the air bubbles in the mixture. Close the lid and place in the water bath canner.
- ❖ Process for 10 minutes.
- ❖ Store in a cool dark place and consume within a year.

Nutrition Calories: 379 Protein: 2.9g Carbs: 96g Fat: 0.4g Sugar: 84.2g

PINEAPPLE JAM

Preparation time: 15 minutes
Cooking time: 1 hour 10 minutes
Servings: 4 pint jars

Ingredients:

- 2 canning bottles
- 1 cup sugar
- 2 fresh lemons, juiced
- 1 medium-sized pineapple, peeled and chopped

Directions:

- ❖ Sterilize the bottles in a water bath canner. Allow the bottles to cool.
- ❖ Add all ingredients in a medium-sized pot and bring to a boil. Reduce the heat and simmer to an hour until the liquid has evaporated and the mixture thickens.
- ❖ Set off the heat and allow to slightly cool before transferring into the bottles.
- ❖ Remove the air bubbles and close the lid.
- ❖ Set in a water bath canner and process for 10 minutes.
- ❖ Consume within a year.

Nutrition Calories: 216 Protein: 1.3g Carbs: 56.3g Fat: 0.3g Sugar: 47.3g

CHERRY JAM

Preparation time: 15 minutes
Cooking time: 60 minutes
Servings: 4 pint jars

Ingredients:

- 4 canning bottles
- 2 pounds cherries, stems removed and pitted
- 2 1/2 cups sugar
- Juice from 1 lemon, freshly squeezed
- 2 drops of almond extract

Directions:

- ❖ Sterilize the bottles in a water bath canner. Allow the bottles to cool.
- ❖ Place all ingredients in a saucepan and cook for 40 minutes or until the mixture thickens. Continue swirling to prevent the bottom from burning.
- ❖ Turn off the heat and remove from the pot to slightly cool.
- ❖ Transfer to the bottles. Remove the air bubbles and close the lid.

- ❖ Set in a water bath canner and process for 10 minutes.
- ❖ Consume within a year.

Nutrition Calories: 331 Protein: 1.9g Carbs: 83.6g Fat: 0.6g Sugar: 78.7 g

RASPBERRY JAM

Preparation time: 15 minutes
Cooking time: 27 minutes
Servings: 6 half pint jars

Ingredients:

- 4 canning bottles with lid
- 4 cups crushed ripe raspberries
- 1 tablespoon fresh lemon juice
- 6 1/2 cups sugar
- 1/2 teaspoon unsalted butter
- 3-ounce pectin

Directions:

- ❖ Sterilize the bottles in a water bath canner. Allow the bottles to cool.
- ❖ Macerate the raspberries and run through a colander to remove the seeds.
- ❖ Place the strained raspberries in a pot and stir in the lemon juice, sugar, and butter.
- ❖ Set on the heat to medium and bring to a rolling boil for 10 minutes. Reduce the heat to simmer for 5 minutes before adding the pectin. Allow to simmer for another 2 minutes.
- ❖ Turn off the heat to cool.
- ❖ Transfer the jam to sterilized bottles and remove the air bubbles.
- ❖ Close the lid.
- ❖ Bring in a water bath canner and process for 10 minutes.
- ❖ Consume within a year.

Nutrition Calories: 581 Protein: 1.4g Carbs: 148g Fat: 0.4g Sugar: 5.9g

PLUM BUTTER

Preparation time: 15 minutes
Cooking time: 25 minutes
Servings: 12 half pint jars

Ingredients:

- 6 canning bottles
- 6 pounds Italian plums, halved and pits removed
- 4 cups sugar
- 1 1/2 teaspoons ground cinnamon
- 1/2 teaspoons ground cloves

Directions:

- ❖ Sterilize the bottles in a water bath canner. Allow the bottles to cool.
- ❖ Place the plums, sugar, cinnamon, and cloves in a saucepan.
- ❖ Set on the heat and bring to a rolling boil for 10 minutes. Reduce the heat to low and continue stirring until the mixture becomes thick.
- ❖ Turn off the heat to cool.
- ❖ Transfer the jam to sterilized bottles and remove the air bubbles. Close the lid.
- ❖ Set in a water bath canner and process for 10 minutes.
- ❖ Consume within a year.

Nutrition Calories: 332 Protein: 3.8 g Carbs: 86.2g Fat: 0.2g Sugar: 83.2g

APPLE PIE JAM

Preparation time: 15 minutes
Cooking time: 27 minutes
Servings: 8 half pint jars

Ingredients:

- 6 canning bottles
- 4 cups diced apples
- 2 tablespoons lemon juice, freshly squeezed
- 1 1/4 teaspoon ground cinnamon
- 1/4 teaspoon ground ginger
- 1/4 teaspoon ground nutmeg
- 4 cups granulated sugar
- 1 cup packed brown sugar
- 1/2 teaspoon unsalted butter
- 1 box pectin

Directions:

- ❖ Sterilize the bottles in a water bath canner. Allow the bottles to cool.
- ❖ Place the apples, lemon juice, cinnamon, ginger, nutmeg, sugar, and butter in a saucepan.
- ❖ Turn on the heat and allow simmering for 15 minutes. Stir in the pectin and simmer for 2 minutes. Keep swirling to avoid the mixture from burning.
- ❖ Turn off the heat to cool.
- ❖ Transfer the mixture to sterilized bottles and remove the air bubbles. Close the lid.
- ❖ Set in a water bath canner and process for 10 minutes.
- ❖ Consume within a year.

Nutrition Calories: 275 Protein: 0.2g Carbs: 70.6g Fat: 0.3g Sugar: 66.9g

STAR FRUIT JAM

Preparation time: 15 minutes
Cooking time: 30 minutes
Servings: 3 pint jars

Ingredients:

- 2 canning bottles
- 1 1/4 pounds carambolas or star fruit, edges trimmed and chopped
- 1 cup water
- 2 cups white sugar
- Juice from 1 lemon, freshly squeezed

Directions:

- ❖ Sterilize the bottles in a water bath canner. Allow the bottles to cool.
- ❖ Place all ingredients in a saucepan. Set on the heat and bring the mixture to a simmer. Stir for 20 minutes or until the mixture is thick and the liquid has reduced.
- ❖ Set off the heat and allow the mixture to cool down.
- ❖ Transfer the mixture to sterilized bottles and remove the air bubbles. Close the lid.
- ❖ Bring in a water bath canner and process for 10 minutes.
- ❖ Consume within a year.

Nutrition Calories: 241 Protein: 1.5g Carbs: 60.3g Fat: 0.5g Sugar: 54.6g

NECTARINE BROWN SUGAR JAM

Preparation time: 15 minutes
Cooking time: 25 minutes
Servings: 8 half pint jars

Ingredients:

- 6 to 8 canning bottles
- 4 pounds nectarines, peeled, seeded and chopped
- 1 1/2 cup brown sugar, lightly packed
- 4 tablespoons lemon juice
- 1/2 teaspoon cinnamon
- 1/4 teaspoon ground ginger

Directions:

- ❖ Sterilize the bottles in a water bath canner. Allow the bottles to cool.
- ❖ Place all ingredients in a big saucepan and bring to a rolling boil for 5 minutes. Set the heat to low and parboil for another 10 minutes. Keep stirring until the mixture thickens.
- ❖ Set off the heat and allow to cool slightly.
- ❖ Transfer the mixture to sterilized bottles and remove the air bubbles. Close the lid.

- ❖ Bring in a water bath canner and process for 10 minutes.
- ❖ Consume within a year.

Nutrition Calories: 259 Protein: 2.5g Carbs: 65.2g Fat: 0.8g Sugar: 58.1g

STRAWBERRY JAM

Preparation time: 15 minutes
Cooking time: 1 hour and 20 minutes
Servings: 4 half pint jars

Ingredients:

- 2 pints jar
- 2 pounds ripe strawberries, hulled and cleaned
- 2 1/2 cups sugar
- 1 tablespoon freshly squeezed orange juice

Directions:

- ❖ Sterilize the bottles in a water bath canner. Allow the bottles to cool.
- ❖ Chop the strawberries and place all ingredients in a large pan. Let it sit for an hour until the sugar is dissolves and the mixture become watery.
- ❖ Heat over the stove using medium flame and bring to a boil. Make sure to stir constantly and mashing with the ladle to macerate. Cook for 10 minutes then allow to cool.
- ❖ Place the strawberry jam in sterilized bottles.
- ❖ Set in a water bath canner and process for 10 minutes.
- ❖ Consumer within a year.

Nutrition Calories: 318 Protein: 1.6g Carbs: 80.2g Fat: 0.7g Sugar: 73g

PEACH SPICE JAM

Preparation time: 5 minutes
Cooking time: 15-25 minutes
Servings: 2 pint jars

Ingredients:

- 8-9 large peaches, pitted
- 3 cups sugar
- Juice and rind of 1/2 lemon
- 1/4 teaspoon allspice (optional)
- 1/4 teaspoon cloves (optional)

Directions:

- ❖ Detach pits and imperfect parts from peaches.
- ❖ In a large kettle, parboil peaches with just enough water to keep them from burning. When peaches are softened, put them through a food mill.
- ❖ To a deep saucepan or cooking pot, attach the peaches and enough water to submerge. Boil until softened. Drain water.
- ❖ Transfer to a blender or food processor. Blend well to make puree.
- ❖ To the pot or pan, add the puree and other ingredients.
- ❖ Boil the mixture till thermometer reads 220F; cook over medium-low heat until firm and thick. Swirl continually to prevent scorching.
- ❖ Spill the hot mixture into pre-sterilized jars directly or with a jar funnel. Keep headspace of 1/4 inch from the jar top.
- ❖ To detach tiny air bubbles, set a nonmetallic spatula and swirl the mixture gently.
- ❖ Wipe the sealing edges. Secure the jars with the lids and adjust the bands/rings to seal and prevent any leakage.
- ❖ Set the jars in a cool, dry and dark place. Allow them to cool down completely.
- ❖ Store in your refrigerator for later use.

Nutrition Calories: 435 Protein: 5.1g Carbs: 11.4g Fat: 1.4g Sugar: 86.3g

RHUBARB ORANGE JAM

Preparation time: 5 minutes
Cooking time: 45 minutes
Servings: 3-4 pint jars

Ingredients:

- 2 cups white sugar
- 2 teaspoons grated orange zest
- 21/2 pounds rhubarb, chopped
- 1/2 cup water
- 1/3 cup orange juice

Directions:

- ❖ In a deep saucepan or cooking pot, merge the rhubarb, sugar, orange zest, orange juice and water.
- ❖ Boil the mixture till thermometer reads 220F; cook for about 45 minutes over medium-low heat until firm and thick. Stir continually to prevent scorching.
- ❖ Spill the hot mixture into pre-sterilized jars directly or with a jar funnel. Keep headspace of 1/4 inch from the jar top.
- ❖ To detach tiny air bubbles, insert a nonmetallic spatula and stir the mixture gently.
- ❖ Wipe the sealing edges and lose the jars with the lids and adjust the bands/rings to seal and prevent any leakage.
- ❖ Set the jars in a cool, dry and dark place. Allow them to cool down completely.

❖ Store in your refrigerator for later use.

Nutrition Calories: 322 Protein: 15g Carbs: 23g Fat: 2.1g Sugar: 22g

BLACKBERRY JAM

Preparation time: 15 minutes
Cooking time: 30 minutes
Servings: 10 pint jars

Ingredients:
- 5 cups blackberries
- 2 cups sugar
- 2 tablespoons lemon juice

Directions:
❖ Sterilize the bottles in a water bath canner. Allow the bottles to cool.
❖ Place all ingredients in a saucepan. Set to a boil while stirring constantly for 10 minutes. Reduce the heat to simmer until the sauce thickens.
❖ Set off the heat and allow to cool slightly.
❖ Transfer the mixture to sterilized bottles and remove the air bubbles. Close the lid.
❖ Set in a water bath canner and process for 10 minutes.
❖ Consume within a year.

Nutrition Calories: 196 Protein: 1.7g Carbs: 49.7g Fat: 0.2g Sugar: 44.9g

HONEYBERRY JAM

Preparation time: 15 minutes
Cooking time: 25 minutes
Servings: 6 half pint jars

Ingredients:
- 2 cups honeyberry fruit
- 2 cups sugar

Directions:
❖ Sterilize the bottles in a water bath canner. Allow the bottles to cool.
❖ Place all ingredients in a saucepan. Macerate the berries using a potato masher or a ladle.

❖ Turn on the heat to medium high and bring to a boil while stirring constantly. Reduce the heat the medium low and allow to simmer for another 15 minutes or until the mixture thickens.
❖ Set off the heat and allow the mixture to slightly cool.
❖ Transfer the mixture to sterilized bottles and remove the air bubbles. Close the lid.
❖ Bring in a water bath canner and process for 10 minutes.
❖ Consume within a year.

Nutrition Calories: 190 Protein: 0.3g Carbs: 48.9g Fat: 0.01g Sugar: 47.4g

BLUEBERRY VANILLA JAM

Preparation time: 15 minutes
Cooking time: 22 minutes
Servings: 22 half pint jars

Ingredients:
- 6 large canning bottles
- 1 1/4 pounds blueberries, rinsed and stems removed
- 3/4 cup granulated sugar
- 2 tablespoons lemon juice
- 1/2 vanilla bean pod, seeds scraped
- 1 teaspoon pectin

Directions:
❖ Sterilize the bottles in a water bath canner. Allow the bottles to cool.
❖ Place all ingredients except for the pectin in a pot and mash until the blueberries are macerated.
❖ Set on the heat and bring to a boil for 10 minutes while stirring constantly. Remove the vanilla bean pod and stir in the pectin. Continue stirring for another 2 minutes until the mixture becomes thick.
❖ Ladle into the sterilized jars and leave 1/4 inch of headspace. Remove the air bubbles and screw the lid on.
❖ Place in a water bath canner and follow the general instructions for water bath canning.
❖ Process for10 minutes.
❖ Consume within a year and keep refrigerated once the bottles are opened.

Nutrition Calories: 38 Protein: 0.19g Carbs: 9.2g Fat: 0.2g Sugar: 8.7g

MANDARIN ORANGE JAM

Preparation time: 15 minutes
Cooking time: 22 minutes
Servings: 5 pint jars

Ingredients:
- 5 bottling jars with lid
- 2 pounds mandarin oranges, peeled and seeded (about 10 to 12 oranges)

- Juice from 1 lemon, freshly squeezed
- 1 cup sugar

Directions:
- ❖ Sterilize the bottles in a water bath canner.
- ❖ Chop the mandarin oranges roughly. Place the ingredients except the pectin in a pot and heat over medium flame. Stir constantly for 10 minutes to avoid burning at the bottom.
- ❖ Stir in pectin and stir for another 2 minutes.
- ❖ Set off the heat and allow to cool.
- ❖ Transfer the orange jam into the sterilized bottles and make sure that there is 1/4 headspace left. Remove the air bubbles. Close the lid.
- ❖ Place the bottles in the water bath canner. Process for 10 minutes.
- ❖ Consume within a year.

Nutrition Calories: 169 Protein: 1.3g Carbs: 41.6g Fat: 0.2g Sugar: 35g

FIG JAM

Preparation time: 15 minutes
Cooking time: 25 minutes
Servings: 3 half pint jars

Ingredients:
- 1-pint jar
- 1-pound black figs
- 3/4 cup granulated sugar
- 1/4 cup water
- Juice from 1/2 small lemon, freshly squeezed
- 1 teaspoon pure vanilla extract

Directions:
- ❖ Sterilize the bottle in a water bath canner. Allow the bottles to cool.
- ❖ Place the figs in a blender and puree until smooth. Place the pureed figs in a pot and add in the rest of the ingredients.
- ❖ Bring to a boil over medium flame while stirring constantly. Cook for 10 minutes and remove from the heat.
- ❖ Allow to cool before transferring into the sterilized bottle.

- ❖ Follow the general instructions for water bath canning and can for 15 minutes.
- ❖ Consume within a year.

Nutrition Calories: 357 Protein: 3.8 g Carbs: 92g; Fat: 1.1g Sugar: 72.8g

JALAPEÑO PEPPER JELLY

Preparation time: 90 minutes
Cooking time: 20 minutes
Servings: 5 half pint jars

Ingredients:
- 1 Cup, chopped green bell pepper
- 1/3 Cup of chopped jalapeño pepper
- 4 Cups of sugar
- 1 Cup of cider vinegar
- 1 Packet of pectin, about 6 ounces

Directions:
- ❖ Merge all the ingredients together in a large saucepot, and let it boil for about five minutes.
- ❖ Next, let it cool to room temperature for about one hour, and then put them into jars.
- ❖ Set the jars sit in a water bath for five minutes, and then let them sit at room temperature for about twelve to 24 hours before storing.

Nutrition Calories: 651 Fat: 26 g Carbs: 93 g Protein: 17 g Sodium: 112 mg

CHAPTER 2

MARMALADES

LEMON HONEY MARMALADE

Preparation time: 10 minutes
Cooking time: 40 minutes
Servings: 12 pint jars

Ingredients:

- 8 cups lemons, chopped
- 6 oz. liquid pectin
- 1 1/2 cups water
- 4 cups sugar
- 2 cups honey

Directions:

- ❖ Add lemons, sugar, water, and honey in a saucepan and bring to boil over medium heat.
- ❖ Reduce heat and simmer for 30 minutes.
- ❖ Add pectin and boil for 5 minutes. Stir constantly.
- ❖ Remove pan from heat. Ladle the marmalade into the jars. Leave 1/2-inch headspace. Remove air bubbles.
- ❖ Secure jars with lids and process in a boiling water bath for 10 minutes.
- ❖ Remove jars from the water bath and let it cool completely.
- ❖ Check seals of jars. Label and store.

Nutrition Calories: 468 Fat 0.4 g Carbohydrates 127.5 g Sugar 116.6 g Protein 1.7 g Cholesterol 0 mg

ZUCCHINI MARMALADE

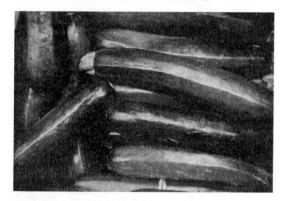

Preparation time: 10 minutes
Cooking time: 15 minutes
Servings: 12 pint jars

Ingredients:

- 4 cups shredded zucchini
- 5 cups sugar
- 1 orange, peel, cut into segments and remove seeds

Directions:

- ❖ Add orange segments and orange peel in the food processor and process until chopped.

- ❖ Add zucchini, sugar, and orange in a saucepan and bring to boil over medium heat for 10-15 minutes or until thickened.
- ❖ Detach pan from heat and let it cool completely.
- ❖ Pour marmalade in a clean jar. Secure jar with lid and store in the refrigerator.

Nutrition Calories: 326 Fat 0.1 g Carbohydrates 86.4 g Sugar 85.4 g Protein 0.6 g Cholesterol 0 mg

CARROT MARMALADE

Preparation time: 10 minutes
Cooking time: 40 minutes
Servings: 48 pint jars

Ingredients:

- 2 cups grated carrots
- 2 1/2 cups sugar
- 2 cups water
- 1 orange
- 1 lemon

Directions:

- ❖ Shred orange and lemon in a large saucepan.
- ❖ Add remaining ingredients into the saucepan and bring to boil over medium heat.
- ❖ Set heat to low and parboil for 30 minutes or until thickened.
- ❖ Once marmalade is thickened then remove the pan from heat.
- ❖ Ladle the marmalade into the clean and hot jars. Leave 1/2-inch headspace. Remove air bubbles.
- ❖ Secure jars with lids and process in a boiling water bath for 5 minutes.
- ❖ Remove jars from the water bath and let it cool completely.
- ❖ Check seals of jars. Label and store.

Nutrition Calories: 43 Fat 0 g Carbohydrates 11.3 g Sugar 11 g Protein 0.1 g Cholesterol 0 mg

STRAWBERRY MARMALADE

Preparation time: 10 minutes
Cooking time: 20 minutes
Servings: 12 pint jars

Ingredients:

- 4 cups strawberries, crushed
- 6 cups sugar
- 6 tbsp. pectin
- 1 lemon

Directions:

- ❖ Cut lemon peel and reserved lemon juice and pulp. Add lemon peel in a small pot with water and boil for 5 minutes. Drain lemon peels.

- Add strawberries, sugar, pectin, lemon peel, lemon juice, and lemon pulp into the large stockpot. Stir well and bring to boil. Stir until sugar is dissolved.
- Set heat to high and boil for 1 minute. Stir constantly.
- Remove pot from heat.
- Ladle the marmalade into the clean and hot jars. Leave 1/2-inch headspace. Remove air bubbles.
- Secure jars with lids and process in a boiling water bath for 10 minutes.
- Remove jars from the water bath and let it cool completely.
- Check seals of jars. Label and store.

Nutrition Calories: 396 Fat 0.1 g Carbohydrates 104 g Sugar 102 g Protein 0.3 g Cholesterol 0 mg

ONION MARMALADE

Preparation time: 10 minutes
Cooking time: 25 minutes
Servings: 4 pint jars

Ingredients:

- 2 large onions, sliced
- 1 tbsp. red wine vinegar
- 1/3 cup red wine
- 1 tsp. sugar
- 1/4 cup olive oil
- Pinch of salt

Directions:

- Warmth oil in a small saucepan over medium heat.
- Add onion and cook for 10-15 minutes or until onion is softened.
- Add sugar and cook for 5 minutes. Attach wine and cook until wine is reduced.
- Remove pan from heat. Add vinegar and salt and mix well.
- Pour marmalade in a clean jar. Secure jar with lid and store in the refrigerator.

Nutrition Calories: 159 Fat 12.7 g Carbohydrates 8.6 g Sugar 4.4 g Protein 0.8 g Cholesterol 0 mg

TOMATO LEMON MARMALADE

Preparation time: 10 Minutes
Cooking time: 20 Minutes
Servings: 9 Half-Pints

Ingredients:

- 4 Cups (4 apples) chopped peeled tart apples
- 5 Medium ripe tomatoes
- 6 Cups sugar
- 2 Medium seeded and finely chopped lemons
- 8 Whole cloves
- 2 1/4 Teaspoons ground ginger

Directions:

- Prepare the tomatoes by peeling them, slicing them into quarters and then chopping them.
- Set chopped tomatoes in a colander to drain before placing in a Dutch oven.
- Add the lemons and apples to the Dutch oven, cook for fifteen minutes on moderate heat, stirring often. Stir in ginger and sugar.
- Place cloves in cheesecloth bag and tie; add to the mixture.
- Bring the mixture to a complete rolling boil; stirring often, and cook until the sugar has melted. Simmer on low for forty minutes, stirring frequently.
- Discard the spice bag and ladle the hot marmalade into nine sterilized hot half-pint jars with a 1/4 inch headspace.
- Remove the air bubbles with a plastic knife, adjusting the headspace and wipe the rims.
- Place the jars into the canner with simmering water, just enough to cover it; bring to a full boil, and process it for ten minutes.
- Detach the jars and place them on a padded work surface. Let it cool.
- Enjoy!

Nutrition Calories: 142 Protein: 0 g Fiber: 1 g Fat: 0 g Carbs: 36 g

STRAWBERRY AND BLACKBERRY MARMALADE

Preparation time: 15 minutes
Cooking time: 5 minutes
Servings: 4 pint jars

Ingredients:

- 1 lemon
- 13/4 cups fresh strawberries, hulled and crushed
- 1 cup fresh blackberries, crushed
- 11/2 teaspoons freshly squeezed lemon juice
- 3 tablespoons powdered pectin
- 31/2 cups sugar

Directions:

- ❖ Prepare a hot water bath. Set the jars in it to keep warm. Clean the lids and rings in hot, soapy water, and set aside.
- ❖ Wash the lemon well with warm, soapy water. With a sharp knife, cut away half of the rind from the lemon, removing as much of the pith (white inner membrane) as possible. Slice the rind into thin strips, and then cut the strips into 1/4-inch-long pieces.
- ❖ In a small saucepot set over high heat, combine the lemon rind with enough water to cover. Bring to a boil. Strain and reserve the rind.
- ❖ In a medium saucepot set over high heat, combine the strawberries, blackberries, lemon rind, and lemon juice. Slowly stir in the pectin. Set the mixture to a full, rolling boil.
- ❖ Add the sugar. Return the mixture to a full, rolling boiling over high heat. When the jam cannot be stirred down, set a timer for 1 minute and stir constantly. Turn off the heat.
- ❖ With the heat off, stir the marmalade for 1 minute more to ensure even distribution of the rind before filling the jars. Skim off any foam.
- ❖ Ladle the marmalade into the prepared jars, leaving 1/4 inch of headspace. Use a nonmetallic utensil to remove any air bubbles. Clean the rims clean and seal with the lids and rings.
- ❖ Bring the jars in a hot water bath for 10 minutes. Set off the heat and let the jars rest in the water bath for 10 minutes.
- ❖ Carefully detach the jars from the hot water canner. Set aside for 12 hours.
- ❖ Check the lids for proper seals. Detach the rings, wipe the jars, name and date them, and transfer to a cupboard or pantry. Refrigerate and use within 3 weeks. Properly secure jars will last in the cupboard for 12 months.

Nutrition Calories:: 49 Fat: 0.2g Carbs: 8.7g, Protein: 3.6g Sugars: 4.9g

GRAPEFRUIT MARMALADE WITH VANILLA

Preparation time: 25 minutes
Cooking time: 60 minutes
Servings: 4 pint jars

Ingredients:

- 3 grapefruits
- 3 cups sugar
- 1 whole vanilla bean

Directions:

- ❖ Prepare a hot water bath. Set the jars in it to keep warm. Clean the lids and rings in hot, soapy water, and set aside.
- ❖ Wash the grapefruits well with warm, soapy water. With a sharp knife, remove the grapefruit rind. Stack into piles and slice into strips. Mince the strips.
- ❖ In a small saucepan over medium heat, merge the minced rind with enough water to cover. Bring to a simmer. Cook for 20 minutes, or until tender.
- ❖ While the rind cooks, remove any remaining pith from the grapefruit with your hands or a knife. Working on a bowl to catch the juice, slice along the membranes, removing each grapefruit segment individually. attach the segments to the bowl with the juice. When finished, squeeze the remaining membranes over the bowl to collect any additional juice. Discard the membranes and seeds.
- ❖ Strain the rind, reserving 2 cups of the cooking liquid.
- ❖ In a medium saucepot set over medium-high heat, combine the reserved cooking liquid, sugar, rind, and the grapefruit segments in their juices. Bring to a full, rolling boil. Cook for 35 to 45 minutes until it reaches 220°F (104°C), measured with a candy thermometer.
- ❖ Add the vanilla bean seeds. Turn off the heat. Use the plate test to determine if the marmalade sets. If not, return the pot to the burner and cook in 5-minute increments until it sets to your liking.
- ❖ With the heat off, stir the marmalade for 1 minute to evenly distribute the rind. Skim off any foam.
- ❖ Ladle the marmalade into the prepared jars, leaving 1/4 inch of headspace. Use a nonmetallic utensil to remove any air bubbles. Wipe the rims clean and seal using the lids and rings.
- ❖ Set the jars in a hot water bath for 10 minutes. Set off the heat and bring the jars rest in the water bath for 10 minutes.
- ❖ Carefully detach the jars from the hot water canner. Set aside to cool for 12 hours.
- ❖ Check the lids for proper seals. Detach the rings, clean the jars, label and date them, and transfer to a cupboard or pantry.
- ❖ Use within 3 weeks.

Nutrition Calories: 149 Fat: 0.4 g Carbs: 37.7 g Protein 1.3 g

BLUEBERRY ORANGE MARMALADE

Preparation time: 15 minutes
Cooking time: 25 minutes
Servings: 3 pint jars

Ingredients:

- 1/2 cup water
- 1/8 teaspoon baking soda
- 1 small orange, peeled and chopped
- 1 small lemon, peeled and chopped
- 2 cups blueberries, crushed
- 21/2 cups sugar

- 1/2 (6-ounce) package liquid fruit pectin

Directions:

- ❖ In a saucepan or cooking pot, merge the water and baking soda.
- ❖ Boil the mixture; cook for about 10 minutes over low heat. Stir continually to prevent scorching.
- ❖ Add the sugar, berries, lemon and orange.
- ❖ Boil the mixture; cook for about 5 minutes over medium-low heat. Stir continually to prevent scorching.
- ❖ Mix in the pectin and simmer for about 1 minutes over medium-low heat until firm and thick. Stir continually to prevent scorching.
- ❖ Spill the hot mixture into pre-sterilized jars directly or with a jar funnel. Keep headspace of 1/4 inch from the jar top.
- ❖ To detach tiny air bubbles, insert a nonmetallic spatula and stir the mixture gently.
- ❖ Clean the sealing edges with a damp cloth. Secure the jars with the lids and adjust the bands/rings to seal and prevent any leakage.
- ❖ Set the jars in a hot water bath for 10 minutes.
- ❖ Set the jars in a cool, dry and dark place. Allow them to cool down completely.
- ❖ Store in your refrigerator and use within 10 days.

Nutrition Calories: 393 Fat 0.1 g Carbohydrates 104.1 g Sugar 99.8 g Protein 0.4 g Cholesterol 0 mg

ORANGE MARMALADE

Preparation time: 15 minutes
Cooking time: 15 minutes
Servings: 2 pint jars

Ingredients:

- 1/2 cup water
- 4 medium navel oranges, peeled and cut into small pieces
- 2 cups sugar

Directions

- ❖ Add the orange pieces to a blender or food processor. Blend well.
- ❖ In a deep saucepan, combine the orange mixture, water and sugar.

- ❖ Set the mixture till thermometer reads 220F; cook for about 12–15 minutes over medium heat until firm and thick. Stir continually to prevent scorching.
- ❖ Spill the hot mixture into pre-sterilized jars directly or with a jar funnel. Keep headspace of 1/4 inch from the jar top.
- ❖ To detach tiny air bubbles, insert a nonmetallic spatula and stir the mixture gently.
- ❖ Clean the sealing edges with a damp cloth. Secure the jars with the lids and adjust the bands/rings to seal and prevent any leakage.
- ❖ Set the jars in a cool, dry and dark place. Allow them to cool down completely.
- ❖ Store in your refrigerator and use within 10 days.

Nutrition: Carbohydrates: 1 g Fat: 0 g Protein: 1 g Sodium: 727 mg Calories: 4g

SUPER TANGY MARMALADE

Preparation time: 5 minutes
Cooking time: 30 minutes
Servings: 3 pint jars

Ingredients:

- 31/2 cups white granulated sugar
- 1 cup limes, unpeeled and thinly sliced
- 1 cup lemons, unpeeled and thinly sliced
- 3 cups water

Directions:

- ❖ In a deep saucepan or cooking pot, merge the citrus slices and water.
- ❖ Boil the mixture; simmer for a few minutes over low heat.
- ❖ Mix in the sugar.
- ❖ Boil the mixture and cook for about 25–30 minutes over medium heat until firm and thick. Swirl continually to prevent scorching.
- ❖ Spill the hot mixture into pre-sterilized jars directly or with a jar funnel. Keep headspace of 1/4 inch from the jar top.
- ❖ To detach tiny air bubbles, insert a nonmetallic spatula and stir the mixture gently.
- ❖ Clean the sealing edges with a damp cloth. Secure the jars with the lids and adjust the bands/rings to seal and prevent any leakage.
- ❖ Set the jars in a cool, dry and dark place. Allow them to cool down completely.
- ❖ Store in your refrigerator and use within 10 days.

Nutrition Calories: 37 Protein: 1.9g Carbs: 7.4g Fat: 0.8g Sugar: 1.3g

MIXED CITRUS MARMALADE

Preparation time: 15 Minutes
Cooking time: 20 Minutes plus Overnight Chilling
Servings: 10 Half-Pints

Ingredients:

- 1 Pound Oranges, thinly sliced and seeds detached
- 1 Pound Grapefruit, thinly sliced and seeds detached
- 1 Pound Lemons, thinly sliced and seeds detached
- 8 Cups sugar
- 2 Quarts water

Directions:

- ❖ Combine in a large mixing bowl the oranges, grapefruit, lemons and 2 quarts water; cover and chill overnight.
- ❖ Place the fruit mixture in a Dutch oven; bring to a complete rolling boil. Remove cover; simmer on low heat for about ten to fifteen minutes until tender.
- ❖ Add the sugar, stir and boil. Cook for forty to fifty-five minutes, stirring often until thickened.
- ❖ Detach from the burner and skim off the foam.
- ❖ Slowly ladle the hot marmalade into sterilized half-pint jars with a one-fourth inch headspace.
- ❖ Remove the air bubbles using a plastic spoon.
- ❖ Clean the rims, adjust the lids and process for five minutes in a canner filled with boiling water. Remove from heat, and let it cool.

Nutrition Calories:: 82 Protein: 0 g Fiber: 0 g Fat: 0 g Carbs: 82 g

CHERRY MARMALADE

Preparation time: 20 minutes
Cooking time: 30 minutes
Servings: 4 pints

Ingredients:

- 4 tbsps. lime
- 4 cup cherries
- 2/3 cup peeled and chopped orange
- 3-1/2 cup sugar

Directions:

- ❖ Take a large pan and mix cherries, orange and juice in it. Make them boil at medium heat. Low the flame and add cove with gentle boiling with frequent stirring for 20 minutes. Keep boiling with slow stirring.
- ❖ Now boil hard with frequent stirring as the mixture gets gel like, for about 30 minutes. Remove the flame.
- ❖ Pour the hot marmalade into sterilized jars. Remove the air bubble by adding more marmalade. Seal them with lids.

Nutrition Calories: 56 Fat: 0 g Carbs: 13 g Protein 1 g

PEAR MARMALADE

Preparation time: 10 minutes
Cooking time: 10 minutes
Servings: 12 pint jars

Ingredients:

- 4 medium ripe pears, peeled and quartered
- 5 1/2 cups sugar
- 1.75oz. pectin
- 1 tbsp. orange zest, grated
- 2 tbsp. lemon juice
- 1/2 cup orange juice
- 8oz. crushed pineapple

Directions:

- ❖ Add pears into the food processor and process until pureed.
- ❖ Add pear puree, pectin, orange zest, lemon juice, orange juice, and pineapple into the saucepan and bring to boil over high heat. Stir constantly.
- ❖ Add sugar and stir well and boil for 1 minute. Stir constantly.
- ❖ Remove pot from heat and let it cool completely.
- ❖ Pour marmalade in a clean jar. Secure jar with lid and store in the refrigerator.

Nutrition Calories: 393 Fat 0.1 g Carbohydrates 104.1 g Sugar 99.8 g Protein 0.4 g Cholesterol 0 mg

RHUBARB MARMALADE

Preparation time: 10 minutes
Cooking time: 35 minutes
Servings: 16 pint jars

Ingredients:

- 6 cups fresh rhubarb, chopped
- 2 medium oranges
- 6 cups sugar

Directions:

- ❖ Grind oranges into the food processor with a peel.
- ❖ Add rhubarb, sugar, and grind oranges into the large saucepan and bring to boil. Reduce heat and simmer for 1 hour.
- ❖ Remove pan from heat. Ladle the marmalade into the jars. Leave 1/4-inch headspace.
- ❖ Secure jars with lids and process in a boiling water bath for 10 minutes.
- ❖ Remove jars from the water bath and let it cool completely.
- ❖ Check seals of jars. Label and store.

Nutrition Calories: 302 Fat 0.1 g Carbohydrates 79.8 g Sugar 77.7 g Protein 0.6 g Cholesterol 0 mg

GINGER ORANGE MARMALADE

Preparation time: 15 minutes
Cooking time: 40 minutes
Servings: 3 pint jars

Ingredients:

- 6-7 bitter oranges
- 2 cups water
- 1 medium lemon
- 3 cups granulated sugar
- 11/2 tablespoons ginger, peeled and finely grated

Directions

- ❖ Remove the skin from the oranges and lemon and cut it into small strips.
- ❖ Cut the oranges and lemon into halves. Juice them, remove the seeds, and set aside the juice but do not discard the pulp.
- ❖ In a deep saucepan or cooking pot, merge the water, pulp, juice and peels.
- ❖ Boil the mixture and simmer for 45–50 minutes until the strips are softened.
- ❖ Mix in the sugar and ginger.
- ❖ Boil the mixture and cook over medium heat until firm and thick. Swirl continually to prevent scorching.
- ❖ Spill the hot mixture into pre-sterilized jars directly or with a jar funnel. Keep headspace of 1/4 inch from the jar top.
- ❖ To detach tiny air bubbles, insert a nonmetallic spatula and stir the mixture gently.

- ❖ Clean the sealing edges with a damp cloth. Secure the jars with the lids and adjust the bands/rings to seal and prevent any leakage.
- ❖ Set the jars in a cool, dry and dark place. Allow them to cool down completely.
- ❖ Store in your refrigerator.

Nutrition Calories: 314 Protein: 0.9 g Carbs: 81.1 g Fat: 0.2 g Sugar: 77.6g

THREE-FRUIT MARMALADE

Preparation time: 15 Minutes
Cooking time: 15 Minutes
Servings: 8 Half-Pints

Ingredients:

- 2 Cups chopped peeled fresh peaches
- 5 Cups sugar
- 1 Medium orange
- 1 Package (1 3/4 ounces) powdered fruit pectin
- 2 Cups chopped peeled fresh pears

Directions:

- ❖ Grate the orange peel. Peel and section the orange fruit. Put the orange sections and peel in a Dutch oven.
- ❖ Stir in pears, peaches and add the pectin; bring it to a full boil on high heat.
- ❖ Stir often and add the sugar. Return to a complete rolling boil, boil again and stir for one minute.
- ❖ Remove from the burner, skimming off the foam.
- ❖ Ladle the hot marmalade into eight sterilized half-pint jars with one-fourth inch headspace.
- ❖ With a plastic spoon, remove the air bubbles, adjusting headspace by pouring the hot mixture if desired.
- ❖ Wipe the rims with cloth, center the lids on the jars and screw on band up to fingertip tight.
- ❖ Place the jars in the canner with enough simmering water to cover the entire jars.
- ❖ Bring water to a full rolling boil and process for ten minutes. Detach the jars from the canner, and let it cool.
- ❖ Serve!

Nutrition Calories: 88 Protein: 0 g Fiber: 0 g Fat: 0 g Carbs: 23 g

ORANGE PINEAPPLE MARMALADE

Preparation time: 35 Minutes
Cooking time: 1 Hour 20 Minutes
Servings: 4 pint jars

Ingredients:

- 2 Cans (8 ounces each) drained crushed pineapple
- 2 Medium oranges
- 2 Tablespoons lemon juice
- 4 Cups sugar

Directions:

- ❖ Wash four one-cup plastic containers and lids, and sterilize them with boiling water. Dry and set aside.
- ❖ Scrape the orange peel, and set aside. Peel off the orange, discarding the white membrane, section the flesh and remove the seeds.
- ❖ Combine in a food processor, the orange sections and zest. Cover and pulse until the orange turns into small bits.
- ❖ Place lemon juice, the orange mixture, sugar and pineapple in a 2 1/2 quart microwave safe bowl with a wide bottom.
- ❖ Microwave the mixture without a cover on high for 2 to 2 1/2 minutes.

- ❖ Stir and heat until bubbly, stir again and microwave for another 1 1/2 to 2 minutes until the middle part is bubbly. Stir and heat for two more minutes, stir often and let cool for ten minutes.
- ❖ Ladle the hot marmalade into plastic containers, leaving a 1/2 inch allowance from the tops.
- ❖ Wipe off the edges with paper towels. Let it cool for 1 hour. Cover the plastic containers and let it stand for four hours at room temperature.
- ❖ Keep refrigerated or keep frozen for up to one year.
- ❖ Thaw for an hour or so in the refrigerator before you serve the marmalade.
- ❖ Enjoy!

Nutrition Calories: 104 Protein: 0 g Fiber: 0 g Fat: 1 g Carbs: 27 g

CHAPTER 3

SALSA AND SAUCES

TOMATO KETCHUP WITH VINEGAR

Preparation time: 25 minutes
Cooking time: 45 minutes
Servings: 2 pint jars

Ingredients:

- 7 pounds (3.2 kg) Roma or other paste tomatoes
- 1 large onion, chopped
- 1 cup apple cider vinegar
- 1/2 cup firmly packed brown sugar
- 2 teaspoons kosher salt
- 1/4 teaspoon cayenne pepper
- 1 teaspoon mustard seed
- 1 teaspoon whole cloves
- 1 teaspoon whole allspice berries
- 1 cinnamon stick, broken

Directions:

- ❖ In a large pot, merge the tomatoes and onion. Bring the mixture to a boil. Reduce the heat to low. Parboil for 30 minutes, or until very soft.
- ❖ Using a food mill, pass the mixture through to purée. Discard the seeds and skins. Rinse the pot, place it on the stove, and return the purée to it.
- ❖ Prepare a hot water bath. Set the jars in it to keep warm. Clean the lids and rings in hot, soapy water, and set aside.
- ❖ Add the cider vinegar, brown sugar, kosher salt, and cayenne pepper to the purée.
- ❖ In a cheesecloth square, combine the mustard seed, cloves, allspice, and cinnamon. Tie securely with kitchen twine into a sachet. Add to the pot. Simmer over low heat for about 1 hour, 30 minutes, or until reduced by half. Remove and discard the sachet.
- ❖ Ladle the hot ketchup into the prepared jars, leaving 1/2 inch of headspace. Clean the rims clean and seal with the lids and rings.
- ❖ Set the jars in a hot water bath for 10 minutes. Se off the heat and let the jars rest in the water bath for 10 minutes.
- ❖ Carefully detach the jars from the hot water canner. Set aside to cool for 12 hours.
- ❖ Check the lids for proper seals. Detach the rings, wipe the jars, label and date them, and set to a cupboard or pantry.
- ❖ Use within 4 weeks.

Nutrition Calories: 37 Protein: 1.9g Carbs: 7.4g Fat: 0.8g Sugar: 1.3g

LIME BLUEBERRY KETCHUP

Preparation time: 5 minutes
Cooking time: 15 minutes
Servings: 3 pint jars

Ingredients:

- 2 cups fresh or frozen blueberries
- 1/3 cup apple cider vinegar
- 2 tablespoons balsamic vinegar
- Juice of 1 lime
- 3/4 cup firmly packed brown sugar
- 1 teaspoon ground cinnamon
- 1/2 teaspoon ground cloves
- 1/2 teaspoon ground ginger
- 1/2 teaspoon salt
- 1/4 teaspoon cayenne pepper

Directions:

- ❖ Prepare a hot water bath. Set the jars in it to keep warm. Wash the lids and rings and set aside.
- ❖ In a medium saucepan, merge the blueberries, cider vinegar, balsamic vinegar, and lime juice. Bring to a boil. Reduce the heat to medium. Simmer for 5 minutes. Set the blueberry mixture through a sieve into a clean saucepan, pressing with a rubber spatula or wooden spoon to extract as much pulp as possible. Discard the seeds.
- ❖ Add the brown sugar, cinnamon, cloves, ginger, salt, and cayenne pepper to the blueberry mixture. Set to a full rolling boil over high heat, stirring to dissolve the sugar. Reduce the heat to medium. Parboil for about 10 minutes more, or until thickened.
- ❖ Ladle the hot blueberry ketchup into the prepared jars, leaving 1/4 inch of headspace. Use a nonmetallic utensil to free any air bubbles. Clean the rims clean and seal with the lids and rings.
- ❖ Set the jars in a hot water bath for 15 minutes. Set off the heat and let the jars rest in the water bath for 10 minutes.
- ❖ Carefully detach the jars from the hot water canner. Set aside to cool.
- ❖ Detach the rings, wipe the jars, label and date them, and transfer to a cupboard or pantry.
- ❖ Refrigerate and use within 3 weeks. Properly secure jars will last in the cupboard for 12 months.

Nutrition Calories:: 22 Total fat: 0.2g Carbs: 3g Protein: 2.8g Sugars: 1g Fiber: 1g

PEACH TOMATO SALSA

Preparation time: 10 minutes
Cooking time: 10 minutes
Servings: 16

Ingredients:

- 2 peaches, peel & chopped
- 1/8 tsp pepper
- 2 tsp brown sugar
- ½ tsp lime juice
- 2 tsp vinegar
- 4 oz. green chilies, chopped
- 1 garlic clove, minced
- ½ tbsp. dried cilantro

- ¼ onion, chopped
- 1 tomato, chopped
- ¼ tsp salt

Directions:

- ❖ Add all ingredients into the large mixing bowl and mix well.
- ❖ Ladle salsa in a clean jar. Seal jar with lid and store in the refrigerator.

Nutrition: Cholesterol 0mg Calories 34 Fat 0.5 g Carbohydrates 7.5 g Sugar 5.2 g Protein 1 g

MANGO PINEAPPLE SALSA

Preparation time: 10 minutes
Cooking time: 30 minutes
Servings: 4

Ingredients:

- 2 mangoes, peeled and chopped
- 2 jalapenos, chopped
- 1 sweet pepper, chopped
- 1 onion, chopped
- 2 garlic cloves, minced
- 1 tsp ginger, grated
- 1/4 cup vinegar
- 1/4 cup lime juice
- 1/3 cup sugar
- 3 cups pineapple, chopped
- 1 1/2 lbs. tomatoes, cored and chopped
- 1/2 tsp salt

Directions:

- ❖ Add all ingredients into the large pot and bring to boil.
- ❖ Reduce heat and simmer for 10 minutes. Stir frequently.
- ❖ Remove pot from heat. Ladle salsa into the clean jars. Leave 1/2-inch headspace.
- ❖ Seal jar with lids. Process in a water bath canner for 20 minutes.
- ❖ Remove jars from the water bath and let it cool completely.
- ❖ Check seals of jars. Label and store.

Nutrition: Cholesterol 0mg Calories 280 Fat 1 g Carbohydrates 70 g Sugar 60 g Protein 4 g

PEPPERS & TOMATO SALSA

Preparation time: 15 minutes
Cooking time: 15 minutes
Servings: 48

Ingredients

- 10 cups tomatoes; peeled, cored, and chopped
- 5 cups onions, chopped
- 5 cups green bell peppers, seeded and chopped

- 2½ cups jalapeño peppers, seeded and chopped
- 3 garlic cloves, chopped finely
- 2 tablespoons fresh cilantro, chopped finely
- 1¼ cups cider vinegar
- 1 tablespoon salt

Directions:

- ❖ In a nonreactive saucepan, add all ingredients over medium-high heat and cook until boiling, stirring continuously.
- ❖ Now set the heat to low and cook for about 10 minutes, stirring frequently.
- ❖ In 6 (1-pint) hot sterilized jars, divide the salsa, leaving about ½-inch space from the top.
- ❖ Slide a small knife around the insides of each jar to remove air bubbles.
- ❖ Wipe any trace of food off the rims of jars with a clean, moist kitchen towel.
- ❖ Close each jar with a lid and screw on the ring.
- ❖ Arrange the jars in a boiling water canner and process for about 15 minutes.
- ❖ Remove the jars from water canner and place onto a wood surface several inches apart to cool completely.
- ❖ After cooling with your finger, press the top of each jar's lid to ensure that the seal is tight.
- ❖ The canned salsa can be stored in the refrigerator for up to 1 month.

Nutrition: Cholesterol 0mg Calories 19 Total Fat 0.2 g Saturated Fat 0 g Sodium 241 mg Total Carbs 3.9 g Fiber 1 g Sugar 2.3 g Protein 0.7 g

PEAR CARAMEL SAUCE

Preparation time: 15 minutes
Cooking time: 30 minutes
Servings: 32

Ingredients

- 2 pounds ripe pears, cored and cut into pieces
- 2 teaspoons vanilla bean paste
- 1 teaspoon sea salt
- 1¾ cups water, divided
- 3 cups granulated sugar

Directions:

- ❖ In a blender, add chopped pears, vanilla bean paste, salt, and ¼ cup of water and pulse until smooth.
- ❖ Transfer the pear puree into a bowl and set aside.
- ❖ In a heavy-bottomed saucepan, add sugar and remaining water over medium-high heat and simmer for about 15–20 minutes, swirling the pan often.
- ❖ Remove the saucepan of sugar syrup from heat and stir in the pear puree.
- ❖ Return the saucepan over medium-low heat and cook for about 5–10 minutes or until the

temperature of caramel sauce reaches between 215°F–225°F, stirring continuously.

- ❖ In 4 (½-pint) hot sterilized jars, divide the sauce, leaving about ½-inch space from the top.
- ❖ Slide a small knife around the insides of each jar to remove air bubbles.
- ❖ Wipe any trace of food off the rims of jars with a clean, moist kitchen towel.
- ❖ Close each jar with a lid and screw on the ring.
- ❖ Arrange the jars in a boiling water canner and process for about 10 minutes.
- ❖ Remove the jars from water canner and place onto a wood surface several inches apart to cool completely.
- ❖ After cooling with your finger, press the top of each jar's lid to ensure that the seal is tight.
- ❖ The canned sauce can be stored in the refrigerator for up to 1 year.

Nutrition: Cholesterol 0mg Calories 87 Total Fat 0 g Saturated Fat 0 g Sodium 58 mg Total Carbs 23.1 g Fiber 0.9 g Sugar 21.5 g Protein 0.1 g

TANGY CRANBERRY SAUCE

Preparation time: 10 minutes
Cooking time: 15 minutes
Servings: 6 pint jars

Ingredients:

- 4 (12-ounces / 340-g) bags fresh cranberries (8 cups)
- 2 cups sugar
- 2 cups water
- 2 cups bottled orange juice
- 2 large oranges, peeled, pith removed, seeded, and chopped
- 1/2 teaspoon ground allspice (optional)
- 1/2 teaspoon ground cloves (optional)

Directions:

- ❖ In a smaller pot, attach lids and rings, 1 tbsp. distilled white vinegar, and water to cover. Boil for 5 minutes, then detach from heat.
- ❖ In a large pot, combine the cranberries, sugar, water, orange juice, oranges, allspice, and cloves. Set to a boil over medium-high heat, stirring often. Set the heat to low and simmer for 15 minutes. Stir often, muddling the orange pieces with your spoon. Remove from heat.
- ❖ Set the hot jars on a cutting board. Using a funnel, ladle the hot sauce into the jars, leaving a 1/2-inch headspace. Detach any air bubbles and add additional sauce if necessary to maintain the 1/2-inch headspace.
- ❖ Clean the jar with a warm washcloth dipped in distilled white vinegar. Set a lid and ring on each jar and hand-tighten.

- ❖ Bring the jars in the water bather, ensuring each jar is covered by at least 1 inch of water. Attach 2 tablespoons distilled white vinegar to the water and turn the heat to high. Set the canner to a boil and process both quarts and pints for 15 minutes. When processed, wait 5 minutes before removing the jars from the canner.

Nutrition Calories: 25 Fat: 0 g Carbs: 6 g Protein 0 g

ENCHILADA SAUCE

Preparation time: 5 minutes
Cooking time: 15 minutes
Servings: 3 pint jars

Ingredients:

- 12 C. halved cored peeled tomatoes (about 24 medium or 8 lb.)
- water
- spices
- bottled lemon juice
- salt (optional)
- 6 tsps. chili powder
- 2 tsps. ground cumin
- 2 tsps. oregano
- 2 tsps. garlic powder
- 2 tsps. ground coriander
- 1 1/2 tsps. seasoning salt

Directions:

- ❖ Set tomatoes in boiling water for 5 minutes before putting it into hot jars containing salt, spice blend and lemon juice.
- ❖ Now pour the cooked liquid over it before sealing the jar.
- ❖ Place jars in hot water for 40 minutes.
- ❖ Tightly seal the jars.

Nutrition Calories: 79 Fat: 0 g Carbs: 21 g Protein 0 g

HONEY MUSTARD

Preparation time: 5 minutes
Cooking time: 15 minutes
Servings: 4 pint jars

Ingredients:

- 3/4 Cup mustard powder
- 1/3 Cup honey
- 1 Cup cider vinegar
- 3 whole eggs, slightly beaten

Directions

- ❖ Combine everything over medium heat in boiling hot water before cooking on low heat for 10 minutes.
- ❖ Pour into sterilized jars and put the jars in boiling water for 10 minutes.

- ❖ Store contents in tightly sealed jars.

Nutrition Calories:: 49 Fat: 0.2g Carbs: 8.7g, Protein: 3.6g Sugars: 4.9g

GREEN SALSA

Preparation time: 5 minutes
Cooking time: 15 minutes
Servings: 3 pint jars

Ingredients:

- 2 lbs. about 8 C. tomatillos
- 2 Cup chopped onions
- 1-4 hot pepper, seeded and chopped
- 1 Cup fresh cilantro, minced
- 4 -8 garlic cloves
- 1/2 Cup lemon juice
- 1/2 Cup lime juice

Directions

- ❖ Set all the ingredients in a large pot along with some oil and bring everything to boil before cooking on low heat for 20 minutes.
- ❖ You can add cumin, oregano, water, oil, lemon thyme, salt, pepper, tarragon, cognac, sugar, tart apples, vinegar, and sweet red peppers to the boiling mixture according to your choice.
- ❖ Pour the mixture into the jars before putting them in hot boiling water for 20 minutes.

Nutrition Calories: 37 Protein: 1.9g Carbs: 7.4g Fat: 0.8g Sugar: 1.3g

SPICY CHUNKY SALSA

Preparation time: 5 minutes
Cooking time: 15 minutes
Servings: 3 pint jars

Ingredients:

- 6 pounds tomatoes
- 3 large green peppers, chopped
- 3 large onions, chopped
- 2 cups of white vinegar
- 1 large sweet red pepper, chopped
- 1 can (12 ounces) tomato paste
- 4 jalapeno peppers, seeded and chopped
- 2 Serrano peppers, seeded and chopped
- 1/2 cup of sugar
- 1/2 cup of minced fresh cilantro
- 1/2 cup of bottled lemon juice
- 3 garlic cloves, minced
- 4 tsp. ground cumin
- 1 tbsp. salt
- 2 tsp. dried oregano
- 1 tsp. hot pepper sauce

Directions:

- ❖ Bring the water into a boil for 2 quarters in a casserole. Dutch oven. Place tomatoes, a couple at a time, in boiling water with a slotted spoon for 30-60 seconds.
- ❖ Remove every tomato and place it in cold water right away. Drain the water and pat it dry. To make 9 cups of tomatoes, peel and coarsely chop them and set them in a stockpot. Mix the remaining ingredients in a mixing dish.
- ❖ Bring to a boil with enough water to cover. Low heat reduction and cooling for 30 minutes, uncovered or until slightly thickened. Fill heated 1-pint jars halfway with the mixture, allowing a 12-inch headspace. Remove air bubbles and, if necessary, correct headspace by adding heated mixture.
- ❖ Clean the rims. Screw on bands until fingertip tight; center lids on jars. Set the jars in a canner filled with simmering water, making sure they are completely covered. Take a boil, and then lower to a simmer for 15 minutes. Remove and chill the jars. Remove them.

Nutrition Calories: 719 Protein: 1.2 g Carbs: 104.5 g Fat: 0.5g Sugar: 97.6g

GREEN TOMATO SALSA

Preparation time: 60 minutes (+standing)
Cooking time: 15 minutes
Servings: 8 pint jars

Ingredients:

- 7 lbs. green tomatoes
- 3 large green peppers, seedless
- 2 large sweet red peppers, seedless
- 4 large onions
- 2 large red onions
- 2 tbsp. celery seed
- 4 tsp. mustard seed
- 4 tsp. canning salt
- 5 cups cider vinegar
- 4 cups sugar

Directions:

- ❖ In a food processor, process tomatoes, peppers, and onions until finely chopped.
- ❖ Add salt and mix.
- ❖ Divide mixture between two strainers and place each over a bowl. Let stand for 3 hours.
- ❖ Discard liquid from bowls. Place vegetables in a stockpot and stir in sugar, vinegar, celery and mustard seed. Bring to a boil. Simmer for 30-35 minutes or until thickened, uncovered.
- ❖ Scoop the hot mixture in hot sterilized pint jars, leaving 1/4-inch space of the top. Remove air bubbles and if necessary, adjust headspace by adding hot mixture. Wipe the rims carefully. Place

tops on jars and screw on bands until fingertip tight.

❖ Set jars into canner with simmering water, ensuring that they are completely covered with water. Let boil for 15-17 minutes. Remove jars and cool.

Nutrition: Carbohydrates: 9 g Fat: 0 g Protein: 0 g Sodium: 78 mg Calories: 37

CHAPTER 4
CHUTNEYS AND RELISHES

CUCUMBER AND BELL PEPPER RELISH

Preparation time: 15 minutes
Cooking time: 10 minutes
Servings: 4 half pint jars

Ingredients:

- 3 cups diced pickling cucumbers
- 3/4 cup finely sliced red bell pepper
- 3/4 cup finely chopped green bell pepper
- 1 celery stalk, finely chopped
- 1 jalapeño pepper, finely chopped
- 3 tablespoons pickling salt
- 11/2 cups white vinegar
- 1/3 cup sugar
- 1 tablespoon chopped garlic
- 3/4 teaspoon dried thyme

Directions:

- ❖ In a large bowl, merge the cucumbers, red bell pepper, green bell pepper, celery, jalapeño, and pickling salt. Cover with a clean kitchen towel. Let stand at room. Drain in a colander and rinse thoroughly.
- ❖ Set a hot water bath. Bring the jars in it to keep warm. Clean the lids and rings in hot, soapy water, and set aside.
- ❖ In a saucepot set over medium-high heat, merge the white vinegar and sugar. Bring to a boil, swirling until the sugar dissolves.
- ❖ Add the drained vegetables, garlic, and thyme. Return the mixture to a boil.
- ❖ Ladle the relish into the prepared jars, leaving 1/2 inch of headspace.
- ❖ Set the jars in a hot water bath for 10 minutes. Set off the heat and set the jars rest in the water bath.
- ❖ Carefully detach the jars from the hot water canner. Set aside for 12 hours.
- ❖ Check the lids for proper seals. Remove the rings, clean the jars, label and date them, and transfer to a cupboard or pantry.
- ❖ Refrigerate any jars that don't seal properly, and use within 2 months. Properly secure jars will last in the cupboard for 12 months.

Nutrition Calories: 43 Fat 0 g Carbohydrates 11.3 g Sugar 11 g Protein 0.1 g Cholesterol 0 mg

ZUCCHINI RELISH WITH BELL PEPPER

Preparation time: 15 minutes
Cooking time: 15 minutes
Servings: 4 half pint jars

Ingredients:

- 4 cups finely diced zucchini
- 2 cups finely chopped red and/or green bell peppers
- 1 cup finely chopped onion
- 2 tablespoons pickling salt
- 2 cups white vinegar
- 1 cup sugar
- 2 tablespoons prepared horseradish
- 1 teaspoon mustard seed

Directions:

Day 1

- ❖ In a large bowl, merge the zucchini, bell peppers, onion, and pickling salt.
- ❖ Cover with a clean kitchen towel. Let stand at room for 12 hours, or overnight.

Day 2

- ❖ Drain the vegetables in a colander and rinse thoroughly. With clean hands, press out any excess water.
- ❖ Prepare a hot water bath. Set the jars in it to keep warm. Clean the lids and rings in hot, soapy water, and set aside.
- ❖ In a medium saucepot set over medium-high heat, combine the white vinegar, sugar, horseradish, and mustard seed. Bring to a boil, swirling until the sugar dissolves.
- ❖ Add the drained vegetables. Return the mixture to a boil. Reduce the heat to low. Simmer for 10 minutes.
- ❖ Ladle the relish into the prepared jars, leaving 1/4 inch of headspace. Use a nonmetallic utensil to free any air bubbles. Clean the rims clean and seal with the lids and rings.
- ❖ Set the jars in a hot water bath for 10 minutes. Set off the heat and let the jars rest in the water bath.
- ❖ Carefully detach the jars from the hot water canner. Set to cool for 12 hours.
- ❖ Check the lids for proper seals. Remove the rings, wipe the jars, name and date them, and bring to a cupboard or pantry.
- ❖ Refrigerate any jars that don't secure properly, and use within 2 months. Properly secure the jars will last in the cupboard for 12 months.

Nutrition Calories:: 36.4 Total fat: 0.13g Carbs: 8.36g Protein: 1.17g Sugars: 1g

ONION RELISH WITH PIMIENTO

Preparation time: 15 minutes
Cooking time: 14 minutes
Servings: 8 half pint jars

Ingredients:

- 5 pounds (2.3 kg) sweet onions (such as Vidalia or Walla Walla)
- 1/4 cup salt
- 1 pint apple cider vinegar
- 1 teaspoon ground turmeric
- 4 ounces (113 g) chopped pimiento

- 1 cup granulated sugar
- 1 teaspoon pickling spices

Directions:

- ❖ Chop the onions very fine, either by hand or in a food processor.
- ❖ Place the onions into a large glass bowl or shallow casserole dish, sprinkle the salt over the onions, and allow to rest in the refrigerator for 1 hour.
- ❖ Fill the canner with enough water to cover the jars. Boil the water, reduce the heat to low, place the jars in the water, and simmer until ready to use.
- ❖ Drain the liquid from the onions. Combine the onions in a large pot with the vinegar, turmeric, pimiento, and sugar. Tie the pickling spices into a small square of cheesecloth and add to the pot.
- ❖ Set the onion mixture to a boil, and allow them to cook until the onions are transparent.
- ❖ Pack the onions with the cooking liquid into the canning jars, leaving 1/2 inch of headspace.
- ❖ Remove air bubbles, wipe the rims, center the lids, and screw on the bands and adjust until they are fingertip tight.
- ❖ Set the jars in the canner and bring to a boil. Be sure there is at least 1 inch of water covering the jars.
- ❖ Process for 10 minutes, adjusting for altitude. Detach the jars from the canner and cool.

Nutrition Calories: 25 Fat: 0 g Carbs: 6 g Protein 0 g

SPICY TOMATO RELISH

Preparation time: 5 minutes
Cooking time: 20 minutes
Servings: 3 pint jars

Ingredients:

- 6 tomatoes
- 10g Indian chili powder plus 1 tbsp.
- 1 tbsp. sugar
- 1 tbsp. salt
- 4 tbsp. sesame seed oil

Directions:

- ❖ Dice the tomatoes and them in a Dutch oven.
- ❖ Add all other ingredients and cook over medium heat for 30 minutes or until the mixture thickens.
- ❖ The oil should be separating from the mixture on the side. Scoop the oil with a spoon and put in the satirized pint jar.
- ❖ Process the jars in hot water for 10 minutes then cool completely.
- ❖ Store in a cool dry place.

Nutrition Calories:: 40 Total fat: 3.5g Carbs: 2g Protein: 0g Sugars: 2g Fiber: 0.5g Sodium: 150mg Potassium: 100mg

JALAPENO PINEAPPLE RELISH

Preparation time: 10 minutes
Cooking time: 40 minutes
Servings: 8 pint jars

Ingredients:

- 8 cups pineapple, diced
- 4 jalapeno peppers, seeded and diced
- 1 cup vinegar
- 1 onion, diced
- 1 1/2 tsp. ground coriander
- 1/2 cup sugar
- 1/2 cup water
- Salt

Directions:

- ❖ Add jalapeno, pineapple, and onion into the food processor and process for 2-3 times to finely chop.
- ❖ Add pineapple mixture into the large pot.
- ❖ Add remaining ingredients and stir well and cook over medium heat. Bring to boil.
- ❖ Reduce heat, and simmer for 25 minutes.
- ❖ Ladle relish into the jars. Leave 1/2-inch headspace.
- ❖ Seal jar with lids. Set in a water bath canner for 15 minutes.
- ❖ Remove jars from the water bath and let it cool completely.
- ❖ Check seals of jars. Label and store.

Nutrition Calories: 144 Fat 0.4 g Carbohydrates 35 g Sugar 30 g Protein 1 g Cholesterol 0 mg

TOMATILLO RELISH WITH PEPPER

Preparation time: 14 minutes
Cooking time: 25 minutes
Servings: 6 pint jars

Ingredients:

- 12 cups chopped tomatillos
- 3 cups finely chopped jicama

- 3 cups chopped onion
- 6 cups chopped plum-type tomatoes
- 1 1/2 cups chopped green bell pepper
- 1 1/2 cups chopped red bell pepper
- 1 1/2 cups chopped yellow bell pepper
- 1 cup canning salt
- 2 quarts water
- 6 tablespoons whole mixed pickling spice
- 1 tablespoon crushed red pepper flakes (optional)
- 6 cups sugar
- 6 1/2 cups cider vinegar (5%)

Directions:

- ❖ Detach husks from tomatillos and wash well.
- ❖ Skin jicama and onion. Clean all vegetables well before trimming and chopping. Set chopped tomatillos, jicama, onion, tomatoes, and all bell peppers in a 4-quart saucepot.
- ❖ Set canning salt in water. Spill over prepared vegetables.
- ❖ Warmth to boiling; parboil 5 minutes. Drain thoroughly for about 15 to 20 minutes.
- ❖ Set pickling spice and optional red pepper flakes on a clean, double-layer, 6 inch-square piece of 100% cotton cheesecloth.
- ❖ Set corners together and tie with a clean string. (Or use a purchased muslin spice bag.)
- ❖ Merge sugar, vinegar and spices in a saucepan; set to a boil.
- ❖ Attached drained vegetables. Return to boil; set heat and simmer, uncovered, 30 minutes. Remove spice bag.
- ❖ Set hot relish mixture into hot pint jars, giving 1/2-inch headspace.
- ❖ Detach air bubbles and adjust headspace if needed.
- ❖ Clean rims of jars with a dampened clean paper towel. Adjust lids and process.

Nutrition Calories: 88 Protein: 0 g Fiber: 0 g Fat: 0 g Carbs: 23 g

CHILE RELISH WITH ONION

Preparation time: 20 minutes
Cooking time: 20 minutes
Servings: 6 pint jars

Ingredients:

- 20 red chilies, stemmed, halved, seeded, and coarsely chopped
- 10 green chilies, stemmed, halved, seeded, and coarsely chopped
- 1 tablespoon canning salt
- 2 pounds (907 g) onions, peeled and chopped
- 1 1/2 cups apple cider vinegar
- 1 1/2 cups sugar

Directions:

- ❖ Set a hot water bath. Bring the jars in it to keep warm. Clean the lids and rings in hot, soapy water, and set aside.
- ❖ In a food processor, process the chilies into a coarse paste. Transfer to a bowl. Add the canning salt and enough boiling water to cover. Let stand for 10 minutes. Drain.
- ❖ In a preserving pot or saucepot set over medium-high heat, mix together the ground chiles and onions. Add the vinegar and sugar. Bring to a boil. Boil for 20 minutes.
- ❖ Ladle the relish into the prepared jars, leaving 1/2 inch of headspace.
- ❖ Set the jars in a hot water bath for 15 minutes. Set off the heat and let the jars rest in the water bath for 10 minutes.
- ❖ Carefully detach the jars from the hot water canner. Set aside to cool for 12 hours.
- ❖ Check the lids for proper seals. Detach the rings, wipe the jars, label and date them, and transfer to a cupboard or pantry, use within 1 month.

Nutrition: Carbohydrates: 1 g Fat: 0 g Protein: 1 g Sodium: 727 mg Calories: 4

SPICY CORN RELISH

Preparation time: 15 minutes
Cooking time: 35 minutes
Servings: 4 pint jars

Ingredients:

- Fresh corn on the cob (about 18)
- Red bell peppers, sliced, 2 cups
- 1 1/2 cups of diced green peppers
- Jalapeno, 1/2 cup chopped finely (optional)
- Crushed garlic, about 2-3 cloves
- Sea salt, two tablespoons
- Dried mustard powder, four teaspoons
- Brown sugar, 2/3 cups
- Cider vinegar, 4 cups
- 1 cup of water

Directions:

- ❖ To prepare the jars, sterilize a minimum of 10-pint jars (or as many as you can). Shuck the corn and remove the silks from the kernels.
- ❖ This is best to perform against a cutting board, carefully, with a sharp knife. Transfer the kernels into a large cooking pot, preferably stainless steel. Add all the other ingredients into the pot and stir well, then bring the contents to a boil.
- ❖ Continue to mix on occasion until the mixture reaches the boiling point, then reduce to medium-low and simmer for about 18-20 minutes.
- ❖ Set the sterilized jars near the stove and gently scoop the corn relish, while it's hot, with a ladle or large spoon into each jar. Allow for 1/2 inch at the top of each jar and remove any air bubbles inside.

- ❖ Adjust the level of the relish in each jar and ensure that there is no excess liquid on the rim or edges of the jars. Clean this area thoroughly with a paper towel lightly dampened with vinegar. Affix the lids and close them tightly.
- ❖ Place then in the water bath canner and cover them completely, with at least one inch of water over the jars. Bring the canner to a boil, cover, and then process for 15-16 minutes.
- ❖ Remove from the heat and remove the lid to the canner and allow the jars of relish to settle for about 5-7 minutes before transferring them onto a clean cloth or wire rack.
- ❖ All the jars to cool this way, at room temperature, for up to twenty-four hours. After they have cooled, remove the rings from the lids and wipe the jars well. Place them in a cellar or pantry (away from natural light) for up to one year.

Nutrition Calories: 255 Fat 0.3 g Carbohydrates 65 g Sugar 55 g Protein 1.7 g Cholesterol 0 mg

CUCUMBER RELISH

Preparation time: 60 minutes
Cooking time: 60 minutes
Servings: 4 pint jars

Ingredients:

- 8 cups chopped cucumbers— blossom ends and stem removed
- 1 cup onions, chopped
- 2 cup sweet red peppers, chopped
- 2 cup sweet green peppers, chopped
- 1 tbsp. turmeric
- 1/2 cup pickling salt
- 8 cups cold water
- 2 cups brown sugar, to taste
- 4 cups white vinegar

Spice bag:

- 1 tbsp. mustard seed
- 2 med. sticks cinnamon
- 2 tsps. whole cloves
- 2 tsps. whole allspice

Directions

- ❖ Rinse and drain vegetables. Remove stem, seeds, and ribs from peppers. Chop and measure all vegetables. Sprinkle with turmeric.
- ❖ Dissolve salt in water. Pour over vegetables. Let stand 3 hours. Drain. Cover vegetables with more cold water. Let stand 1 hour. Drain well. Add spice bag and sugar to vinegar. Heat to boiling. Simmer for about 10 minutes.
- ❖ Remove spice bag. Pour syrup on top of vegetables. Let stand overnight. Heat until hot throughout. If too dry, add a bit more vinegar.

- ❖ Allow to boil, stirring to distribute heat. Package the hot relish into sterilized, hot jars, allowing 1/4 inch of headspace. Wipe the jar's rim; set a warm lid in place and tighten. Place in a bath canner with boiling water and process for 10 minutes.

Nutrition Calories: 318 Fat: 1 g Carbs: 1 g Protein 0 g

CRANBERRY RELISH

Preparation time: 15 minutes
Cooking time: 15 minutes
Servings: 2 pint jars

Ingredients:

- 2 cups fresh cranberries, chopped
- 6 Medjool dates, pitted and chopped
- 1/2 shallot, finely diced
- 1 orange, seeded and chopped
- 4 sage leaves, finely chopped
- 2 tablespoons brown sugar
- 1 cup red wine vinegar
- 1/4 cup sugar
- 1 tablespoon salt

Directions

- ❖ Add the cranberries, dates, shallots, sage leaves and orange to a medium bowl and toss well to combine then set aside. Merge the v... r, sugar and salt in a small sauce pan over medium to high heat and bring to a boil. Set the heat to simmer for 10 minutes then remove from heat. Scoop the cranberry relish three quarter way into the storage cans and top with the vinegar mixture, leaving 1/4inch head space.
- ❖ Tightly seal the cans and place in a 15 minute water bath the let cool in a dry place.

Nutrition Calories:: 81 Total Fat: 0.1 g Carbs: 21.6 g Sugars: 17 g Protein: 0.6 g

RHUBARB CHUTNEY

Preparation time: 15 minutes
Cooking time: 15 minutes
Servings: 6 pint jars

Ingredients:

- 8 cups sliced rhubarb
- 6 cups sliced onion
- 2 cups raisins
- 7 cups light brown sugar
- 4 cups apple cider vinegar
- 2 tbsps. salt
- 2 tsps. cinnamon
- 2 tsps. ginger
- 1 tsp. ground cloves
- 1/8 tsp. cayenne pepper

Directions:

- ❖ Mix all the components together in a large pot.
- ❖ Boil, then simmer gently until the liquid is slightly thickened.
- ❖ Pour into sterile jars and wipe the rims.
- ❖ Tighten the lids and process in a hot water bath for 10 minutes.

Nutrition Calories: 58 Fat: 1g Carbs: 12g Protein 0g

MANGO CHUTNEY

Preparation time: 15 minutes
Cooking time: 45 minutes
Servings: 4 pint jars

Ingredients:

- 6 cups sliced green mangos
- 1/2 lb. fresh ginger
- 31/2 cups currants
- 8 cups sugar
- 2 cups vinegar
- 3 cups ground cayenne pepper
- 1 cup salt

Directions:

- ❖ Peel the ginger and halve it.
- ❖ Slice one half of the ginger into thin slices; chop the other half of the ginger roughly.
- ❖ Grind the sliced ginger with half of the currants using a blender until well combined. Place all in a saucepan, except the mangoes.
- ❖ Cook over medium heat for 15 minutes.
- ❖ Meanwhile, to set 6 cups, cut, halve, pit, and slice the green mangos.
- ❖ After 15 minutes of cooking, attach the mangos and parboil for another 30 minutes until the mangos are tender.
- ❖ Pour into shot glasses, clean the rims, and screw the lids and rings together.
- ❖ Use the boiling water bath process: pints and quarts for 10 minutes in both.

Nutrition: Calories 37 Fat: 0g Carbs: 12g Protein 0g

RHUBARB CHERRY CHUTNEY

Preparation time: 15 minutes
Cooking time: 35 minutes
Servings: 6 pint jars

Ingredients:

- 2 lbs. chopped fresh rhubarb
- 2 cups chopped cherries
- 1 chopped apple
- 1 chopped red onion
- 1 chopped celery rib
- 3 minced garlic cloves
- 1 tbsp. chopped crystallized ginger
- 2 cups brown sugar
- 1 cup red wine vinegar
- 3/4 tsp. ground cinnamon
- 1/2 tsp. ground coriander
- 1/4 tsp. ground cloves

Directions:

- ❖ In a 6-quart stockpot, combine all ingredients and allow to boil.
- ❖ Simmer 30 minute while uncovered.
- ❖ Transfer to covered containers. If freezing, use freezer-safe containers and fill to within 1/2-inch of tops.
- ❖ Freeze up to 12 months or refrigerate up to 3 weeks. Before serving, thaw frozen salsa in the refrigerator.

Nutrition: Calories: 102 Carbs: 27g Fat: 0g Protein: 0g

GARLICKY LIME CHUTNEY

Preparation time: 10 minutes
Cooking time: 60 minutes
Servings: 3 pint jars

Ingredients:

- 12 limes, scrubbed and cut into 1/2-inch dice
- 12 garlic cloves, thinly sliced lengthwise
- 1 (4-inch) piece fresh ginger, peeled and thinly sliced
- 8 green chili peppers (jalapeños or Serrano's), stemmed, seeded, and thinly sliced
- 1 tablespoon chili powder
- 1 cup distilled white vinegar
- 3/4 cup sugar

Directions:

- ❖ Prepare a hot water bath. Bring the jars in it to keep warm. Clean the lids and rings in hot, soapy water, and set aside.
- ❖ In a medium saucepan, combine the limes, garlic, ginger, chiles, and chili powder, stir well, and bring to a simmer.
- ❖ Add the vinegar and sugar, return to a simmer, and cook, stirring occasionally, until the limes are

tender and the mixture is thick to mound when dropped from a spoon, about 70 minutes. Remove from the heat.

- ❖ Ladle the chutney into the prepared jars, leaving 1/4 inch of headspace. Use a nonmetallic utensil to free any air bubbles. Clean the rims and seal with the lids and rings.
- ❖ Set the jars in a hot water bath for 20 minutes. Set off the heat and let the jars rest in the water bath.
- ❖ Carefully detach the jars from the hot water canner. Set aside to cool for 12 hours.
- ❖ Check the lids for proper seals. Remove the rings, wipe the jars, label and date them, and transfer to a cupboard or pantry.
- ❖ For the best flavor, allow the chutney to rest for 3 days before serving. Set in refrigerator any jars that don't seal properly, and use within 6 weeks. Properly secure jars will last in the cupboard for 12 months. Once opened, refrigerate and consume within 6 weeks.

Nutrition Calories: 58 Fat: 1g Carbs: 12g Protein 0g

CILANTRO CHUTNEY

Preparation time: 45 minutes
Cooking time: 10 minutes
Servings: 5 pint jars

Ingredients:

- 1/2 cup of yogurt (this can be omitted or replaced with a vegan-based version of yogurt)
- Lemon juice, three tablespoons
- Cilantro with stems removed (small branches can be left intact), one bunch
- Mint leaves, about one cup packed
- Ginger, sliced (2 teaspoons)
- Sea salt, 1/2 teaspoon
- One garlic clove
- One medium-sized jalapeno, sliced finely
- Sugar, 1/2 teaspoon

Directions:

- ❖ Merge all the ingredients above in a blender with one tablespoon of water.
- ❖ Taste and add more spice as needed, then pour it into a sterilized jar and store in the refrigerator. If you want to substitute the yogurt for a non-dairy alternative, you can add coconut or soy-based yogurt. Tofu is another option to consider.
- ❖ If you wish to preserve for a longer time frame, omit the yogurt entirely and store the chutney in a jar for up to one month in your refrigerator.

Nutrition: Calories: 88 Carbs: 22g Fat: 0g Protein: 1g

INDIAN APPLE CHUTNEY

Preparation time: 14 minutes
Cooking time: 20 minutes
Servings: 6 pint jars

Ingredients:

- 2 pounds of apples (medium in size)
- 1 cup of diced onions (finely diced)
- Allspice, two teaspoons
- Ginger, ground or fresh, about two tablespoons
- Raisins, about 7 cups or two pounds
- Red bell pepper, chopped finely, about one cup
- Mustard seeds, about three tablespoons
- Curry powder, about two teaspoons
- Pickling salt, two teaspoons
- 1 clove of garlic, crushed
- 2 hot peppers, seeds removed and diced finely
- 4 cups of malt vinegar
- Brown sugar, about 4 cups (or less, if you prefer less sugar)

Directions:

- ❖ To prepare, wash, and scrub the apples, then peel, core, and slice. Place the apples in a large cooking pot and cover with water. Wash and slice the onions, removing all the skin, and add to the cooking pot.
- ❖ Repeat the same process with the peppers and add them into the pot with the onions and apples. Pour the remaining ingredients into the cooking pot, including the malt vinegar, and bring the contents to a boil. Once this point is reached, cook for about 2 minutes, then reduce to a simmer and stir often.
- ❖ Continue this process until the apples are tender, which can take up to one hour. Place the mixture into sterilized jars and adjust to allow for one inch of space at the top. Clean down the rims of the jars before scooping the contents of the chutney into the jars. Place the lids on tightly and process in a water bath canner for 10-11 minutes. Allow the jars to cool on a wire rack or cloth overnight, then store in a pantry or fruit cellar for up to one month.

Nutrition: Calories: 47 Fat: 0g Carbs: 11.1g Protein 0g

PLUM TOMATO CHUTNEY

Preparation time: 15 minutes
Cooking time: 15 minutes
Servings: 4 pint jars

Ingredients:

- 4 tomatoes, chopped
- 6 plums, seeded and chopped
- 2 green chilies, chopped
- 4 tablespoons fresh ginger, grated

- 1 teaspoon lemon zest
- Juice of 1 lemon
- 2 bay leaves
- Pinch of salt
- 1/2 cup plus 2 tbsp. brown sugar
- 2 teaspoons vinegar
- Pinch black pepper
- 4 tsps. vegetable oil

Directions:

❖ Heat the oil in a deep saucepan. Add the bay leaves, ginger and green chilies, and stir. Add the tomatoes, plums. Add the salt, zest, lemon juice and vinegar. Stir in the sugar and pepper, cover, and cook for 3 minutes.

❖ Spoon the chutney into sterilized jars, leaving a 1/2 inch headspace. Wipe the edge of the jar rim clean and add the lid. Process these in a boiling water bath for 10 minutes.

Nutrition Calories: 70 Fat: 0 g Carbs: 31 g Protein 1 g

CURRIED APPLE CHUTNEY

Preparation time: 15 minutes
Cooking time: 15 minutes
Servings: 10 pint jars

Ingredients:

- 2 quarts apples, peeled, cored and chopped
- 2 pounds raisins
- 4 cups brown sugar
- 1 cup onion, chopped
- 1 cup sweet pepper, chopped
- 3 tbsps. mustard seed
- 2 tbsps. ground ginger
- 2 tsps. allspice
- 2 tsps. curry powder
- 2 tsps. salt
- 2 hot red peppers, chopped
- 1 clove garlic, minced
- 4 cups vinegar

Directions:

❖ In a large saucepan, mix all of the ingredients together. Set to a boil and simmer for 1 hour.

❖ Spoon the chutney into sterilized jars, leaving a 1/2 inch headspace. Wipe the jars' edge rim clean and add the lid. Set jars in a water bath for 10 minutes.

Nutrition Calories: 23 Fat: 0 g Carbs: 11 g Protein 0 g

CONCLUSION

Water bath canning nowadays is used primarily for home canning to preserve food's flavor and nutritional value. It is a very safe way to preserve food because it does not use any chemicals. The only things that are in the jars are the acid and other preservatives if you choose. This method produces good results in preserving food from bacteria because the jars are boiled whole, killing all harmful germs and microorganisms that cause spoiling or decay. The steps use steam under pressure to cook food that is placed into a sealed jar. The jars are then placed into boiling water for a specified time to sterilize and seal the jars.

Water bath canning is a technique that requires you to use water to sterilize jars and covers during the sealing process. This method of properly preserving foods uses high heat and pressure as two-part barriers for keeping bacteria out of food, typically done in a boiling water bath canner. Food preserved using this technique retains its natural color, flavor, nutritional value, texture, and other properties. Water bath canning is one of the safest ways of preserving food. Canning is a method of food preservation that uses heat to destroy microorganisms that cause food spoilage and the growth of harmful bacteria. While this is done through heat, it does not cook or pasteurize the food. Instead, it creates an acidic environment that inhibits the growth of food-spoiling microorganisms.

The jars must be boiled and then placed into a water bath to be sterilized. Before canning, you should make sure that your jars are clean, free from rust or other debris, and screw on tight. Store them upside down, so the mouth is at the bottom of the jar. Place lids on the jars and place them in a boiling water canner for about 30 minutes.

Thank you for using this book to learn about water bath canning. Make sure to always follow proper steps and safety procedures while canning food. Make sure that you have the felicitous equipment and do not ignore any steps in this process. As long as you come after the instructions carefully and safely, you'll be sure to enjoy food that has been preserved adequately for months to come.

BOOK 5

PICKLING AND FERMENTING COOKBOOK

__ for Preppers __

1000 Days of Recipes to Preserve Fruits, Vegetables,
Meat, and Fish Before the Food Riot Starts.

INTRODUCTION

Foods and beverages that have undergone fermentation can require some getting used to. Words like "aged" and "cured" on food containers will be a helpful indicator while searching for fermented foods.

Making fermented food at home is simple. This book teaches you how to ferment proteins, legumes, vegetables, fruits, dairy products, sourdough, alcoholic and nonalcoholic beverages, and even your own vinegar.

You don't need to consume a whole meal of fermented foods to reap their health advantages and enjoy their flavors. Simply adding some sauerkraut to your sausage enhances the flavor while providing health benefits. The same is true for eating some miso soup beforehand or adding some pickles to a sandwich.

Your health will improve more quickly as you consume and prepare fermented foods. Naturally, sharing what you know with others would only be fair if you've begun to appreciate the benefits of such foods. Encourage your friends to learn more about fermented foods by letting them sample the healthy foods you made yourself.

Due to its health advantages, fermentation is experiencing a rebirth in the modern world. Probiotics are abundant in fermented foods and beverages and aid in improving gut health. You might wish to start fermenting your own food for a variety of additional reasons as well. Beyond the benefits to health and food preservation, fermented food simply tastes fantastic!

In the past, pickling and other preservation methods were essential, even lifesaving. Only recently have people been able to keep food for lengthy periods using temperature control reliably; in the past, they had to come up with inventive ways to prevent rotting. Pickles have been a staple of ancient trip fare for millennia, nourishing many families during the lean winter months. Fermented pickles have a distinct flavor and scent that cannot be replicated using vinegar-brine procedures. Fermented pickles are also the healthiest sort of pickled food because they contain living bacteria and probiotics that are created during the fermenting process.

Don't worry if you've never fermented anything before. This book will teach you the fundamental methods and instructions you need to master the fermentation process. After you have mastered these methods, you can graduate to more complicated projects. We'll cover the fundamentals of hygienically and adequately fermenting food, what kinds of foods you can ferment, and how to do it. So, whether you're an experienced fermenter or new to the process, this guide has something for you.

This guide covers you, so don't worry!

CHAPTER 1

INTRODUCTION TO PICKLING AND FERMENTING

Food that has undergone biochemical changes due to the activity of enzymes or microbes, resulting in significant modifications to the food, is referred to as fermented food.

However, according to microbiologists, fermentation is a type of energy-producing microbial metabolism in which an organic or carbohydrate substrate undergoes incomplete oxidation while acting as an electron acceptor. This indicates that fermentation includes the procedures involved in the lactic acid bacteria or yeasts that manufacture ethanol from organic acids.

Regardless of these classifications, food that lactic acid-producing microbes have impacted is considered to be fermented food. To put it more plainly, food is considered to be fermented if it has aged with yeast and/or bacteria.

Many people may be unaware that the most typical foods they eat are fermented. For instance, fermented grapes are used to make wine, fermented milk is used to make cheese and yogurt, fermented soybeans are used to make miso and tempeh, and fermented grains are used to make most bread and beer. In addition, countless other delicious and healthy foods and beverages are fermented.

Ancient civilizations used fermentation as their primary means of food preservation, even after a culture had passed away. It follows that people in ancient times could eat fermented food even after several months or years. Additionally, it has been shown that the fermentation process not only preserved the nutritional value of food but also unlocked a wide range of textures and flavors that enhance the enjoyment of the dish.

Many ancient people's fermented foods have been improved with health benefits, opening the door for other people and businesses to improve their fermentation techniques. They also recorded the causes and results of their fermentation processes simultaneously.

They were aware that the effectiveness of the fermentation process depends on how effectively the food is fermented in response to the process. A range of amino acids, minerals, and vitamins are among the many nutrients produced and released throughout time by fermentation.

It is a process in which bacteria, yeast, and other microbes manufacture enzymes that cause organic molecules to be chemically changed into simpler chemicals. The enzymes break down complex chemical molecules into simpler substances and nutrients. Food that has undergone fermentation has a particular texture, taste, and flavor that enhances the original product and makes it easier for humans to digest. Typically, in groups or individually, yeasts, molds, or bacteria trigger fermentation processes.

All bacteria have specialized metabolic genes that produce enzymes that can digest particular subtypes of sugar compounds. Different types of microorganisms are present during the fermentation process in varying concentrations. Together, they produce the desired fermented byproduct for you. The type and quantity of bacteria utilized in the fermentation process will affect the flavor of specific fermented foods.

DIFFERENT FORMS OF FERMENTATION

Alcohol Fermentation

Alcohol is produced when yeasts break down the pyruvate molecules found in carbohydrates. Alcoholic fermentation is the most well-known type of fermentation. Humans have long savored the byproducts of wine, beer, and other beverages.

Acetic Fermentation

Sour vinegar and other condiments are created from fruit or grain sugars. When the fermentation of alcohol is finished, this procedure begins. The most frequent result of acetic acid production is vinegar. Because of this, apple cider and apple cider vinegar are different products.

Lactic Acid Fermentation

Lactic acid is formed as a result of the digestion of sugars or carbohydrates. This fermenting technique is said to be the earliest. Most civilizations worldwide use fermented milk products consumed for generations.

You must remember that food fermentation is a form of controlled degradation when you start working on it. Fermentation produces potent smells and odors that may appeal to certain people but not others. These dishes are not fresh, but they are also not bad. By consuming fermented foods, you can enhance your body's digestion of other foods and prevent harmful bacteria from flourishing inside you. Your taste will determine the type of fermented food you consume. Try a few different fermentations using this method to see which ones best fit your taste. They're a great way to improve your health and reduce food waste.

BENEFITS OF FERMENTATION

Foods that have undergone fermentation have many advantages. Compared to their unfermented counterparts, most foods are more nutrient-rich when fermented. Let's examine some of these meals' benefits.

Enhanced Gut Health

Probiotics are added to food during fermentation, increasing their quantity. These bacteria can treat stomach aches and digestive issues as well as balance the microbiota in the gut. According to studies, probiotics can help with some IBS or irritable bowel syndrome symptoms. Most people worldwide with this illness exhibit either modest or severe symptoms. Fermented foods, like cheese and yogurt, for example, can lessen symptoms like bloating, according to research by Guyonnet D et al. on adults.

Additionally, they might increase stool frequency, which reduces constipation. Further, fermented foods can lessen the intensity of gas and diarrhea. You should consider including fermented foods in your diet if you have digestive troubles or stomach problems.

Enhanced Immunity

Your immune system and intestinal health are closely intertwined. You have a lower chance of getting illnesses like the common cold, the flu, fever, etc., thanks to the bacteria in your gut. Additionally, these nutrients boost immunity. Fermented foods boost your immunity since they include a lot of probiotics. Consuming probiotic foods can also help you recover from infections more quickly. Most fermented foods are high in iron, zinc, and vitamin C. Your immune system is known to be strengthened by these foods.

Enhanced Digestion

Foods are easier for the body to digest because fermentation breaks down different meal components. For instance, lactose, a natural sugar in milk, is converted into galactose and glucose during fermentation. These latter are basic sugars that are simple for your body to process. You can eat fermented foods, including cheese, yogurt, and kefir, if you have lactose sensitivity. Additionally, the process of fermentation aids in the destruction or breakdown of chemical compounds like lectins and phytates into smaller and more palatable ones. These are frequently located in grains, legumes, nuts, and seeds. As a result, your body has no trouble digesting meals like tempeh, made from fermented legumes or beans.

Loss of Weight

Additionally, studies indicate a connection between particular probiotic strains and weight loss. Lactobacillus gasseri and Lactobacillus rhamnosus are two of these strains that have a reputation for lowering abdominal fat.

HOW DOES PICKLING WORK, AND WHAT IS IT?

Although this question initially looks straightforward, clarifying the processes you want to take place is crucial. This contrasts with merely hoping for the best and tossing some vegetables in a jar. You can confidently follow a recipe if you understand the pickling procedure. Or, even better, you can develop the confidence to disregard a recipe and create your own peculiar, fascinating, and, most importantly, palatable inventions.

The method of pickling involves immersing the edible product you're trying to preserve in an acidic solution. Usually, vinegar is used for this, although brine—a salt solution—is occasionally applied. The solution is edible to humans, but the most crucial component is unfriendly to microbes. Since you probably intend to eat this item, using an inedible solution defeats the point.

The term "pickling" typically relates to the use of this solution to preserve fresh plants; however, there are some exceptions, including pickled eggs. Meat can also be preserved similarly, which is known as curing. We'll concentrate on fresh produce.

The vinegar method is easy to use and understand, which is why it's so well-liked. Because vinegar is so acidic, it takes care of your preserving job. Since vinegar typically has a pH of 2 or 3, it generates a climate unfriendly to dangerous germs.

Of course, pickling can be done with acidic liquids other than vinegar. The most popular acid used is simply vinegar. For instance, using a technique we'll discuss later, limes and lemons can be pickled in their acidic juice.

Things may get weird when it comes to the brine solution approach. Salt is not acidic. So how do we define pickling in this context? The brine helps a fermentation process that results in the production of lactic acid rather than immediately pickling the food. The lactic acid preserves the food.

Meals that have been pickled have the obvious advantage of not spoiling as quickly as fresh foods. Pickling alters the flavor, consistency, and even nutritional value of food and preserving it.

You don't have to pickle everything, so don't stress. However, you might be tempted to once you see how simple and helpful it is.

Health Advantages of Pickling

Given the minimum work required for pickling, the health advantages are enormous. Pickles are made from plants, rich in healthy nutrients like vitamins and minerals, and have little fat and calories.

Let's take a moment to consider the lowly dill pickle. This is the classic pickle that we are all accustomed to. Additionally, it pairs amazingly well with your preferred sandwich. In its most basic form, a dill pickle is a cucumber that has been pickled with dill.

According to an analysis of its nutritional value, one whole dill pickle has 23% of the necessary daily quantity of vitamin K. You need this vitamin to thrive since it is vital. It is used by the body to aid in blood clotting and stop excessive bleeding. It has also been connected to healthy bones.

Vitamin A intake should be between 21% and 24% of the daily recommended value. The immune system is strengthened by vitamin A, which also benefits and protects the eyes and the skin. Retinol, another name for it, is frequently found in vitamin supplements and is occasionally used in skin treatments.

7% of adults should consume calcium daily for strong bones, teeth, and nerves.

Potassium, a mineral and an electrolyte, accounts for 5% of the daily recommended intake. Potassium is a multi-tasking mineral that supports the health of your heart rhythm, muscles, nerves, blood pressure, and even your body's natural pH balance.

Vitamin C preserves cells and keeps them healthy, promotes wound healing, and maintains the health of the skin, blood vessels, bones, and cartilage, in 3-4% of the daily recommended allowance.

Pickles are the tastiest option if you have to choose between eating a few of them daily or popping a multivitamin. Dill pickles include a lot of beta-carotene, crucial for lowering your risk of heart disease, stroke, cancer, respiratory disorders, other diseases, and all of these vitamins and minerals. Additionally, they are loaded with antioxidants, which aid in lessening the adverse effects of free radicals on the body. These consequences include a variety of unpleasant chronic diseases, heart disease, cancer, and inflammation. Simply said, consuming more antioxidants will benefit your overall health.

Enhancing the Flavor of Pickles

Discovering just how wonderful pickled food can be is one of the most thrilling aspects of pickling at home. Pickles might sometimes be overlooked as a tiny component of your diet, serving only as a condiment for a certain sandwich or meal. People frequently find it challenging to come up with ideas for what to do with all of the pickles, especially now that alternative food preservation techniques are available.

However, this does not have to be the case. There are no restrictions on how to use pickles or what foods to serve them. Instead, consider them a flavor enhancer that can be added to nearly anything.

Cooking involves many different aspects, but one of them is the idea of balancing various flavors. These flavors include acid and salt. Many savory recipes contain acid, such as vinegar or lemon juice. Even tomatoes contribute a small amount of acid to the dish. Acidity contrasts with other flavors and helps food to be balanced. Since salt is a flavor enhancer, it draws attention to other flavors. A typical tip is adding a tiny touch of salt to something sweet to highlight the sweetness without overdoing the salt to give it a salty flavor.

Why Have We Been Discussing Flavor Theory?

Pickles are usually acidic and salty. You can rely on those two; however, the recipe may require additional tastes. As a result, you can add some pickle to almost any dish and, in addition to bringing the flavors together, elevate the dish to new heights by adding a layer of complexity. For this reason, pickles are frequently used in meals across many cultures as an ingredient or a side dish.

Even if you don't want to use the pickle itself, vinegar can be substituted in a recipe with pickling brine. Additionally, you may use pickling brine in marinades to give the food you're marinating incredible, nuanced flavors. Making your own pickles enables you to experiment with cooking much more, and experimenting is where things can get a lot more delicious and enjoyable.

The type of vinegar used alters the pickled food's texture and flavor, whether it be cucumbers, onions, or something else entirely. You see, the acid in the vinegar affects your meals in several ways. The fact that it makes the environment within the jar uninhabitable for microorganisms is the most visible of these effects. But the lovely process of osmosis also turns the vegetable itself acidic. As a result, the water inside the vegetable is pulled into the acidic pickling solution, while the acid in the solution is absorbed into the vegetable. This occurs because the vegetable is significantly less acidic than the vinegar. This increases the acidity of the vegetable, keeping harmful germs from destroying your product while decreasing the acidity of the solution. The veggie becomes crisper since it contains less moisture. Despite logic stating that a watery vegetable preserved in liquid should be squishy and mushy, dill pickles remain crisp rather than soggy. They give sharpness to your dish that might not otherwise be present, which is another reason they are so enjoyable to eat.

You may read about how wonderful home pickling is, but the only way to believe it is to do it yourself. So, let's go over the details of the pickling procedure before trying out a few international recipes.

EVERYTHING YOU SHOULD KNOW BEFORE PICKLING

The art of pickling dates back over 4,000 years. It was rumored that pickles were a component of Cleopatra's beauty regimen. Even Julius Caesar's soldiers received pickles as a source of energy. The average American consumes 9 pounds of pickles annually, making pickles a vital component of the national identity. While neither Cleopatra nor Napoleon's claims are strongly supported by science, pickled foods are a healthy, economical, and enjoyable way to enjoy the flavor of fresh food all year round.

What Exactly is Pickling?

Pickling is the anaerobic fermentation process used to preserve food in brine or vinegar, which can hold perishables for months. The two methods of pickling that are most frequently used are the water bath canning process, which involves preserving vegetables in a vinegar-brine, or wild fermentation, which calls for fermentation tools like a pickling crock or a fermentation kit like the Perfect Pickler.

Beginners may find it intimidating to begin the pickling process at home, but with a few inexpensive tools and ingredients, we can all quickly pickle like masters in no time.

Before Pickling

Although it's understandable if you want to start immediately, pickling requires some preparation. Equipment must be obtained, ingredients must be located, and safety regulations must be followed.

Safety comes first because it will determine the tools and components that are required:

- Check it before you consume it, just like you should with everything you intend to eat. Throw away your pickle if you notice that it smells bad, is discolored, or has mold developing on it. Although it is regrettable to have to discard anything like this, food poisoning is a much worse condition.
- Before utilizing it, make sure everything is clean. Jars and lids, in particular, fall under this. Before usage, run a load through the dishwasher or wash in hot, soapy water. Jars can also be sterilized by baking them for around fifteen minutes at 320–350°F (160–180°C).
- Pickle brine shouldn't be reused because it would have been diluted, making it harder to measure a healthy brine. Pickling liquid should always be acidic enough to kill any microorganisms.
- Different pickling procedures used in various recipes have an impact on storage. Always keep quick pickles in the refrigerator. Other pickles should be sealed, kept in a cool, dark location, and ideally kept in the refrigerator once they are opened.

CHAPTER 2
FRUITS RECIPES

FIVE SPICE APPLE CHUTNEY

Preparation time: 10 minutes
Fermentation time: 3 days
Servings: 4

Ingredients:

- 3 c. cored, coarsely chopped apples
- ½ c. chopped pecans
- ¼ c. lemon juice
- ½ c. pure water
- ½ c. raisins
- ½ tsp. sea salt
- 2 – 4 tbsp. whey liquid
- 2 tbsp. sucanat or rapadura or any other natural sweetener of your choice
- 2 tsp. five spice blend

Directions:

- ❖ Add apples, pecans, lemon juice, water, raisins, salt, whey, sweetener, and five spice. Blend into the mixing bowl and mix well.
- ❖ Spoon the mixture into the jar. Tighten the lids and place them on your countertop for two to three days.
- ❖ Stir daily. Remove any mold that may appear on top.
- ❖ Chill until ready to use. Use within 2 – 3 weeks.
- ❖ Make sure to put the name and date on the jar.

Nutritional values: Calories: 138, Carbohydrates: 32.2 g, Protein: 3.8 g, Fat: 0.4 g, Fiber: 7.4 g, Sugar: 14.6 g

SPICY PEAR CHUTNEY

Preparation time: 15 minutes
Fermentation time: 3 days
Servings: 1 quart

Ingredients:

- 1 ½ to 2 pears, cored, chopped
- ¼ c. chopped cashews or pecans
- Juice of ½ to 1 lemon
- ½ tbsp. grated ginger
- ¼ c. filtered water
- 1 hot chili pepper, fresh or dried, chopped

Directions:

- ❖ Add pears, cashews, lemon juice, ginger, water, raisins, salt, onion, and chili pepper into a bowl and stir well.
- ❖ Spoon the mixture into the jar. Press the fruits down so that the water comes up. Tighten the lids and place them on your countertop for two to three days.
- ❖ Stir daily. Remove any mold that may appear on top.
- ❖ Chill until ready to use. It can last for two to three weeks.
- ❖ Make sure to put the name and date on the jar.

Nutritional values: Calories: 302, Fat: 7 g, Carbs: 26 g, Protein 35

CURRIED MANGO GINGER CHUTNEY

Preparation time: 15 minutes
Fermentation time: 2 – 3 days

Ingredients:

- 6 c. peeled, diced ripe mango
- 4 cloves of garlic, minced
- ½ c. minced fresh cilantro
- 4 tsp. curry powder
- 6 tbsp. whey liquid
- 1 tsp. red pepper flakes or crushed peppercorns
- 5 tsp. minced fresh ginger
- 1 sweet red onion, minced
- 4 tbsp. lemon juice
- 2 tsp. sea salt
- 4 basil leaves, chopped

Directions:

- ❖ Add mango, garlic, cilantro, curry powder, red pepper flakes, onion, lemon juice, ginger, salt, and basil into a bowl and stir well.
- ❖ Spoon the mixture into the jars. Tighten the lids and place them on your countertop for 2 – 3 days.
- ❖ Stir daily. Remove any mold that may appear on top.
- ❖ Chill until ready to use. Use within 2 – 3 weeks.
- ❖ Make sure to put the name and date on the jar.

Nutritional values: Calories: 302 , Fat: 7 g, Carbs: 26 g, Protein 35

BRANDIED FRUIT

Preparation time: 60 minutes
Fermentation time: 40 days
Servings: About 1 quart

Ingredients:

- 4 ½ c. diced fruits (use any one type of fruit or mixture of fruits) of your choice
- 2 ½ c. firmly packed light brown sugar
- 2 ½ c. sugar
- 2 c. brandy

Directions:

- ❖ Add fruits, brown sugar, and sugar into a bowl and mix well. Cover the bowl and place it on your countertop for an hour. Toss the fruit mixture after every 15 minutes.
- ❖ Transfer the mixture into the jar. Add brandy and stir. The fruits should be covered in brandy. Fasten the lid.
- ❖ Place the jar in a dry, cool area for about 40 days.

- ❖ This jar is to be placed at room temperature. It can last for four months.
- ❖ Add more fruits to replace the used ones when you use some fruits. If you add a cup of fruit, add ¼ cup of white sugar and ¼ cup of brown sugar and some brandy to cover the fruits.

Nutritional values: Calories: 138, Carbohydrates: 32.2 g, Protein: 3.8 g, Fat: 0.4 g, Fiber: 7.4 g, Sugar: 14.6 g

FIGS WITH ONIONS & CARDAMOM FERMENT

Preparation time: 10 minutes
Fermentation time: 6 days
Servings: 2 quarts

Ingredients:

- 4 tbsp. sea salt
- 16 to 20 whole, firm figs
- 2 sticks cinnamon
- 10 to 12 cardamom pods, slightly crushed
- 1 tbsp. organic green tea leaves
- 7 c. boiled water
- 1 small shallot or red onion, thinly sliced

Directions:

- ❖ Combine salt and boiling water in a bowl.
- ❖ Add onion, green tea leaves, and spices into the jar. Place the figs in the jar. There should be enough figs to fill the jar up to the top, leaving 2 inches of headspace.
- ❖ Place the fermentation lid on the jar without using the spring. Fasten the moat and mason ring. The moat is to be filled and the cap placed on the bottle.
- ❖ Set aside the jar on your countertop for 5 to 6 days. Now remove the fermentation lid and place the original lid of the jar.
- ❖ Place the jar in the refrigerator for 2 to 3 days.
- ❖ The figs are ready to use now.
- ❖ Keep the jar refrigerated. It can last for about a month.

Nutritional values: Calories: 199, Fats: 27 g, Carbs: 10.8 g, Protein: 27 g, Fiber: 10 g

MIXED FRUIT CHUTNEY

Preparation time: 15 minutes
Fermentation time: 3 days
Servings: 4

Ingredients:

- 2 c. chopped mixed fruit of your choice
- ½ red pepper, chopped
- 2 small cloves of garlic, minced
- ¼ c. raisins
- Juice of a lemon
- Zest of a lemon, grated
- ½ tsp. mustard seeds
- Salt to taste
- ½ c. chopped red onion
- ½ jalapeño, minced (optional)
- 1 tbsp. minced fresh ginger
- 2 tbsp. ginger bug
- ¼ tsp. ground cinnamon
- ½ tbsp. sugar

Directions:

- ❖ Add fruits, onion, sugar, ginger, garlic, mustard, ginger bug, salt, red pepper, cinnamon, lemon juice, and zest into a bowl. Mix until well combined. Add more seasonings if required.
- ❖ Transfer into a jar.
- ❖ If there isn't sufficient liquid in the jar (the liquid in the jar should cover the fruits), pour three to four tablespoons of water into the jar.
- ❖ Tighten the lids and place them on your countertop for 2 – 3 days.
- ❖ Stir daily. Remove any mold that may appear on top.
- ❖ Chill until ready to use. Use within 2 – 3 weeks.
- ❖ Make sure to put the name and date on the jar.

Nutritional values: Calories: 199, Fats: 27 g, Carbs: 10.8 g, Protein: 27 g, Fiber: 10 g

PEACH CHUTNEY

Preparation time: 15 minutes
Fermentation time: 2 – 3 days
Servings: 2 quarts

Ingredients:

- 8 peaches, pitted, chopped
- 1 c. chopped pecans
- ½ c. lemon juice (about 5 lemons)
- 1 c. raisins
- 1 ¼ tbsp. sea salt or to taste
- 2 onions, chopped
- 2 hot peppers, sliced
- 2 tbsp. grated fresh ginger
- 2 c. water

Directions:

- ❖ Add peaches, pecans, lemon juice, raisins, onion, hot pepper, and ¼ tablespoon of salt and ginger into the mixing bowl and mix well.
- ❖ Spoon the mixture into the jar. Tighten the lids and shake the jar.
- ❖ Add water and one tablespoon of salt into a bowl and stir until salt dissolves completely.
- ❖ Pour the brine into the jar, all over the mixture. Press the vegetables with a spoon so that the liquid comes up. Place the jar someplace warm, without sunlight falling on it.
- ❖ Taste it after two days and decide if you want to ferment it for a couple more days.
- ❖ If you are happy with the fermentation, place the jar in the refrigerator until use. Use within 2 – 3 weeks.
- ❖ Make sure to label the bottles with their name and date.

Nutritional values: Calories: 138, Carbohydrates: 32.2 g, Protein: 3.8 g, Fat: 0.4 g, Fiber: 7.4 g, Sugar: 14.6 g

RUMTOPF

Preparation time: 30 minutes
Fermentation time: 6 months
Servings: 6 quarts

Ingredients:

To start Rumtopf:

- 1 lb. mixture of soft fruits like cherries, raspberries, plums, berries, peaches, red and black currants
- 4 c. strong dark rum
- 6 oz. sugar

To add later:

- Dark rum, if required
- ½ lb. seasonal fruit of your choice (to be added every month for 4 – 5 months)
- 3 oz. sugar (to be added each time ½ lb. fruit is added)

Directions:

- ❖ Start making this recipe 4 – 6 months before Christmas.
- ❖ If the fruits you use have pits or stones, remove them, and add them to a bowl.
- ❖ Add sugar and toss well. Stir in the rum.
- ❖ Once well combined, cover and set aside for 8 – 9 hours.
- ❖ Transfer the fruit mixture into the jar.
- ❖ Place fermentation weights in the jar. Fasten the lid. Place the jar in a dry, cool place.
- ❖ Add seasonal fruit and sugar every 3 – 4 weeks and mix well. Add rum if necessary to cover the fruits. Place fermentation weights in the jar. Fasten the lid. You mustn't forget to place the jar someplace cool and dry each time.

Nutritional values: Calories: 199, Fats: 27 g, Carbs: 10.8 g, Protein: 27 g , Fiber: 10 g

SPICED PICKLED CHERRIES

Preparation time: 20 minutes
Fermentation time: 30 days
Servings: 2 quarts

Ingredients:

- 2 lb. cherries, discard stems, rinsed, pat dried
- 2 c. water
- 4 tsp. black peppercorns
- 1 tsp. red pepper flakes (optional)
- 2 c. cider vinegar
- ⅔ c. sugar
- 2 tsp. coriander seeds
- 1 stick of cinnamon, broken into 4 pieces
- 4 – 6 whole cloves
- 4 pods cardamom

Directions:

- ❖ Pour vinegar and water into a saucepan. Add sugar and spices and place the saucepan over medium flame.
- ❖ When it begins to boil, lower the flame and simmer for 10 – 12 minutes.
- ❖ Meanwhile, make sure that the cherries are well dried. Remove the pit from the cherries. It can be done easily with a cherry pitter.
- ❖ Add the cherries along with the juice into the jars. Add equal quantities in each jar.
- ❖ Drizzle equal amounts of the vinegar mixture into the jars, ensuring a piece of cinnamon, cardamom, and a clove in each jar.
- ❖ Fasten the lid and place the jar on your countertop to cool completely.
- ❖ Place the jar in the refrigerator for 1 -4 weeks, depending on how you like it.
- ❖ It can last for 2 – 3 months.

Nutritional values: Calories: 183, Fats: 23 g, Carbs: 21 g, Protein: 23 g, Fiber: 3 g

UMEBOSHI (PICKLED UME PLUM)

Preparation time: 15 minutes
Fermentation time: 60 days
Servings: 2 quarts

Ingredients:

- 2 lb. unripe ume plums or apricots, remove stems
- ½ c. neutral alcohol like vodka
- 4 oz. salt
- 10 – 20 red shiso or perilla leaves (optional)

Directions:

- ❖ Add plums into a large bowl. Pour enough water to cover the plums. Let it soak for 9 – 10 hours.
- ❖ Place a layer of plums in the jar. Sprinkle a little salt over it. Repeat this layering of plums and salt until all of it is added.
- ❖ Fasten the lid and place the jar on your countertop. Let it ferment for three weeks.
- ❖ Now take out the plums from the jar and retain the liquid from the jar.
- ❖ Place the plums on a screen, without overlapping, in the sun during the day. Take it back to your countertop during the night. Do this (drying in the sun) for three days.
- ❖ By the end of 3 days, the plums would have shrunk, and salt will be visible on the plums.
- ❖ Now add the plums back into the jar. Add the red shiso leaves as well and mix.
- ❖ Fasten the jar's lid and place it at room temperature for 1 – 2 months.
- ❖ It is now ready to use.

Nutritional values: Calories: 183, Fats: 23 g, Carbs: 21 g, Protein: 23 g, Fiber: 3 g

LACTO-FERMENTED RASPBERRY PRESERVES

Preparation time: 10 minutes
Fermentation time: 2 days
Servings: 3 quarts

Ingredients:

- 12 c. fresh raspberries
- 3 tsp. sea salt
- 6 tsp. Pomona's pectin
- ¾ c. palm sugar or Rapadura
- 12 tbsp. whey liquid
- 6 tsp. calcium water (which comes along with the pectin)

Directions:

- ❖ Add raspberries, salt, pectin, sugar, whey liquid, and calcium water into a bowl and mash with the potato masher until raspberries are crushed. Let a few remain chunky.
- ❖ Transfer into the jar. Ensure that there is at least an inch of headspace on top.
- ❖ Fasten the lid and place the jar at room temperature for several days.
- ❖ You might find some scum on top. Remove it if it is there.
- ❖ When active fermentation stops, place the jar in the refrigerator.
- ❖ It can last for two months. To make it last longer, transfer the berries into a freezer-safe container and freeze. It can last for 6 – 8 months.
- ❖ Make sure to put the name and date on the jar.

Nutritional values: Calories: 138, Carbohydrates: 32.2 g, Protein: 3.8 g, Fat: 0.4 g, Fiber: 7.4 g, Sugar: 14.6 g

FERMENTED STRAWBERRY PRESERVES

Preparation time: 20 minutes
Fermentation time: 3 days
Servings: 2 quarts

Ingredients:

- 8 c. sliced strawberries
- 2 small green apples, grated
- Juice of a lemon
- 1 c. honey
- 1 tsp. Himalayan pink salt
- 4 tbsp. whey liquid

Directions:

- ❖ Add strawberries, apples, lemon juice, and honey into the pot and mix well, mashing slightly with the back of a spoon.
- ❖ Cook over low heat. Do this until the sauce thickens. Then, take the pot away from the heat and set aside to completely cool.
- ❖ Add whey and salt and mix well.
- ❖ Fasten the fermentation lid and place the jar at room temperature for 2 – 3 days or until you are satisfied with the fermentation.
- ❖ Remove this lid, place the jar's original lid, and fix it tightly.
- ❖ Chill until ready to use.
- ❖ Make sure to put the name and date on the jar.

Nutrition values: Calories: 361, Total Fat: 16.3 g, Saturated Fat: 4.9 g, Cholesterol: 114 mg, Sodium: 515 mg, Total Carbs: 19.3 g, Fiber: 0.1 g, Sugar: 18.2 g, Protein: 33.3 g

STRAWBERRY CHIA JAM

Preparation time: 15 minutes
Fermentation time: 2 days

Ingredients:

- 4 c. organic strawberries
- 4 tbsp. chia seeds

- ½ c. kombucha or whey liquid or water kefir
- 4 tbsp. sugar or honey
- 4 tsp. sea salt

Directions:

- ❖ Add strawberries into a bowl. Scatter sugar and salt over it. Chill overnight.
- ❖ Transfer the strawberries to the pan. Place the pan over medium flame. Stir constantly until sugar dissolves.
- ❖ Turn up the heat and bring it to a rapid boil. Allow it to boil for 5 minutes. Turn off the heat and set aside for 10 to 12 minutes to cool.
- ❖ Stir in chia seeds and kombucha. Let it cool for another 10 minutes.
- ❖ Spoon the mixture into jam jars. Tighten the lids and place them on your countertop for two days. Open the jar on the second day to remove any built-up gasses.
- ❖ Refrigerate the jam until use. It can last for two months.
- ❖ Make sure to label the jars with their name and date.

Nutrition values: Calories: 350, Total Fats: 24 g, Carbs: 6 g, Protein: 26 g, Fiber: 2 g

CHIA PLUM JAM

Preparation time: 20 minutes
Fermentation time: 3 days
Servings: 5 ounces

Ingredients:

- 1 lb. red, ripe, firm plums, pitted, chopped
- ½ tbsp. Kombucha or whey liquid or sauerkraut juice
- ¼ c. chia seeds + 1 – 2 tbsp. extra if required
- 2 – 4 mint sprigs
- ¼ c. raw honey
- ¼ tsp. salt
- A tiny pinch of ground cardamom (optional)
- A tiny pinch of ground cloves (optional)

Directions:

- ❖ Combine plum, salt, honey, kombucha, mint, and ¼ cup of chia seeds into a bowl.
- ❖ Add spices if used and mix well.
- ❖ Spoon the mixture into jam jars. Tighten the lids and place them in a cool, dark area for three days. Open the jar on the second and third day and stir the jam. Do this at least twice daily.
- ❖ Discard the mint sprigs.
- ❖ If you think the jam is not thick enough, add 1 – 2 tablespoons of chia seeds and mix well. Tighten the lid of the jar.
- ❖ Refrigerate the jam until use. It can last for two months.
- ❖ Make sure to label the jars with their name and date.

Nutrition values: Calories: 350, Total Fats: 24 g, Carbs: 6 g, Protein: 26 g, Fiber: 2 g

BLUEBERRY JAM

Preparation time: 10 minutes
Fermentation time: 2 days
Servings: About 2 cups

Ingredients:

- 1 lb. blueberries
- ½ tsp. sea salt
- 6 tbsp. honey or sucanat
- 3 tbsp. whey or water kefir

Directions:

- ❖ Add strawberries, salt, and honey into the saucepan and mix well, mashing slightly with the back of a spoon.
- ❖ Cook for 5 minutes on low heat in a saucepan. Remove from the heat and set aside to cool completely.
- ❖ Add whey and mix well.
- ❖ Spoon the mixture into jam jars. Tighten the lids and place them on your countertop for two days. Open the jar on the second day to remove any built-up gasses.
- ❖ Refrigerate the jam until use. It can last for two months.
- ❖ Make sure to label the jars with their name and date.

Nutrition values: Calories: 170, Total Fats: 19.2 g

Carbs: 0.5 g, Protein: 35 g, Fiber: 0 g

RHUBARB & BLOOD ORANGE JAM

Preparation time: 15 minutes
Fermentation time: 4 – 5 days
Servings: 1 quart

Ingredients:

- 1 ½ lb. rhubarb, thinly sliced
- Juice of 1 blood orange
- Zest of 1 blood orange, grated
- 5.3 oz. agave nectar or honey or maple syrup
- 2 star anise
- 2 bay leaves, torn

- 4 pods of cardamom
- 2 tsp. raw apple cider vinegar with mother
- ½ tsp. Himalayan pink salt

Directions:

- ❖ Add rhubarb, bay leaves, cardamom, star anise, orange juice, zest, salt, and honey into the saucepan and mix well.
- ❖ Over low heat, place the pot and cook until rhubarb is soft, mashing slightly with the back of a spoon as it begins to soften.
- ❖ Turn off the heat and let it completely cool.
- ❖ Add apple cider vinegar and mix well.
- ❖ Spoon the mixture into jam jars. Tighten the lids and place them on your countertop for 4 – 5 days.
- ❖ Refrigerate the jam until use. It can last for two months, unopened. If you open the jar, use it within 12 – 13 days.
- ❖ Make sure to label the jars with their name and date.

Nutrition values: Calories: 138, Carbohydrates: 32.2 g, Protein: 3.8 g, Fat: 0.4 g, Fiber: 7.4 g, Sugar: 14.6 g

APRICOT JAM

Preparation time: 15 minutes
Fermentation time: 3 days
Servings: 4

Ingredients:

- 8 c. diced apricots, peeled and cored
- ¼ c. lemon juice
- 6 c. sugar

Directions:

- ❖ In a large stock pot, mix all ingredients and stir until the sugar is dissolved.
- ❖ Once at a rolling boil, let it boil for about 30 minutes, then remove from heat and put into jars.
- ❖ Let the jars sit in a water bath for about 10 minutes.
- ❖ Let cool completely before storing.

Nutrition values: Carbs: 250.86 g, Fat: 1.9 g, Protein: 7.09 g, Calories: 971

FIG AND PEAR JAM

Preparation time: 15 minutes
Fermentation time: 3 days
Servings: 4

Ingredients:

- 2 c. Pears (chopped)
- 2 c. Figs (fresh and chopped)
- 4 tbsp. Ball® Classic Pectin
- 2 tbsp. Lemon juice (Bottled)
- 15 ml. Water

- 3 c. Sugar

Directions:

- ❖ In a 4L Stainless-steel Dutch oven, add pears, figs, pectin, lemon juice, and water. Boil the mixture on a high flame with continuous stirring.
- ❖ Add sugar and stir until dissolved. Bring the mixture to boil and boil hard for 1 minute. Remove from the flame.
- ❖ Transfer the hot jam into a hot jar using a ladle. Leave ¼ inch space on the top. Remove air bubbles. Clean the rim of the glass jar. Place the lid and apply a band around the lid. Adjust to ensure that the lid is tight. In the water bath canner with boiling water, place the jar.
- ❖ Process the jars for about 10 minutes.
- ❖ Turn the canner off and take off the lid. Keep the jars in the canner for 5 minutes.
- ❖ Take away the jars and allow to cool. Store in the refrigerator.

Nutrition values: Carbs: 250.86 g, Fat: 1.9 g, Protein: 7.09 g, Calories: 971

KIWI JAM

Preparation time: 15 minutes
Fermentation time: 3 days
Servings: 4

Ingredients:

- 3 c. kiwi (peeled and chopped)
- 6 tbsp. Pectin
- 1 c. unsweetened pineapple juice
- 4 c. white granulated sugar

Directions:

- ❖ In a 4L Stainless-steel Dutch oven, add kiwi, pectin, and pineapple juice. Mix properly and bring it to a boil.
- ❖ Put in sugar and constantly stir until it dissolves. Boil the mixture hard for 1 minute. Remove from the flame.
- ❖ Transfer the hot jam into a hot jar using a ladle. Leave ¼ inch space on the top. Remove air bubbles. Clean the rim of the glass jar. Place the lid and apply a band around the lid. Adjust to ensure that the lid is tight. In the water bath canner with boiling water, place the jar.
- ❖ Process the jars for about 10 minutes.
- ❖ Turn the canner off and take off the lid. Keep the jars in the canner for 5 minutes.
- ❖ Take away the jars and allow to cool. Store in the refrigerator.

Nutrition values: Calories: 280, Total Fats: 23 g, Carbs: 6 g, Protein: 27 g, Fiber: 0.5 g

PICKLED GRAPES

Preparation time: 10 minutes
Fermentation time: 2 days
Servings: 1 quart

Ingredients:

- 16 oz. seedless red grapes stemmed and picked over
- 12 oz. apple cider vinegar
- 8 oz. water
- 8 oz. raw sugar
- ½ slivered small red onion
- 1 tsp. whole black peppercorns
- 1 bay leaf
- 1 star anise pod
- ⅓ oz. yellow mustard seeds
- 1 whole allspice
- 1 cinnamon stick

Directions:

- ❖ Place grapes in a jar of 32 ounces and set them aside.
- ❖ Mix the rest of the ingredients in a saucepan and bring to a boil.
- ❖ Reduce heat to low. Let cook for 10 minutes or until the onion is tender.
- ❖ Remove pan from heat and cool mixture for 15 minutes.
- ❖ Pour liquid over the grapes and swirl the jar to combine the brine.
- ❖ Seal the jar and chill in the refrigerator for 24 hours before eating.

Nutrition values: Calories: 280, Total Fats: 23 g, Carbs: 6 g, Protein: 27 g, Fiber: 0.5 g

PLUM ORANGE JAM

Preparation time: 15 minutes
Fermentation time: 3 days
Servings: 4

Ingredients:

- 10 c. chopped plums, skinless
- 1 c. orange juice

- 1 package pectin
- 3 c. sugar
- 3 tbsp. Grated orange zest
- 1½ tsp. Ground cinnamon

Directions:

- ❖ In a Dutch oven, combine plums and orange juice, then bring to a boil.
- ❖ Turn down the heat. Simmer while covered for 5-7 minutes or until softened, stirring occasionally.
- ❖ Stir in pectin. Bring to a rolling boil, stirring constantly.
- ❖ Stir in sugar, cinnamon, and orange zest, letting it boil for 1 minute. Stir until sugar completely dissolves.
- ❖ Remove from heat and skim off foam.
- ❖ Into hot sterilized half-pint jars, scoop the hot mixture. Leave a ¼-inch space on the top. Remove any air bubbles and, if needed, adjust headspace with a hot mixture. Wipe the rims cleanly. Screw on bands until fingertip tight and place tops on jars.
- ❖ Place jars into a canner with boiling water, ensuring they are completely covered with water. Let boil for 5 minutes. Remove jars and cool.

Nutrition values: Carbohydrates: 13 g, Fat: 0 g, Protein: 0 g, Calories: 50

PEACH JAM

Preparation time: 15 minutes
Fermentation time: 3 days
Servings: 8 quarts

Ingredients:

- 4 ¼ c. crushed peaches
- ¼ c. lemon juice
- 7 c. sugar
- ½ bottle liquid pectin (1.5 oz.)

Directions:

- ❖ Place the crushed peaches in a large pot. Add the sugar and the lemon juice and bring to a boil, constantly stirring, for 1 minute. Remove the pot from heat and stir in the pectin.
- ❖ Pour the mixture into sterile jars and adjust the lids. Process for 5 minutes in a boiling water bath.

Nutrition values: Carbohydrates: 185.1 g, Fat: 0.25 g, Protein: 1.04 g, Calories: 713

FERMENTED BLUEBERRIES WITH SALT

Preparation time: 15 minutes
Fermentation time: 8 days
Servings: 21 oz.

Ingredients:

- 21.2 oz. blueberries
- 0.4 oz. 2% salt

Equipment:

- Glass bowl
- Jar
- Fermentation weights

Directions:

- ❖ Crush the blueberries lightly if desired.
- ❖ Combine blueberries and salt in a bowl. Transfer into the jar.
- ❖ Place fermentation weights in the jar. Loosely cover the jar with the lid. Set aside on your countertop.
- ❖ Taste a bit of the blueberry daily. When satisfied with the taste, fasten the lid, and refrigerate until use. This method can be used for any other berries as well.

Nutrition values: Calories: 280, Total Fats: 23 g, Carbs: 6 g, Protein: 27 g, Fiber: 0.5 g

FERMENTED BLUEBERRIES IN SUGAR BRINE

Preparation time: 15 minutes
Fermentation time: 4 days
Servings: 4 quarts

Ingredients:

- 4 c. blueberries
- 1 ½ tsp. salt
- 18 tbsp. filtered water
- 12 tbsp. kombucha or whey or water kefir
- 12 tbsp. organic cane sugar

Equipment:

- Saucepan
- Large Mason's jar
- Fermentation weights

Directions:

- ❖ Pour water into a saucepan and place the saucepan over medium flame. When the water is slightly heated, turn off the heat.
- ❖ Combine salt and sugar in the jar. Add water into the jar and stir until sugar dissolves completely. Let it cool to room temperature.
- ❖ Add blueberries and kombucha and stir.
- ❖ Place fermentation weights in the jar. Loosely cover the jar with the lid. Set aside on your countertop.
- ❖ Taste a bit of the blueberry daily. When satisfied with the taste, fasten the lid, and refrigerate until use. This method can be used for any other berries as well.

Nutrition values: Calories: 280, Total Fats: 23 g, Carbs: 6 g, Protein: 27 g, Fiber: 0.5 g

FERMENTED STRAWBERRIES

Preparation time: 10 minutes
Fermentation time: 4 days
Servings: 1 quart

Ingredients:

- 4 c. sliced strawberries
- 2 tbsp. sugar (optional)
- ½ c. culture (ginger bug or kombucha or water kefir)
- 4 tbsp. filtered water

Equipment:

- Jar (1-quart size)
- Cheesecloth
- Fermentation weights

Directions:

- ❖ Add strawberries and culture into the jar and stir. Stir in sugar if using. You can use honey as well. If you are using honey, do not add the culture.
- ❖ Add water and stir. When you place fermentation weights over the strawberries, the strawberries should be covered with water. Add more water if required.
- ❖ Keep the jar covered with cloth. Place the jar on your countertop or kitchen cupboard for 2 – 4 days. Make sure that there is no sunlight falling on the jar.
- ❖ Place in the refrigerator until use. It can last for three weeks.

Nutrition values: Calories: 138, Carbohydrates: 32.2 g, Protein: 3.8 g, Fat: 0.4 g, Fiber: 7.4 g, Sugar: 14.6 g

LACTO-FERMENTED PEACHES WITH HONEY AND PURPLE BASIL

Preparation time: 15 minutes
Fermentation time: 6 days

Ingredients:

- 4 c. chopped peaches
- 1 tbsp. Himalayan pink sea salt
- 2 c. loosely packed purple basil, discard stems
- 2 tbsp. honey
- Spices of your choice (optional)

Directions:

- ❖ Combine peaches, honey, basil, and salt in the jar. Add spices if using. Close the lid and set it aside in a warm area for 4 – 6 days. Make sure that there is no sunlight falling on the jar.

❖ Taste for fermentation on the 4th day. If you are satisfied, shift the jar into the refrigerator. Else continue fermenting, tasting it daily for fermentation.

Nutrition values: Carbs: 250.86 g, Fat: 1.9 g, Protein: 7.09 g, Calories: 971

FERMENTED MIXED BERRIES

Preparation time: 5 minutes
Fermentation time: 2 days

Ingredients:

- 4 c. mixed berries of your choice
- 1 tsp. packaged starter culture or 4 tbsp. fresh whey liquid
- ½ tsp. fine ground salt
- 4 tbsp. honey
- Filtered water, as required

Equipment:

- Glass jar
- Fermentation weights

Directions:

❖ Place berries in the jar. Combine honey and whey if used in a bowl and pour over the berries.
❖ Pour enough water to fill the jar, about 1 ½ inch below the top. Press the berries onto the bottom of the jar with a wooden spoon. Pour more water if required.
❖ Place fermentation weights over the berries.
❖ Keep the jar covered with the lid. Place the jar on your countertop or kitchen cupboard for 2 – 4 days. Make sure that there is no sunlight falling on the jar.
❖ Place in the refrigerator until use. It can last for 4 – 8 weeks.

Nutrition values: Calories: 213, Total Fat: 7.5 g, Saturated Fat: 1.1 g, Cholesterol: 20 mg, Sodium: 297 mg, Total Carbs: 10.4 g, Fiber: 0.2 g, Sugar: 0.1 g, Protein: 13.1 g

SPICED PROBIOTIC APPLES

Preparation time: 15 minutes
Fermentation time: 2 days
Servings: 2 quarts

Ingredients:

- 6 sweet, crunchy apples, cut into ¼-inch thick slices
- ½ tsp. ground cloves
- 2 tsp. ground cinnamon
- 2 tsp. freshly grated ginger
- Purified water, as required
- 1 packet starter culture

Equipment:

- Bowl
- Large jar (2-quart size)
- Fermentation weights

Directions:

❖ Add a little warm water and starter to a bowl and mix until it dissolves completely. Set aside to cool completely.
❖ Place apples and all the spices in a jar and stir. Pour the starter mixture and stir.
❖ Pour enough water to fill the jar, about 1 ½ inch below the top. Stir until well combined.
❖ Place fermentation weights over the apples.
❖ Keep the jar covered with the lid. Place the jar on your countertop or kitchen cupboard, in a cool and dry place, for 1 to 2 days. Make sure that there is no sunlight falling on the jar.
❖ Place in the refrigerator until use. It can last for about two weeks.

Nutrition values: Calories: 138, Carbohydrates: 32.2 g, Protein: 3.8 g, Fat: 0.4 g, Fiber: 7.4 g, Sugar: 14.6 g

FERMENTED CRANBERRIES

Preparation time: 15 minutes
Fermentation time: 5 days
Servings: 2 quarts

Ingredients:

- 24 oz. whole cranberries
- 2 inches ginger, grated
- 2 tbsp. whey liquid or brine from another ferment
- 6 whole cloves
- 2 sticks cinnamon
- Juice of 4 tangerines or 2 oranges
- 4 tbsp. raw honey or maple syrup
- 1 tsp. salt, non-iodized
- Non-chlorinated water, as required

Directions:

❖ Place cranberries in a bowl and mash them with a potato masher. Add the mashed cranberries into the jar. Add whey, salt, ginger, cloves, and cinnamon.
❖ Stir well. Stir in tangerine juice and honey.
❖ Place fermentation weights over the apples.
❖ Keep the jar covered with the fermentation lid. Place the jar on your countertop or kitchen cupboard, in a cool and dry place, for 4 to 5 days. Make sure that there is no sunlight falling on the jar.
❖ Place in the refrigerator until use. It can last for about two weeks.

Nutrition values: Carbs: 250.86 g, Fat: 1.9 g, Protein: 7.09 g, Calories: 971

FERMENTED SWEET PLUMS

Preparation time: 20 minutes
Fermentation time: 4 days
Servings: 2 quarts

Ingredients:

- 2 tsp. sea salt
- 20 to 25 organic firm plums, pitted, cut into wedges
- 3 to 4 tsp. of spices like juniper berries, cardamom, dried lavender, etc. (optional)
- 4 c. filtered water

Directions:

- ❖ Combine salt and water in the jar. Let the salt dissolve completely. This is the brine.
- ❖ Add plums and spices and stir well. The plum should be covered in brine. Tap the jar lightly on the countertop.
- ❖ Close the jar with the fermentation lid. Place the jar at room temperature to ferment for about 5 days.
- ❖ Taste and decide if you are satisfied with the fermentation. If satisfied, remove the fermentation lid, tighten the jar's original lid, and refrigerate until use. Otherwise, continue fermenting until you are happy with it.

Nutrition values: Calories: 213, Total Fat: 7.5 g, Saturated Fat: 1.1 g, Cholesterol: 20 mg, Sodium: 297 mg, Total Carbs: 10.4 g, Fiber: 0.2 g, Sugar: 0.1 g, Protein: 13.1 g

APPLE SALSA

Preparation time: 15 minutes
Fermentation time: 2 days
Servings: ½ quart

Ingredients:

- 1 – 2 large, crisp apples, cored, cut into bite-size cubes, peel if desired
- ½ jalapeño, sliced
- ¼ tsp. Allspice
- ½ tsp. salt
- ¼ c. packed, finely chopped red onion
- 1 tsp. grated ginger (optional)
- 1 tbsp. lemon juice
- 1 c. water

Directions:

- ❖ Scatter ginger on the bottom of the jar.
- ❖ Combine apples, jalapeño, salt, allspice, onion, and lemon juice in a bowl. Transfer into the jar.
- ❖ Place the fermentation weights on the apples. Add water if required. The liquid should cover the apples.
- ❖ Tighten the lid of the jar and set it aside on your countertop to ferment for 1 – 2 days.

- ❖ If you are satisfied with the fermentation, shift the jar into the refrigerator. Chill until ready to be used.

Nutrition values: Carbs: 250.86 g , Fat: 1.9 g, Protein: 7.09 g, Calories: 971

FERMENTED CHERRIES

Preparation time: 20 minutes
Fermentation time: 2 days
Servings: 1 quart

Ingredients:

- 1 lb. cherries, pitted (do not use overripe cherries)
- 1 c. filtered water
- ¾ tbsp. kosher salt

Directions:

- ❖ Combine salt and cherries in the jar.
- ❖ Place fermentation weights in the jar. Add water into the jar. Cover the jar with a fermentation lid. Tighten the lid. Set aside on your countertop for 1 – 2 days.
- ❖ Taste it on the 2nd day. When satisfied with the taste, fasten the lid, and refrigerate until use. It can last for a week.

Nutrition values: Calories: 280, Total Fats: 23 g, Carbs: 6 g, Protein: 27 g, Fiber: 0.5g

CRANBERRY RELISH

Preparation time: 10 minutes
Fermentation time: 2 days
Servings: 1 quart

Ingredients:

- 24 oz. cranberries
- ¼ c. diced shallot
- 2 tbsp. chopped rosemary
- 2 oranges, quartered with peel, deseeded
- 2 tsp. salt
- 2 tbsp. balsamic vinegar
- ½ c. sugar or honey
- 1 c. finely chopped raisins or currants
- 2 – 4 tbsp. ground chia seeds (optional)

Directions:

- ❖ Add oranges, shallots, cranberries, salt, and rosemary into the food processor and give short pulses until chopped into smaller pieces. Do not blend for long.
- ❖ Transfer into the jar. Tighten the lid and place it in a cool, dark area for 24 hours. If you are satisfied with the fermentation, add raisins and vinegar and mix well. If you are not satisfied, ferment it for a couple of days. Stir a couple of times daily.

- If you want to thicken the relish, add ground chia seeds, and mix well. Tighten the lid and chill until use.
- It can last for a month. Make sure to label the jar with the name and date.

Nutrition values: Calories: 170, Total: Fats 19.2 g, Carbs: 0.5 g, Protein: 35 g, Fiber: 0 g

FERMENTED PINEAPPLE SALSA

Preparation time: 10 – 15 minutes
Fermentation time: 12 hours
Servings: 1 quart

Ingredients:

- 4 c. chopped pineapple
- 4 green onions, thinly sliced
- Pepper to taste
- 2 jalapeño peppers, finely chopped
- Salt to taste
- 4 tbsp. whey liquid

Directions:

- ❖ Add pineapple, green onion, jalapeño, salt, pepper, and whey into the jar and stir until well combined.
- ❖ Cover the jar with cheesecloth and fasten it with a rubber band. Set aside on your countertop to ferment for 8 to 12 hours.
- ❖ Refrigerate until use. It can last for a week.

Nutrition values: Calories: 138, Carbohydrates: 32.2 g, Protein: 3.8 g, Fat: 0.4 g, Fiber: 7.4 g, Sugar: 14.6 g

LACTO-FERMENTED SALSA WITH ARONIA BERRIES

Preparation time: 10 minutes
Fermentation time: 3 days
Servings: 3 cups

Ingredients:

- 2 c. diced tomatoes
- ½ tsp. sea salt
- ¼ c. diced bell pepper
- ½ c. whole Aronia berries
- ½ tbsp. minced garlic
- ¼ c. diced onion
- 2 tbsp. whey liquid (optional)
- 1 tbsp. lemon juice
- 1 mild pepper, finely chopped

Directions:

- ❖ Add tomatoes, bell pepper, onion, mild pepper, salt, garlic, whey liquid, and lemon juice into the jar and stir well.

- ❖ Tighten the lid. Set aside on your countertop to ferment for 2 – 3 days. You can drain the liquid from the jar if desired; stir well and use it.
- ❖ Now close the lid of the jar. Refrigerate until use. It can last for about two weeks.

Nutrition values: Carbs: 250.86 g, Fat: 1.9 g, Protein: 7.09 g, Calories: 971

SPICY FERMENTED PINEAPPLE

Preparation time: 15 minutes
Fermentation time: 4 days
Servings: ½ quart

Ingredients:

- ½ whole pineapple, peeled, cut into wedges
- ½ tbsp. whey liquid
- Water, as required
- ½ small jalapeño, thinly sliced
- 1 tsp. sea salt

Directions:

- ❖ Scatter jalapeños in the jar. Place pineapple wedges as well. Sprinkle salt over it.
- ❖ Drizzle whey and water. Pour enough water to fill up to about ½ inch below the neck.
- ❖ Fasten the lid. Set aside on your countertop for 2 – 4 days. Make sure there is no sunlight falling on the jar.
- ❖ Refrigerate until use. It can last for a week.

Nutrition values: Calories: 138, Carbohydrates: 32.2 g, Protein: 3.8 g, Fat: 0.4 g, Fiber: 7.4 g, Sugar: 14.6 g

SUMMER FRUIT SALSA

Preparation time: 15 minutes
Fermentation time: 3 days
Servings: 1 quart

Ingredients:

- 1 lb. Roma tomatoes, finely chopped
- 1 peach, pitted, diced
- 1 pear, peeled, cored, diced
- ½ c. finely chopped green bell pepper
- ½ c. chopped onion
- ½ hot pepper, deseeded, sliced (optional)
- 1 tbsp. tomato paste
- ½ tbsp. salt or to taste
- 1 clove of garlic, peeled, minced
- ¼ tsp. ground cumin
- 1 tbsp. kombucha

Directions:

- ❖ Add tomatoes, pear, peach, bell pepper, onion, hot pepper, tomato paste, salt, garlic, cumin, and cider vinegar with mother into the jar and stir well.
- ❖ Place fermentation weights in the jar. Cover the jar with cheesecloth and fasten it with a rubber

band. Set aside on your countertop to ferment for 2 – 3 days. You can drain the liquid from the jar if desired; stir well and use it.
- ❖ Now close the lid of the jar. Refrigerate until use. It can last for four weeks.

Nutrition values: Calories: 138, Carbohydrates: 32.2 g, Protein: 3.8 g, Fat: 0.4 g, Fiber: 7.4 g, Sugar: 14.6 g

TOMATO SALSA

Preparation time: 10 minutes
Fermentation time: 3 days
Servings: 1 quart

Ingredients:

- 1 ½ lb. Roma tomatoes, finely chopped
- ½ c. chopped green bell pepper
- ½ c. chopped onion
- ½ hot pepper, deseeded, sliced (optional)
- 1 tbsp. tomato paste
- ½ tbsp. salt or to taste
- 1 clove of garlic, peeled, minced
- ¼ tsp. ground cumin
- 1 tbsp. cider vinegar with mother

Directions:

- ❖ Add tomatoes, bell pepper, onion, hot pepper, tomato paste, salt, garlic, cumin, and cider vinegar with mother into the jar and stir well.
- ❖ Place fermentation weights in the jar. Cover the jar with cheesecloth and fasten it with a rubber band. Set aside on your countertop to ferment for 2 – 3 days. You can drain the liquid from the jar if desired; stir well and use it.
- ❖ Now close the lid of the jar. Refrigerate until use. It can last for four weeks.

Nutrition values: Calories: 116, Total Fat: 2.2 g, Saturated Fat: 1.1 g, Cholesterol: 51 mg, Sodium: 87 mg, Total Carbs: 2.3 g, Fiber: 0.6 g, Sugar: 1.1 g, Protein: 19.7 g

LACTO-FERMENTED PEACH SALSA

Preparation time: 15 minutes
Fermentation time: 3 – 5 days
Servings: 4 quarts

Ingredients:

- 4 c. peeled, pitted, chopped very ripe peaches
- ⅔ c. chopped purple onion
- ¾ c. fresh lemon juice
- 2 tsp. red pepper flakes
- Freshly ground pepper to taste
- 2 large ripe tomatoes, finely chopped
- 10 mint leaves, chopped
- ¼ c. chopped cilantro
- ¼ tsp. cayenne pepper
- 2 tsp. sea salt

Directions:

- ❖ Add tomatoes, onion, peaches, mint leaves, cilantro salt, garlic, red pepper flakes, cayenne pepper, and lemon juice into the jar and stir well.
- ❖ Tighten the lid. Set aside on your countertop to ferment for 3 – 5 days. You can drain the liquid from the jar if desired; stir well and use it.
- ❖ Now close the lid of the jar. Refrigerate until use. It can last for about four weeks.

Nutrition values: Calories: 213, Total Fat: 7.5 g, Saturated Fat: 1.1 g, Cholesterol: 20 mg, Sodium: 297 mg, Total Carbs: 10.4 g, Fiber: 0.2 g, Sugar: 0.1 g, Protein: 13.1 g

APPLE PIE JAM

Preparation time: 15 minutes
Fermentation time: 3 – 5 days
Servings: 4 quarts

Ingredients:

- 1 c. water
- 5 c. sugar
- ½ tsp. butter
- 4 large Golden Delicious apples, peeled and sliced
- 3 oz. liquid fruit pectin
- 1½ tsp. ground cinnamon
- 1 tsp. ground nutmeg
- ¼ tsp. ground mace

Directions:

- ❖ In a Dutch oven, mix the apples and water. Cover and cook over medium heat until the apples are tender.
- ❖ Add butter and sugar and bring the mixture to a rolling boil over high heat, stirring continuously.
- ❖ Stir in the pectin. Allow the mixture to boil for 1 minute while stirring.
- ❖ Remove the oven from heat and skim off foam. Stir in the spices.
- ❖ Carefully pack the mixture into hot jars, leaving ¼ inch of space at the top.
- ❖ Run a knife or spatula along the top to remove air bubbles.
- ❖ Clean the rims of the jars, and screw on the lids and rings. Process in boiling water for 10 minutes.
- ❖ Remove the jars and cool.

Nutrition values: Calories: 138, Carbohydrates: 32.2 g, Protein: 3.8 g, Fat: 0.4 g, Fiber: 7.4 g, Sugar: 14.6 g

PEACH MANGO JAM

Preparation time: 15 minutes
Fermentation time: 3 – 5 days
Servings: 4 quarts

Ingredients:

- 2 lb. peaches, peeled and chopped
- 2 c. mangoes, peeled and chopped
- 5 c. sugar
- ¼ c. lemon juice
- 3 oz. liquid fruit pectin (half a small pouch)

Directions:

- ❖ Place peaches and lemon juice in a large pot and heat.
- ❖ Crush the peaches with a potato masher until pulpy. Add the mangoes and sugar.
- ❖ As soon as the mixture boils, stir in pectin. Boil for one minute, stirring constantly.
- ❖ Remove from heat. Spoon into hot jars and wipe down the rims.
- ❖ Screw on lids and bands and process in boiling water for 15 minutes. Remove and cool.

Nutrition values: Calories: 116, Total Fat: 2.2 g, Saturated Fat: 1.1 g, Cholesterol: 51 mg, Sodium: 87 mg, Total Carbs: 2.3 g, Fiber: 0.6 g, Sugar: 1.1 g, Protein: 19.7 g

ORANGE MARMALADE

Preparation time: 15 minutes
Fermentation time: 3 – 5 days
Servings: 4 quarts

Ingredients:

- 3 lb. oranges
- 2 lemons
- 3 c. sugar

Directions:

- ❖ Wash and dry the fruit and peel the skins.
- ❖ Chop the peels. Cover the skins with water and refrigerate overnight.
- ❖ Keep the fruit in sealed containers in the fridge.
- ❖ The next day, coarsely chop the fruit, throwing out seeds.
- ❖ Drain the water from the skins and place them in a stock pot. Add the fruit and simmer for 2 hours, stirring occasionally.
- ❖ Add the sugar and cook for 30 minutes more. It will thicken.
- ❖ Place in hot jars and do a boiling bath for 20 minutes. Remove to cool.

Nutrition values: Calories: 116, Total Fat: 2.2 g, Saturated Fat: 1.1 g, Cholesterol: 51 mg, Sodium: 87 mg, Total Carbs: 2.3 g, Fiber: 0.6 g, Sugar: 1.1 g, Protein: 19.7 g

APPLE CHUTNEY

Preparation time: 15 minutes
Fermentation time: 3 – 5 days
Servings: 4 quarts

Ingredients:

- 10 medium apples, peeled, cored, and chopped
- 1 c. onions, chopped
- 2 jalapeno peppers, chopped
- 1 lb. raisins
- 2 c. brown sugar
- 2 c. white sugar
- 2 tbsp. ground ginger
- 2 tbsp. ground cinnamon
- 2 tsp. salt
- 2 c. white vinegar

Directions:

- ❖ Combine everything in a large pot and simmer until thick, for about an hour.
- ❖ Spoon into hot jars, leaving ½ inch at top, and process in a boiling bath for 20 minutes.
- ❖ Remove from water to cool.

Nutrition values: Calories: 116, Total Fat: 2.2 g, Saturated Fat: 1.1 g, Cholesterol: 51 mg, Sodium: 87 mg, Total Carbs: 2.3 g, Fiber: 0.6 g, Sugar: 1.1 g, Protein: 19.7 g

CHOCOLATE RASPBERRY JAM

Preparation time: 15 minutes
Fermentation time: 5 days
Servings: 4 quarts

Ingredients:

- 6 pints of fresh raspberries
- 3 squares of unsweetened chocolate
- 4 c. sugar
- ½ tsp. butter
- 2 oz. dry pectin

Directions:

- ❖ In a large pot, crush berries with a potato masher.
- ❖ Chop the chocolate squares into smaller pieces and add to the berries.
- ❖ In a separate bowl, combine the sugar and the pectin. Once it's combined, add it to the pot and stir continuously.
- ❖ Add the butter and bring the mixture to a boil for 1 minute, stirring.
- ❖ Remove pan from heat and spoon into hot jars, skimming off any foam that is created on top. Wipe down the jars, add the tops and the bands, and process in a boiling water bath for 10 minutes.

- ❖ Remove the jars and cool.

Nutrition values: Calories: 116, Total Fat: 2.2 g, Saturated Fat: 1.1 g, Cholesterol: 51 mg, Sodium: 87 mg, Total Carbs: 2.3 g, Fiber: 0.6 g, Sugar: 1.1 g, Protein: 19.7 g

FERMENTED ORANGES

Preparation time: 15 minutes
Fermentation time: 2 days
Servings: ½ quart

Ingredients:

- 1 ½ lb. organic oranges, cut into quarters along with skin but leave it intact at one of the ends (either stem side or bottom)
- 1-inch ginger, peeled, thinly sliced
- ¼ c. salt
- 1 tbsp. whey liquid
- Filtered water, as required

Directions:

- ❖ Scatter ½ tablespoon of salt on the bottom of the jar. Scatter some salt inside the cut part of the orange. Place ginger slices in between the orange quarters and place the oranges in the jar.
- ❖ Drizzle whey over it. Pour enough water to fill up the jar. Leave about 1 ½ inch of space on top of the jar.
- ❖ Place fermentation weights in the jar if desired. Cover the jar with the fermentation lid. Set aside on your countertop to ferment for 1 – 2 weeks.
- ❖ Once the active bubbling stops, remove the fermentation lid, fasten the jar's original lid, and refrigerate until use.
- ❖ It can last for a year. The longer it is refrigerated, the better it tastes.

Nutrition values: Carbs: 250.86 g, Fat: 1.9 g, Protein: 7.09 g, Calories: 971

SWEET PICKLE RELISH

Preparation time: 15 minutes
Fermentation time: 3 – 5 days
Servings: 4 quarts

Ingredients:

- 4 lb. cucumbers
- 1 red onion
- 4 cloves of garlic, minced
- 2 tsp. dried dill seed
- 2 tsp. mustard seed
- 2 tsp. celery seed
- ¼ c. kosher salt
- 3 c. white vinegar
- ¾ c. sugar

Directions:

- ❖ Slice the cucumbers lengthwise. Remove seeds. Dice the garlic, cucumber, and onion by hand, or use your food processor.
- ❖ Place all the vegetables in a pot and cover with salt. Allow it to sit for about 2 hours. Stir occasionally. Drain the mixture until all the liquid is released.
- ❖ In a pot over low heat, combine the vinegar, sugar, dill, celery, and mustard. Bring to a boil, and then add the vegetable mixture. Simmer for 15 minutes.
- ❖ Remove from heat and spoon into hot jars. Wipe the rims and settle the lids and bands.
- ❖ Process in a boiling bath for 10 minutes. Allow cooling.

Nutrition values: Calories: 213, Total Fat: 7.5 g, Saturated Fat: 1.1 g, Cholesterol: 20 mg, Sodium: 297 mg, Total Carbs: 10.4 g, Fiber: 0.2 g, Sugar: 0.1 g, Protein: 13.1 g

APPLE JUICE

Preparation time: 15 minutes
Fermentation time: 3 days
Servings: 2 quarts

Ingredients:

- 18 organic apples, cored, chopped into chunks
- ¼ tsp. sea salt
- 2 tsp. powdered culture starter or 4 tbsp. whey

Directions:

- ❖ Juice the apples in a juicer. Measure out 2 quarts of the juice. If the juice doesn't measure 2 quarts, juice some more apples. Pour into the mason jars.
- ❖ Stir in starter culture or whey and salt.
- ❖ Tighten the lid of the jars. Keep the jars at room temperature for three days. Make sure it is not under sunlight. Shake the jar a couple of times every day.
- ❖ Refrigerate until use. Make sure to label the jar with the date of preparation and expiry date.
- ❖ It can last for a month.

Nutrition values: Carbs: 250.86 g, Fat: 1.9 g, Protein: 7.09 g, Calories: 971

TROPICAL SALSA

Preparation time: 10 minutes
Fermentation time: 2 – 3 days
Servings: 1 quart

Ingredients:

- 1 large ripe mango, peeled, diced
- 1 ½ lb. Roma tomatoes, finely chopped
- ½ hot pepper, deseeded, sliced (optional)
- 1 tbsp. Tomato paste
- ½ tbsp. salt or to taste
- 1 clove of garlic, peeled, minced
- ¼ tsp. ground cumin
- 1 tbsp. whey liquid

Directions:

- ❖ Add tomatoes, mango, hot pepper, tomato paste, salt, garlic, cumin, and cider vinegar with mother into the jar and stir well.
- ❖ Place fermentation weights in the jar. Cover the jar with cheesecloth and fasten it with a rubber band. Set aside on your countertop to ferment for 2 – 3 days. You can drain the liquid from the jar if desired; stir well and use it.
- ❖ Now close the lid of the jar. Refrigerate until use. It can last for four weeks.

Nutrition values: Calories: 138, Carbohydrates: 32.2 g, Protein: 3.8 g, Fat: 0.4 g, Fiber: 7.4 g, Sugar: 14.6 g

ORANGE JUICE

Preparation time: 15 minutes
Fermentation time: 2 days
Servings: 2 quarts

Ingredients:
- 5 c. freshly squeezed orange juice
- 2 c. filtered water
- 1 tsp. Culture starter or 4 tbsp. whey
- ¼ tsp. salt

Directions:
- ❖ Add orange juice into a 2-quarts glass jar. Stir in culture starter or whey and salt.
- ❖ Add water and stir. Fill up to the neck of the jar, making sure to leave at least an inch of space. Tighten the lid of the jar.

- ❖ Place the jar at room temperature for two days. Make sure it is not under sunlight.
- ❖ Shake the jar a couple of times every day.
- ❖ Place in the refrigerator until use. Make sure to label the jar with the date of preparation and expiry date.
- ❖ It can last for a month.

Nutrition values: Calories: 321, Total Fats: 11 g, Carbs: 28 g, Protein: 31 g, Fiber: 1 g

TEPACHE

Preparation time: 10 minutes
Fermentation time: 2 – 3 days
Servings: 2 quarts

Ingredients:
- 2 whole, ripe pineapples, peeled, chopped (retain the peels)
- 10 whole cloves
- 2 qt. of purified water or more if required
- 2 c. raw cane sugar
- 2 cinnamon sticks
- 1 to 2 tsp. brewer's yeast (optional)

Directions:

- ❖ Add pineapple peels and pieces into the canning jar.
- ❖ Scatter cloves, sugar, and cinnamon over it. Pour water and brewer's yeast. Stir well.
- ❖ Close the jars with the fermentation lids. If you do not have fermentation lids, cover the jar with cheesecloth.
- ❖ Place the jar at room temperature for 2 - 3 days.
- ❖ After 24 hours (on the 2nd day), open the jar and discard the white-colored froth floating on top.
- ❖ Make sure it is not under sunlight.
- ❖ Shake the jar a couple of times every day.
- ❖ After another 24 hours (on the 3rd day), taste the liquid and decide if you would like to store it or ferment it for another day.
- ❖ Place a strainer over a pitcher and pour the liquid into the pitcher. Transfer the Tepache into the jar. Taste the tepache and add more sugar if desired. Make sure to label the jar with the date of preparation and expiry date.
- ❖ Pour into a glass jar and refrigerate until use.
- ❖ It can last for a year.
- ❖ You can serve it as it is or dilute it with water and serve.

Nutrition values: Carbs: 250.86 g, Fat: 1.9 g, Protein: 7.09 g, Calories: 971

SIMPLE LACTO-FERMENTED BEVERAGE

Preparation time: 15 minutes
Fermentation time: 2 days
Servings: About 1 quart

Ingredients:

- 0.8 oz. Grainfields B.E. Wholegrain liquid
- 3 ¾ c. cranberry or blackberry or blackberry or grape juice

Equipment:

- Mason's jar (1 quart)

Directions:

- ❖ Pour juice (any one of the suggested juice) and Grainfields into Mason's jar and fasten the lid.
- ❖ Shake the jar a couple of times. Invert the jar as well, a couple of times to mix well.
- ❖ Place the jar at 77°F. Let it ferment for two days. Remove the lid after every 12 hours to check for fermentation.
- ❖ Pour into a glass jar and refrigerate until use.
- ❖ It can last for about a week.

Nutrition values: Calories: 321, Total Fats: 11 g, Carb: 28 g, Protein: 31 g, Fiber: 1 g

CHAPTER 3
VEGETABLE RECIPES

CABBAGE SAUERKRAUT

Preparation time: 15 minutes
Fermentation time: 3 days
Servings: 4 quarts

Ingredients:

- 2 medium heads of green cabbage (about 3 lb. each), thinly sliced into ribbons
- 2 tbsp. caraway seeds (optional)
- 3 tbsp. kosher salt
- 3 tbsp. dill (optional)

Equipment:

- Bowl
- 2 Masons jars (1 ½ quart each)
- Fermentation weights
- Rubber band
- Cotton cloth

Directions:

- ❖ Add salt and cabbage into a bowl and toss well. Massage the cabbage using your hands for about 8 – 10 minutes. In a while, the cabbage will become softer and will release water.
- ❖ Add caraway seeds and dill and stir well. Transfer the cabbage into the jar. Place one large cabbage leaf on top of the sliced cabbage and place the fermentation weight on the cabbage leaf.
- ❖ Keep the jar covered with cloth and fasten it with a rubber band. Set aside the jar for 24 hours.
- ❖ Press the cabbage every 2 hours or so. The cabbage should sink in the liquid.
- ❖ Once 24 hours have passed, check for the liquid in the jar; if it is not over the cabbage, combine two cups of water and two teaspoons of salt in a bowl and pour as much as required to keep the cabbage below the water level.
- ❖ Cover it with the cloth again and place it at room temperature for 3 – 10 days. Make sure that there is no sunlight falling on the jar.
- ❖ Taste the sauerkraut daily, from the 3rd day. When you are happy with the fermentation, remove the fermentation weights. Place the original lid of the jar and fasten the lid.
- ❖ Transfer the jar to the refrigerator. It can last for 4 – 5 months.
- ❖ If you see any scum or mold floating, remove it.

Nutrition values: Calories: 213, Total Fat: 7.5 g , Saturated Fat: 1.1 g , Cholesterol: 20 mg, Sodium: 297 mg, Total Carbs: 10.4 g, Fiber: 0.2 g, Sugar: 0.1 g, Protein: 13.1 g

VEGETABLE SAUERKRAUT

Preparation time: 15 minutes
Servings: 1 quart

Ingredients:

- 4 c. finely grated or chopped red or green cabbage
- ½ medium beet, finely shredded
- 1 ½ tbsp. grated ginger
- 2 medium carrots, finely shredded
- 2 cloves of garlic, minced
- 1 ½ tbsp. grated, fresh turmeric
- 1 tsp. Sea salt or more to taste

Equipment:

- Bowl
- 1 Masons jar (1 ½ qt. size)
- Fermentation weights
- Rubber band
- Cotton cloth

Directions:

- ❖ Add salt and cabbage into a bowl and toss well. Massage the cabbage using your hands for about 8 – 10 minutes. In a while, the cabbage will become softer and will release water.
- ❖ Add beets, ginger, garlic, turmeric, and carrots and stir well. Massage the vegetables once again.
- ❖ Transfer the vegetables into the jar. Place one large cabbage leaf on top of the vegetables and the fermentation weight on the cabbage leaf.
- ❖ Keep the jar covered with cloth and fasten it with a rubber band. Set aside the jar for 24 hours.
- ❖ Press the mixture every 2 hours or so. The vegetable mixture should sink into the liquid.
- ❖ Once 24 hours have passed, check for the liquid in the jar; if it is not over the mixture, combine two cups of water and two teaspoons of salt in a bowl and pour as much as required to keep the mixture below the water level.
- ❖ Cover it with the cloth again and place it at room temperature for 3 – 10 days. Make sure that there is no sunlight falling on the jar.
- ❖ Taste the sauerkraut daily, from the 3rd day. When you are happy with the fermentation, remove the fermentation weights. Place the original lid of the jar and fasten the lid.

- Transfer the jar to the refrigerator. It can last for 4 – 5 months.
- If you see any scum or mold floating, remove it.

Nutrition values: Calories: 100, Total Fats: 9 g, Carbs: 75 g, Protein: 7 g, Fiber: 1 g

APPLE & DAIKON RADISH SAUERKRAUT

Preparation time: 15 minutes
Fermentation time: 3 days
Servings: 4 quarts

Ingredients:

- One head of green cabbage, cut into thin ribbons
- 4 medium daikon radishes with some of its greens, cut into matchsticks
- 2 firm apples, cored, cut into matchsticks
- 4 tbsp. pickling spice blend
- 2 tbsp. Himalayan pink salt

Equipment:

- Bowl
- 2 Masons jars (1 ½ quart each)
- Fermentation weights
- Rubber band
- Cotton cloth

Directions:

- Add radish, apple, salt, and cabbage into a bowl and toss well. Sprinkle the pickling spice, blend over the mixture, and toss well.
- Massage the mixture using your hands for about 8 – 10 minutes. In a while, the mixture will become softer and will release water.
- Pound the mixture with a pestle until well-mashed.
- Transfer the mixture into the jar. Place one large cabbage leaf on top of the mixture and place the fermentation weight on the cabbage leaf.
- Keep the jar covered with cloth and fasten it with a rubber band. Set aside the jar for 24 hours.
- Press the mixture with a wooden spoon every 2 hours or so. The mixture should sink into the liquid.
- After 24 hours, check for the liquid in the jar; if it is not over the mixture, combine two cups of water and two teaspoons of salt in a bowl and pour as much as required to keep the mixture below the water level.
- Cover it with the cloth again and place it at room temperature for 3 – 15 days. Make sure that there is no sunlight falling on the jar.
- Taste the sauerkraut daily, from the 3rd day. When you are happy with the fermentation, remove the fermentation weights, and fasten the original lid of the jar.

- Transfer the jar to the refrigerator. Let it remain in the refrigerator for at least a week before serving. It can last for 4 – 5 months.
- If you see any scum or mold floating, remove it.

Nutrition values: Calories: 321, Total Fats: 11 g, Carbs: 28 g, Protein: 31 g, Fiber: 1 g

EASY FERMENTED VEGETABLES

Preparation time: 15 minutes
Fermentation time: 5 days
Servings: 4 quarts

Ingredients:

- 2 tbsp. Himalayan Sea salt or pickling salt
- 5 c. small cauliflower florets
- 2 carrots, cut into strips
- 20 cloves of garlic, peeled
- 2 tbsp. black peppercorns
- 2 qt. water
- 12 radishes, quartered
- 2 c. green beans, trimmed, cut into 2-inch pieces
- 10 whole green chilies

Equipment:

- Bowl
- 1 Masons jar (2 ½ qt. size)

Directions:

- Add salt and water into a bowl and mix well until salt dissolves completely.
- Add all the vegetables and black peppercorns into the jar. Pour brine over the vegetables in the jar. The vegetables should be covered in water so add more water if required.
- Fasten the lid of the jar and place it on your countertop for 2 to 3 days. Transfer the jar into the refrigerator when you are happy with the fermentation. Let it remain in the refrigerator for at least a few days before serving. It can last for about one month.
- If you see any scum or mold floating, remove it.

Nutrition values: Calories: 321, Total Fats: 11 g, Carbs: 28 g, Protein: 31 g, Fiber: 1 g

BASIL LEAVES

Preparation time: 15 minutes
Fermentation time: 3 days
Servings: 4 quarts

Ingredients:

- Basil, whole leaves
- Salt, non-iodizing

Directions:

- ❖ Mix basil leaves with salt and massage lightly. A brown juice will come out, and leaves will shrink, which is expected.
- ❖ Put leaves in the jar and squeeze out bubbles as much as possible.
- ❖ Cover with a weight to keep basil under the brine. Add water as needed.
- ❖ Throw the lid on (not too tight) and let ferment at room temperature for 1-2 weeks.
- ❖ Once the preferred taste is achieved, tighten the lid, and put it in the fridge.

Nutrition values: Calories: 182, Total Fats: 9 g, Carbs: 10 g, Protein: 27 g, Fiber: 0.2 g

FERMENTED CARROTS WITH GALANGAL AND LIME

Preparation time: 15 minutes
Fermentation time: 5 days
Servings: 4 quarts

Ingredients:

- 2 lb. carrots, cut into ¼-inch thick slices
- 2 tbsp. grated lime zest
- 2 tbsp. thinly sliced galangal or ginger
- 4 tsp. pickling salt

Equipment: 1 Masons jar (2 ½ qt. size)

Directions:

- ❖ Add pickling salt and water into the saucepan. Place the saucepan over medium flame and mix well until salt dissolves completely. Turn off the flame and let the solution cool completely.
- ❖ Add all the vegetables and black peppercorns into the jar. Pour brine over the vegetables in the jar. The vegetables should be covered in water so add more water if required.
- ❖ Fasten the lid of the jar and place it on your countertop for 2 to 3 days. Transfer the jar into the refrigerator when you are happy with the fermentation. Let it remain in the refrigerator for at least a few days before serving. It can last for about one month.
- ❖ If you see any scum or mold floating, remove it.

Nutrition values: Calories: 213, Total Fat: 7.5 g, Saturated Fat: 1.1 g, Cholesterol: 20 mg, Sodium: 297 mg, Total Carbs: 10.4 g, Fiber: 0.2 g, Sugar: 0.1 g, Protein: 13.1 g

GREEN BEANS

Preparation time: 15 minutes
Fermentation time: 3 days
Servings: 5 quarts

Ingredients:

- 1 tsp. non-iodized salt
- 2 cloves of garlic, crushed
- ½ tsp. red chili flakes
- ½ tsp. mustard seeds
- 2 lb. green beans

Directions:

- ❖ Add mustard seeds and red chili flakes to the jar.
- ❖ Pack in green beans and add crushed garlic halfway through.
- ❖ Add in the remaining green beans, leaving 2 inches of headspace.
- ❖ Add brine (one cup of water to one teaspoon of salt) until beans are covered.
- ❖ Place the weight on the beans to keep them submerged. Then, seal the jar with a lid.
- ❖ Set on the kitchen counter to ferment at room temperature. For half a gallon jar, it takes ten days to ferment.
- ❖ Unseal jars to release the gas buildup every day before sealing again.
- ❖ The beans are ready when the brine becomes foggy and then clear up again. Store in fridge.

Nutrition values: Calories: 182, Total Fats: 9 g, Carbs: 10 g, Protein: 27 g, Fiber: 0.2 g

LACTO-FERMENTED DILL PICKLED CUCUMBERS

Preparation time: 15 minutes
Fermentation time: 3 days
Servings: 4 quarts

Ingredients:

- 2 tbsp. mustard seeds
- 2-3 tbsp. pickling spices
- 1-2 tsp. dried thyme
- 1 white onion, chopped
- 8 garlic cloves
- Salt, non-iodized
- 3 lb. small cucumbers

Directions:

- ❖ Clean and trim ends of cucumbers.

- ❖ In a big pot, add water and salt, and bring to a boil. Each quart of water needs 2 tbsp of salt. Make sure the salt completely dissolves.
- ❖ When water starts boiling, remove from pot and let cool.
- ❖ Place dill on the bottom of the jar, add some onion, a couple of garlic cloves, a few mustard seeds, thyme, and pickling spices.
- ❖ Add cucumbers to the bowl, leaving 2 inches of headspace. Add more garlic and onions on top, then dill.
- ❖ Pour brine over, submerging everything.
- ❖ Seal the jars and place them outside at a warm temperature. You should see bubbles after a few days and unseal them a bit to let the gas out before sealing again.
- ❖ Allow fermenting for about six days. The liquid should become cloudy. After the third day, do a taste test.
- ❖ Throw in the fridge when at the right texture and taste.

Nutrition values: Calories: 100, Total Fats: 9 g, Carbs: 75 g, Protein: 7 g, Fiber: 1 g

LACTO-FERMENTED LETTUCE

Preparation time: 15 minutes
Fermentation time: 3 days
Servings: 4 quarts

Ingredients:

- Lettuce
- Sea salt
- Water

Directions:

- ❖ Wash lettuce and discard any brown leaves.
- ❖ Layer lettuce in a large vessel, sprinkle lightly with salt, and add another layer. For every quart of lettuce, use 2 tbsp salt. Mix and salt all layers and add more salt until you can taste the saltiness.
- ❖ Weigh down the veggies in an open bowl or crock.
- ❖ The brine will begin to form, and the lettuce should be covered in brine after 24 hours. If not, add some brine (one-quart water to one tablespoon of salt). Lettuce should be 2 inches below the brine.
- ❖ Ferment for several days until the right texture and taste are achieved, then move to jars and cold storage.

Nutrition values: Calories: 210, Total Fats: 21 g, Carbs: 9.3 g, Protein: 18 g, Fiber: 0 g

PICKLED ONIONS

Preparation time: 15 minutes
Fermentation time: 3 days
Servings: 4 quarts

Ingredients:

- 3 c. onions, peeled
- 2 tbsp. salt
- 4 c. water

Directions:

- ❖ Prepare the onions and add them to the jar, leaving 1-inch headspace.
- ❖ Combine salt and water and pour into the jar.
- ❖ Seal jar with lid and store in a dark place. Open once a day to release gas before sealing again.
- ❖ Repeat for 3-4 weeks until there are no more bubbles.
- ❖ Store in fridge.

Nutrition values: Calories: 210, Total Fats: 21 g, Carbs: 9.3 g, Protein: 18 g, Fiber: 0 g

PICKLED ZUCCHINI

Preparation time: 15 minutes
Fermentation time: 3 – 5 days
Servings: 4 quarts

Ingredients:

- 5 sterilized canning jars with lids and rings
- 1 extra-large sliced zucchini, peeled and cut into thirds
- 1 sliced onion
- 1 sliced carrot
- 5 peeled and sliced garlic cloves
- 1 bunch of fresh dill, chopped
- 15 whole allspice berries
- 5 bay leaves
- 15 whole black peppercorns
- ½ oz. mustard seed

For the Brine:

- 32 oz. water
- 8 oz. white vinegar
- 1 oz. salt
- 10 oz. superfine sugar

Directions:

- ❖ Remove seeds from the zucchini and slice into thin strips
- ❖ Sterilize jars following the canning method.
- ❖ Evenly distribute onion, carrot, garlic, and dill between the jars. Add zucchini to the jars and pack vertically.
- ❖ Evenly distribute peppercorns, berries, mustard, and bay leaves in the jars.
- ❖ Pour brine ingredients into a pan and bring to a boil. Stir for 1-2 minutes until sugar and salt dissolve.
- ❖ Remove brine from heat and spoon into jars, leaving ¼" of space at the top.
- ❖ Seal jars according to the method for canning

Nutrition values: Calories: 100, Total Fats: 9 g, Carbs: 75 g, Protein: 7 g, Fiber: 1 g

REFRIGERATOR RAINBOW CARROT PICKLES

Preparation time: 15 minutes
Fermentation time: 3 – 5 days
Servings: 4 quarts

Ingredients:

- 32 oz. Multi-colored carrots, scrubbed but not peeled
- ⅓ oz. White sugar
- ⅔ oz. pickling salt, divided
- ½ tsp. whole cloves
- 8 oz. water
- 12 oz. white wine vinegar
- 4 oz. honey

Directions:

- ❖ Rinse carrots and drain. Slice carrots in ⅛" thick medallions and discard the tops.
- ❖ Place carrots in a colander placed in a large bowl. Pour sugar and one teaspoon of salt into the carrots and toss. Let the mixture sit for 1 hour, rinse and drain.
- ❖ Place cloves in a non-reactive 96-ounce pot on medium heat. Shake the pan for 1 minute until cloves are fragrant.
- ❖ Slowly pour water into the pot. Add vinegar, honey, and the rest of the salt to the mixture and stir. Bring to a boil.
- ❖ Add carrots and cook for 8 minutes, often stirring, until mixture returns to a simmer.
- ❖ Scoop carrots into sterilized jars and pack them into the jars. Pour brine over the carrots, leaving ½" of space on the top of the jar. Apply and seal lids.
- ❖ Place in the refrigerator for 24-48 hours before serving.
- ❖ Stores for one month in the refrigerator.

Nutrition values: Calories: 188, Total Fat: 8.5 g, Saturated Fat: 3 g , Cholesterol: 102 mg , Sodium: 115 mg, Total Carbs: 20.2 g, Fiber: 2.1 g, Sugar: 14.9 g, Protein: 32.7 g

SPICY DILL AVOCADO PICKLES

Preparation time: 15 minutes
Fermentation time: 3 – 5 days
Servings: 4 quarts

Ingredients:

- 10 oz. distilled white vinegar
- 8 oz. filtered water
- 4 oz. white sugar
- 1 tsp. brown mustard seeds
- 1 tsp. rock salt
- 1 tsp. fresh dill, chopped
- ½ tsp. habanero pepper flakes
- ½ tsp. whole black peppercorns
- 2 habanero peppers
- 1 smashed garlic clove, cut in half
- 2 peeled unripe avocados, sliced into eighths

Directions:

- ❖ Mix vinegar and water in a pan.
- ❖ Add sugar, salt, mustard, dill, pepper, and pepper flakes. Bring mixture to a boil. Stir until sugar and salt dissolve.
- ❖ Remove pan from heat and cool for 15 minutes.
- ❖ Evenly distribute habanero peppers and garlic cloves between 2 jars
- ❖ Pour hot liquid into the jars, leaving ¼" of space at the top
- ❖ Place in the refrigerator for 24-48 hours before using.

Nutrition values: Calories: 188, Total Fat: 8.5 g, Saturated Fat: 3 g , Cholesterol: 102 mg, Sodium: 115 mg, Total Carbs: 20.2 g, Fiber: 2.1 g , Sugar: 14.9 g, Protein: 32.7 g

TANGY PICKLED ONIONS

Preparation time: 15 minutes
Fermentation time: 3 days
Servings: 4 quarts

Ingredients:

- 4 canning jars with lids and rings, 1 pint

- 1 tsp. celery seed
- 1 tsp. yellow mustard seed
- 4 whole allspice berries
- 1 tsp. black peppercorns
- 40 oz. trimmed green onions, trimmed, sliced into 3" pieces
- 24 oz. water
- 24 oz. white vinegar
- ¾ oz. kosher salt

Directions:

- ❖ Combine celery, mustard seeds, peppercorns, and allspice in a bowl and stir well.
- ❖ Evenly distribute spice mixture among the sterilized canning jars.
- ❖ Pack onions in the jars vertically.
- ❖ Combine vinegar, water, and salt in a saucepan and bring to a boil. Pour hot brine into the jars, leaving ½" of space at the top. Seal and process jars.
- ❖ Store jars in a cool dark place for one month before consuming.

Nutrition values: Calories: 188, Total Fat: 8.5 g, Saturated Fat: 3 g , Cholesterol: 102 mg , Sodium: 115 mg, Total Carbs: 20.2 g , Fiber: 2.1 g, Sugar: 14.9 g, Protein: 32.7 g

WHITE KIMCHI

Preparation time: 15 minutes
Fermentation time: 3 days
Servings: 4 quarts

Ingredients:

- 1 head napa cabbage
- 1 ½ oz. salt
- 8 oz. water and more to cover
- 8 oz. white radish, thinly grated
- 2 sliced green onions, cut into thin strips diagonally
- 2 minced garlic cloves
- 2 slices of fresh ginger
- 1 tsp. granulated sugar
- 1 tsp. white vinegar
- 1 tsp. salt
- 3 pinches of dried Korean red pepper threads

Directions:

- ❖ Keeping the leaves attached, slice cabbage along the length and then into quarters.
- ❖ Rinse cold water and sprinkle 1 ½ ounce of salt between the cabbage leaves.
- ❖ Put cabbage in a bowl and pour in enough water to cover. Let the cabbage stand for 5 hours until the leaves are tender.
- ❖ Place salted cabbage in a colander and rinse with cold water 4-5 times. Drain in the colander for 20 minutes.

- ❖ Mix 8 ounces of water, onions, radish, ginger, garlic, and sugar. Also, add one teaspoon of salt, vinegar, and pepper threads to a large bowl.
- ❖ Distribute radish mixture between the cabbage leaves except for the large outer leaves.
- ❖ Reserve juice from the radish mix.
- ❖ Peel each large outer leaf, but leave it attached to the core.
- ❖ Fold the inner leaves of the cabbage in half.
- ❖ Wrap the outer leaf around the inner leaves and pack them into the sterilized canning jars.
- ❖ Pour the juice into the jars, leaving ¼" of space at the top.
- ❖ Seal jars and store them at room temperature for 24 hours.
- ❖ Slice cabbage into 2" pieces.

Nutrition values: Carbs: 250.86 g, Fat: 1.9 g, Protein: 7.09 g, Calories: 971

LEMONY PICKLED MUSHROOMS

Preparation time: 15 minutes
Fermentation time: 3 days
Servings: 4 quarts

Ingredients:

- 24 oz. sliced fresh mushrooms
- 4 sprigs of fresh thyme
- ½ thinly sliced serrano pepper

For the Brine:

- 8 oz. white wine
- 4 oz. water
- 1 ¼ oz. kosher salt
- ½ oz. white sugar
- 4 thinly sliced cloves of garlic
- 20 whole black peppercorns
- 12 coriander seeds
- 3 x 1" strips lemon zest

Directions:

- ❖ Fill sterilized jars with mushrooms leaving ¼ of the jars empty at the top. Top with a sprig of thyme and pepper slices.
- ❖ Combine the rest of the ingredients in a small pan on medium-low heat. Simmer for 5 minutes until sugar dissolves. Stir occasionally. Remove the pan from heat and pour the mixture into each jar evenly.
- ❖ Seal and process jars. Store in the refrigerator for two days before consuming.

Nutrition values: Calories: 376, Fat: 16 g, Carb: 22 g, Proteins: 35 g

PICKLED TURNIPS

Preparation time: 15 minutes
Fermentation time: 3 days

Servings: 4 quarts

Ingredients:

- 2 peeled turnips, cut into ½" wedges
- 1 thinly sliced small beet
- 2 chopped cloves of garlic
- 8 oz. distilled white vinegar
- 8 oz. water
- 1 tsp. sea salt
- 1 tsp. white sugar

Directions:

- ❖ Evenly divide beet, turnip, and garlic between two mason jars (16 ounces)
- ❖ Divide turnips, garlic, and beet between two 16-ounce Mason jars.
- ❖ Bring sugar, water, and vinegar to a boil in a pan and boil for 2-3 minutes. Remove the pan from heat and pour the hot liquid over the mixture in the jars. Leave ½" of headspace.
- ❖ Seal and process jars. Store in the refrigerator for one week before consuming.

Nutrition values: Calories: 376, Fat: 16 g, Carb: 22 g, Proteins: 35 g

REMADE PICKLES

Preparation time: 15 minutes
Fermentation time: 3 days
Servings: 4 quarts

Ingredients:

- 32 oz. Polish dill pickles, slice into thick pieces
- 16 oz. white sugar
- 4 oz. cider vinegar
- 2 oz. brown sugar, packed
- 2 oz. cold water
- ½ oz. pickling spice

Directions:

Transfer pickle slices back to the original jar.

- ❖ Combine the rest of the ingredients in a saucepan and bring to a boil. Cook and stir for 2 minutes until a syrup forms.
- ❖ Pour syrup over the pickles in the jar and cool to room temperature. Place lid on jar and store in the refrigerator for two weeks before consuming.

Nutrition values: Calories: 376, Fat: 16 g, Carb: 22 g, Proteins: 35 g

BLACK-EYED PEAS

Preparation time: 15 minutes
Fermentation time: 3 days
Servings: 4 quarts

Ingredients:

- 1 ½ lb. dried black-eyed peas, soaked overnight and drained
- 6 tbsp. onions, chopped
- 4 tsp. dried thyme
- 1 ½ tsp. kosher salt
- 30 peppercorns

Directions:

- ❖ Add black-eyed peas and enough water to cover over high heat in a Dutch oven and cook until boiling.
- ❖ Now set the heat to low and cook for about 30 minutes.
- ❖ Drain the black-eyed peas, reserving cooking liquid.
- ❖ In 3 (1-pint) hot sterilized jars, divide the black-eyed peas, onion, thyme, salt, and peppercorn.
- ❖ Fill each jar with hot cooking liquid, leaving a 1-inch space from the top.
- ❖ Run a knife around the inside of each jar to remove any air bubbles.
- ❖ Wipe any trace of food off the rims of jars with a clean, moist kitchen towel.
- ❖ Close each jar with a lid and screw on the ring.
- ❖ Carefully place the jars in the pressure canner and process at 10 pounds pressure for about 75 minutes.
- ❖ Remove the jars from the pressure canner and place them onto a wood surface several inches apart to cool completely.
- ❖ After cooling with your finger, press the top of each jar's lid to ensure the seal is tight.
- ❖ Store these canning jars in a cool, dark place.

Nutrition values: Calories: 116, Total Fat: 2.2 g, Saturated Fat: 1.1 g, Cholesterol: 51 mg, Sodium: 87 mg, Total Carbs: 2.3 g, Fiber: 0.6 g, Sugar: 1.1 g, Protein: 19.7 g

GREEN BEANS

Preparation time: 15 minutes
Fermentation time: 3 days
Servings: 4 quarts

Ingredients:

- 2 lb. green beans per quart
- Water
- Salt (optional)
- Ball glass preserving jars with lids and bands

*To ensure safe processing, simultaneously process at least 2-quart jars or 4-pint jars in the pressure canner.

Directions:

- ❖ Prepare pressure canner. Heat jars in simmering water until ready for use. Do not boil. Wash lids in warm soapy water and set bands aside.
- ❖ Wash and rinse beans thoroughly. Remove string, trim ends, and break or cut freshly gathered beans into 2-inch pieces. Place prepared beans in a large

saucepan and cover with boiling water. Boil for 5 minutes.

- ❖ Pack hot beans into hot jars, leaving 1-inch headspace. Add one teaspoon of salt to each quart jar or ½ a teaspoon to each pint jar, if desired.
- ❖ Ladle boiling water over beans leaving 1-inch headspace. Remove air bubbles. Wipe rim. Center hot lid on jar. Apply band and adjust until fit is fingertip tight.
- ❖ Process filled jars in a pressure canner at 10 pounds pressure, 20 minutes for pints, and 25 minutes for quarts, adjusting for altitude. Remove jars and cool. Check lids for seal after 24 hours. The lid should not flex up and down when the center is pressed.

TIP: The processing time given applies only to young, tender pods. Beans that have almost reached the "shell-out" stage require a longer time for processing. Increase processing time by 15 minutes for pints and 20 minutes for quarts.

Nutrition values: Carbohydrates: 33.16 g, Fat: 0.91g, Protein: 6.35 g, Calories: 168

SWEET & SOUR BEANS

Preparation time: 15 minutes
Fermentation time: 3 days
Servings: 4 quarts

Ingredients:

- 1 lb. navy beans
- ½ c. leeks, chopped
- 2 c. water
- 2 c. ketchup
- 1 c. maple syrup
- ½ c. molasses
- 2 tbsp. brown sugar
- 1½ tsp. mustard powder
- Salt and ground black pepper, as needed
- ½ c. white vinegar

Directions:

- ❖ Add beans and enough water to cover over high heat in a Dutch oven and cook until boiling.
- ❖ Remove the pan of beans from heat and set aside, covered for about 30–45 minutes.
- ❖ Drain the beans, and then add enough fresh water to cover.
- ❖ Add the leeks and cook for about 15–20 minutes.
- ❖ Remove the pan of beans from heat and drain water.
- ❖ In a nonreactive saucepan, add two cups of water and remaining ingredients (except for vinegar) and bring to a gentle boil, stirring continuously.
- ❖ Remove the pan of the cooking mixture from heat and stir in vinegar.
- ❖ In 4 (1-pint) hot sterilized jars, divide the beans.

- ❖ Fill each jar with hot vinegar, leaving a 1-inch space from the top.
- ❖ Run a knife around the inside of each jar to remove any air bubbles.
- ❖ Wipe any trace of food off the rims of jars with a clean, moist kitchen towel.
- ❖ Close each jar with a lid and screw on the ring.
- ❖ Carefully place the jars in the pressure canner and process at 10 pounds pressure for about 75 minutes.
- ❖ Remove the jars from the pressure canner and place them onto a wood surface several inches apart to cool completely.
- ❖ After cooling with your finger, press the top of each jar's lid to ensure the seal is tight.
- ❖ Store these canning jars in a cool, dark place.

Nutrition values: Calories: 188, Total Fat: 8.5 g, Saturated Fat: 3 g , Cholesterol: 102 mg, Sodium: 115 mg, Total Carbs: 20.2 g, Fiber: 2.1 g, Sugar: 14.9 g, Protein: 32.7 g

CORN RELISH

Preparation time: 15 minutes
Fermentation time: 3 days
Servings: 4 quarts

Ingredients:

- 9 c. fresh sweet corn
- 2 c. chopped onions
- 1 c. chopped green peppers
- ½ c. chopped red peppers
- 1 c. sugar
- 2 tbsp. Salt
- 1 ½ tbsp. Celery seed
- 1 ½ tbsp. Mustard seed
- 1 tbsp. Turmeric
- 3 c. cider vinegar

Directions:

- ❖ Cut corn from ears. Remove stems, seeds, and ribs from peppers. Combine chopped vegetables, sugar, salt, spices, and vinegar.
- ❖ Bring to a boil. Cover and simmer for 15 minutes, occasionally stirring to prevent scorching.
- ❖ Ladle hot relish into hot, sterilized jars, leaving ¼ inch of headspace. Wipe the jar's rim, set a warm lid, and tighten.
- ❖ Place in a bath canner with boiling water and process for 15 minutes.

Nutrition values: Calories: 21, Fat: 0.2 g, Carbs: 4.7 g, Protein: 0 g

BACON BEANS

Preparation time: 15 minutes
Fermentation time: 3 days
Servings: 4 quarts

Ingredients:

- 3 slices of thick-cut bacon
- 2 pints of canned green beans

Directions:

- Boil green beans in water for 10 minutes, then drain.
- Fry bacon until crispy in a skillet over medium-high heat.
- Remove bacon and reserve about half of the grease.
- Chop bacon finely and return to skillet.
- Add drained beans to skillet and cook for 5 minutes, stirring and tossing.

Nutrition values: Calories: 129.3, Fat: 4.7 g, Carbs: 1.3 g, Protein: 8.7 g

SPLIT PEA SOUP

Preparation time: 15 minutes
Fermentation time: 3 days
Servings: 4 quarts

Ingredients:

- 1 lb. Yellow, dry split peas
- 2 qts. Water
- 4 tsp. Lime juice
- ¾ c. peeled and sliced carrots
- 1 c. peeled and chopped onions
- 2 cloves of garlic peeled, minced
- ½ tsp. Cayenne pepper
- 1 tsp. Cumin seed and coriander
- 1 tsp. Salt
- 1 tsp. Sugar (optional)

Directions:

- Allow the water with split peas to boil in a large stockpot. Let it gently simmer without cover until the peas become soft; this will take about an hour.
- Add the remaining ingredients and allow it to continue simmering for 30 minutes more. Check the consistency and thin out the water if necessary.
- Ladle it into jars and leave a headspace of 1 inch. Put a cap on and seal.
- Put it in a canner with hot water of 2-3 inches and allow a processing time of 90 minutes at high pressure.

Nutrition values: Calories: 158, Fat: 2.8 g, Carbs: 26 g, Protein: 8.3 g

CANNED DILL GREEN BEANS

Preparation time: 15 minutes
Fermentation time: 3 days
Servings: 4 quarts

Ingredients:

- 5 c. water
- 5 c. cider vinegar
- ½ c. pickling salt
- Garlic
- Dill seed
- Mustard seed
- Red pepper flakes
- 4 lb. yellow or green beans

Directions:

- Boil water with pickling salt and vinegar to form a brine.
- Add ½ a teaspoon of dill seed, ¼ teaspoon of red pepper flakes, one clove of garlic, and ½ a teaspoon of mustard seed to each jar.
- Fill jars, packed tightly, with beans; leave 1-inch space at the top.
- Pour boiling brine over beans to the top of the jar.
- Close lids and place them into the pressure canner.
- Place on rack in the pressure canner and fill to just below the rings of the jars with hot water.
- Close and heat to boiling, then put the weighted pressure gauge on top of the canner and reduce heat.
- Process at 11psi for 5 to 10 minutes.
- Let cool to room temperature.

Nutrition values: Calories: 60, Fat: 0 g, Carbs: 0 g, Protein: 1.1 g

CHICKPEAS

Preparation time: 15 minutes
Fermentation time: 3 days
Servings: 4 quarts

Ingredients:

- 1 lb. dried chickpeas, soaked for 18 hours and drained
- 1 tsp. salt

Directions:

- Add beans and enough water to cover over high heat in a Dutch oven and cook until boiling.
- Now set the heat to low and cook for about 30 minutes.
- Drain the chickpeas, reserving cooking liquid.
- In 2 (1-pint) hot sterilized jars, divide the chickpeas and sprinkle with salt.
- Fill each jar with hot cooking liquid, leaving a 1-inch space from the top.
- Run a knife around the inside of each jar to remove any air bubbles.
- Wipe any trace of food off the rims of jars with a clean, moist kitchen towel.
- Close each jar with a lid and screw on the ring.

- Carefully place the jars in the pressure canner and process at 10 pounds pressure for about 90 minutes.
- Remove the jars from the pressure canner and place them onto a wood surface several inches apart to cool completely.
- After cooling with your finger, press the top of each jar's lid to ensure the seal is tight.
- Store these canning jars in a cool, dark place.

Nutrition values: Calories: 100, Total Fats: 9 g, Carbs: 75 g, Protein: 7 g, Fiber: 1g

DILL PICKLES

Preparation time: 15 minutes
Fermentation time: 3 days
Servings: 4 quarts

Ingredients:

- 4 c. water
- 3 c. vinegar
- 12 heads of fresh dill and leaves
- 4 lb. of pickling cucumbers
- 8 cloves of garlic, peeled (optional)
- 8 small hot chili peppers (optional)
- ¼ c. pickling salt
- 4 tsp. mixed pickling spice

Directions:

- First, start by scrubbing the cucumbers thoroughly and cutting about ¼ inch slice off the blossom end.
- Then, prepare the preserving jars.
- Add water and vinegar into the saucepan and bring to a boil
- Reduce heat but keep it at a simmer
- Work on one jar at a time. Add three dill heads, some leaves, two garlic cloves, two hot peppers, one tablespoon of salt, and one teaspoon of pickling spice to the jar.
- Pack the cucumbers in the jar, wedge them in so none of them floats to the top, and give it one inch of head space. Then, pour in the hot vinegar solution, giving it about ¼ inch of headspace.
- Repeat with other jars. Process for 15 minutes.
- You should have four 1-quart jars.

Nutrition values: Calories: 22, Carbohydrates: 2 g, Sodium: 1,578 mg, Potassium: 151 mg, Sugar: 1 g

GREEN GARLIC BEANS

Preparation time: 15 minutes
Fermentation time: 3 days
Servings: 4 quarts

Ingredients:

- 3 tbsp. Olive oil
- 1 tbsp. Butter
- 1 sliced head of peeled garlic
- ¼ c. grated Parmesan
- 30 oz. Canned green beans, drained

Directions:

- Melt butter with olive oil in a skillet over medium heat.
- Cook garlic for 1 minute in a skillet.
- Add green beans and cook for 10 minutes.

Nutrition values: Calories: 72, Fat: 2.7 g, Carbs: 0 g, Protein: 2 g

KIDNEY BEANS CHILI

Preparation time: 15 minutes
Fermentation time: 3 days
Servings: 4 quarts

Ingredients

- 3 c. dried red kidney beans, soaked overnight and drained
- 1 tbsp. salt
- 2 c. onion, chopped
- 1 c. sweet bell pepper, seeded and chopped
- 6 garlic cloves, minced
- ¼ c. fresh parsley, minced
- 8 c. tomato juice
- ½ c. tomato paste
- 3 tbsp. red chili powder
- 1 tsp. ground black pepper
- 2 tsp. dried thyme
- 2 tsp. ground cumin

Directions:

- Add beans and enough water to cover over high heat in a Dutch oven and cook until boiling.
- Now set the heat to low and cook for about 30 minutes.
- Drain the beans well.

For the sauce:

- Add remaining ingredients over medium heat and cook until boiling in a saucepan.
- Stir in the cooked beans and cook until boiling.
- In 9 (1-pint) hot sterilized jars, divide the beans.

- ❖ Fill each jar with hot sauce, leaving a 1-inch space from the top.
- ❖ Run a knife around the insides of each jar to remove any air bubbles.
- ❖ Wipe any trace of food off the rims of jars with a clean, moist kitchen towel.
- ❖ Close each jar with a lid and screw on the ring.
- ❖ Carefully place the jars in the pressure canner and process at 10 pounds pressure for about 75 minutes.
- ❖ Remove the jars from the pressure canner and place them onto a wood surface several inches apart to cool completely.
- ❖ After cooling with your finger, press the top of each jar's lid to ensure the seal is tight.
- ❖ Store these canning jars in a cool, dark place.

Nutrition values: Calories: 100, Total Fats: 9 g, Carbs: 75 g, Protein: 7 g, Fiber: 1 g

PICKLED CAULIFLOWER

Preparation time: 15 minutes
Fermentation time: 3 days
Servings: 4 quarts

Ingredients:

- 1 tsp. whole cumin seeds
- 2 tsp. whole coriander seeds
- 2 tsp. whole fennel seeds
- 7 c. cauliflowers, split into florets
- 1 c. bell peppers
- 2 c. white wine vinegar
- 2 c. water
- 2 tbsp. pickling salt

Directions:

- ❖ Process 4-pint mason jars
- ❖ Put ¼ tsp cumin, ½ tsp of coriander, and fennel into all four-pint jars. Put the cauliflower and peppers together, and pack tightly into the jars.
- ❖ Put vinegar, water, and salt on a nonreactive pan, then bring up to a boil. Pour the solution over the cauliflower, giving ½ inch headspace.
- ❖ Process the jars in boiling water for 10 minutes.
- ❖ Once done, take out the jars and let cool. Then store in a cool, dark, and dry place for at least three weeks before eating. After consumption, store leftovers in the fridge.

Nutrition values: Calories: 44, Carbohydrates: 6 g, Protein: 2 g, Sodium: 1,781 mg, Potassium: 361 mg, Fiber: 2 g, Sugar: 2 g

PICKLED WILD MUSHROOMS

Preparation time: 15 minutes
Fermentation time: 3 days
Servings: 4 quarts

Ingredients:

- 64 oz. porcini mushrooms, washed and trimmed
- 5 canning jars with lids and rings, 1 pint
- 28 oz. water
- 8 oz. white vinegar
- 1 roughly chopped onion
- ½ oz. superfine sugar
- 1 tsp. salt
- 2 whole allspice berries
- 1 bay leaf
- 6 whole black peppercorns

Directions:

- ❖ Place mushrooms in a large pan and cover with water. Bring water to a boil, remove from heat, and drain.
- ❖ Place mushrooms back in the pan and cover with fresh water. Bring to a boil again, remove from heat again and drain. Slice mushrooms into bite-sized pieces.
- ❖ Pack mushrooms in sterilized jars
- ❖ Combine the rest of the ingredients in a saucepan and bring to a boil. Boil for 5 minutes. Remove the pan from heat and pour the hot liquid over the mushrooms in the jars.
- ❖ Seal and process jars and store them in a cool, dark place for one week before consuming.

Nutrition values: Calories: 138, Total Fat: 0.5 g, Saturated Fat: 0.1 g, Cholesterol: 0 mg, Sodium: 681 mg, Total: 27.1 g, Fiber: 5.9 g, Sugar: 6.3 g, Protein: 8.3 g

SPICY ROSEMARY PICKLED CARROTS

Preparation time: 15 minutes
Fermentation time: 3 days
Servings: 4 quarts

Ingredients:

- 3 c. vinegar
- 3 c. water
- ¼ c. white sugar
- ¼ c. pickling salt/kosher salt
- 2 tbsp. black peppercorns
- 6 cloves of garlic, peeled
- 6 red chili peppers
- 4 lb. carrots, peeled, sliced into 4-inch-long stocks at ½ inch wide
- 6 sprigs of rosemary

Directions:

- ❖ Combine water, sugar, vinegar, salt, and peppercorns in a small pot. Bring to a boil over high heat, reduce the heat to medium, and let simmer for 5 minutes.
- ❖ Add one chili pepper and one clove of garlic into each jar, one at a time.
- ❖ Pack it tightly with carrot stocks and add your rosemary sprig about halfway through.
- ❖ Pour the vinegar solution over the carrots. Give it about ¼ inch of head space.
- ❖ Process for 15 minutes.
- ❖ Remove the jars and let them cool naturally. You should hear the ping as it cools.

Nutrition values: Calories: 58, Carbohydrates: 12 g, Protein: 1 g, Fat: 1 g, Saturated Fat: 1 g, Sodium: 1,480 mg, Potassium: 310 mg, Fiber: 3 g, Sugar: 7 g

TARRAGON PICKLED GREEN BEANS

Preparation time: 15 minutes
Fermentation time: 3 days
Servings: 4 quarts

Ingredients:

- 6 cloves of garlic, thinly sliced
- 36 whole peppercorns, crushed
- 3 lb. green beans, washed and trimmed to 4 inches
- 6 sprigs of fresh tarragon can be substituted with 12 basil sprigs
- 3 ½ c. white wine vinegar, or just white vinegar
- 3 ½ c. water
- 2 tbsp. pickling salt or kosher salt

Directions:

- ❖ Process the lids
- ❖ Then, divide the garlic and peppercorns into 6-pint jars
- ❖ Pack the green beans into the jars tightly and add sprigs of tarragon/basil

- ❖ Heat the water, vinegar, and salt to boil at medium heat. Pour over the green beans in the jars and give it ½ inch headspace.
- ❖ Process for 5 minutes in boiling water. Remove and let cool. You should hear the ping as it cools.

Nutrition values: Calories: 31, Carbohydrates: 6 g, Protein: 1 g, Fat: 1 g, Saturated Fat: 1 g, Sodium: 590 mg, Potassium: 171 mg, Fiber: 2 g, Sugar: 2 g

WHITE BEANS

Preparation time: 15 minutes
Fermentation time: 3 days
Servings: 4 quarts

Ingredients:

- 3 ¼ lb. dried white beans, soaked for 18 hours and drained
- 4 ½ tsp. salt

Directions:

- ❖ Add beans and enough water to cover over high heat in a Dutch oven and cook until boiling.
- ❖ Now set the heat to low and cook for about 30 minutes.
- ❖ Drain the beans, reserving cooking liquid.
- ❖ In 7 (1-pint) hot sterilized jars, divide the beans and sprinkle with salt.
- ❖ Fill each jar with hot cooking liquid, leaving a 1-inch space from the top.
- ❖ Run a knife around the insides of each jar to remove any air bubbles.
- ❖ Wipe any trace of food off the rims of jars with a clean, moist kitchen towel.
- ❖ Close each jar with a lid and screw on the ring.
- ❖ Carefully place the jars in the pressure canner and process at 10 pounds pressure for about 75 minutes.
- ❖ Remove the jars from the pressure canner and place them onto a wood surface several inches apart to cool completely.
- ❖ After cooling with your finger, press the top of each jar's lid to ensure the seal is tight.
- ❖ Store these canning jars in a cool, dark place.

Nutrition values: Calories: 72, Fat: 2.7 g, Carbs: 0 g, Protein: 2 g

ZUCCHINI BREAD AND BUTTER PICKLES

Preparation time: 15 minutes
Fermentation time: 3 days
Servings: 4 quarts

Ingredients:

- 1 c. cider vinegar
- ½ c. honey
- 1 tbsp. mustard seeds
- 1 tsp. celery seeds
- ½ tsp. red chili flakes
- ½ tsp. ground cumin
- 1 tbsp. finely milled sea salt
- 1 lb. young zucchini, thickly sliced
- 1 c. red bell pepper, sliced, seeded
- 1 c. sliced onion

Directions:

- ❖ On a medium saucepan, pour in vinegar and honey. Heat the solution to dissolve the honey, and then add celery, mustard, chili flakes, sea salt, and cumin. Then, bring to a rolling boil before adding zucchini, onion, and red bell pepper.
- ❖ Stir and cook for five minutes until everything is nicely heated.
- ❖ Use a pair of tongs to split the veggies evenly between the jars, then top with the brine. Give it a ½-inch head space.
- ❖ Process for 10 minutes.
- ❖ After that, remove and let cool naturally.
- ❖ Leave it for 24 hours before storing it in a cool, dark, and dry place. Allow it seven days before consumption or storage.

Nutrition values: Calories: 68, Carbohydrates: 15 g, Protein: 1 g, Sodium: 588 mg, Potassium: 172 mg, Fiber: 1 g, Sugar: 13 g

PICKLED BEETS

Preparation time: 15 minutes
Fermentation time: 3 days
Servings: 4 quarts

Ingredients:

- 2 c. water
- 2 c. white vinegar
- 2 c. sugar
- 1 tsp. salt
- 3 ½ lb. dark red beets
- 1-2 yellow or white onions

Directions:

- ❖ Wash the beets and place them in a large kettle covered with water. Bring to a boil and let them cook until tender. You know they're ready when

you can insert the knife with just a bit of resistance. Test and remove individually.
- ❖ After they're cooked, drain, let cool and use a knife to remove the skin.
- ❖ On the stove, combine the water, white vinegar, sugar, and salt, and bring to a simmer.
- ❖ Start a large kettle with water on high heat to process your jars.
- ❖ Slice up the onions and beets and put them in the jar. Make sure there are onions on top of the beets. Give it about ½-inch of headspace.
- ❖ Bring the brine to a hard boil, fill the jars, and maintain headspace.
- ❖ Process for 10 minutes.
- ❖ Once done, remove the jars from the kettle and let cool completely and naturally.

Nutrition values: Calories: 68, Carbohydrates: 15 g, Protein: 1 g, Sodium: 588 mg, Potassium: 172 mg, Fiber: 1 g, Sugar: 13 g

PICKLED ASPARAGUS

Preparation time: 15 minutes
Fermentation time: 3 days
Servings: 4 quarts

Ingredients:

- 3 tbsp. canning salt
- ¼ c. honey
- 3 ¼ c. water
- 4 c. white vinegar
- 3 lb. fresh asparagus
- 1 clove of garlic
- ½ tsp. turmeric
- ½ tsp. red pepper flakes
- 1 tsp. whole coriander seeds
- 1 tsp. mustard seeds

Directions:

- ❖ Combine water, vinegar, honey, and salt in a 4-quart kettle. Bring to a boil and then reduce to a simmer.
- ❖ Add the garlic turmeric, red pepper flakes, coriander seeds, and mustard seed into each jar. Trim the asparagus as needed, at ½ headspace.
- ❖ Add the hot brine to cover the asparagus, keeping the same headspace.
- ❖ Process for 15 minutes.
- ❖ Then, remove your jars and let cool for 12 hours before consumption or storage. Good up to a year.

Nutrition values: Calories: 138, Total Fat: 0.5 g, Saturated Fat: 0.1 g, Cholesterol: 0 mg, Sodium: 681 mg, Total: 27.1 g, Fiber: 5.9 g, Sugar: 6.3 g, Protein: 8.3 g

CUCAMELON PICKLES

Preparation time: 15 minutes

Fermentation time: 3 days
Servings: 4 quarts

Ingredients:

- 20 oz. cucamelons
- 2 green chile peppers, cut in half with seeds removed
- 2 sprigs of fresh dill
- ½ oz. yellow mustard seeds
- ½ oz. dill seed
- ⅓ oz. crushed black peppercorns
- 6 oz. water
- 6 oz. apple cider vinegar
- ½ oz. coarse salt

Directions:

- ❖ Sterilize a jar and combine melon, peppers, dill, mustard, dill seeds, and peppercorns in the jar.
- ❖ Bring water, salt, and vinegar to a boil in a pan, stirring for 1 minute until salt dissolves.
- ❖ Remove pan from heat and cool.
- ❖ Pour hot liquid into the jar until cucamelons are covered completely. Before consuming, seal the jar and leave it for 3-4 days in a cool, dark place.

Nutrition values: Calories: 18, Carbohydrates: 2.9 g, Sodium: 839.3 mg, Potassium: 4.9 mg, Fiber: 0.1 g, Sugar: 2.8 g

EASY PICKLED RADISHES

Preparation time: 15 minutes
Fermentation time: 3 days
Servings: 4 quarts

Ingredients:

- 4 oz. water
- 4 oz. rice vinegar
- 4 oz. white sugar
- 1 tsp. salt
- 12 oz. thinly sliced radishes

Directions:

- ❖ Combine water, vinegar, salt, and sugar in a microwaveable bowl. Heat on high for 90 seconds, stirring every 30 seconds until sugar dissolves completely.
- ❖ Place radishes in a jar and pour the hot liquid over the radishes. Let stand for 2-4 hours before eating.

Nutrition values: Calories: 40, Carbohydrates: 8.2 g, Protein: 1.2g, Potassium: 266.4 mg, Fiber: 1.3 g, Sugar: 4.7 g

PICKLED CURRY CAULIFLOWER

Preparation time: 15 minutes
Fermentation time: 3 days
Servings: 4 quarts

Ingredients:

- 1 ½ tbsp. canning salt
- 4 c. vinegar
- 3 c. water
- 3 tsp. cumin seeds
- 3 tsp. turmeric
- 3 tsp. curry powder
- 5 lb. cauliflower
- 6 Serrano peppers

Directions:

- ❖ With a 4-quart kettle, combine the water, salt, and vinegar. Bring to a simmer over medium-low heat and whisk to help dissolve the salt. Keep hot until ready to use.
- ❖ Pack jars with cauliflower. Add ½ teaspoon of cumin seeds, turmeric, curry flower, and 1 Serrano pepper into each jar.
- ❖ Pour hot brine into the jars, leaving ½ inch headspace.
- ❖ Process for 12 minutes.
- ❖ Remove from water and let cool for 12 hours.

Nutrition values: Calories: 34, Carbohydrates: 5.3 g, Protein: 2 g, Fat: 0.4 g, Saturated Fat: 0.1 g, Polyunsaturated Fat: 0.1 g, Sodium: 467.2 mg, Potassium: 303.5 mg, Fiber: 2.2 g, Sugar: 1.9 g

PICKLED PICO DE GALLO JICAMA

Preparation time: 15 minutes
Fermentation time: 3 days
Servings: 4 quarts

Ingredients:

- 36 oz. water
- 8 oz. white vinegar
- 2 ½ oz. pickling salt
- 3 juiced Key limes
- 1 oz. pico de gallo seasoning mix

- 4 canning jars with lids and rings, 1 pint
- 1 large peeled jicama, sliced into matchsticks
- 1 sliced Key lime, cut into eight pieces

Directions:

- ❖ Combine vinegar, water, pickling salt, lime juice, and seasoning mix in a large saucepan and bring to a boil. Stir and boil until salt dissolves.
- ❖ Sterilize jars. Pack jicama and slices of lime in the jars. Pour hot liquid into the jars and seal. Process and store in a cool, dark place for two weeks before eating.

Nutrition values: Calories: 18, Carbohydrates: 2.9 g, Sodium: 839.3 mg, Potassium: 4.9 mg, Fiber: 0.1 g, Sugar: 2.8 g

PICKLED SALAD

Preparation time: 15 minutes
Fermentation time: 3 days
Servings: 4 quarts

Ingredients:

- 8 diced zucchinis
- 4 diced cucumbers
- 1 diced sweet onion
- 2 diced red bell pepper
- 2 diced green bell pepper
- 2 minced jalapeno peppers
- 8 oz. of sea salt
- Enough water to cover
- 16 oz. white sugar
- 16 oz. rice vinegar
- 4 oz. white vinegar
- ⅓ oz. ground turmeric
- ⅓ oz. yellow mustard seed
- 1 tsp. dried rosemary
- 1 tsp. garlic powder
- 1 tsp. onion powder
- 12 canning jars with lids and rings, 1 pint

Directions:

- ❖ Combine zucchini, onion, cucumber, bell peppers, and jalapenos in a large bowl and toss. Add salt and enough water to cover, wrap the bowl in plastic, and chill in the freezer overnight. Then drain and rinse vegetables in a colander.
- ❖ Combine the rest of the ingredients in a large stock pot and bring to a boil.
- ❖ Sterilize jars and pack vegetables evenly in the jars. Pour the brine over the vegetables and seal, and process.
- ❖ Store in a cool, dark place for 2-4 days before consuming.

Nutrition values: Calories: 18, Carbohydrates: 2.9 g, Sodium: 839.3 mg, Potassium: 4.9 mg, Fiber: 0.1 g, Sugar: 2.8 g

QUICK PICKLED RADISHES

Preparation time: 15 minutes
Fermentation time: 3 days
Servings: 4 quarts

Ingredients:

- 10 thinly sliced radishes
- 5 ½ oz. white wine vinegar
- 2 ½ oz. water
- 1 star anise pod
- ½ oz. white sugar
- 1 tsp. salt
- ½ tsp. black peppercorns
- ½ tsp. cumin seed

Directions:

- ❖ Place radishes in a canning jar.
- ❖ Combine vinegar and water in a pan on medium heat and whisk in sugar and salt for 5 minutes until dissolved.
- ❖ Remove the pan from heat and add the rest of the ingredients.
- ❖ Stir and let stand for 5-10 minutes to cool.
- ❖ Pour hot liquid over the radish in the jar. Seal the jar and cool radishes to room temperature. Put in the refrigerator overnight before eating.

Nutrition values: Calories: 188, Total Fat: 8.5 g, Saturated Fat: 3 g, Cholesterol: 102 mg, Sodium: 115 mg, Total Carbs: 20.2 g, Fiber: 2.1 g, Sugar: 14.9 g, Protein: 32.7 g

SPICY DILL PICKLES

Preparation time: 15 minutes
Fermentation time: 3 days
Servings: 4 quarts

Ingredients:

- ½ tsp. red pepper flakes
- 10 cloves of garlic, peeled and smashed
- 5 tsp. dill seed, separated
- 2 tbsp. canning salt
- 3 tbsp. honey
- 4 c. water
- 1 c. white vinegar
- 3 c. apple cider vinegar
- 11 lb. cucumber

Directions:

- ❖ Combine both kinds of vinegar, honey, salt, and water. Bring to a boil, then reduce to a simmer.
- ❖ Cut ½ inch off each end of the cucumbers and discard. Slice ¼-inch slices and set aside. If you are not using fresh cucumber, soak in ice water for 2 hours.
- ❖ Add one smashed garlic clove and one hot pepper or ½ red pepper flakes to each jar. Pack cucumbers in and give it ½ inch headspace. Add ½ teaspoon dill seed on top.
- ❖ Pour brine over, giving the same headspace.
- ❖ Process your jars in boiling water for 10 minutes.
- ❖ Remove and let cool naturally for 12 hours. Then, store in a dark and dry place for two weeks before consumption or storage.

Nutrition values: Calories: 40, Carbohydrates: 8.2 g, Protein: 1.2g, Potassium: 266.4 mg, Fiber: 1.3 g, Sugar: 4.7 g

WATER KIMCHI

Preparation time: 15 minutes
Fermentation time: 3 days
Servings: 4 quarts

Ingredients:

- ½ sliced napa cabbage, cut into 1" pieces
- 1 tsp. sea salt
- ½ tsp. Korean red pepper powder
- 40 oz. water
- ½ oz. sweet rice flour
- ½ yellow onion, chopped
- ½ peeled and cored Asian pear, thinly sliced
- 3 sliced green onions, 1" pieces
- 6 sliced cloves of garlic
- 3 pieces of fresh ginger, sliced
- ¼ tsp. Splenda

Directions:

- ❖ Sprinkle cabbage and red pepper powder over cabbage in a large bowl. Toss to coat and let stand for 1-2 hours until cabbage is wilted.
- ❖ Combine water and flour in a large stockpot and bring to a boil. Boil for 5 minutes. Remove pot from heat and let stand for 5-10 minutes.

- ❖ Mix onion, pear, and green onions in a 64-ounce jar. Add cabbage, ginger, garlic, and Splenda. Pour the water and flour mixture into the jar and seal. Let stand at room temperature for two days before consuming. Store in refrigerator once opened.

Nutrition values: Calories: 18, Carbohydrates: 2.9 g, Sodium: 839.3 mg, Potassium: 4.9 mg, Fiber: 0.1 g, Sugar: 2.8 g

PICKLED CABBAGE AND PEPPER

Preparation time: 15 minutes
Fermentation time: 3 days
Servings: 4 quarts

Ingredients:

- 2 finely shredded heads of cabbage
- 1 ½ oz. salt
- 32 oz. water
- 32 oz. vinegar
- 12 oz. white sugar
- 8 oz. vegetable oil
- ½ oz. turmeric, ground
- ½ oz. celery seed
- ½ oz. mustard seeds
- 10 chopped onions
- 10 chopped sweet red peppers

Directions:

- ❖ Put cabbage in a large non-reactive bowl and sprinkle with salt. Toss the mixture, cover the bowl with wrap, and chill in the refrigerator overnight.
- ❖ Place cabbage in a colander and drain excess liquid.
- ❖ Mix vinegar, water, oil, sugar, celery, turmeric, and mustard seeds in a large stockpot. Bring mixture to a boil. Add cabbage, onions, and sweet peppers to the pot and bring back up to a boil. Reduce heat and simmer the mixture for 45 minutes until the vegetables are tender.
- ❖ Transfer mixture to sterilized jars and seal and process. Store in a cool, dark area.

Nutrition values: Calories: 40, Carbohydrates: 8.2 g, Protein: 1.2g, Potassium: 266.4 mg, Fiber: 1.3 g, Sugar: 4.7 g

CHAPTER 4

MEAT AND FISH RECIPES

CURED FERMENTED BEEF

Preparation time: 15 minutes
Fermentation time: 3 days
Servings: 4 quarts

Ingredients:

- 1 lb. ground beef
- 3.5 lb. cooked, sliced pork skin
- ½ tsp. salt or to taste
- 2 – 3 cloves garlic, peeled
- A handful of Vietnamese cilantro leaves
- 1 package of Nam powder seasoning mix
- 3 tbsp. sugar
- Crushed black pepper to taste
- Thai chili to taste

Equipment:

- Pan
- Large bowl

Directions:

- ❖ Add pork skin and ⅛ teaspoon of salt into a pan. Place the pan over medium flame and cook for a couple of minutes. Turn off the heat and rinse the skin in cold water. Shake the skin to remove extra water.
- ❖ Add the skin into a bowl. Add beef, sugar, pepper, and seasoning mix and mix well.
- ❖ Cover and set aside for 24 hours. The color of the meat will change to brown in 24 hours.
- ❖ Line a baking pan with cling wrap. Spread the meat mixture in the pan and spread it well. Wrap the meat with cling wrap. Spread it evenly with your hands.
- ❖ Place something heavy on the wrapped meat and set it aside for 24 hours.
- ❖ Unwrap the meat. Chop into bite-size pieces.
- ❖ Slice the garlic and chili into thin slices. Chop the cilantro into small pieces.
- ❖ Combine garlic, cilantro, and chili in a bowl and mix well.
- ❖ Add the chopped meat to the bowl and toss until the meat is well coated with the mixture.
- ❖ You can make the same recipe using ground pork instead of ground beef.

Nutritional values: Calories: 18, Carbohydrates: 2.9 g, Sodium: 839.3 mg, Potassium: 4.9 mg, Fiber: 0.1 g, Sugar: 2.8 g

MEAT GARUM

Preparation time: 15 minutes
Fermentation time: 3 days
Servings: 4 quarts

Ingredients:

- 1.1 lb. lean meat, cut into pieces such that it fits in the meat grinder
- 1 ¾ c. of water
- 4.2 oz. kosher salt
- 3.5 oz. koji rice

Equipment:

- Meat grinder
- Fermentation container with lid
- Dehydrator
- Storage jar
- Cheesecloth

Directions:

- ❖ Combine meat and koji rice and add to the meat grinder. Grind the meat and add to a bowl. Add salt and mix well.
- ❖ Add water and mix until well combined. Transfer the mixture into the fermentation container. Press the mixture onto the bottom of the container.
- ❖ Close the lid and place the container in the dehydrator. Adjust the temperature to 140° F. Check every few hours and remove any fat that floats. Do this for the initial seven days and every week after that until you will not find any fat floating. You may need to skim off the fat for about three weeks.
- ❖ Once there is no fat floating, after about 1 – 2 days, tiny bubbles will be visible in the meat. This means that fermentation has started. Strain the garum after 70 days using a wire mesh strainer and place the liquid in the refrigerator. Skim off any fat that is floating.
- ❖ Line the strainer with cheesecloth. Strain the mixture once again. Transfer into the storage jar. Make sure to label the jar with the name and date of preparation.
- ❖ Refrigerate until use.

Nutrition values: Calories: 188, Total Fat: 8.5 g, Saturated Fat: 3 g, Cholesterol: 102 mg, Sodium: 115 mg, Total Carbs: 20.2 g, Fiber: 2.1 g, Sugar: 14.9 g, Protein: 32.7 g

FERMENTED THAI PORK SAUSAGE

Preparation time: 15 minutes
Fermentation time: 3 days
Servings: 4 quarts

Ingredients:

- 1.1 lb. lean, minced pork meat, trimmed of fat
- 12 – 15 cloves of garlic
- 1 tsp. sugar
- ½ c. cooked, sticky rice
- 6.2 oz. pork skin
- 1 ¼ tbsp. sea salt
- ½ tsp. monosodium glutamate
- 20 bird's eye chilies
- White vinegar to clean
- Rough sea salt to clean

Equipment:

- Meat grinder
- Banana leaves of plastic wrap to wrap the sausages
- Saucepan

Directions:

- ❖ Mince the meat in a meat grinder.
- ❖ Using salt and vinegar, clean the pork skin. Rub the skin very well and rinse under running water.
- ❖ Repeat the previous step a few times until the skin turns smooth.
- ❖ Boil some water in a saucepan and add pork skin to it. Boil until the skin turns clear, and when you pinch it, it should break. This stage should reach in about 30 – 40 minutes.
- ❖ Remove the skin and place it on your cutting board. Cut into thin strips of about 1 ½ inch in length.
- ❖ Add minced pork, garlic, salt, monosodium glutamate, sugar, rice, and pork skin into a bowl and mix until well incorporated.
- ❖ Place the banana leaves (7 – 8 leaves) on your countertop. Divide the sausage mixture into 7 – 8 equal portions and shape into sausages (like a log). Place one sausage on each leaf at the corner, parallel to the tip of the corner. Place a bird's eye chili on each and roll it a couple of rounds. Fold the sides inwards and continue rolling till the end. Place it with the seam side facing down.

- ❖ Ferment it at 85° F for 3 – 5 days and humidity at 50%.

Nutrition values: Calories: 138, Total Fat: 0.5 g, Saturated Fat: 0.1 g, Cholesterol: 0 mg, Sodium: 681 mg, Total: 27.1 g, Fiber: 5.9 g, Sugar: 6.3 g, Protein: 8.3 g

SALMON GRAVLAX

Preparation time: 15 minutes
Fermentation time: 3 days
Servings: 4 quarts

Ingredients:

- 1 ½ lb. salmon fillet, rinsed
- 1 tsp. coriander seeds
- 1 tbsp. fennel seeds
- 3 tbsp. kosher salt
- ¾ oz. vodka
- ½ bunch dill, chopped
- ½ tbsp. freshly ground pepper or to taste
- 1 tbsp. sugar
- 1 tsp. grated lemon zest
- 1 tbsp. chopped cilantro

Directions:

- ❖ Dry the salmon by patting with paper towels.
- ❖ Combine salt, spices, cilantro, dill, vodka, and lemon zest in a bowl.
- ❖ Place two cling wrap sheets stacked on your cutting board. Place the salmon on the center of the sheet with the skin side facing down.
- ❖ Spread the spice mixture over the salmon and wrap the salmon. Wrap more cling wrap over the salmon and place it on a plate. Place something heavy over it.
- ❖ Place the salmon and the weight in the refrigerator for 12 – 16 hours.
- ❖ It is now ready to use. It can last a week but ensure it remains wrapped in the refrigerator.

Nutrition values: Calories: 138, Total Fat: 0.5 g, Saturated Fat: 0.1 g, Cholesterol: 0 mg, Sodium: 681 mg, Total: 27.1 g, Fiber: 5.9 g, Sugar: 6.3 g, Protein: 8.3 g

FERMENTED BEEF JERKY

Preparation time: 15 minutes
Fermentation time: 3 days

Servings: 4 quarts

Ingredients:

- 2 lb. lean beef meat (or turkey or lamb or goat meat), trimmed of fat

For Kombucha Marinade:

- 1 c. wine
- 4 tsp. sea salt or fine salt
- ½ c. organic sugar
- ½ tsp. freshly ground pepper
- 2 tbsp. liquid smoke
- 3 c. kombucha vinegar
- 2 heads of garlic, minced
- ½ c. Worcestershire sauce
- 2 tsp. mustard seeds, slightly cracked
- 2 tsp. oregano
- 2 tsp. basil

Equipment:

- Glass container
- Dehydrator

Directions:

- ❖ If the meat is fresh, place it in the freezer for about an hour. If the meat is frozen, remove it from the freezer and let it sit on your countertop to defrost for 3 hours.
- ❖ To make the marinade: Add wine, sugar, and kombucha vinegar into the glass bowl and stir until sugar has dissolved. Kombucha vinegar is over-processed kombucha tea, i.e., it is fermented for longer than necessary.
- ❖ Add the rest of the ingredients for the marinade and mix well.
- ❖ Trim off the fat from the meat. Cut into ¼-inch slices along the grain.
- ❖ Add the meat into the bowl of marinade and stir well. Cover the bowl and chill for 12 – 15 hours.
- ❖ Transfer the meat into the dehydrator trays, set the temperature to 155° F, and dehydrate until crispy. It should take 14 – 16 hours, depending on the thickness of the slices.
- ❖ Turn the meat slices over for four hours.
- ❖ Alternately, you can place the slices on a baking sheet and bake in the oven at the lowest available setting. If your oven does not have an option of less than 155° F, keep the door slightly ajar while baking.
- ❖ Let the jerky cool completely.
- ❖ Transfer into a glass jar. Make sure to label the jar with the name and date of preparation.

Nutrition values: Calories: 188, Total Fat: 8.5 g, Saturated Fat: 3 g, Cholesterol: 102 mg, Sodium: 115 mg, Total Carbs: 20.2 g, Fiber: 2.1 g, Sugar: 14.9 g, Protein: 32.7 g

FERMENTED LIVER

Preparation time: 15 minutes
Fermentation time: 3 days
Servings: 4 quarts

Ingredients:

- 1 c. chopped chicken liver
- Fermenting liquid from kimchi or sauerkraut or whey liquid or kombucha

Directions:

- ❖ Place the liver in the jar. Pour enough fermenting liquid into the jar to cover the liver.
- ❖ Fasten the lid and place it on your countertop for 24 hours.
- ❖ Refrigerate until use. Make sure to label the jar with the name and date of preparation.

Nutrition values: Calories: 138, Total Fat: 0.5 g, Saturated Fat: 0.1 g, Cholesterol: 0 mg, Sodium: 681 mg, Total: 27.1 g, Fiber: 5.9 g, Sugar: 6.3 g, Protein: 8.3 g

FERMENTED BEEF LIVER PATE

Preparation time: 15 minutes
Fermentation time: 3 days
Servings: 4 quarts

Ingredients:

- 2 lb. raw beef liver
- Rosemary
- Cloves of garlic, peeled
- 2 tsp. Himalayan salt
- 4 tbsp. whey liquid
- 2 egg yolks
- 1 large sweet onion, chopped
- 2 tsp. peppercorns

Equipment:

- Food processor
- Mason's jar

Directions:

- ❖ Add meat, spices, rosemary, yolks, onion, and whey into the food processor and process until smooth.
- ❖ Transfer into the jar. Cover with a plastic lid and place it on your countertop at room temperature for 24 hours.
- ❖ Shift the jar into the refrigerator. Make sure to label the jar with the name and date of preparation.

Nutrition values: Calories: 22, Fat: 18 g, Carb: 0 g, Proteins: 22 g

BASIC SALAMI

Preparation time: 15 minutes
Fermentation time: 3 days
Servings: 4 quarts

Ingredients:

- 2 lb. pork shoulder or wild boar meat
- 0.8 oz. salt
- 1 tsp. sugar
- 1 tbsp. minced garlic
- 2 tbsp. distilled water
- ½ lb. pork fatback
- 0.1 oz. Instacure No.2
- ½ tbsp. coarsely ground pepper
- Red wine
- ½ tsp. FRM=52 starter culture or T-SPX culture

Equipment:

- Hot casings (about 1 ½ inches diameter)
- Bowls
- Meat grinder
- Airtight containers
- Fermentation plastic container
- Sausage stuffer

Directions:

- ❖ Take out about ⅓ pound of pork and finely dice it. The rest of the fat, pork fatback, and meat should be cut into bigger pieces (chop them so they can go into the grinder) and place the fat and meat chunks in different airtight containers (separate containers for the finely diced meat).
- ❖ Sprinkle salt over the meat chunks and toss well. Place the containers in the refrigerator. The sinew and silver skin should be trimmed as well.
- ❖ The following day, place the fat and the grinder parts in the freezer. Add garlic, Instacure, sugar, and ¼ tbsp. into the meat container and toss well. Place this container in the freezer as well. Take out the containers after 1 ½ hours.
- ❖ Now, set up your grinder with the coarse die and add the finely chopped meat into the grinder. Grind the meat and place the meat in a bowl.
- ❖ Fix the fine die and grind the chopped meat. Add it back into the container. Next, grind the chopped fat and add it back into its container. Place the

containers in the freezer once again. Let the fat and meat chill until it is 35°F.
- ❖ In the meantime, add starter culture and distilled water to a bowl. Stir until it dissolves completely.
- ❖ Add the meat, fat, wine, starter mixture, and ¼ tbsp. of pepper into the fermentation container.
- ❖ Mix using your hands for a couple of minutes. Place the container in the refrigerator. Now run the sausage casing under warm water for a couple of minutes.
- ❖ Insert one end of the casing into the sausage stuffer. Stuff the casing with the meat mixture, ensuring you do not like stuff until the end. (You need about 6 inches on the other end of the casing to tie it up).
- ❖ Press the casing gently to remove any air bubbles. Sterilize a needle and prick the casing at a few places for the air to escape.
- ❖ Tie the bottom end into a knot. Remove the sausage from the sausage stuffer and knot this end as well. Fasten it once again with kitchen twine.
- ❖ Now hang the sausage on some hook or nail in a warm and moist area of 35°F -85°F.
- ❖ Spray some water over the sausage 1 – 2 times a day. Do this for 2 – 3 days.
- ❖ Now hang the sausages in an area where the temperature is 50°F to 60°F and humidity of 80% to 90%. You may need a humidifier to maintain the humidity.
- ❖ Let it remain like this for one week. Spray the sausage with water once daily.
- ❖ Next, let the humidity be reduced to 70% to 80% and let it remain for one week.
- ❖ Next, let the humidity be reduced to 65% - 70% and let it remain like this for 2 – 3 more weeks.
- ❖ The salami is ready to eat now. If you want to store it for longer, vacuum seals the sausage and refrigerate it until use. Make sure to label the jar with the name and date of preparation.

Nutrition values: Calories: 188, Total Fat: 8.5 g, Saturated Fat: 3 g, Cholesterol: 102 mg, Sodium: 115 mg, Total Carbs: 20.2 g, Fiber: 2.1 g, Sugar: 14.9 g, Protein: 32.7 g

FINOCCHIONA

Preparation time: 15 minutes
Fermentation time: 3 days
Servings: 4 quarts

Ingredients:

- 2 ½ lb. fatty pork or wild boar shoulder
- 0.8 oz. salt
- 1 tsp. sugar
- ½ tbsp. minced garlic
- ½ tbsp. ground fennel seeds or fennel pollen
- 2 tbsp. distilled water
- 0.1 oz. Instacure No.2
- ½ tbsp. coarsely ground pepper

- ½ tbsp. fennel seeds
- 3 tbsp. ouzo or any anise-flavored liqueur
- ½ tsp. FRM=52 starter culture or T-SPX culture

Equipment:

- Hot casings (about 1 ½ inches diameter), 7.5 feet
- Bowls
- Meat grinder
- Airtight containers
- Fermentation plastic container
- Sausage stuffer

Directions:

- ❖ Take out about ⅓ pound of pork and finely dice it. The rest of the fat and meat should be cut into bigger pieces (chop them so they can go into the grinder) and place the fat and meat chunks in different airtight containers (separate containers for the finely diced meat).
- ❖ Sprinkle salt over the meat chunks and toss well. Place the containers in the refrigerator. The sinew and silver skin should be trimmed as well.
- ❖ The following day, place the fat and the grinder parts in the freezer.
- ❖ Add garlic, sugar, spices, Instacure, and ¼ tbsp. Pepper into the meat container and toss well. Place this container in the freezer as well. Take out the containers after 1 ½ hours.
- ❖ Now, set up your grinder with the coarse die and add the finely chopped meat into the grinder. Grind the meat and place the meat in a bowl. Fix the fine dice and grind the chopped meat. Add it back into the container.
- ❖ Next, grind the chopped fat and add it back into its container. Place the containers in the freezer once again. Let the fat and meat chill until it is 35°F.
- ❖ In the meantime, add starter culture and distilled water to a bowl. Stir until it dissolves completely.
- ❖ Add the meat, fat, liqueur, starter mixture, ouzo, and ¼ tbsp. of pepper into the fermentation container. Mix using your hands for a couple of minutes. Place the container in the refrigerator.
- ❖ Run the sausage casings under warm water. Insert one end of the casing into the sausage stuffer. Stuff the casing with the meat mixture, ensuring you do not stuff up to the end. (You need about 6 inches on the other end of the casing to tie it up).
- ❖ Press the casing gently to remove any air bubbles. Sterilize a needle and prick the casing at a few places for the air to escape.
- ❖ Tie the bottom end into a knot. Remove the sausage from the sausage stuffer and knot this end as well. Fasten it once again with kitchen twine.
- ❖ Hang the sausage on some hook or nail in a warm and moist area of 67°F -80°F. Spray some water over the sausage every 6 – 7 hours a day. Do this for three days.
- ❖ Now hang the sausages in an area where the temperature is 50°F to 60°F and humidity 70% to 80%. You may need a humidifier to maintain the moisture.
- ❖ Let it remain like this for three weeks. Spray the sausage with water once daily.
- ❖ You can hang it for a couple of weeks more if desired.
- ❖ The salami is ready to eat now. If you want to store it for longer, vacuum seal the sausage and refrigerate it until use. Otherwise, freeze until ready to use. Make sure to label the jar with the name and date of preparation.

Nutrition values: Calories: 22, Fat: 18 g, Carb: 0 g, Proteins: 22 g

AUTHENTIC ROMAN GARUM FISH SAUCE

Preparation time: 15 minutes
Fermentation time: 3 days
Servings: 4 quarts

Ingredients:

- 1 lb. small, raw fish, rinsed and drained
- ½ tbsp. dried oregano
- Sea salt or pickling salt as required (mentioned in the directions)

Equipment:

- Fermenting container
- Bowl
- Strainer
- Storage container
- Cotton cloth or cheesecloth

Directions:

- ❖ After you drain the fish, check the weight of the fish. Weigh out salt, 20% of the importance of the drained fish.
- ❖ Combine salt, oregano, and fish in a bowl. Cover and set aside for 30 minutes.
- ❖ Mix well and transfer into the fermenting container. Stir once daily.
- ❖ Slowly, with the passing of days, only bones will be visible in the container, as the fish would have fully dissolved.
- ❖ Strain the mixture into a bowl using a coarse strainer. Discard the bones and any solids.
- ❖ Now line the strainer with a cotton cloth and strain the mixture a few times.
- ❖ Pour into the storage container. Refrigerate until use. It can last for a couple of years or until it turns cloudy. Discard it once it turns cloudy. Make sure to label the jar with the name and date of preparation.

Nutrition values: Calories: 118, Total Fats: 9.1 g, Carbs: 4 g, Protein: 7.3 g, Fiber: 0.6 g

ROASTED CHICKEN WING GARUM

Preparation time: 15 minutes
Fermentation time: 3 days
Servings: 4 quarts

Ingredients:

- 3.3 oz. chicken wings
- 2.2 oz. chicken bones
- 8 oz. salt
- 8.5 oz. pearl barley koji

Directions:

- ❖ Fill a pot with water (about 6 – 8 cups) and add bones into it. Place the pot over medium flame and let it boil.
- ❖ Skim off any scum that rises on top. Lower the heat and cook for about 1 ½ - 2 hours. Strain the stock and let it cool.
- ❖ Meanwhile, prepare a baking sheet by lining it with parchment paper. Spread the chicken wings on the baking sheet.
- ❖ Bake the chicken wings in an oven that has been preheated to 355° F for about 40 – 45 minutes. Turn the wings every 12 – 15 minutes, roasting them evenly. Take out the baking sheet and let it cool completely.
- ❖ Now weigh the roasted chicken wings and use only 1.1 pounds (chop them into smaller pieces). Use the rest of the wings in another recipe or as a snack with a dip of your choice.
- ❖ Place koji in the food processor bowl and process until it is broken down into smaller pieces. Transfer into the fermentation container.
- ❖ Add chicken wings, salt, and 28 ounces of chicken stock into the fermentation container and mix well.
- ❖ Place a sheet of cling wrap on top of the liquid. Place the lid of the container and fix it less than fully tight. Place the container for fermentation at 140°F or place it in a rice cooker on the "Keep warm" mode for four weeks.
- ❖ Remove any fat visible on top daily. Stir it well after discarding the fat. Do this for the first seven days.
- ❖ Next, remove the fat and stir the mixture only once a week for the next three weeks. Strain the mixture into a bowl using a fine wire mesh strainer. Discard any solids.
- ❖ Now line the strainer with a cotton cloth and strain the mixture a few times. Pour into the storage container. Refrigerate until use. Make sure to label the jar with the name and date of preparation.

Nutrition values: Calories: 118, Total Fats: 9.1 g, Carbs: 4 g, Protein: 7.3 g, Fiber: 0.6 g

VEGAN MINCEMEAT

Preparation time: 15 minutes
Fermentation time: 3 days
Servings: 4 quarts

Ingredients:

- 1 lb. dates, pitted, chopped
- 20 oz. raisins
- Juice of ½ orange
- Zest of ½ orange, grated
- Juice of ½ lemon
- Zest of ½ lemon, grated
- 1 apple, cored, grated along with the peel
- 1 oz. walnuts, chopped
- 2.5 oz. currants
- ½ tsp. ground cinnamon
- ⅛ tsp. ground nutmeg
- ½ tsp. ground ginger
- ⅛ tsp. ground cloves
- 2 tbsp. cider vinegar
- 1 tbsp. brandy (optional)
- 1 tbsp. cultured apple cider vinegar with mother

Equipment:

- Bowl
- Mason's jar

Directions:

- ❖ Combine apple, dates, raisins, walnuts, currants, spices, lemon, orange juice, and zest in a bowl and mix well.
- ❖ Add one tablespoon of cider vinegar and mix well.
- ❖ Add brandy and cultured apple cider vinegar and mix well.
- ❖ Transfer into the jar. Drizzle remaining cider vinegar on top. Fasten the lid and set it aside on your countertop for 24 hours in a cool and dark area.
- ❖ Shift the jar into the refrigerator. Let it remain in the refrigerator for two weeks.
- ❖ The mincemeat is now ready to use.
- ❖ Add brandy just before serving.

Nutrition values: Calories: 290, Fat: 36 g, Carb: 43 g, Proteins: 50 g

BEEF MEATBALLS

Preparation time: 15 minutes
Fermentation time: 3 days
Servings: 4 quarts

Ingredients:

- 6 lb. ground beef
- 6 c. soft breadcrumbs
- 6 large eggs
- 1½ c. water
- 1 c. onion, chopped finely
- 1 tbsp. salt
- ¼ tsp. ground black pepper
- 8 c. hot chicken broth

Directions:

- ❖ In a glass bowl, add all ingredients (except for broth) and mix until just combined. Set aside for about 15–30 minutes.
- ❖ Preheat your oven to 425°F. Lightly grease two shallow baking dishes.
- ❖ Make 1-inch balls from the mixture. Arrange the meatballs onto the prepared baking dishes in a single layer.
- ❖ Bake for approximately 15 minutes. In 8 (1-pint) hot sterilized jars, divide the meatballs.
- ❖ Pack each jar with hot broth, leaving a 1-inch space from the top. Run a knife around the inside of each jar to remove any air bubbles.
- ❖ Wipe any trace of food off the rims of jars with a clean, moist kitchen towel.
- ❖ Close each jar with a lid and screw on the ring. Carefully place the jars in the pressure canner and process at 10 pounds pressure for about 75 minutes.
- ❖ Remove the jars from the pressure canner and place them onto a wood surface several inches apart to cool completely.
- ❖ After cooling with your finger, press the top of each jar's lid to ensure the seal is tight. Store these canning jars in a cool, dark place.

Nutrition values: Calories: 525, Total Fat: 15.3 g, Saturated Fat: 5.3 g, Cholesterol: 222 mg, Sodium: 1,169 mg, Total Carbs: 30.4 g, Fiber: 2 g, Sugar: 3.3 g, Protein: 61.9 g

BEEF IN WINE SAUCE

Preparation time: 15 minutes
Fermentation time: 3 days
Servings: 4 quarts

Ingredients:

- 1 tbsp. vegetable oil
- 2 lb. beef stew meat, cut into 1-inch cubes
- 1 c. carrot, peeled and shredded
- ¾ c. onion, sliced
- 1 large apple; peeled, cored, and shredded
- 2 garlic cloves, minced
- ¾ c. water
- ½ c. red wine
- 2 beef bouillon cubes
- 2 bay leaves
- 1 tsp. salt

Directions:

- ❖ In a cast-iron wok, heat vegetable oil over medium-high heat and sear beef cubes in 2 batches for about 4–5 minutes.
- ❖ Add in the remaining ingredients and stir to combine well. Adjust the heat to high and bring to a full rolling boil.
- ❖ Set the heat to low and cook, covered for about 1 hour, stirring occasionally. Remove the wok of meat mixture from heat and discard the bay leaves.
- ❖ In 3 (1-pint) hot sterilized jars, divide the beef mixture, leaving about 1-inch space from the top.
- ❖ Run a knife around the inside of each jar to remove any air bubbles. Wipe any trace of food off the rims of jars with a clean, moist kitchen towel.
- ❖ Close each jar with a lid and screw on the ring. Carefully place the jars in the pressure canner and process at 10 pounds pressure for about 75 minutes.
- ❖ Remove the jars from the pressure canner and place them onto a wood surface several inches apart to cool completely.
- ❖ After cooling with your finger, press the top of each jar's lid to ensure the seal is tight. Store these canning jars in a cool, dark place.

Nutrition values: Calories: 354, Total Fat: 11.9 g, Saturated Fat: 4.1 g, Cholesterol: 135 mg, Sodium: 706 mg, Total Carbs: 9.4 g, Fiber: 1.7 g, Sugar: 5.8 g, Protein: 46.5 g

CHICKEN MARSALA

Preparation time: 15 minutes
Fermentation time: 3 days
Servings: 4 quarts

Ingredients:

- 6 lb. boneless, skinless chicken, cut into bite-sized pieces
- Salt and ground black pepper, as needed

- 2-3 tbsp. olive oil
- 1 medium onion chopped
- 1 tsp. garlic, chopped
- 1 tsp. dried oregano
- 2 c. dry Marsala wine
- 8 c. chicken broth
- 5 c. mushrooms, sliced

Directions:

- ❖ Rub the chicken pieces with salt and black pepper generously. In a cast-iron wok, heat olive oil over medium-high heat and sear the chicken pieces in 4 batches for about 3–5 minutes.
- ❖ Transfer each cooked chicken batch to a colander to drain excess grease. Add the onion and sauté for about 3–4 minutes in the same wok.
- ❖ Add in the garlic and oregano and sauté for about 1 minute. Stir in the wine and boil for about 1 minute.
- ❖ Stir in the broth and cook until boiling. Set the heat to low and cook for about 3–5 minutes.
- ❖ In 10 (1-pint) hot sterilized jars, divide the chicken pieces and mushrooms.
- ❖ Pack each jar with a hot cooking mixture, leaving a 1-inch space from the top.
- ❖ Run a knife around the inside of each jar to remove any air bubbles. Wipe any trace of food off the rims of jars with a clean, moist kitchen towel.
- ❖ Close each jar with a lid and screw on the ring. Carefully place the jars in the pressure canner and process at 11 pounds pressure for about 75 minutes.
- ❖ Remove the jars from the pressure canner and place them onto a wood surface several inches apart to cool completely.
- ❖ After cooling with your finger, press the top of each jar's lid to ensure the seal is tight. Store these canning jars in a cool, dark place.

Nutrition values: Calories: 259, Total Fat: 6.1 g, Saturated Fat: 1.5 g, Cholesterol: 105 mg, Sodium: 401 mg, Total Carbs: 2.2 g, Fiber: 0.3 g, Sugar: 1 g, Protein: 42 g

BRAISED LAMB

Preparation time: 15 minutes
Fermentation time: 3 days
Servings: 4 quarts

Ingredients:

- 1 sliced onion
- 1 tbsp. Olive oil
- 1 crushed and 1 peeled clove of garlic
- 1 diced red bell pepper
- 2 shredded sprigs of basil
- 1 tsp. Tomato puree
- 1 ½ c. water
- 1 ¾ c. tomato sauce
- 1 lb. canned lamb

Directions:

- ❖ Cook onion in olive oil for 10 minutes in a large pot.
- ❖ Add lamb, red pepper, garlic, and tomato puree to the pot.
- ❖ Add tomato sauce, basil, and water and stir.
- ❖ Cover and simmer on low for 90 minutes.

Nutrition values: Calories: 258, Fat: 17 g, Carbs: 0 g, Protein: 26 g

CHICKEN CACCIATORE

Preparation time: 15 minutes
Fermentation time: 3 days
Servings: 4 quarts

Ingredients:

- 2-3 tbsp. olive oil
- 9 (5 oz.) boneless, skinless chicken thighs, cut in half lengthwise
- 8 c. tomato sauce
- ¾ lb. fresh mushrooms, sliced
- 1 medium onion, sliced
- 3 garlic cloves, minced
- 2 tbsp. dried oregano
- 2 tbsp. dried basil
- 2 c. hot chicken broth

Directions:

- ❖ In a cast-iron wok, heat olive oil over medium-high heat and sear the chicken pieces in 4 batches for about 3–5 minutes.
- ❖ Transfer each cooked chicken batch to a colander to drain excess grease.
- ❖ In a stainless-steel saucepan, add the tomato sauce, mushroom, onions, garlic, and herbs over medium heat and cook for about 15 minutes, stirring occasionally.
- ❖ In 5 (1-pint) hot sterilized jars, divide the chicken pieces and tomato sauce mixture.
- ❖ Pack each jar with hot broth, leaving a 1-inch space from the top.
- ❖ Run a knife around the insides of each jar to remove any air bubbles.
- ❖ Wipe any trace of food off the rims of jars with a clean, moist kitchen towel.

- ❖ Close each jar with a lid and screw on the ring.
- ❖ Carefully place the jars in the pressure canner and process at 11 pounds pressure for about 75 minutes.
- ❖ Remove the jars from the pressure canner and place them onto a wood surface several inches apart to cool completely.
- ❖ After cooling with your finger, press the top of each jar's lid to ensure the seal is tight.
- ❖ Store these canning jars in a cool, dark place.

Nutrition values: Calories: 337, Total Fat: 13.1 g, Saturated Fat: 3.2 g, Cholesterol: 114 mg, Sodium: 968 mg, Total Carbs: 13.8 g, Fiber: 3.9 g, Sugar: 9.6 g, Protein: 41.8 g

MEXICAN TURKEY SOUP

Preparation time: 15 minutes
Fermentation time: 3 days
Servings: 4 quarts

Ingredients:
- 6 c. cooked turkey, chopped
- 2 c. chopped onions
- 8 oz. can of Mexican green chilies, chopped and drained
- ¼ c. taco seasoning mix, packed
- 28 oz. crushed tomatoes with the juices
- 16 c. turkey or chicken broth
- 3 c. corn
- 1 ½ tbsp. extra virgin olive oil

Directions:
- ❖ In a large stockpot, warm olive oil on medium-high heat. Sauté the onions until tender and fragrant, about 2 minutes on medium-high heat. Reduce heat to medium-low.
- ❖ Add taco seasoning and chilies. Cook and stir for another 3 minutes, and add the tomatoes and the broth. Bring to a boil, and then add the corn and the turkey.
- ❖ Reduce heat to low and let simmer for 10 minutes.
- ❖ Ladle equally into the jars.
- ❖ Process pints at 10 pounds for 75 minutes and quarts at 10 pounds for 90 minutes for the weighted gauge of the pressure canner or 11 pounds if the pressure canner has a dial gauge.
- ❖ Remove jars and let cool until it is at room temperature. This may take about a day.

Nutrition values: Carbohydrates: 30.08 g, Fat: 76.84 g, Protein: 63.66 g, Calories: 106

CHICKEN CACCIATORE

Preparation time: 15 minutes
Fermentation time: 3 days
Servings: 4 quarts

Ingredients:
- 3 tbsp. olive oil

- 8 (8 c.) large breasts boneless, skinless chicken breasts, cut into 2-inch cubes
- 12 (6 c.) boneless, skinless chicken thighs, cut into 2-inch pieces
- 1 tbsp. dried oregano
- 1 tbsp. dried basil
- 1 tsp. dried thyme
- 1 tsp. dried rosemary, crushed
- 1 tsp. coarse sea salt
- ½ tsp. ground black pepper
- 1 c. red wine
- 4 c. diced tomatoes, with their juice
- 4 c. tomato juice
- 2 c. sliced white mushrooms
- 3 c. coarsely chopped sweet onion
- 1½ c. large red bell pepper, chopped
- ½ c. celery stalk, chopped
- 6 garlic cloves, minced
- ¾ c. tomato paste (6 oz.)
- 1 tbsp. granulated sugar

Directions:
- ❖ In a thick-bottomed stockpot, combine the oil and the chicken breasts and thighs. Mix well to coat the chicken. Cook the chicken on medium-high heat for 3 minutes, stirring often.
- ❖ Add the oregano, basil, thyme, rosemary, salt, and pepper. Mix well and cook for an additional 3 minutes. Add the red wine, cover the stockpot, and let cook for five more minutes undisturbed.
- ❖ Add the tomatoes, Tomato Juice, mushrooms, onion, bell pepper, celery, and garlic. Mix well and bring to a boil. Boil for 5 minutes. Add the tomato paste and sugar, mixing well to distribute paste. Boil for an additional 5 minutes. Remove from the heat.
- ❖ Using a slotted spoon, fill each hot jar three-quarters full with the chicken and vegetables. Ladle, the hot tomato sauce over the mixture, leaving 1 inch of headspace.
- ❖ Remove any air bubbles and add additional sauce if necessary to maintain the 1 inch of headspace.
- ❖ Wipe the rim of each jar with a warm washcloth dipped in distilled white vinegar. Place a lid and ring on each jar and hand tighten.
- ❖ Place jars in the pressure canner, lock the pressure canner lid, and bring to a boil on high heat. Let the canner vent for 10 minutes. Close the vent and continue heating to achieve 11 PSI for a dial gauge and 10 PSI for a weighted gauge.
- ❖ Process quart jars for 1 hour 30 minutes and pint jars for 1 hour 15 minutes.

Serving Tip: This dish is traditionally served over pasta noodles, flat or spaghetti, and topped with fresh chopped parsley and shaved Parmesan cheese. For a fun kick, use V8® juice, regular or spicy, instead of Tomato Juice.

Nutrition values: Carbohydrates: 42.14 g, Fat: 43.8 g, Protein: 37.12 g, Calories: 701

SOUR CHICKEN

Preparation time: 15 minutes
Fermentation time: 3 days
Servings: 4 quarts

Ingredients:

- 3 20 oz. cans of pineapple chunks
- 1¼ c. white vinegar
- ½ c. water
- ⅓ c. soy sauce
- ¼ c. ketchup
- ¾ c. brown sugar
- 1 tsp. ginger powder
- 4½ lb. boneless, skinless chicken breasts, cut into 1-inch bite-sized pieces
- 3 large bell peppers (red and green), seeded and chopped
- 2 medium onions, chopped

Directions:

- ❖ Drain the cans of pineapple, reserving the juice into a bowl.
- ❖ In a nonreactive saucepan, add 2½ cups of reserved pineapple juice, vinegar, water, soy sauce, ketchup, brown sugar, and ginger powder over medium-high heat and cook until boiling, stirring continuously.
- ❖ In 10 (1-pint) hot sterilized jars, divide the chicken pieces, onions, bell peppers, and pineapple.
- ❖ Pack each jar with hot cooking liquid, leaving a 1-inch space from the top.
- ❖ Run a knife around the inside of each jar to remove any air bubbles.
- ❖ Wipe any trace of food off the rims of jars with a clean, moist kitchen towel.
- ❖ Close each jar with a lid and screw on the ring.
- ❖ Carefully place the jars in the pressure canner and process at 11 pounds pressure for about 75 minutes.
- ❖ Remove the jars from the pressure canner and place them onto a wood surface several inches apart to cool completely.
- ❖ After cooling with your finger, press the top of each jar's lid to ensure the seal is tight.
- ❖ Store these canning jars in a cool, dark place.

Nutrition values: Calories: 276, Total Fat: 7.7 g, Saturated Fat: 2.1 g, Cholesterol: 91 mg, Sodium: 365 mg, Total Carbs: 20.2 g, Fiber: 1.7 g, Sugar: 15.8 g, Protein: 30.6 g

PICKLED TROUT

Preparation time: 15 minutes
Fermentation time: 3 days
Servings: 4 quarts

Ingredients:

- 5 lb. trout fillets
- 2½ tsp. salt

Directions:

- ❖ In 10 (½-pint) hot sterilized jars, divide the trout and salt, leaving a 1-inch space from the top.
- ❖ Run a knife around the insides of each jar to remove any air bubbles.
- ❖ Wipe any trace of food off the rims of jars with a clean, moist kitchen towel.
- ❖ Close each jar with a lid and screw on the ring.
- ❖ Carefully place the jars in the pressure canner and process at 10 pounds pressure for about 100 minutes.
- ❖ Remove the jars from the pressure canner and place them onto a wood surface several inches apart to cool completely.
- ❖ After cooling with your finger, press the top of each jar's lid to ensure the seal is tight.
- ❖ Store these canning jars in a cool, dark place.

Nutrition values: Calories: 215, Total Fat: 9.6 g, Saturated Fat: 1.7 g, Cholesterol: 84 mg, Sodium: 368 mg, Total Carbs: 0 g, Fiber: 0 g, Sugar: 0 g, Protein: 30.2 g

STROGANOFF

Preparation time: 15 minutes
Fermentation time: 3 days
Servings: 4 quarts

Ingredients:

- 1 lb. canned beef
- 2 sliced onions
- 8 oz. Sliced mushrooms
- 1 tsp. Worcestershire sauce
- ¼ c. butter
- One clove of chopped garlic
- ½ tsp. Salt
- 1 ½ c. beef broth
- 1 ½ c. sour cream
- ¼ c. all-purpose flour
- 3 c. egg noodles, hot cooked

Directions:

- ❖ In a skillet over medium heat, cook mushrooms, garlic, and onions for 10 minutes in butter.
- ❖ Remove vegetables and cook beef in the same skillet until browned.
- ❖ Stir in Worcestershire, salt, and 1 c. broth, and bring to a boil.
- ❖ Reduce heat to low. Cover and simmer for 15 minutes.
- ❖ Stir remaining broth into flour, then stir mixture into beef in skillet.
- ❖ Add onion mixture to skillet and allow to boil for about 1 minute, stirring.
- ❖ Stir in sour cream and heat but do not boil.
- ❖ Serve over hot cooked egg noodles.

Nutrition values: Calories: 340, Fat: 9 g, Carbs: 44 g, Protein: 20 g

SALMON PATTIES

Preparation time: 15 minutes
Fermentation time: 3 days
Servings: 4 quarts

Ingredients:

- 2 beaten eggs
- 14 oz. Canned salmon
- ¼ c. Italian breadcrumbs
- ¼ c. dry potato flakes
- 1 minced clove of garlic
- 1 minced onion
- ¼ tsp. Celery salt
- ¼ tsp. Dill weed
- 2 tbsp. Olive oil

Directions:

- ❖ Combine eggs in a large bowl with salmon, breadcrumbs, onion, potato flakes, dill, garlic, and celery salt.
- ❖ Form into ten patties by hand.
- ❖ Cook patties in olive oil in a skillet over medium heat for 5 minutes per side.
- ❖ Flip and cook 5 minutes more.

Nutrition values: Calories: 250, Fat: 11 g, Carbs: 2.3 g, Protein: 32 g

CANNED CHICKEN

Preparation time: 15 minutes
Fermentation time: 3 days
Servings: 4 quarts

Ingredients:

- 18 medium boneless and skinless chicken breasts
- 1 ½ tbsp. of salt
- 4 ½ c. of water
- Butter or olive oil for frying in a skillet

Directions:

- ❖ Cook each side of the chicken in a skillet with butter or olive oil for about 8-10 minutes. Remove from heat when the chicken is white and cooked

through. If you poke it with a fork, the juices run clear.
- ❖ Place a ½ teaspoon of salt and two chicken breasts in each pint jar.
- ❖ Fill the jar with water and process for 70 minutes at 10 pounds of pressure for the weighted gauge of the pressure canner or 11 pounds if the pressure canner has a dial gauge.
- ❖ Remove jars, and let cool until it is room temperature, which may take about a day.

Nutrition values: Carbohydrates: 0 g, Fat: 55.09 g, Protein: 5.06 g, Calories: 509

BEEF PAPRIKASH

Preparation time: 15 minutes
Fermentation time: 3 days
Servings: 4 quarts

Ingredients:

- 1 sliced onion
- 2 tbsp. Flour
- ¼ tsp. Black pepper
- ¼ tsp. Salt
- 2 minced cloves of garlic
- 2 chopped red bell peppers
- 2 tbsp. Sweet paprika
- ½ c. beef broth
- 2 tbsp. Tomato paste
- ½ c. sour cream
- 1 tsp. Caraway seeds
- ¼ c. chopped fresh dill
- 2 lb. canned beef

Directions:

- ❖ Place onions in a slow cooker.
- ❖ In a small bowl, toss beef in flour with salt and pepper.
- ❖ Top onions with seasoned beef.
- ❖ Spread over garlic and bell peppers in a slow cooker.
- ❖ Mix paprika, broth, caraway, and tomato paste in a separate small bowl.
- ❖ Pour sauce over the beef.
- ❖ Cover and cook on high for 4 hours or low for 8 hours.
- ❖ Uncover and turn off heat; let stand for 10 minutes.
- ❖ Stir in dill and sour cream.

Nutrition values: Calories: 360, Fat: 22 g, Carbs: 42 g, Protein: 31 g

GROUND TURKEY

Preparation time: 15 minutes
Fermentation time: 3 days
Servings: 4 quarts

Ingredients:

- 4 lb. ground turkey
- 4 tsp. salt

Directions:

- ❖ Add ground turkey and cook until boiling in a large pan of water. Now set the heat to low and cook for about 5 minutes.
- ❖ Drain the meat entirely. In 4 (1-pint) hot sterilized jars, divide the ground turkey and salt.
- ❖ Pack each jar with hot water, leaving a 1-inch space from the top.
- ❖ Run a knife around the insides of each jar to remove any air bubbles. Wipe any trace of food off the rims of jars with a clean, moist kitchen towel.
- ❖ Close each jar with a lid and screw on the ring. Carefully place the jars in the pressure canner and process at 10 pounds pressure for about 75 minutes.
- ❖ Remove the jars from the pressure canner and place them onto a wood surface several inches apart to cool completely.
- ❖ After cooling with your finger, press the top of each jar's lid to ensure the seal is tight. Store these canning jars in a cool, dark place.

Nutrition values: Calories: 221, Total Fat: 12.5 g, Saturated Fat: 2.1 g, Cholesterol: 116 mg, Sodium: 703 mg, Total Carbs: 0 g, Fiber: 0 g, Sugar: 0 g, Protein: 31 g

APRICOT PORK

Preparation time: 15 minutes
Fermentation time: 3 days
Servings: 4 quarts

Ingredients:

- ½ tsp. Salt
- ½ tsp. Dried thyme
- 1 lb. canned pork
- 2 tbsp. Olive oil
- 1 sliced onion
- 1 tbsp. Butter
- 2 tbsp. Apricot jam
- ½ c. chicken broth
- 1 tbsp. Dijon mustard

Directions:

- ❖ Sprinkle pork with salt and thyme on both sides.
- ❖ Cook oil over medium-high heat in a skillet for 3 minutes per side; do not crowd.
- ❖ Remove from skillet, then melt butter in skillet.
- ❖ Cook onion for 3 minutes, then add jam, mustard, and broth.
- ❖ Bring to a boil, stirring continuously.
- ❖ Cover and turn heat to medium-low, then simmer for 5 minutes.
- ❖ Return pork to skillet and stir to coat in sauce.

- ❖ Cover again and simmer for 5 minutes more to heat pork through.

Nutrition values: Calories: 288, Fat: 7 g, Carbs: 26 g, Protein 28 g

COOLED HAM

Preparation time: 15 minutes
Fermentation time: 3 days
Servings: 4 quarts

- Ingredients

- 19 lb. ham, cut into ½-inch chunks

Directions:

- ❖ Heat a lightly greased large cast-iron skillet over medium-high heat and sear ham chunks in 8 batches for about 3–5 minutes.
- ❖ In 10 (1-pint) hot sterilized jars, divide the ham chunks. Pack each jar with hot water, leaving a 1-inch space from the top.
- ❖ Run a knife around the insides of each jar to remove any air bubbles. Wipe any trace of food off the rims of jars with a clean, moist kitchen towel.
- ❖ Close each jar with a lid and screw on the ring. Carefully place the jars in the pressure canner and process at 11 pounds pressure for about 75 minutes.
- ❖ Remove the jars from the pressure canner and place them onto a wood surface several inches apart to cool completely.
- ❖ After cooling with your finger, press the top of each jar's lid to ensure the seal is tight. Store these canning jars in a cool, dark place.

Nutrition values: Calories: 351, Total Fat: 18.5 g, Saturated Fat: 6.3 g, Cholesterol: 123 mg, Sodium: 1,568 mg, Total Carbs: 8.3 g, Fiber: 2.8 g, Sugar: 0 g, Protein: 35.8 g

SMOKY MEATLOAF

Preparation time: 15 minutes
Fermentation time: 3 days
Servings: 4 quarts

Ingredients:

- French bread loaf
- 5 lb. ground beef
- 1 onion, chopped
- 4 large eggs
- 1½ c. ketchup
- 2 tbsp. Worcestershire sauce
- ¾ c. brown sugar
- 2 tbsp. salt
- 1 tbsp. powdered smoke
- 1 tbsp. sage
- 1 tbsp. garlic powder
- ½ tbsp. onion salt
- ½ tbsp. ground black pepper

Directions:

- ❖ Add bread loaf into a food processor and process until crumbed.
- ❖ Add breadcrumbs and remaining ingredients to a large glass bowl and mix until well combined.
- ❖ In 8 (1-pint) hot sterilized jars, divide the beef mixture, leaving about 1-inch space from the top. Run a knife around the insides of each jar to remove any air bubbles.
- ❖ Wipe any trace of food off the rims of jars with a clean, moist kitchen towel.
- ❖ Close each jar with a lid and screw on the ring. Carefully place the jars in the pressure canner and process at 10 pounds pressure for about 75 minutes.
- ❖ Remove the jars from the pressure canner and place them onto a wood surface several inches apart to cool completely.
- ❖ After cooling with your finger, press the top of each jar's lid to ensure the seal is tight. Store these canning jars in a cool, dark place.

Nutrition values: Calories: 347, Total Fat: 10.3 g, Saturated Fat: 3.7 g, Cholesterol: 173 mg, Sodium: 1,268 mg, Total Carbs: 16.3 g, Fiber: 0.4 g, Sugar: 12.7 g, Protein: 45.5 g

PICKLED SHRIMP

Preparation time: 15 minutes
Fermentation time: 3 days
Servings: 4 quarts

Ingredients:

- 8 c. water
- 1 c. vinegar
- 1 c. salt
- 3 tbsp. salt
- 4 lb. shrimp

Directions:

- ❖ Add water, vinegar, and salt to a large stockpot and cook until boiling.

- ❖ Add the shrimp to the boiling water and immediately remove it from the heat. Set aside for about 10 minutes.
- ❖ Transfer the shrimp into a bowl with cold water with a slotted spoon. Drain the shrimp and then peel them.
- ❖ Immediately plunge the shrimp in the same stockpot of water.
- ❖ In 8 (1-pint) hot sterilized jars, divide the shrimp. Fill each jar with hot cooking liquid, leaving a 1-inch space from the top.
- ❖ Run a knife around the insides of each jar to remove any air bubbles. Wipe any trace of food off the rims of jars with a clean, moist kitchen towel.
- ❖ Close each jar with a lid and screw on the ring. Carefully place the jars in the pressure canner and process at 10 pounds pressure for about 45 minutes.
- ❖ Remove the jars from the pressure canner and place them onto a wood surface several inches apart to cool completely.
- ❖ After cooling with your finger, press the top of each jar's lid to ensure the seal is tight. Store these canning jars in a cool, dark place.

Nutrition values: Calories: 138, Total Fat: 1.9 g, Saturated Fat: 0.6 g, Cholesterol: 239 mg, Sodium: 1,690 mg, Total Carbs: 1.9 g, Fiber: 0 g, Sugar: 0.1 g, Protein: 25.8 g

BEEF BONE BROTH

Preparation time: 15 minutes
Fermentation time: 3 days
Servings: 4 quarts

Ingredients:

- 4 lb. (2 kg) meaty beef bones
- 2 qt. (2 L) water
- 2 tbsp. Unfiltered apple cider vinegar (5% acidity)
- 2 tsp. Salt
- 3 garlic cloves (crushed)
- 2 bay leaves
- 1 large onion (quartered)

Directions:

- ❖ Preheat the oven to 200°C. Place beef bones in a large roasting pan and bake for 30 minutes. Removes bones.
- ❖ Reduce temperature to 10°C. Place a Stainless-steel Dutch oven, and add bones, pan drippings, water, vinegar, salt, garlic, bay leaves, and onion. Stir well. Cover and bake for 8 hours.
- ❖ Reduce temperature to 90°C and bake for 8 hours more. Remove bones. In a two-liter bowl, strain the broth using a fine wire-mesh strainer. Skim fat and discard solids. Add water if the broth doesn't measure two liters.
- ❖ Pour broth into a large Dutch oven and let it simmer.

- ❖ Transfer the broth to hot jars. Leave headspace of 1-inch. Clean the rim of the glass jar. Place the lid and apply a band around it. Adjust to ensure that the lid is tight.
- ❖ In a pressure canner, place jars on racks with simmering water (2-inches, 90°C/180°F).
- ❖ Place lid on canner, adjust medium-high heat. Vent steam for 10 minutes at 10/11 pounds (psi for weighted gauge/dial-gauge canner).
- ❖ Process pint jars for 20 minutes or quarts for 25 minutes.
- ❖ Turn off the canner and remove the lid after two minutes when pressure turns zero. Keep the jars in the canner for 10 minutes more.
- ❖ Remove the jars. Reprocess if the jars are not sealed. Cool and store in the refrigerator.

Nutrition values: Calories: 138, Total Fat: 1.9 g, Saturated Fat: 0.6 g, Cholesterol: 239 mg, Sodium: 1,690 mg, Total Carbs: 1.9 g, Fiber: 0 g, Sugar: 0.1 g, Protein: 25.8 g

PORK AND BLACK BEANS

Preparation time: 15 minutes
Fermentation time: 3 days
Servings: 4 quarts

Ingredients:

- 2 ¼ c. dried black beans (16 oz.)
- 4 tbsp. Olive oil, divided
- 1 ½ lb. boneless pork shoulder, surface fat trimmed, cut into 1-inch cubes
- 1 tsp. Coarse Sea salt
- ½ tsp. Ground black pepper
- 2 medium white onions, coarsely chopped
- 2 sprigs fresh epazote, coarsely chopped, or 2 tsps. dried epazote
- 4 c. Chicken Broth
- 2 c. water
- 4 (4 c.) large tomatoes, peeled and diced, with juice
- 2 serrano peppers, finely chopped
- 8 garlic cloves, minced
- 1 tbsp. Chili powder
- 2 tsp. Chopped fresh oregano
- 2 tsp. Chopped fresh basil
- 2 tsp. ground cumin

Directions:

- ❖ Thoroughly rinse and clean the black beans, discarding any disfigured or shriveled beans and any rocks or debris. Set aside.
- ❖ In a thick-bottomed stockpot, heat two tablespoons olive oil on medium-high. Working in batches, place the pork cubes in the oil and lightly brown all sides, about one minute on each side, seasoning each batch with a dash of salt and pepper.

- ❖ Add a tablespoon of oil while browning each batch. Do not cook the pork through. Place the browned pork batches in a bowl and set aside.
- ❖ Add the onions and epazote to the drippings in the stockpot. Sauté until the onions are translucent, about 5 to 8 minutes, then add the broth and two cups water. Bring to a boil.
- ❖ Once the water is at a boil, add the cleaned black beans to the stockpot. Return to a boil and cook for 5 minutes, stirring often.
- ❖ Add the browned pork, tomatoes, serrano peppers, garlic, chili powder, oregano, basil, cumin, salt, and pepper to the stockpot and mix well. Return to a boil for 5 minutes, often stirring to avoid scorching.
- ❖ Ladle the pork and beans into hot jars, leaving 1 inch of headspace. Be sure to give each jar a good ratio of beans and meat.
- ❖ Remove any air bubbles and add additional mixture or liquid if necessary to maintain the 1 inch of headspace.
- ❖ Dip a warm washcloth in distilled white vinegar and wipe the rims of the jars. Set a lid and jar on each and tighten.
- ❖ Set the jars in the pressure canner, place the lid, and allow to boil while on high heat. You can vent for approximately 10 minutes.
- ❖ Lock the vent and heat further to attain a dial gauge of 11 PSI and a weighted gauge of 10 PSI. Process quart jars for 90 minutes and pint jars for around 75 minutes

Nutrition values: Calories: 355.5, Fat: 15 g, Carbs: 20 g, Protein 32.6 g

CHICKEN STOCK

Preparation time: 15 minutes
Fermentation time: 3 days
Servings: 4 quarts

Ingredients:

- 3-4 lb. of Chicken pieces
- 4 qt. Water
- 2 stalks of Celery (leaves attached, cut into 1-inch pieces)
- 2 Onions (medium-sized, quartered)
- 15 Peppercorns
- 3 Bay leaves
- Salt to taste

Directions:

- ❖ In a 6–8-liter pot, add chicken and water and bring it to boil on high flame. Add all remaining ingredients. Reduce heat and cover, then let it simmer for 2 hours or until the chicken becomes tender.
- ❖ Remove from flame. Skim foam. Remove chicken for other use.

- In a large bowl, strain the stock using a fine wire-mesh strainer and cheesecloth.
- Strain the stock through a mesh strainer or several layers of cheesecloth into a large bowl. Cool and refrigerate for easy removal of fat. Remove fat. Pour the stock into a pot and boil.
- Transfer the broth to hot jars. Leave headspace of 1-inch. Clean the rim of the glass jar. Place the lid and apply a band around it. Adjust to ensure that the cover is tight.
- In a pressure canner, place jars on racks with simmering water (2-inches, 90°C/180°F).
- Place lid on canner, adjust medium-high heat. Vent steam for 10 minutes at 10/11 pounds (psi for weighted gauge/dial-gauge canner).
- Process pint jars for 20 minutes or quarts for 25 minutes.
- Turn off the canner. Put away the lid after two minutes when pressure turns zero. Keep the jars in the canner for 10 minutes more.
- Use the unsealed jars within a week.

Nutrition values: Calories: 138, Total Fat: 1.9 g, Saturated Fat: 0.6 g, Cholesterol: 239 mg, Sodium: 1,690 mg, Total Carbs: 1.9 g, Fiber: 0 g, Sugar: 0.1 g, Protein: 25.8 g

SALMON CHOWDER

Preparation time: 15 minutes
Fermentation time: 3 days
Servings: 4 quarts

Ingredients:

- ¾ c. chopped onion
- 3 tbsp. Butter
- ½ c. chopped celery
- 2 c. diced potatoes
- 1 tsp. Garlic powder
- 2 c. chicken broth
- 2 diced carrots
- 1 tsp. Black pepper
- 1 tsp. Salt
- 32 oz. Canned salmon
- 1 tsp. Dried dill weed
- 15 oz. Canned creamed corn
- 12 oz. Canned evaporated milk
- ½ lb. shredded cheddar cheese

Directions:

- Over medium heat, melt butter in a pot.
- Cook celery, onion, and garlic powder for 5 minutes in melted butter.
- Stir in carrots, potatoes, salt, broth, pepper, and dill.
- Bring to a boil, then reduce heat to low.
- Cover and simmer for 20 minutes.
- Stir in milk, cheese, corn, and salmon.
- Cook until cheese melts.

Nutrition values: Calories: 407, Fat: 11 g, Carbs: 21 g, Protein: 32 g

PICKED FISH

Preparation time: 15 minutes
Fermentation time: 3 days
Servings: 4 quarts

Ingredients:

- 5 lb. tuna or salmon
- 5-pint sized mason jars with lids and rings
- Canning salt
- Lemon juice
- One jalapeño pepper

Directions:

- Place one slice of jalapeño pepper into each jar. Fill jars with meat to ½ inch from the top.
- Add ¼ teaspoon canning salt and one teaspoon lemon juice per pint. Use a knife to jiggle meat and remove any air pockets.
- Wipe rim of jar clean. Heat lids in hot water for 3 minutes; place lids on jars and tighten rings slightly.
- In the canner, place the jars and fill with water up to the jar rings.
- Close and lock the pressure canner and bring to a boil over high heat, then add cooking weight to the top.
- After 20 minutes, reduce the heat to medium and cook for 75 minutes.
- Turn off the heat and leave the canner alone until it has cooled completely to room temperature.
- After the canner has cooled, remove jars from the canner and check for sealing.
- If the jars have sealed, store for up to 2 years; if not, use meat immediately.

Nutrition values: Carbohydrates: 1.51 g, Fat: 32.56 g, Protein: 93.79 g, Calories: 700

FERMENTED TUNA

Preparation time: 15 minutes
Fermentation time: 3 days
Servings: 4 quarts

Ingredients:

- 2½ lb. boneless skinless tuna, cut into 4-inch chunks
- 3 tsp. kosher salt

Directions:

- ❖ In 5 (½-pint) hot sterilized jars, divide the tuna chunks and salt.
- ❖ Fill each jar with water, leaving a 1-inch space from the top.
- ❖ Run a knife around the inside of each jar to remove any air bubbles.
- ❖ Wipe any trace of food off the rims of jars with a clean, moist kitchen towel.
- ❖ Close each jar with a lid and screw on the ring.
- ❖ Carefully place the jars in the pressure canner and process at 10 pounds pressure for about 100 minutes.
- ❖ Take away the jars from the pressure canner. Place them onto a wood surface several inches apart to cool completely.
- ❖ After cooling with your finger, press the top of each jar's lid to ensure the seal is tight.
- ❖ Store these canning jars in a cool, dark place.

Nutrition values: Calories: 211, Total Fat: 9.2 g, Saturated Fat: 1.9 g, Cholesterol: 35 mg, Sodium: 754 mg, Total Carbs: 0 g, Fiber: 0 g, Sugar: 0 g, Protein: 30.1 g

FERMENTED FISH STEW

Preparation time: 15 minutes
Fermentation time: 3 days
Servings: 4 quarts

Ingredients:

For the Fish Brine:

- 8 c. water
- ½ c. salt
- 2 lb. boneless, skinless fish, cut into 1-inch pieces

For the Stew:

- 3 c. water
- 6 large tomatoes
- 2 garlic cloves
- 2 tsp. sugar
- ½ tsp. celery salt
- Pinch of cayenne pepper
- 4 c. potatoes, peeled and cubed
- ½ c. onion, chopped roughly
- ¼ c. pimiento, chopped
- 3 cooked bacon slices, crumbled
- 1 tbsp. fresh lemon juice

Directions:

For the brine: Dissolve salt in water in a large glass bowl. Add fish pieces and soak for about 1 hour. Drain fish pieces.

For the stew:

- ❖ In a stockpot, add water, tomatoes, garlic, sugar, salt, celery salt, and cayenne pepper over medium-high heat and cook until boiling.
- ❖ Now set the heat to low and cook for about 20 minutes.
- ❖ Add in remaining ingredients and stir to combine.
- ❖ Now adjust the heat to medium-high and cook until boiling.
- ❖ Cook for about 5 minutes.
- ❖ In 5 (1-pint) hot sterilized jars, divide the stew, leaving about ½-inch space from the top.
- ❖ Slide a small knife around the insides of each jar to remove air bubbles.
- ❖ Wipe any trace of food off the rims of jars with a clean, moist kitchen towel.
- ❖ Carefully place the jars in the pressure canner and process at 10 pounds pressure for about 100 minutes.
- ❖ Take away the jars from the pressure canner. Place them onto a wood surface several inches apart to cool completely.
- ❖ After cooling with your finger, press the top of each jar's lid to ensure the seal is tight.
- ❖ Store these canning jars in a cool, dark place.

Nutrition values: Calories: 230, Total Fat: 6.5 g, Saturated Fat: 1.9 g, Cholesterol: 47 mg, Sodium: 2,000 mg, Total Carbs: 15.6 g, Fiber: 2.9 g, Sugar: 4.8 g, Protein: 26.7 g

FERMENTED FISH BROTH

Preparation time: 15 minutes
Fermentation time: 3 days
Servings: 4 quarts

Ingredients:

- 2 tbsp. unsalted butter
- 2 medium onions, sliced thinly
- 2 medium carrots, sliced thinly
- 4 celery stalks, sliced thinly
- 2 dried bay leaves
- 6–8 sprigs of fresh thyme
- ¼ c. fresh parsley, chopped
- 2 tbsp. black peppercorns
- 1 cod head split lengthwise, gills removed and rinsed
- 3 lb. fish bones, cut into 2-inch pieces and rinsed

- ¼ c. dry white wine
- 8 c. of hot water

Directions:

- ❖ Melt the butter in a heavy-bottomed stockpot over medium heat and cook the onions, carrots, celery, fresh herbs, bay leaves, and peppercorns for about 8 minutes, stirring frequently.
- ❖ Add the remaining ingredients (except for water) and cook for about 10–15 minutes.
- ❖ Stir in the water and cook until boiling. Adjust the heat to medium and simmer, covered for about 10–15 minutes, skimming off the foam from the top occasionally.
- ❖ Remove the pan of broth from heat and, through a strainer, strain it. In four (1-pint) hot sterilized jars, divide the broth, leaving about ½-inch space from the top.
- ❖ Slide a small knife around the insides of each jar to remove air bubbles.
- ❖ Wipe any trace of food off the rims of jars with a clean, moist kitchen towel.
- ❖ Carefully place the jars in the pressure canner and process at 10 pounds pressure for about 20 minutes.
- ❖ Take away the jars from the pressure canner. Place them onto a wood surface several inches apart to cool completely.
- ❖ After cooling with your finger, press the top of each jar's lid to ensure the seal is tight. Store these canning jars in a cool, dark place.

Nutrition values: Calories: 116, Total Fat: 2.2 g, Saturated Fat: 1.1 g, Cholesterol: 51 mg, Sodium: 87 mg, Total Carbs: 2.3 g, Fiber: 0.6 g, Sugar: 1.1 g, Protein: 19.7 g

CONCLUSION

Thank you for reading this book! These recipes are sure to have something that will fit your needs. When you are craving a dill pickle or a savory pickled vegetable, give one of these simple dishes a try to fill your jars with tasty treats for the family.

This is an ideal book for people who are already fermenting and want to learn more, individuals who are just beginning and want to understand more about the process, and those who may not be extremely interested in health but simply want to experiment with making great food. You can discover something in this book that interests you no matter who you are or your background. The book itself includes many delectable recipes that use products that have undergone fermentation. It also demonstrates how to use fermentation techniques to enhance the flavor and appeal of food. The manual includes basic fermentation information, step-by-step recipes, and useful hints. Not everyone knows what to do when starting on the fermentation adventure.

While fermented foods contribute to a healthy diet, most people have started eating them because of their taste. The flavors of these foods are induced by the microbes that break the sugar in the food. Some common fermented foods include Asian miso, sauerkraut, kimchi, kvass, Russian kefir, and wine. People across the globe are embracing these foods and welcoming them to their diet.

It's simple to incorporate fermented foods into your diet. Replace your ordinary bread with a fresh slice of sourdough bread. Kefir is good to drink, and yogurt is preferable to milk. Smoothie recipes benefit from both. Why not even attempt some naturally fermented foods like pickled cucumbers, beets, onions, salsa, sauerkraut, and even kimchi?

Enjoy your fermented recipes!

BOOK 6

FREEZE DRYING FOR BEGINNERS

How to Freeze Dry and Preserve Nutrient Dense Food Safely
at Home to Be Prepared for the Next 3 Years.
1000 Days of Tasty Recipes and Log Book Included.

INTRODUCTION

We have numerous options for food preservation methods to extend the shelf-life of food consumed at home or in your food business. You can use cooling, freezing, canning, sugaring, salting, and even vacuum packaging. Furthermore, food preservation experts constantly research new techniques to expand our options.

We must prioritize the safest food preservation techniques, which have been learned through centuries of trial and error, as these will help us preserve the quality and cleanliness of stored food. The good news is that you can do it in any situation with the right instructions and resources.

Food preservation refers to the techniques used to prepare food for safe, long-term storage, whether consumed at home, in a professional kitchen or sold directly to customers. Preserved food will be safe and delicious to eat in the future because preservation techniques limit bacterial growth and other spoilage.

Food preservation is essential for three reasons:

1. Pathogenic bacteria – Pathogenic bacteria, such as E. coli, Salmonella, and other pathogens, pose a significant risk of food spoilage during long-term storage. Bacteria only require heat, moisture, and time to reproduce quickly in food, but food preservation limits one or more of these factors, halting their proliferation.
2. To keep the food of the highest quality – Food quality degrades over time due to spoilage. In many cases, moderate spoilage does not make food unsafe to eat, but it drastically alters its flavor, texture, and appearance. Proper food preservation may preserve some of these characteristics and the nutritional value of specific foods.
3. To save money – Food is expensive both at home and at work. Ideally, you should avoid purchasing more food than you can eat. Nonetheless, various safe preservation techniques allow you to store vegetables, fruits, meat, and other foods much past their expected expiration date, eliminating the need to discard them.

Specific food preservation techniques may be challenging to master, but once you do, you will almost certainly feel a sense of accomplishment and pride. You will also better understand food hygiene issues and best practices because many food preservation techniques require precision and care to ensure food safety. This book will discuss the best method for preserving food: freeze-drying. Let's get started without further ado.

CHAPTER 1

FREEZE DRYING
BASICS

Freeze-drying is a food preservation technique that removes all fluid from a specific food without affecting its taste. Agricultural products are dried to reduce the amount of water in them. At the same time, freeze-drying is a preservation technique in which the sample material is frozen below its glass transition temperature, and then frozen water dissolves as the process pressure and temperature are reduced.

Freeze-drying is a modern dehydration technique that removes moisture efficiently while causing minor structural deformation in the product. Because of the low process enthalpy, it is a less severe thermal process degrades heat-sensitive compounds minimally while protecting thermo-liable constituents. The product is freeze-dried at low and high temperatures.

Freeze-drying requires a two-step process that starts with freezing your food. When food is frozen, it undergoes a vacuum cycle. This cycle will convert all ice gems formed during freezing into a fume. The fume is removed from the food and is safe for consumption now and in the future without losing its tone or taste.

In addition to freezing, there is an ancient method known as freeze-drying that you can use to preserve your food. Freeze-drying, contrary to what the name implies, is not the same as the methods previously discussed. Technically, freeze-drying is a type of dehydration.

The Incan empire once spanned the harsh terrain of the Andes. They thrived in that harsh, unforgiving landscape, which was bitterly cold at night but also windy and dry. They developed Chuo, a freeze-dried potato that could sustain their massive armies for years. It was created by Altiplano villagers from Peru and Bolivia's high plateaus. There are two kinds of Chuo: black and white. The former is made by freezing harvested bitter potatoes overnight and crushing them with their feet during the day to remove the skin and squeeze out the liquids until they are completely dehydrated. In contrast, the latter is made by soaking or submerging the potatoes in freezing waters of local streams and rivers and then drying them out in the sun.

Chuos are still eaten in the Andes today. Locals adore it, but the flavor is difficult for visitors to adjust to. By simply adding water, Chuos can be eaten as if you are eating freeze-dried mashed potatoes. The locals add it to other local dishes where a potato can be used, such as the local chili or aji. It can also be ground into powder to make flour that can thicken stews and soups. The long shelf life can also save the livelihoods of locals who rely on a good harvest to survive. If the crops fail this year, they will have stored chuo to help them get by.

So, what about this method makes the food last so long? The chalk-like dehydrated potatoes of the Andes are said to rival the shelf life of modern freeze-dried food. Heat is used to extract moisture from food during dehydration. Dehydration will remove approximately 95% of the water content from the food, whereas freeze-drying will remove about 99% of the water content. As a result, your food will have a longer shelf life and taste better than your dehydrated counterparts. Despite the name, freeze-dried foods do not need to be stored in the freezer or even the refrigerator. When packaged correctly in airtight and vacuum-sealed mylar bags, freeze-dried foods can last long, even if kept in a cupboard.

Furthermore, because the water content of the food items is extracted, freeze-dried food rehydrates easily and quickly, making it the ideal way to process food that you intend to store for an extended period. Rehydrated freeze-dried food can be used in the same way as fresh food. If you freeze-dried raw bacon, rehydrate it with just a bowl of fresh potable water, and it'll be ready to cook just like regular freshly bought bacon. Cooked foods like stews, roasts, soups, and stir-fried dishes can also be freeze-dried with little flavor or quality loss. Furthermore, freeze-dried food should be consumed within four months of opening.

As a result, NASA prefers this method when packing food for our astronauts to take into space. It is delivered into space in small bags that astronauts can quickly rehydrate with just a little water. Preppers also like this method for preserving meats and other cooked foods for their bunkers and go bags because it keeps them fresh indefinitely. The disadvantage is that raw food items must be rehydrated to be consumed safely, but meals cooked before freeze-drying are generally safe to consume when opened and rehydrated. However, because it is dehydrated, it will absorb water from other sources, such as your saliva or the inside of your stomach, so that you will rehydrate the food one way or another.

In natural disasters that only last a few days without access to freshwater, freeze-dried food will be extremely useful, if not life-saving. However, in disasters where you will be without clean water for days or weeks, consumption of freeze-dried food should be limited, and water should be saved for drinking. Backpackers and climbers should also avoid freeze-dried food. Activities that cause you to sweat profusely and expend a great deal of energy dehydrate your body; furthermore, eating freeze-dried food will not only contribute to dehydration in your body but will also "back up" your gastrointestinal tract by absorbing more water as it exits your body. Bring plenty of water and electrolyte-rich drinks if you're climbing or camping with freeze-dried food to help you rehydrate properly.

When food is freeze-dried, it goes through a process known as lyophilization. Food will be chilled to temperatures well below freezing. The water content is removed when vacuum pressure is applied to the food. It is extracted as vapor, which condenses back into ice in the machine's condenser. The temperature is then gradually raised to allow the remaining moisture in the food to be extracted while retaining the structure of the food, which helps rehydrate the food in the future.

Compared to regular freezing in the freezer, rapid freezing will preserve the quality of your food the best because it produces smaller ice crystals. Because liquid nitrogen flash freezes the items, minor damage to the quality of the meats, poultry, and fish occurs, allowing them to retain their quality quite effectively. In addition, unlike regular freezing, the extremely low temperature will be able to kill any bacteria or pathogen that could cause your food to spoil.

You can also go old school and do it the Inca way, flash freezing it and leaving it to dry out in the sun, hoping for the best.

Finally, compared to dehydrating, the latter is far more cost-effective for home use. Unless you spend thousands of dollars on equipment, freeze-drying cannot be done at home. Unless you own a farm or intend to start a freeze-drying business, it is best to stick to standard freezing and dehydration.

The following are some of the reasons why people freeze dry food:

1. Frozen foods are superior to canned and dehydrated foods.
2. Freeze-drying retains nutritional value better than other drying methods, supporting consumers' desire for whole-food nutrition.
3. The freeze-drying process preserves the original raw material's color and shape, assuring consumers that they are eating natural fruits and vegetables.
4. The freeze-drying process eliminates the possibility of bacterial growth by removing the water in the product.
5. Freeze-dried foods require less time to prepare. Simply pour in some hot, boiling water, wait a few minutes, and you're ready to go.
6. Freeze-dried foods have a longer shelf life of up to 25 years.
7. Freeze-dried food is a great solution for people who cannot eat candy due to braces or dentures.
8. Freeze-dried food is a great solution for people who cannot eat candy due to sensitive teeth.
9. Freeze-dried foods are lightweight and inexpensive to transport. The food's nutritional value, flavor, and size are all preserved, and these foods can be stored for months or years. Unlike dehydrated foods, freeze-dried foods can be quickly rehydrated. Trekkers, hikers, and backpackers benefit greatly from freeze-dried foods.
10. Freeze-dried foods can be used as emergency supplies on a rainy day.

SCIENCE BEHIND FREEZE-DRYING

The structure shrinks and deforms less when it is frozen. A vacuum pump can create a vacuum by lowering the pressure below the triple point of water and monitoring the pressure with sensors such as a capacitance manometer throughout the process. Heating plates provide the latent heat of sublimation. Using a refrigerated condenser, the vacuum pump draws sublimated vapors from the process chamber and condenses them to ice. The drying rate slows because the ice/sublimation front moves backward when ice molecules sublime.

Low pressure or vacuum slows the rate of diffusion. When ice is removed from a porous structure, the volume reduction is negligible compared to other drying methods. During drying, evaporated vapors can be recovered by condensing in a refrigerated condenser. The microscopic porous structure aids reconstitution by efficiently regaining maximum water, improving product quality, allowing for the recovery of crispy texture, and shortening the rehydration cycle time.

The shelf life of freeze-dried products containing 2% MC is about two days. The final product does not require refrigeration due to the high quality of its end products. If the resistance occurs at the mouth of the pore, pore blockage kinetic theory can be investigated to improve the quality of dried products. The drying process should maximize component retention (ascorbic acid, nutrients, vitamins), preserve nutritional and sensory values, and reduce processing time and capital costs. Freeze-drying is used for solid (fruits, vegetables, and meat) and liquid raw materials (homogenous solutions). The freeze-drying process is completed in three major stages, with no raw material pre-treatment required.

Using a plate, blast, immersion, or liquid blast freezing method, water in a sample food is frozen below its eutectic temperature. It is considered successful freezing when 95 percent of the water is converted to ice. Freezing affects the distribution of pore size. The optimal freezing rate must be chosen because it affects the drying rate and final product quality. The eutectic point can be determined using thermal analysis techniques such as cryo-microscopy, differential scanning calorimetry, and time versus temperature curve methodologies. The freezing rate governs crystal growth and ice morphology. Slow freezing results in larger crystals, a porous structure, and an increased drying rate, damaging the product's tissues and reducing rehydration efficiency. Accelerated freezing produces small ice crystals that promote intense nucleation while permitting easy reconstitution and rapid drying.

Initial Drying

The process chamber pressure is lower (13.5 270Pa absolute) than the ice vapor pressure in the sample material to sublime ice. Conduction and radiation through the lower and upper plates provide latent sublimation heat. As a result of initial drying or ice sublimation, a dry layer forms on the top surface of the sample product. Diffusion through this partial dry layer or heat movement through the frozen and dry layers determines the drying rate. A refrigerated condenser condenses diffused vapors, and a vacuum pump is used to remove non-condensable gases. This is the longest stage of the freeze-drying process.

During initial drying, a temperature range of -20 to +20 is maintained. Heat transfer can only occur through conduction or radiation because convection lacks its medium due to the absence of air. The product is heated to a temperature below its glass transition temperature. In initial drying, the condenser temperature should be lower than the product temperature. The maximum heat should be less than its eutectic temperature, which raises the pressure difference between the condenser and the product. Heat transfer stops when the product and shelf temperatures become the same, resulting in lower system pressure and condenser temperature values due to no evaporated load. The end of initial drying can be accurately determined using comparative pressure measurement methods.

Freeze-drying preserves the nutritional value, heat-sensitive compounds, color, shape, texture, size, aroma, and flavor of agricultural products. The ongoing development of freeze-drying, as well as future aspects, make its application very feasible. The primary process parameters vary depending on the chemistry of the subjected product. Freeze-drying is an ancient technique that has evolved and continues to improve. However, freeze-drying has a high process and fixed cost. The freeze dryer freezes the product's water before applying the latent sublimation heat to sublimate the frozen water and then increasing the heat to remove any remaining water.

FREEZE DRYING WITH A FREEZE DRYER MACHINE

If you're planning a large-scale freeze-drying empire or simply want to try freeze-drying, one of these machines might be worth investing in. A freeze-drying machine will undoubtedly be a worthwhile investment if you own a farm or a fruit farm. It is important to note that if you need to prepare food for storage quickly, having a freeze dryer in your home will not save you much time. If you want something quick and efficient, other methods are preferable. Overloading the trays and containers of a freeze dryer is not permitted. The drying time will vary between one day for thin slices of meat and fruits and three days for thicker and larger chunks of food.

To get into the deep end of freeze-drying, you must first understand that three steps must occur for a satisfying freeze-dried product to be produced. You can buy a freeze-drying machine or rig something together if you're daring by following YouTube tutorials. Numerous resources are available to teach you how to set up a vacuum chamber in your home.

The first step in creating a DIY home freeze-drying rig is to freeze. You'll need a heavy-duty freezer that can withstand temperatures as low as -30°F or even lower. As previously stated, you can also flash freeze the items with liquid nitrogen for this stage. Second, you'll need an airtight vacuum-sealed chamber and a vacuum pump to extract moisture from your food. This second stage is known as initial drying or sublimation. Finally, there is desorption, also known as secondary drying. Attach a thermostat and a heater to the rig so that you can gradually add heat to the chamber to draw the remaining moisture out. This step is required so that you can adjust the temperature inside the chamber to repeat the sublimation process. A humidity sensor is also needed to determine whether all of the moisture has been removed from your food items.

Armed with this knowledge, you should now ask yourself a few questions before beginning your freeze-drying adventure. What are you going to do with it? Will it only be used for camping or backpacking? Do you buy bulk and plan to freeze-dry cooked items for your family's meals? Or are you a doomsday prepper preparing for the end of the world or nuclear fallout?

Whatever your reason, even a home freeze-drying machine will be an expensive purchase. It is highly preferable to consider your reasons. You don't want to spend a thousand dollars on equipment that will only be used once and collect dust in your basement or garage. Additionally, these machines are large and heavy, taking up much space in your kitchen.

One of the best ways to preserve your groceries or surplus garden harvest is to freeze-dry them. Sublimation removes water from food by converting it from a solid to a vapor or gas. Freeze-drying is one of the best ways to preserve food because it retains almost all nutritional value.

Canning and dehydrating food changes the flavor and color and reduces the nutritional content by half. Freeze-dried foods can be stored in the refrigerator, pantry, or cellar for up to 25 years. They're small and lightweight, making them ideal for quick camping meals or an emergency food supply. Most homeowners can access a home freezer and dry ice if they do not have a freeze-dryer.

PREPARATION OF FREEZE-DRIED FOOD

Before freeze-drying your food, select the freshest options. The food should then be chopped into small pieces or bits to remove moisture. Cooked meals, on the other hand, can be frozen entirely.

If you can afford it, a freeze-dryer is an excellent option because it is explicitly designed for freeze-drying. There are numerous dryers to choose from, so make sure you get an affordable one. The advantage of these dryers is that they come with various trays for different meals.

Follow the procedures below to freeze-dry your goods. Remember to test your meals before storing them if you use this method:

1. Place your meals in the trays, ensuring they do not exceed the tray's height.
2. Place the trays in the dryer after closing the doors (Some models have two doors).
3. Freeze the food between -40 and -50 degrees Fahrenheit.
4. Allow 24 hours for the procedure to be completed.
5. After they're done, place the food in Mylar bags and seal them.

How Does a Home Freeze Dryer Work?

The following is an excerpt from "The Good, the Bad, and the Ugly of Home Freeze Drying":

- First, you get a sturdy freezer (Harvest Right units can reach -30°F or lower).
- Second, you pair it with an airtight chamber capable of maintaining a vacuum (no oxygen) at all times.
- Finally, you connect a vacuum pump powerful enough to remove zebra stripes.

- Install a heater and thermostat to cycle the temperature up and down for many hours, repeating the sublimation process.
- Fifth, connect a humidity sensor to confirm that the water has evaporated and the cycle is complete.

Many goods, such as dairy products, whole meals (hot dishes, cream-based soups, etc.), and leftovers, cannot be preserved conventionally but can be frozen at home. Fruits, vegetables, meats, and seafood can also be preserved.

USING A MACHINE TO FREEZE DRY

Freeze-drying food with a machine is about as simple as it gets. You wash the food you intend to save and cut them into smaller pieces. When the food is ready, place it on the machine's tray, turn it on, and use the machine as the manufacturer directs.

When the food has finished drying, place it in a fixed plastic pack and store it. Although drying food varieties with a machine is quick and easy, it is quite expensive.

You can expect to spend a significant amount of money. If you want to take the easier route and use this strategy to protect your food, be prepared to contribute.

People who are new to freeze-drying food benefit from having a home freezer. This is an even better option if you have a deep freezer. However, your standard home freezer will continue to work.

1. Place the food on a tray or dish after being spread out.
2. Place the tray in the freezer to freeze the food at the coldest temperature possible.
3. Allow the food to freeze for 2–3 weeks or until entirely freeze-dried.
4. After completing the procedure, store it in an airtight storage bag in your freezer or pantry.

FREEZE DRYING WITHOUT A MACHINE

Freeze-drying with a machine is simple, but doing it without a machine isn't too tricky.

The primary difference between using a machine and not one is the amount of time the interaction takes. If you dry food without a machine, you should prepare it as you usually would before securing it with another method.

When the food is finished, place it on an air-drying rack so the air can completely circle it.

Place the plate in a deep cooler and leave it there. The food will immediately freeze. The food will become dry in a matter of weeks.

You will notice that the food has wholly dried by removing one piece. If the food doesn't change color as it defrosts, you'll know the interaction is finished.

HOW TO FREEZE-DRY FOOD WITH DRY ICE

Use protective equipment for this process because dry ice can burn your skin.

Place the food in a freezer bag and freeze it with dry ice. If you leave it open, the escaping air could cause your bag to explode. Pile a lot of dry ice on top of the freezer bag and leave it for 24 hours to dry. After 24 hours, the container or freezer will be filled with carbon dioxide, so do this in a well-ventilated area. Carbon dioxide inhalation in confined spaces can be fatal. If successful, frozen food must be stored in vacuum-sealed airtight containers with no moisture allowed to enter the bag.

It saves time to use dry ice instead of frozen food. This is because dry ice quickly evaporates moisture from the meal. Fill freezer bags with the food. Place the bags in the fridge. Freeze the bags for 24 hours, completely wrapped in dry ice. Remove and store the bags after they have entirely freeze-dried.

Items that are ideal for freezing with dry ice:

- Broth: Take a handful and use it for cooking or flavoring.
- Citrus juice can be used in beverages, seasonings, and dressings.
- Coffee/Tea: Use cool beverages like iced coffee and iced tea without diluting them.

- Herbs: Combine 2 cups fresh herbs and 1 cup water in a blender until smooth, then pour into trays. Frozen herbs are convenient for incorporating into cooked or pureed foods such as soups, sauces, and marinades.

Yogurt can be stored in the freezer for 2 to 3 months. You can blend it into a smoothie as a creamier alternative to ice.

FREEZE-DRYING FOOD USING LIQUID NITROGEN

If you want to freeze dry items at home, another method that will undoubtedly come up when you search the internet is liquid nitrogen. Of course, liquid nitrogen quickly freezes food when it comes into contact with it. Liquid nitrogen, at -320°F, will freeze anything it comes into contact with and should be handled cautiously. Often, liquid nitrogen will be used as a faster way to bring the food to a temperature below freezing before a vacuum pump can extract all of the moisture from the food. If you don't have a drying machine, you can still flash freeze your food before storing it in the freezer with liquid nitrogen.

INSTRUCTIONS FOR STORING FREEZE-DRIED FOOD

Currently, your food options are freeze-dried. What would be a fantastic next step for you? When food sources have finished drying, place them in a plastic sack or compartment that seals.

There is no compelling reason to keep the items in the refrigerator or cooler. If all else is equal, store them in a cool place with temperatures no higher than 75°F.

This could be a root cellar, storage room, or bureau in many homes.

Food security did not appear to be this simple for many years, but we are fortunate. You can dry your food for long-term storage in just a few hours.

You can also store it for an extended period without any special requirements. You may have considered freeze-drying if you're looking for a simple way to save food.

CHAPTER 2

FREEZING - THE MOST EFFECTIVE METHOD TO FREEZE DRY FOOD

Freezing food is a simple process that requires no special equipment, making it ideal for beginners. Prepare your vegetables by blanching or cooking them before freezing. This process inhibits enzyme activity while maintaining high quality. Blanching involves heating your vegetables and immersing them in cold water to stop cooking. Blanching time in boiling water is expected to be three minutes.

Freeze-drying appears to be an excellent method of food preservation, leading you to believe it is extremely perplexing. In any case, freeze-drying food has been around for a long time. It is straightforward and can be refined with or without a machine.

Vacuum sealing frozen products prevents ice crystal formation and can increase the shelf life of frozen items by three to five times. Non-vacuum-sealed items are rarely placed in the freezer. On the other hand, fruits can be frozen "as is" or added with a bit of sugar or antioxidants to help extend storage life and slow discoloration. If you want to freeze fruits and vegetables for long-term storage, consider freezing them on a cookie sheet and then vacuum-sealing them. This helps prevent ice crystal formation, which can increase the storage life of your frozen fruits and vegetables by up to 5 times.

Freezing is one of the most straightforward and convenient methods of food preservation and one of the oldest, along with dehydration. Before the invention of modern home appliances, communities in the far north or near mountain ranges discovered that food did not spoil in freezing temperatures. The power of cold temperatures gave rise to ice boxes (literally, metal boxes stuffed with ice), which eventually evolved into the refrigeration we have today.

Because freezing lowers the temperature of food, micro-organisms can no longer function, and enzymes act at a much slower rate. It's worth noting that I didn't say it "kills" the micro-organisms; they're still there, just not moving. Enzymes will also be present and working much slower, but they will still function, implying that decay will occur much more slowly. Because spoilage elements are still present, once an item thaws, it begins to spoil quickly.

The goal of freezing food is not only to keep it fresher for longer but also to preserve its quality. With this in mind, you should place your food in the freezer with as little air as possible. Food deteriorates due to a leak when exposed to air from outside or within the container.

You can freeze anything you can process in a jar and even more, but deciding which method to use requires weighing the benefits and drawbacks of freezing food. Freezing is ideal for seafood, berries, and other perishable produce (like broccoli). Freezing preserves much of the nutritional value, color, and texture of foods, but there are drawbacks to be aware of. A freezer has limited space; you cannot choose to freeze everything. And, unlike other methods, freezing necessitates defrosting and, in some cases, cooking. It's also difficult to transport unless you have a portable freezer.

Frozen foods, on the other hand, have a shelf life of 3 to 1 year when properly stored. When the temperature of your freezer fluctuates (due to a malfunction, power outage, or being left open for too long), the quality of the frozen items inside can suffer. If there is a prolonged rise in temperature, it is critical to check all frozen items (especially meat) to ensure that they are still frozen. If the item has completely thawed, you should prepare it within the next few days or refreeze it. Label these items with the date and the word "refrozen."

Frozen foods can last for months if properly stored. Because germs cannot develop when food is frozen, food stored in the freezer can be consumed for almost indefinite periods. However, its quality will quickly deteriorate and become unappealing, so most frozen foods should be consumed within a few months to a year.

- To freeze food securely, set the freezer to a temperature between -18°C and -22°C.
- Place food in airtight containers or freezer bags before freezing. Meat is especially prone to freezer burn and becomes unusable if not properly packaged.
- Items should be frozen only before their best-before or use-by dates.
- Never refreeze defrosted food because it allows germs to grow between thawings.
- Consume it right away or refrigerate it for up to 24 hours.
- Defrost the freezer frequently to avoid ice accumulation. You should be able to store frozen items in the refrigerator for a few hours while the freezer defrosts.

Foods should be labeled with the date they were frozen. You can check the expiration date to see if you should eat the food before it spoils. To determine the shelf life of frozen foods, use our online guide.

THE FREEZING PROCEDURE

Freezing isn't rocket science; you've almost certainly done it before, but there are ways to do it better. This is how.

1. Clean Out Your Freezer

If you want to maximize your freezer and use your freezing skills to the fullest, you must first overhaul your freezer. Empty it, assess everything inside, and decide which items are old and/or will be used in a reasonable amount of time. Be honest: are you going to use everything in there? It's also fine, to begin with, an empty freezer so you can fill it with purpose. After you've emptied it, thoroughly clean it, and make sure it has a thermometer, either built into the unit or one you add.

2. Select and Prep Your Ingredients

Select the best and most fresh ingredients you can find. Fruit should be at its peak of flavor, vegetables should be young, and meats should be of the highest possible quality. Wash everything thoroughly but do not soak anything because retained water expands as the item freezes, breaking food tissues and cell walls and reducing quality. As needed, pre-treat. Freeze 101.

3. Divide Your Frozen Items Into Portions

You can portion things however you want if you have the proper vessels to place them in. This allows you to freeze quantities based on how much you want to eat or serve.

Refrigerate animal proteins until ready to cut, and work in small batches as you package them to avoid contamination and quality loss.

Cut fruits and vegetables to your liking and place them in a single layer on a parchment paper-lined tray to freeze. Freeze liquid ingredients in pint or quart containers or heavy-duty resealable plastic bags. If you're freezing in a bag, seal it and place it on a rimmed baking sheet to freeze; once frozen, stack the bags to store.

4. Put Labels On Your Packages

On each package, label your items and include the date frozen. If you want, include words like "spicy," "sugar-free," or "contains nuts."

5. Change Out Your Frozen Foods

Place new freezer items in the back of the freezer and older items in the front. This policy, known as "FIFO" (first in, first out), ensures that older food is used first, reducing waste. Make a raw protein section on the bottom or separate it from other items in the freezer. This reduces the risk of cross-contamination if a meat container breaks or leaks.

However, unlike smoking or curing, freezing does not kill bacteria that can cause food to spoil. Because freezing only stops or slows bacterial growth, spoilage can still occur if your items are not appropriately frozen. To avoid this, food must be frozen quickly and kept at a temperature below 0°F at all times.

By keeping your freezer temperature at or below 0°F, you can not only stop the growth of bacteria that can cause spoilage but also reduce changes in the texture, nutritional value, and flavor of your foods.

THINGS TO CONSIDER BEFORE FREEZING YOUR FOOD

Arrange items in your freezer, so there is enough space between them for cold air to circulate, allowing for an even freeze—only stack items on top of each other when they are completely frozen. At the same time, avoid opening and closing your freezer multiple times daily. The constant temperature fluctuation will cause the items inside the freezer to thaw and freeze repeatedly. Even minor changes in the freezer will cause the smaller ice crystals to grow larger over time, causing further damage to the meat's cell structure and, in the long run, a softer and mushier texture. Temperature changes will also cause water to seep out of the meat, making it less juicy and healthier.

When freezing cooked meat, including the sauce, gravy, or marinade in the bag. This can also help to prevent moisture loss and freezer burn. Before storing it in the freezer, you should also allow pre-cooked food to cool to room temperature. Still, hot food takes a lot more energy to cool down and freeze, raising your electricity bill. Allowing your items to cool to room temperature slows the freezing process and helps maintain their quality.

Some loose food items, such as fruits and vegetables and lower-priced meat, can be tray-packed. Tray-packed items are first arranged in a tray to be quickly frozen so that individual pieces do not touch one another or in one thin layer that is easily broken up when frozen. Afterward, the items are collected and placed in a smaller container or bag for easier access. Berries, broccoli, chopped chicken, chicken wings, patties, and nuggets are all examples of tray-packable foods.

If you don't already have a vacuum sealer, you don't need to buy one if you're only freezing a few items for your home. It is important to note that this is not vacuum packing because you will be unable to remove all of the air from the bag. To do so, fill a large bowl halfway with water and place your meat in a resealable freezer bag. Zip it almost up until you have about a quarter-inch left open. Submerge the bag slowly in the water, slowly pulling down until all the air is pushed out and only the tip left open is above the water.

Butter and margarine can also be frozen when cut and separated by smaller pieces of parchment or baking paper. While the butter or margarine is still cool, cut it into smaller flat squares—place parchment paper between the layers and freeze.

Try to portion the items according to the number of servings you intend to use. This will keep your food from spoiling due to repeated thawing.

Because water expands when frozen, your food will do the same. To prevent leakage, give your meats some wiggle room when packing them in resealable plastic bags. Before putting your items in the fridge, ensure they are correctly labeled. This will save you significant time searching for the right items. It also reduces the time the freezer is left open while you search.

Defrost or thaw food in the refrigerator, with a tray or plate underneath to catch the juices. Food should not be left to thaw in a warm place because it will spoil. Consider the enzymes responsible for its breakdown when freezing food. These enzymes are responsible for hastening the ripening or maturing of plants and the breakdown of cellular structures in meats. If these reactions are allowed to continue, the food's color, flavor, and texture will change. To avoid this, many people blanch the food quickly or add ascorbic acid to prevent browning.

Blanching is the process of quickly immersing food in boiling water for 30 seconds to a minute, followed by rapid cooling in an ice bath. This is mainly done with vegetables, stopping and inactivating the enzymes while also killing any micro-organisms on the surface. Blanching your vegetables allows you to store them for longer periods and takes up less space in your freezer.

Chemical compounds such as ascorbic acid, also known as Vitamin C, can prevent browning on fruits typically eaten raw and thus cannot be blanched. Lemon juice can be substituted for vitamin C if it is unavailable.

The most common issue people face when it comes to meat is rancidity. Freezing meat that will be cooked in a few weeks is fine, especially if it has already been vacuum-packed and frozen. However, if you plan to store fresh meats from the butcher for an extended period, it is best to trim the excess fat and place them in an airtight wrap or a vacuum-sealed plastic bag. This extra step will also help prevent freezer burn, which is damage to meat or other food caused by moisture loss and exposure to air. While the meat is still safe to eat, it may develop dark or gray spots, and the surface may resemble leather. On the other hand, fruits and vegetables will have their water content converted into ice crystals, shriveling and drying out.

Another factor to consider is the food's texture. When water freezes, it expands, so when you freeze food, the cell walls break down or rupture as the water inside them freezes. When the food has finally thawed, it will have a softer or mushy texture. Because of their higher water content, some vegetables and fruits exhibit this effect more than meat. As a result, if you find frozen fruit chunks in your freezer, serving them while they are still partially frozen is best.

Cooking the food beforehand softens the cell walls, reducing the adverse effects. Food that is quickly frozen can produce better results. According to research, the larger the ice crystals, the longer it takes for the food to freeze. As a result, it will cause more cell damage. However, rapidly freezing the food results in smaller ice crystals, which reduces cell damage. This is why flash freezing is often used to preserve the quality of freshly caught seafood for the journey to your table. This is also done to all types of meat typically sold chilled in supermarkets, thawed ahead of time for the shopper's convenience.

Fortunately, this method is not limited to large manufacturers. You can also do rapid freezing at home without any special equipment. All you need is a freezer; fortunately, the freezer in your refrigerator will suffice most of the time.

MAINTAINING QUALITY WHEN FREEZING

You can take steps to ensure higher quality results when freezing, such as pre-treating produce, blanching, and preventing discoloration and freezer burn. Some items, for example, must be pre-treated to maintain their structure in cold temperatures. Similarly, most vegetables should be blanched before freezing, which can be accomplished by lightly steaming or boiling them. Blanching inhibits enzyme activity.

Some fruits, such as cut apples, darken when exposed to air. Apply one of three options to the fruit before freezing to prevent discoloration: lemon juice, salt water (2 teaspoons salt to 2 cups water), or a salt-vinegar solution (1 tablespoon salt + 1 tablespoon vinegar and 2 quarts water). This is especially important when working with lighter-colored fruits.

Freezer burn is another food-quality concern when it comes to freezing. Dehydration in frozen food is referred to as freezer burn. It may be found on the edges of frozen items where there is air exposure. It is not harmful but can affect the product's texture and flavor. Limiting the air to which a product is exposed by removing as much air as possible from the bags (vacuum sealing is ideal) or leaving only 12 inches of headspace in containers. Wrapping items tightly in aluminum foil or plastic wrap and taping them well also helps avoid freezer burn.

TOOLS AND EQUIPMENT

Some of these are required (such as the freezer!) while others are optional.

Containers

Heavy-duty resealable plastic bags, plastic pint or quart containers, or other tougher plastic containers can be used. Many use "deli cups" from restaurant supply stores. It all depends on the size of the items you're storing and how efficiently these storage containers use the freezer space. Use heavy-duty foil and wrap it in plastic wrap to prevent tearing. And, as much as I love using glass for preservation projects, it is brittle.

Pack meat in appropriate containers. Different foods necessitate slightly different containers. Use caution when using large containers because they will cause the items to freeze slowly, which is counterintuitive to our goal. As a general rule, freezer containers should be food grade, moisture-proof, waterproof, durable, odorless, leakproof, and designed for the freezer. This means they should not crack or become brittle after prolonged use in the freezer.

Freezer-grade containers include plastic resealable freezer bags, rigid and resealable metal, glass, or plastic containers, and flexible or soft plastic/silicone containers. Carefully read the back labels of any containers you intend to purchase. They should be clearly labeled as freezer-safe. Most manufacturers would also include temperature limits for their products. Choose items that can withstand temperatures as low as 0°F.

Rigid containers hold liquids, soft foods, and easily broken down foods. The straight and hard sides make it simple to remove the food with a wet towel applied to the outside surface of the container. Most of them are also meant to nest or stack on top of one another. Metal and plastic are the most common materials used to make these containers. glass is another option; however, it should be noted that it has been tested for freezer use. Regular glass containers, such as canning jars can easily crack when temperatures drop below freezing. When using rigid containers, ensure the lids are tightly closed and airtight. If they are not, use freezer tape (tape designed for temperatures below freezing). Masking tapes should not be used because they may not adhere correctly.

The resealable plastic freezer bags and wraps that are widely available in stores are the most commonly used. Heavy-duty aluminum foil can also be used in a pinch. To avoid puncturing, keep them away from sharp objects and corners inside the freezer – using cardboard dividers in the freezer can protect the plastic wraps and aluminum foils. These bags are ideal for drier foods such as chops and steaks, as well as raw meat, fish, poultry, fruits, and vegetables.

Another container that has recently gained popularity on social media is the resealable silicone container, which can also be used as a freezer container. Because it is a hybrid of rigid, softer, more flexible wraps and bags, many people prefer it. Additionally, it is more durable than plastic freezer bags and is an environmentally friendly alternative to freezer bags.

Freezer

There are two types of freezers: upright and chest. Most of us are probably used to upright freezers. It is either a refrigerator/freezer combination or a stand-alone freezer. There are numerous size, style, and appearance variations. Because they are taller rather than wider, the uprights take up less space. However, these freezers are typically much smaller (especially when attached to a refrigerator) and lose cold air quickly when opened. If you need to do some serious freezing, chest freezers are ideal. They are larger and remain cold even when the door is opened because cool air tends to sink to the bottom. They do require more floor space. Whichever you choose, place it away from heat sources, such as your oven, and leave 2 to 4 inches between the back of the unit and the wall to allow for good airflow, which means the appliance won't have to work as hard to keep the temperature cold.

Ice-Cube Tray Made of Silicone

Although there is a long list of things that can be frozen in ice cube trays, you can also use these trays to portion out items that have a big impact in small doses, like lemon juice. Silicone ice cube trays are preferred because they make it easier to remove items from these trays.

Bags and Vacuum Sealer

A vacuum sealer machine removes all of the air from a specially designed bag; the bag conforms to a frozen item, cutting out oxygen. Simple sealers cost between $70 and $1,000 for commercial-grade sous vide sealers. Vacuum sealers are ideal for expensive items like meats and proteins because they ensure that as little air as possible comes into contact with the item, resulting in less freezer burn. This is also an excellent method for preparing single portions of large batch items; you can maximize storage space by eliminating unused space.

FREEZING MEAT AT HOME

If you intend to freeze fresh meats at home, turn on the freezer and keep the temperature inside well below freezing – around -10°F or even lower – for a few hours ahead of time.

Meat that will be used within a week or so can be frozen in its original packaging; however, meat that will be stored for an extended period must be properly packaged and sealed. When storing meats for an ample time, keep them away from air and in an airtight or vacuum-sealed freezer bag to avoid freezer burn.

When working with fresh meats you have just brought home from the store, and you must work quickly and efficiently so that the meat does not have enough time to thaw while working thoroughly. Keep your countertop, hands, utensils, and equipment clean to avoid contamination. To prevent food poisoning, you must exercise extreme caution when handling raw poultry. Also, to keep your family safe, remember to clean and disinfect afterward.

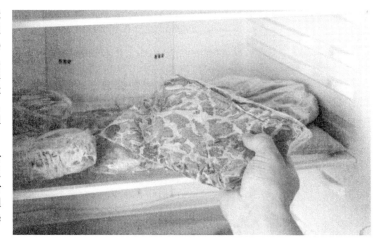

To maintain the quality of the meat, the freezer temperature must be kept below 0°F even after the initial freeze is complete. Allowing food to be stored in a freezer at temperatures above 0°F may result in spoilage and shorter shelf life. Food that has been frozen should be kept frozen.

Place it in the coldest part of the freezer, usually against the walls. Take care not to crowd the area. Cramming your freezer with unfrozen food all at once will result in a slow freeze.

Red Meat

If you are a hunter or butcher, freezing your red meats may be the simplest and quickest thing you can do with them when you have a large quantity and have yet to find the time or the right recipe to make your summer sausage.

Most butchers and delis will gladly freeze your meat for you. It's ideal if you don't want to cook your meat immediately. Put them in the freezer when you get home.

Red meat can be frozen relatively easily. Simply keep them away from moisture and air to maintain their quality. Remove any excess fat and, if possible, all of the bones. It may arrive wrapped in plain butcher paper when you buy fresh meat from the butcher or the store. Meats wrapped in butcher paper or other paper wraps in the store cannot be relied on to prevent freezer burn.

If you don't intend to use them within a week of purchasing them, take them out and rewrap them in a freezer bag or a freezer-safe container. If you don't intend to remove the butcher paper, simply wrap them in a freezer-grade wrap or place them in a freezer-proof bag. Items purchased vacuum sealed and frozen, on the other hand, would require rewrapping. It's fine to refreeze them when you get home.

Furthermore, if you are storing or packing multiple individual cuts of meat in one package or container, place freezer paper or baking paper in between each piece to prevent them from freezing together for easier thawing. Tray packing smaller chunks of meat or cut pieces of poultry is also an option. Tray packing means freezing your meats in a baking tray, arranged, so they do not touch. Cover the tray with freezer-safe plastic wrap and place in the freezer until completely frozen. These can then be placed in smaller, more compact containers for easier storage.

Salted meats such as hams and luncheon meats should not be stored in the freezer even if they are already cured. You will notice that the salt in the cured meats causes your meat to go rancid faster. For other cured meats, such as hotdogs and luncheon meats, freezing temperatures cause the emulsions inside to break down and leak, causing the meat to "weep."

Lower temperatures will cause cooked meat to dry out much faster than raw meat. It is therefore strongly advised to store it in the sauce in which it was cooked. Submerge or coat your meats in gravy before sealing them in a bag or container. After thawing, your meats will retain their freshness while also becoming more flavorful from having had more time to absorb the sauce. However, remember that meats frozen in sauces or marinades will last much less time than fresh raw meat. Try to finish them within three months.

Poultry

When selecting poultry that is best for freezing, choose whole, fresh, and unblemished birds. To ensure freshness, choose plump and odorless ones. You can certainly buy poultry that has already been butchered, but it is well worth your time to learn how to cut up your poultry correctly. It is far easier than it appears and far easier than butchering beef or pork.

Pull and separate the legs and wings from the body before separating the thigh from the drumstick. Split the ribcage in half, separating the back from the breast. If desired, cut the breast in half to make smaller servings.

When selecting the right poultry to freeze, consider how you intend to cook it. Choose more flavorful birds if you want to cook stews. Young poultry, on the other hand, is ideal for roasting and frying.

Before freezing your poultry, prepare it according to how you intend to use it in the future. Birds cut up for specific recipes must be chopped up before freezing. The same is true for cooked birds in half or whole. However, the stuffing inside stuffed poultry should not be frozen. The stuffing is more likely to contain toxic bacteria during thawing and refreezing. The filling can be frozen separately from the poultry. The giblets, gizzard, heart, liver, and neck should also be packed separately because they spoil faster, in about two weeks. These are excellent for making gravy or stuffing.

Pack chopped-up birds in the same manner as you would other red meats. Place freezer paper between individual portions to make separation easier when taking them out. You can also tray individual pack pieces of poultry, which, like red meats, come wrapped in butcher paper when purchased fresh from butcher shops and stores. These papers will not keep your birds from getting burned in the freezer. If you intend to keep these birds in your freezer for more than a week, rewrap or overwrap them until they arrive vacuum-sealed. If they are, do not open them; simply place them in the freezer.

Fish

Fish is much more challenging to prepare than red meat because it spoils quickly. If you catch them fresh, in addition to gutting, descaling, and cleaning them, you should also salt them or dunk them in an ascorbic acid solution to improve their shelf life. So, if you buy them from a fishmonger, ask them to gut, clean, and descale the fish. This will speed up your freezing preparation when you get home.

Freshly caught fish must be frozen immediately, so if you're out on the lake and don't plan on returning home soon, keep your fish packed deep within a large cooler filled with crushed ice. When you get home, thoroughly wash the fish in fresh potable water, then descale it by gently running the back of your knife back and forth against the skin. To remove the entrails, cut the fish's belly. When cutting, be careful not to puncture the innards, as this will impart a bitter taste to your fish. Remove the fish's head and rinse everything in fresh potable water again, paying particular attention to the fish's stomach cavity.

The back and dorsal fins are then removed with a sharp knife. Cut from the base, not leaving any fin stumps in the fish. To remove all the fins cleanly, cut along the side of the fish. Rinse the fish in water once more. After taking larger fish out of the freezer, it is recommended that they be chopped up or filleted for easier cooking. Larger fish, such as tuna or salmon, and large Spanish mackerels, should be cut into 34-inch-thick crosswise steaks.

Cut the back of a medium-sized fish, from the collarbone to the tail, to fillet it. Make another cut along the fish's tail, flattening the knife and slicing the flesh off, running the knife along the spine from the tail to the collarbone. Flip the fish over and repeat the procedure on the other side. Feel for fish bones stuck inside the flesh by running the back of your knife along the fish's spine. Pull out all of the fish bones with a tweezer.

To improve the quality of the fish, pre-treat it before freezing. This will reduce rancidity and the likelihood of flavor change. Dip fish with high-fat content, such as tuna, salmon, mackerel, trout, and mullet, in an ascorbic acid solution for 20 to 30 seconds.

To make the solution, combine two teaspoons of crystalline ascorbic acid and one quart of fresh potable water. Immerse lean fish like snapper, grouper, flounder, cod, croaker, redfish, whiting, and most freshwater species like bass, catfish, and crappie in brine for 20 to 30 seconds. The brine solution combines 14 cups of salt and 1 quart of fresh and cold potable water. This solution will firm the flesh and reduce drip loss when thawing the fish.

After pre-treatment, you have three options for freezing fish. The most convenient method is to wrap it in freezer wrap or place it in a freezer bag. Remove the air from the bag and place it directly in the freezer. For easier thawing, place freezer paper or baking paper between individual slices before freezing, just as you would with individual pieces of meat and poultry.

You can also put it in a rigid container and cover it with fresh potable water before freezing it. Cover the container tightly with an airtight lid or freezer-safe wrap after covering all parts of the fish with water.

You can also use the ice glaze method. This method is primarily used with vacuum-packed, frozen fish commonly found in supermarkets. To do this, unwrap and separate the fish (whole, cut, or filleted) in a tray and freeze. Once completely frozen, quickly immerse the fish or individual pieces of it in very cold, fresh potable water, then place it back in the freezer. Dunk and refreeze the fish several times until a uniform and visible layer of hard ice coats it. This will form a thin layer of water on the fish's surface, protecting it from the harsh environment of the freezer. Afterward, place the ice-glazed fish in a freezer bag and freeze it. Also, keep individual pieces separate from one another.

Fish roe, a delicacy in and of itself, should be frozen separately. Roe is the most perishable part of the fish and should be carefully removed from the stomach cavity and thoroughly washed with fresh potable water. To prepare the egg sacs for freezing, pierce them in several places with a clean and disinfected needle, then dunk them in an ascorbic acid solution like you would with fatty fish. A dip of 20 to 30 seconds would suffice. This will also reduce the rancidity and flavor change effect on the fish eggs when stored in the freezer. After that, freeze the egg sacs in individual freezer wraps or bags. Remember to use up the roe within three months.

Game

To prevent spoilage when storing fresh-caught wild game in the freezer, field dress and process large animals such as deer, antelope, and moose. As with other red meats, butcher and clean the meat before freezing it. Remove the bloodshot meat and discard it before freezing the meat. This will spoil faster and should be thrown away.

Squirrels and rabbits, for example, should be skinned, dressed, and refrigerated or chilled as soon as possible after being killed. Refrigerate it for a day or two until the meat is pliable and no longer rigid. Prepare or cut the meat as you intend to cook it in the future—pack and freeze as you would any other red meat.

Duck, geese, dove, quail, and pheasant should be bled, plucked of feathers, gutted, cleaned, and refrigerated or chilled immediately after shooting. Remember to trim or cut off any excess fat to prevent rancidity, especially on geese and ducks. Pack and freeze these game birds in the same manner as you would other poultry.

THAWING

To avoid the growth of bacteria that can cause spoilage, it is strongly advised to thaw meat, fish, and poultry in the refrigerator. Meats such as steaks and other large cuts of meat and whole poultry should be partially thawed before being placed in a pot or oven to cook. Larger pieces of meat and poultry can be partially thawed to avoid being overdone on the outside and undercooked or raw on the inside.

Frozen meats, fish, and poultry that will be breaded or battered before cooking, on the other hand, should be partially thawed so that the breading batter adheres to the surface. It is preferable to thaw frozen food before completely deep-frying it. Because of the high heat and short cooking time, the outside will be cooked quickly while the inside or center will remain frozen.

Cooking frozen meat takes a long time and should be done slowly over low heat. Cooking at high temperatures results in unbalanced cooking: the surface will char or cook quickly, but the inside will remain cold and frozen. If this is possible with chilled or refrigerated items, the likelihood of serving a charred but frozen inside roast with frozen meats is higher. Depending on the size of the cuts, frozen food will generally take half or twice the time that chilled or room temperature meat, fish, or poultry would.

There are three methods for thawing meats, poultry, and fish straight from the freezer. The quickest and safest method would be to thaw the sealed packages in the refrigerator. Place it on a tray or other container to catch drippings and keep meltwater from flooding your fridge. Smaller cuts will, of course, thaw much faster, taking only a few hours, but larger whole birds and larger cuts of meat may take a day or more to defrost thoroughly.

Submerging the sealed package in a bowl of room temperature water is an old method for thawing or defrosting frozen food. Replace the water every half hour until the item is completely defrosted. To avoid spoilage, the items must be cooked immediately after being thawed using this method.

When you buy microwaves, many of them come with a defrost function. As long as they fit inside the oven, these can also be used to defrost meats, fish, and poultry. You may need to turn and flip the items while defrosting to ensure that everything thaws evenly. Food defrosted in the microwave must be cooked immediately after defrosting, like food defrosted by submerging it in water.

Frozen meats, fish, and poultry should never be left to defrost at room temperature. This causes the bacteria to multiply rapidly, contaminating your food.

Before defrosted raw food items can be safely frozen again, they must be completely defrosted and cooked. Thawing or defrosting and then freezing again will result in larger ice crystals than desired. The meat's cell walls will rupture, causing the meat's quality to deteriorate over time. Cook them after defrosting to reduce moisture, flavor, and quality loss before freezing them again. However, it is perfectly safe to defrost an item inside the refrigerator and then change your mind and need to freeze it again. However, doing so will reduce the quality of the meat.

FLASH FREEZING

Individual food portions should be flash-frozen in a single layer on a parchment-lined tray to allow for easy separation. For easier storage, place the frozen items in heavy-duty resealable plastic bags. The following are the best flash freeze items:

- Avocado
- Banana
- Snap or shelled beans
- Berries
- Coconut
- Kernels of corn
- Flours
- Grains (raw and cooked)
- Seeds and nuts
- Shelled peas
- Stone fruits

The greater the surface area of an item, the greater its exposure to the elements and the shorter its storage time. A cut of meat, for example, will keep longer than ground beef. Similarly, preparing animal proteins before freezing reduces storage time compared to freezing them in their raw state. Foods with a high-fat content will also have a shorter storage life.

Beans and grains don't have their section here, but that doesn't mean they can't be frozen. On the contrary, they are excellent for freezing. The rules are the same regardless of the type of cooking. Cooked grains can be flash-frozen by spreading them on a parchment-lined baking sheet and freezing them. Transfer to a labeled heavy-duty resealable plastic bag once frozen. Freeze beans in their cooking liquid in a pint or quart-size container or flat in a bag in the same manner. They will keep in the freezer for six months. Thaw in the refrigerator overnight, microwave, or reheat on the stovetop in a covered container over low heat.

Meat, Poultry, and Proteins

Thaw meats and proteins in the fridge for best quality—this could take overnight or several days, depending on the size of the pieces. Some frozen items, such as dinners and casseroles, can be cooked directly from the freezer. You can also place the meat in its wrapping in a bowl of cool water on the counter, changing the water frequently to keep it cool. Alternatively, you can thaw in the microwave at 50% power, but check it often so it doesn't start to cook.

Item	Months To Keep Frozen
Bacon and sausage	1 to 2
Casseroles	2 to 3
Egg whites or egg substitute	12
Frozen dinners and entrées	3 to 4
Gravy, meat, or poultry	2 to 3
Ham, hot dogs, lunch meats	1 to 2
Meat, cooked	2 to 3
Meat, uncooked ground	3 to 4
Meat, uncooked roasts	4 to 12
Meat, uncooked steaks, or chops	4 to 12
Poultry, cooked	4
Poultry, uncooked giblets	3 to 4
Poultry, uncooked parts	9
Poultry, uncooked whole	12
Soups and stews	2 to 3
Wild game, uncooked	8 to 12

Fruits

Many fruits can be flash-frozen and then kept frozen, but some foods benefit from pre-treatment. All of these fruits will keep in the freezer for nine months to a year in general but check them periodically to ensure they aren't developing freezer burn and that the packaging is still intact. You can use these straight from the freezer for baking or smoothies or heat them up for sauces and compotes. Fruit that has been frozen can also be a tasty and refreshing snack. Remember that their texture will be softer than fresh fruits, so choose a cooking method that considers this.

Type of Food	Prep Notes
Apples	Peel, core, slice, and dip into acidulated water; can sprinkle with sugar or turn into applesauce
Apricots	Pit; ascorbic acid dip; sugar sprinkle (optional); can puree
Bananas	Peel and slice; ascorbic acid dip; can mash
Blueberries	Blanch for 30 seconds for a firm texture; sugar sprinkle for a soft texture; can crush/puree
Cherries	Stem and pit; sugar sprinkle
Citrus	Peel, segment, or pull apart; sugar sprinkle (optional); can juice
Cranberries	Blanch for 30 seconds for a firm texture; sugar sprinkle for a soft texture; can crush/puree
Figs	Peel (optional); sugar sprinkle (optional); can crush
Grapes	Sugar sprinkle (optional); can juice
Guava	Peel and cut; sugar sprinkle (optional); can puree (add lemon juice)
Loquats	Cut and seed; acidulated water; can puree (add juice)
Mango	Peel and slice; sugar sprinkle (optional); can puree
Melons	Peel, remove soft areas, cube, slice, or ball; sugar sprinkle (optional); can crush (add lemon juice)
Peaches and nectarines	Peel, pit, and slice; acidulated water dip; sugar dip; can crush/puree
Pears	Peel, core, and slice; acidulated water dip; sugar sprinkle (optional); can puree
Persimmons	Peel and cut; can puree (add juice)
Pineapple	Peel, remove eyes/core; dice or slice; sugar sprinkle (optional); can crush
Plums	Cut and pit; acidulated water dip; sugar dip; can puree (use juice)
Rhubarb	Cut into 1-to 2-inch pieces; blanch for 1 minute; sugar sprinkle (optional); can puree (cook in boiling water)

Vegetables

Most vegetables must be pre-treated in some way before freezing. Vegetables can be stored in the freezer for nine months to a year, but check them regularly to ensure they don't develop freezer burn and that the packaging is still intact. For a quick side dish, stir into casseroles, roast straight from the freezer, or heat on the stovetop or microwave. Like fresh fruit, the texture of vegetables will be softer than when cooked, so use a cooking method that takes this into account.

Type of Food	Prep Notes
Asparagus	Trim and blanch
Beets	Roast or boil until thoroughly cooked; peel. If small, freeze whole, or quarter and flash freeze
Broccoli and cauliflower	Separate florets, chop stems, blanch
Broccoli rabe	Trim, chop, and blanch
Brussels sprouts	Halve large sprouts, keep small ones whole; blanch
Carrots	Slice or chop; blanch
Celery	Slice or chop
Corn	Blanch on the cob, then cut off kernels
Eggplant	Slice or halve (if small), salt for 30 minutes, then roast until tender
Fennel bulb	Core, slice, and roast until tender, or chop and freeze (the texture will suffer if you don't pre-cook, so this is appropriate for soups and casseroles)
Garlic	Roast whole, then puree or mash the cloves; freeze in ice-cube trays
Ginger	Grate or juice and freeze in ice-cube trays, or freeze, whole and unpeeled, in plastic wrap—to use, grate from frozen
Green beans	Trim and blanch
Hardy greens	Sauté, cool, and freeze in a heavy-duty resealable plastic bag
Herbs	Blend with water or oil and freeze in ice-cube trays
Leeks	Slice or chop
Mushrooms	Slice or chop, dip in acidulated water, then steam blanch, sauté, or roast
Okra	Trim and blanch
Onions and shallots	Slice or chop
Parsnips	Slice or chop, then blanch
Peppers, sweet and hot	Slice, chop, or leave whole if small; can roast before freezing
Potatoes	Peel, chop, blanch, or roast (do not need to cook fully)
Scallions	Puree or finely chop, mix with water or oil; freeze in ice-cube trays
Spinach and other tender greens	Sauté, cool, and freeze in a heavy-duty resealable plastic bag
Squash, summer	Slice ½ inch thick and blanch
Squash, winter	Roast and mash, or cube and blanch until fully cooked
Sweet potatoes	Peel, chop, blanch, or roast (do not need to cook fully)
Tomatillos	Remove husks, score, freeze whole or roast and freeze
Tomatoes	Blanch and peel, or freeze whole or chopped, or roast and freeze

Troubleshooting

Issue	Root Cause	Solution	Keep/Toss
The surface of food is light-colored; food is tough or dried out	Freezer burn; food exposed to air	• Seal food tightly, making sure there are no tears/rips • Use vacuum-seal bags • Remove as much air as possible from the bag	Keep, but taste and consistency will be altered
Brownish color in vegetables	No blanching	Blanch vegetables before freezing	Keep, but taste and consistency will be altered
Food is mushy	• Freezer burn; food exposed to air • Temperature fluctuation • Food too large or dense when frozen	• Seal food tightly, making sure there are no tears/rips • Use vacuum-seal bags • Remove as much air as possible from the bag • Freeze foods at 0°F or below and maintain the temperature during storage • Freeze smaller portions	Toss
Watery/gummy consistency in fruits	• Freezer burn; food exposed to air • Temperature fluctuation • Food too large or dense when frozen	• Seal food tightly, making sure there are no tears/rips • Use vacuum-seal bags • Remove as much air as possible from the bag • Freeze foods at 0°F or below and maintain the temperature during storage • Freeze smaller portions	Toss
Discoloration in fruits	No pre-treatment	Light-colored fruits need to be treated in sugar syrup or citric acid.	Safe, but the taste and appearance will be altered

HOW TO PROPERLY STORE FROZEN FOOD

Although frozen food can be stored for long periods, its quality and nutrition degrade over time. Even though food can be stored in the freezer indefinitely, don't try to keep it for 50,000 years. Eating beef sitting in the back of your freezer for over a decade is still dangerous. Here's a convenient list that shows how long food can be kept in the freezer.

Seafood

- 2 to 3 months for fatty fish (perch, salmon, and mackerel).
- 3 to 6 months for lean fish (flounder, cod, and sole).
- 4 to 6 months for cooked fish
- 2 months for smoked fish (sealed and vacuum-packed)
- 3 to 6 months for shellfish (e.g., mussels, oysters, scallops)
- 3 to 5 months for shrimp
- 2 months for cooked crab

Processed Meat

- 1 to 2 months for bacon
- 1 to 2 months for luncheon meat (open/sealed package or deli-sliced)
- 3 to 4 months for burgers and ground meat patties (beef, pork, poultry, veal, lamb, and other meats)
- 1 to 2 months for (opened or sealed) hot dogs
- 1 to 2 months for raw sausages (made from beef, chicken, pork, or turkey)
- 1 to 2 months for cooked sausages (made from beef, chicken, pork, or turkey)
- 2 months of pre-frozen sausages (made from beef, chicken, pork, or turkey)
- 5 to 6 months for fresh ham, uncooked and uncured
- 3 to 4 months for fresh ham, cooked and uncured
- 1 to 2 months for fresh ham cured, cooked, and vacuum sealed (unopened)
- 1 month for country ham
- Canned and unopened (labeled "keep refrigerated"): no need to freeze; it will last 6 to 9 months in the fridge
- 1 to 2 months if canned and opened (shelf-stable)
- 1 month for Italian and Spanish hams (Parma, Prosciutto, Serrano, and so on)
- 2 to 3 months for lamb and beef fresh ground meat
- 1 to 2 months for pork fresh ground meat
- 6 to 12 months for beef slices, fresh whole (for steaks and chops)
- 3 to 6 months for pork slices, fresh whole (for steaks and chops)
- 1 to 2 months for veal and lamb slices, fresh whole (for steaks and chops)
- 6 to 12 months for fresh beef (for roasts)
- 3 to 6 months for fresh pork (for roasts)
- 6 to 9 months for fresh lamb and veal (for roasts)

Poultry

- 12 months for a whole chicken
- 6 months for chopped or cut chicken
- 12 months for a whole turkey
- 6 months for chopped or cut turkey
- 6 months for an entire goose and duck
- 3 months for giblets
- 8 to 12 months for uncooked wild game

Pre-Cooked and Cooked Food

- 3 months for stews or casseroles (meat, poultry, and fish)
- 3 months for meat pies
- 8 months for fruit pies (unbaked)
- 2 to 4 months for baked fruit pies
- 3 months for bread
- 3 months for the cake

- 3 months for cookies (baked and unbaked)
- 6 to 9 months for dairy butter
- 12 months for margarine
- 1 month for fresh milk
- 2 months for heavy cream
- 1 month for whipped cream
- 2 months for ice cream
- 5 to 8 weeks for organic and natural cheeses
- 4 months for processed cheeses

Eggs

- 12 months for raw beaten eggs (raw eggs keep better in the freezer when beaten)
- 12 months for Raw eggs (in shells); however, keep refrigerated until thawed.

Overall, food appropriately stored in subzero temperatures will keep you going for a long time, if not indefinitely, but be careful if the frozen item has been sleeping in the back of a freezer for years. Avoid eating food that appears and smells off or rotten to avoid food poisoning.

CHAPTER 3

RECIPES TO HELP YOU GET STARTED WITH YOUR FREEZE-DRYING PROCESS

TERIYAKI MARINADE

Preparation time: 10 minutes
Cooking time: 35 minutes
Servings: 1 cup

Ingredients:

- ⅓ c. soy sauce
- ⅓ c. rice wine vinegar
- 3 tbsp. olive oil
- 2 tbsp. light brown sugar
- 1 tsp. thinly sliced garlic or ½ teaspoon garlic powder
- 1 tsp. grated peeled fresh ginger or ½ teaspoon ground ginger

Directions:

- ❖ In a medium bowl, large measuring cup, or jar, combine the soy sauce, vinegar, oil, sugar, garlic, and ginger. Whisk well to combine.
- ❖ If you are freezing the marinade alone, pour it into a plastic pint container, or freeze flat in a heavy-duty resealable plastic bag.
- ❖ If you are freezing the marinade with chicken, tofu, or tempeh, place the protein in a vacuum or heavy-duty resealable plastic bag. Pour the marinade into the bag. Close the bag, removing as much air as possible.
- ❖ Place the bag on a flat dish in the freezer for 3 hours or until frozen solid. Check the bag to ensure there are no leaks—label and use within three months.

TOMATO PASTE

Preparation time: 30 minutes, plus 1 hour to cool
Cooking time: 4 to 26 hours
Servings: 4 half-pints or 32 ice cubes

Ingredients:

- 12 lbs. tomatoes, cored and chopped (4 quarts); if you don't have a food mill, blanch and peel the tomatoes before coring and chopping
- 2 bay leaves
- ½ tsp. Diamond Crystal kosher salt (optional)

Directions:

- ❖ If using a food mill, skip this step. In a large pot over high heat, cook the chopped tomatoes for 30 minutes, stirring frequently and crushing them with a wooden spoon to break them down and make them soft. Press the cooked tomatoes through a fine-mesh sieve into a slow cooker.
- ❖ If using a food mill, pass the raw tomatoes through a food mill into a slow cooker.
- ❖ Add the bay leaves to the cooker, cover the cooker, and cook on high heat for 2 hours. After 2 hours, the puree should be bubbling.

- ❖ Turn the lid slightly to the side so there is an opening for air to escape, or use two wooden spoons to prop up the lid. The objective is to have air flowing out of the cooker while keeping the puree hot so it can reduce. Cook for 24 hours, checking it and stirring every so often. The paste is ready when it holds its shape on a spoon.
- ❖ Alternatively, place the puree in a saucepan, add the bay leaves, and place the pan over medium heat. Cook for 1½ to 2 hours, frequently stirring to avoid burning. When the paste is thick and coats the spoon, remove it from the heat and let it cool for 1 hour.
- ❖ Taste the paste; add the salt if using.
- ❖ Once cooled, remove the bay leaves from the paste, spoon the paste into an ice-cube tray, and freeze for 1 hour.
- ❖ Transfer the cubes into a heavy-duty resealable plastic bag when the paste is frozen. Keep frozen, labeled, for up to 6 months. If you have vacuum-sealed bags, portion the cubes into groups of 4 and vacuum seal the bags for freezing.

CHICKEN BONE BROTH

Preparation time: 15 minutes
Cooking time: 8 hours 30 minutes (stovetop); 15 hours 30 minutes (slow cooker)
Makes: 4 quarts

Ingredients:

- 20 c. water
- Bones from 1 whole roasted chicken, picked clean of meat
- 1 yellow onion, quartered
- 1 celery stalk halved
- 3 carrots, roughly chopped
- 3 garlic cloves, peeled
- 1 bay leaf
- 2 tsp. Diamond Crystal kosher salt (optional), divided, plus more as needed

Directions:

- ❖ In a slow cooker, combine the water, bones, onion, celery, carrots, garlic, bay leaf, and one teaspoon of salt (if using). Cover the cooker and cook on high heat for 10 to 15 minutes until the liquid starts to boil. If 20 cups of water are too much for your slow cooker, just cover the bones with water.
- ❖ Once the broth boils, turn the slow cooker temperature to low. If you are making this on the stovetop, combine the ingredients in a large stockpot over high heat and bring it to a boil. Reduce the heat to low, partially cover the pot with a lid, and simmer for 6 to 8 hours. With either appliance, maintain a simmer or low boil.
- ❖ Check the broth at the 5-hour mark. You should start to see the chicken fat on the top of the broth and the vegetables softening.

- After the 10-hour mark, the broth will start to become ready. The chicken bones should be brittle, and you can crush them easily.
- By hour 15, the vegetables will almost disintegrate upon touching them. Taste the broth and turn off the heat.
- Using a fine-mesh strainer set over a large heatproof bowl, filter out all the bones and vegetables from the broth. Taste the broth. Add the remaining teaspoon of salt (if used), stir, and taste again. If you need more salt, add it to taste.
- Pour the broth into four quart-size plastic containers, leaving 1½ inches of headspace to allow the broth to expand while freezing—freeze, labeled, for up to 6 months.

SPINACH AND PARMESAN FRITTATAS

Preparation time: 15 minutes
Cooking time: 35 minutes
Servings: 12 frittatas

Ingredients:

- 2 tbsp. olive oil or butter, divided
- 1 c. chopped onion
- 1 (16-ounce) package frozen spinach, thawed, squeezed dry, and chopped
- 12 large eggs
- ½ tsp. Diamond Crystal kosher salt
- ½ tsp. freshly ground black pepper
- ¾ c. grated parmesan cheese
- 1 tbsp. dried parsley or dill (optional)

Directions:

- Preheat the oven to 350°F. Coat a 12-cup muffin tin, or two 6-cup tins, using one tablespoon of oil.
- Heat the remaining one tablespoon of oil over medium heat in a small skillet. Add the onion and cook for about 8 minutes, stirring, until soft.
- Add the spinach and cook for 2 minutes, just until hot. Evenly distribute the vegetable mixture among the prepared cups.
- Whisk the eggs, salt, and pepper in a large bowl until blended. Whisk in the cheese and dried herbs, if desired.
- Pour the egg mixture into a large measuring cup and evenly distribute it into the muffin tin, using all the custard.
- Bake for 25 minutes until the eggs are lightly browned on the top and sizzling on the sides.
- Let cool to room temperature. Remove the cooled frittatas from the tin and place them into a heavy-duty resealable plastic bag—freeze, labeled, for up to 3 months.
- To reheat, microwave on high power for 2 minutes.

VEGAN SOUP

Preparation time: 20 minutes
Cooking time: 30 minutes
Servings: 1 cup

Ingredients:

- 4 tbsp. of olive oil
- 2 c. chopped leeks, white part only (from approximately three medium leeks)
- 2 tbsp. finely minced garlic, Kosher salt
- 2 c. carrots, peeled and chopped into rounds (about two medium)
- 2 c. peeled and diced potatoes
- 2 c. fresh green beans, broken or cut into 3/4-inch pieces
- 2 qt. of chicken or vegetable broth
- 4 c. peeled, seeded, and chopped tomatoes
- 2 ears of corn, kernels removed
- ½ tsp. freshly ground black pepper
- ¼ c. packed, chopped fresh parsley leaves
- 1 to 2 tsp. freshly squeezed lemon juice

Directions:

- In a sizable, heavy-bottomed stockpot, warm the olive oil over medium-low heat.
- Once hot, add the leeks, garlic, and a dash of salt, and cook for 7 to 8 minutes, or until they start to soften.
- Stirring occasionally, add the carrots, potatoes, and green beans. Cook for 4 to 5 minutes.
- Add the stock, increase the heat to high, and bring to a simmer. Once simmering, add the tomatoes, corn kernels, and pepper.
- Reduce the heat to low, cover, and cook until the vegetables are fork-tender, approximately 25 to 30 minutes.
- Remove from heat and add the parsley and lemon juice—season to taste with kosher salt. Serve immediately.

PEA, SCALLION, AND GINGER RAMEN SOUP

Preparation time: 15 minutes
Cooking time: 12 minutes
Servings: 2 cups

Ingredients:

- 1 tbsp bouillon granules
- 1 tbsp powdered soy sauce
- ½ tsp ground ginger
- ⅛ tsp ground garlic
- 1/8 teaspoon freshly ground black pepper
- ¼ cup freeze-dried peas
- 2 tbsp freeze-dried scallions
- 1/2 cup Ramen noodles (broken).
- 1¾ cups boiling water (divided)

Directions:

- ❖ Mix the bouillon powder, ground soy sauce, powdered garlic, fresh ginger, freeze-dried scallions and ramen noodles together in a Ziplock bag or jar that holds 1 quart. Mix well.
- ❖ Mix the ingredients in a bowl or mug with a 2+ cup capacity.
- ❖ Stir in half the boiling water and mix well until it is all incorporated. Stir in the remaining boiling water.
- ❖ Cover with a towel and let it rest for between 8-10 minutes.
- ❖ To freeze-dry the soup. First, spoon it onto the tray, and then spread it out to a thickness of approximately half an inch. Following the half-inch guideline when filling the tray is a solid starting point. Overfilling the tray will cause condensation within the freeze drier. After the food has been placed on the tray, now, place the tray into the freeze dryer's rack.
- ❖ Put in the insulating pad, and close and secure the door. Push start. Freeze dryers include a built-in reminder to make sure the drain valve is shut. Push Continue, and it will start.
- ❖ After it's done, extract the soup from the freeze dryer.
- ❖ Place it in a Mylar bag with an oxygen-absorbing packet, seal it, and label it with the date.

NOTE: I have used Freeze Dryer to freeze-dry all the recipes. But for your convenience, you can use any of the methods mentioned in chapter 2.

POTATO AND CHIVE FREEZE DRIED SOUP

Preparation time: 5 minutes
Cooking time: 15 minutes
Servings: 2 cups

Ingredients:

- ⅓ cup instant potato flakes
- 2 tbsp grated Parmesan cheese canned and dried
- 1 ½ tsp cornstarch
- 1 tbsp freeze-dried chives
- 2 tbsp bouillon granules ¼ cup powdered milk
- 1/8 tsp onion powder
- 1/8 Tsp garlic powder
- 1/8 teaspoon freshly ground black pepper
- ⅛ tsp salt
- 1 3/4 cups boiling water (divided).

Directions:

- ❖ Add the instant potato chips, frozen cheese, cornstarch and freeze dried herbs, bouillon powder granules milk powder, powdered milk powder, onion powder, garlic powder, fresh ground black pepper salt, and powdered milk to a

zip lock bag or jar with a 1 quart capacity. Mix well.
- ❖ Mix the ingredients in a 2+ cup mug or bowl.
- ❖ Stir in half the boiling water and mix well until it is all incorporated. Stir in the remaining boiling water.
- ❖ Cover with a towel and let it rest for between 8-10 minutes.
- ❖ To freeze-dry the soup. First, spoon it onto the tray, and then spread it out to a thickness of approximately half an inch. Place the tray into the freeze dryer's rack.
- ❖ Put in the insulating pad, and close and secure the door. Push start.
- ❖ After it's done, extract the soup from the freeze dryer.
- ❖ Put it in a Mylar bag with an oxygen-absorbing packet, seal it, and label it with the date.

STUFFED PEPPER SOUP

Preparation time: 5 minutes
Cooking time: 15 minutes
Servings: 2

Ingredients:

- ¼ cup instant 1-minute rice
- 1/4 cup frozen-dried green bell peppers
- 1/4 cup frozen-dried red bell peppers
- 1/4 cup frozen-dried orange bell pepper
- 1/4 cup frozen-dried ground beef
- 1/4 cup frozen-dried tomato powder
- 3 cups boiling water (divided).
- To serve, pinch of oregano
- Serve with a pinch of thyme
- Splash of pepper sauce (to serve)

Directions:

- ❖ To a zip lock bag, or jar, add the instant rice, freeze green bell peppers and red bell peppers as well as freeze dried orange bell peppers, frozen-dried ground beef and freeze dried tomato paste. Mix well.
- ❖ Mix the ingredients in a 3+ cup mug or bowl.
- ❖ Stir in half the water. Continue stirring until it is completely dissolved. Add the remaining boiling water to the bowl and stir.
- ❖ Cover with a towel and let it rest for between 8-10 minutes.
- ❖ Season the soup by adding a pinch of oregano, thyme, and a splash pepper sauce.
- ❖ To freeze-dry the soup. First, spoon it onto the tray, and then spread it out to a thickness of approximately half an inch. Place the tray into the freeze dryer's rack.
- ❖ Put in the insulating pad, and close and secure the door. Push start.
- ❖ After it's done, extract the soup from the freeze dryer. Put it in a Mylar bag with an oxygen-absorbing packet, seal it, and label it with the date.

THAI COCONUT MILK SOUP WITH RICE

Preparation time: 5 minutes
Cooking time: 10 minutes
Servings: 2

Ingredients:

- ½ cup powdered coconut milk
- 1½ tbsp bouillon granules)
- 1 tsp powdered soy sauce ½ tsp brown sugar
- 2 tsp cornstarch
- ½ tsp dried basil
- ½ tsp ground ginger
- ⅛ tsp ground garlic
- Ground cayenne in a pinch
- 1/5 tsp powdered lime juice crystals powder
- ¼ cup chopped freeze-dried mushrooms
- 1 tbsp freeze-dried scallions
- 2 tbsp freeze-dried peas
- 1/4 cup instant 1-minute Rice
- 1 3/4 cups boiling water (divided).

Directions:

- ❖ You can add the powdered coconut milk and bouillon powder granules, as well as brown sugar, cornstarch or dried ginger, ground garlic, cayenne pepper, lime juice crystals and freeze-dried mushrooms, freeze -dried scallions and freeze-dried peas to a jar, or Ziplock bag that holds a 1-quart jar. Mix the ingredients together by stirring or massaging them until they are well combined.
- ❖ Mix the ingredients in a 2+ cup mug or bowl.
- ❖ Stir in half the boiling water and mix well until it is all incorporated. Stir in the remaining boiling water.
- ❖ Cover with a towel and let it rest for between 8-10 minutes.
- ❖ To freeze-dry the soup and rice. First, spoon them onto the trays, and then spread it out to a thickness of approximately half an inch. Place the trays into the freeze dryer's rack.
- ❖ Put in the insulating pad, and close and secure the door. Push start.
- ❖ After it's done, extract the trays from the freeze dryer. Put it in a Mylar bag with an oxygen-absorbing packet, seal it, and label it with the date.

CHICKEN NOODLE SKILLET MEAL IN A JAR

Preparation time: 5 minutes
Cooking time: 10 minutes
Servings: 2

Ingredients:

- 2 cups egg noodles
- 1 tbsp minced, dehydrated onions
- 1/3 cup instant non-fat dried milk
- 1 1/2 teaspoons Italian seasoning
- ½ tsp salt
- ¼ tsp pepper
- ¼ cup butter powder
- 1/2 cup freeze-dried vegetable mix
- ⅓ cup cheese powder
- 1 cup frozen-dried diced chicken
- 3½ cups water

Directions:

- ❖ In a large-mouthed Mason Jar, layer the ingredients according to recipe order: egg noodles, minced onion, non-fat dry milk, Italian seasoning, salt and pepper, butter powder. To settle, shake gently.
- ❖ Place a canning lid over the jar. Seal it with a vacuum seal. Add a ring and tighten by hand, taking care to not overtighten.
- ❖ You can label the jar with the date and keep it dry in a cool, dry place.
- ❖ Once you're ready to cook, transfer the contents of the jar to a skillet.
- ❖ Bring to boil the water. Reduce the heat and simmer for between 12-15 minutes, stirring occasionally.
- ❖ Remove the pan from the heat. Allow the sauce to cool for about 3-5 minutes. Enjoy and serve.
- ❖ To freeze-dry the meal. First, spoon it onto the tray, and then spread it out to a thickness of approximately half an inch. Place the tray into the freeze dryer's rack.
- ❖ Put in the insulating pad, and close and secure the door. Push start.
- ❖ After it's done, extract the tray from the freeze dryer. Put it in a Mylar bag with an oxygen-absorbing packet, seal it, and label it with the date.

EGG FRIED RICE

Preparation time: 5 minutes
Cooking time: 15 minutes
Servings: 2

Ingredients:

- 1 cup freeze-dried mixed veggies
- 1 vegetable bouillon cube
- ½ tsp ground ginger
- ½ tsp brown sugar
- ¼ tsp garlic powder
- 2 Single-portion sachets with soy sauce. Instant rice in 60 seconds
- 1/4 cup whole eggs crystals Water (as required)

Directions:

- ❖ Prepare three Ziplock bags while you are at home.

- ❖ Combine the mixed vegetables with the bouillon cubes, ground ginger, sugar and garlic powder in the first bag.
- ❖ You can add the rice to another bag, and the egg crystals in the third.
- ❖ Combine the egg crystals and 3 ounces of water in a saucepan. Stir well to combine.
- ❖ Place the pot on the stovetop and, using low heat, cook the eggs crystals, stirring constantly. Once the egg is cooked, take it out of the pot and place it on a plate.
- ❖ To the pot, add 1 1/4 cups water and the contents from the first Ziplock bag. Reduce the heat to low and let the vegetables simmer for 5 minutes.
- ❖ Stir in the rice. Remove the pot from the heat. Cover the pot with a lid. Let the pot cool for five minutes.
- ❖ Mix the egg back into the pot. Stir the eggs well to combine and heat the eggs.
- ❖ To freeze-dry the rice. First, spoon them onto the trays, and then spread it out to a thickness of approximately half an inch. Place the trays into the freeze dryer's rack.
- ❖ Put in the insulating pad, and close and secure the door. Push start.
- ❖ After it's done, extract the trays from the freeze dryer. Put it in a Mylar bag with an oxygen-absorbing packet, seal it, and label it with the date.

JAMBALAYA WITH ORZO

Preparation time: 5 minutes
Cooking time: 12 minutes
Servings: 6

Ingredients:

- 1 cup orzo pasta
- ½ cup freeze-dried vegetables
- 2 tbsp tomato powder
- 1 tbsp Cajun seasoning
- 1 tsp salt
- 1 tbsp olive oil
- 3 ounces spicy smoked sausage
- 2½ cups water

Directions:

- ❖ When you get home, put the orzo pasta and freeze-dried vegetables, tomato powder, Cajun seasoning and salt in a Ziplock container. Separately pack the oil and spicy-smoked sausage.
- ❖ Add the contents of the Ziplock bag outside your home to a pan.
- ❖ Add the water to the pan. Then, heat the oil in the pan and continue cooking for about 8-10 minutes until the orzo becomes al dente.
- ❖ While the sausage is heating, cut it and place it in a pan.
- ❖ To freeze-dry the meal. First, spoon it onto the trays, and then spread it out to a thickness of

approximately half an inch. Place the trays into the freeze dryer's rack.
- ❖ Put in the insulating pad, and close and secure the door. Push start.
- ❖ After it's done, extract the trays from the freeze dryer. Put it in a Mylar bag with an oxygen-absorbing packet, seal it, and label it with the date.

PASTA CARBONARA

Preparation time: 5 minutes
Cooking time: 7 minutes
Servings: 2

Ingredients:

- 4 ounces uncooked angel hair pasta
- ½ tsp salt
- 1 tbsp olive oil
- 2 tbsp whole eggs crystals
- 2 tbsp grated, dried and canned Parmesan cheese
- ½ tsp black pepper
- 2 ounces bacon jerky

Directions:

- ❖ At home, place the angel hair pasta, salt, and oil in a large Ziplock bag. In a separate container, add the oil.
- ❖ In a second Ziplock bag, add the egg crystals and grated Parmesan cheese. As needed, repackage the bacon jelly.
- ❖ Add the pasta and salt outside your home to the crockpot. Add enough water to cover the pasta and then add the olive oil. Bring to a boil, and cook the pasta until it is al dente.
- ❖ Reduce the heat to low and add the egg crystals, Parmesan cheese and stir well. If too much of the mixture has boiled, you may need to add some water.
- ❖ Turn off the heat source and add the bacon jerky. Serve and enjoy.
- ❖ To freeze-dry the pasta. First, spoon it onto the trays, and then spread it out to a thickness of approximately half an inch. Place the trays into the freeze dryer's rack.
- ❖ Put in the insulating pad, and close and secure the door. Push start.
- ❖ After it's done, extract the trays from the freeze dryer. Put it in a Mylar bag with an oxygen-absorbing packet, seal it, and label it with the date.

THAI RED CURRY RICE WITH COCONUT MILK SAUCE

Preparation time: 5 minutes
Cooking time: 8 minutes
Servings: 3

Ingredients:

- ½ cup instant 60-second rice
- 1/4 cup frozen-dried mixed vegetables
- ¼ cup freeze-dried chicken
- 3 tbsp coconut milk powder 2 tbsp Thai Red Curry Powder
- 1 tbsp peanut butter powder
- 1 tbsp peanuts (chopped)
- ½ sachet crystallized lime
- ½ tsp salt
- ¾ cup water
- 1 tbsp oil

Directions:

- ❖ At home, combine the dry ingredients in a Ziplock bag (rice, freeze-dried mixed veggies, freeze-dried chicken, powdered milk, curry powder, powdered peanut butter, peanuts, lime, and salt). Shake to combine. Double bag for transport to prevent the curry from infiltrating your purse or backpack.
- ❖ Outside your home, bring the water to a boil.
- ❖ Add the Ziplock bag's contents to the pot along with the oil and stir to combine.
- ❖ Cover with a lid and simmer for 4-6 minutes, until the rice, chicken, and veggies are rehydrated.
- ❖ To freeze-dry the meal. First, spoon it onto the trays, and then spread it out to a thickness of approximately half an inch. Place the trays into the freeze dryer's rack.
- ❖ Put in the insulating pad, and close and secure the door. Push start.
- ❖ After it's done, extract the trays from the freeze dryer. Put it in a Mylar bag with an oxygen-absorbing packet, seal it, and label it with the date.

APPLE CRISP

Preparation time: 5 minutes
Cooking time: 8 minutes
Servings: 2

Ingredients:

- 1½ cups freeze-dried apples
- 3 tbsp brown sugar
- 1 tsp ground cinnamon
- ¼ tsp ground cloves
- ⅓ cup granola
- ¼ cup walnuts (chopped)

Directions:

- ❖ While at home, add the apples, followed by the sugar, ground cinnamon, and ground cloves, to a Ziplock bag.
- ❖ Using a second smaller Ziplock bag, combine the granola with the chopped walnuts.
- ❖ Outside your home, transfer the apple mixture to a cookpot.
- ❖ Add approximately 3 cups of water to the mixture, and stir to combine. Light a stove, and cook over moderate to low heat until the apples start to soften and the sugar is dissolved. You will need to

stir the mixture to thicken and add a drop of more water if necessary.

- ❖ When the apple mixture is ready, take the pot off the heat.
- ❖ Scatter the granola and walnuts over the granola and enjoy.
- ❖ To freeze-dry the apple crisps. First, spoon it onto the trays, and then spread it out to a thickness of approximately half an inch. Place the trays into the freeze dryer rack.
- ❖ Put in the insulating pad, and close and secure the door. Push start.
- ❖ After it's done, extract the tray from the freeze dryer. Put it in a Mylar bag with an oxygen-absorbing packet, seal it, and label it with the date.

FETA CHEESE TOPPED MOUSSAKA

Preparation time: 5 minutes
Cooking time: 2 hours
Servings: 2

Ingredients:

- 4 large aubergines (thinly sliced diagonally)
- Olive oil
- 2 pound 2 ounces minced lamb
- 2 large-size onions (peeled, chopped)
- 4 cloves garlic (peeled, crushed)
- 4 tbsp tomato puree
- 1 tsp ground cinnamon
- 1½ tbsp dried mixed herbs
- 2 (14½ ounce) cans chopped tomatoes

Topping:

- 2 large-size eggs
- 17½ ounces plain Greek yogurt
- 7 ounces Greek feta cheese (crumbled)
- Black pepper
- 2 tbsp Parmesan cheese (finely grated)

Directions:

- ❖ Preheat the main oven to 425 degrees F.
- ❖ Brush one side of the sliced aubergines with a drop of oil and arrange on 2 large baking sheets.
- ❖ In batches, if necessary, roast the aubergine in the preheated oven for 20 minutes, flipping over halfway and brushing with a drop more oil. Roast until fork tender and golden. Set to one side in a bowl and repeat with the remaining aubergine.
- ❖ Reduce the oven temperature to 395 degrees F.
- ❖ In the meantime, heat a large casserole dish over high heat. When sufficiently hot add the lamb mince and cook while breaking the meat up using the back of a spoon for 5 minutes.
- ❖ Stir in the onions along with the garlic and cook until the lamb is browned and the onions, softened; this will take around 5 minutes.

- Transfer the lamb mixture to a colander to drain away any fat, return to the dish.
- Next, add the tomato puree, cinnamon, and mixed herbs, cook for 60 seconds.
- Stir in the canned tomatoes, to combine. Add sufficient cold water to one empty can to fill it halfway full and tip the contents into the dish.
- Season and rapidly simmer, while occasionally stirring for 15 minutes, until the majority of the liquid has evaporated.
- In the meantime, prepare the topping. In a bowl, combine the eggs with the Greek yogurt. Stir in the feta cheese and season liberally with pepper.
- Layer the moussaka. Evenly divide half of the lamb mince between two, deep 2-quart oven and freezer safe dishes.
- Evenly divided the roasted aubergines between the two dishes and arrange on top of the mince. Season and repeat the layers, finishing with aubergine.
- Divide the topping between them, evenly spread to cover the aubergine layer. Scatter Parmesan over the top.
- Set one moussaka aside to completely cool, for freezing.
- Place the second moussaka on a baking tray and cook in the preheated oven for between 35-40 minutes, until the cheese is golden and the meat is piping hot. You may need to cover the moussaka in foil to avoid it browning too quickly.
- Serve and enjoy.
- To freeze-dry the meal. First, spoon it onto the tray, and then spread it out to a thickness of approximately half an inch. Place the tray into the freeze dryer's rack.
- Put in the insulating pad, and close and secure the door. Push start.
- After it's done, extract the tray from the freeze dryer. Put it in a Mylar bag with an oxygen-absorbing packet, seal it, and label it with the date.

TOMATO SOUP WITH WHOLE WHEAT ORZO

Preparation time: 5 minutes
Cooking time: 30 minutes
Servings: 4

Ingredients:

- 2 tbsp olive oil
- 1 medium-size onion (peeled and chopped)
- 1¼ cups uncooked whole wheat orzo pasta
- 2 (14 ounces) cans chopped whole tomatoes with juice
- 3 cups low-salt chicken broth
- 2 tsp dried oregano
- ¼ tsp salt
- ¼ tsp freshly ground black pepper

- Greek feta cheese (crumbled)
- Fresh basil (chopped, to serve)
- Crusty bread (to serve)

Directions:

- In a large pan, over moderate heat, heat the oil.
- Add the onion to the pan and sauté for 3-5 minutes, until tender.
- Add the whole wheat orzo and cook while stirring until lightly toasted.
- Stir in the drained tomatoes, chicken broth, dried oregano, salt, and black pepper. Bring to boil.
- Turn the heat down and simmer, while covered for 15-20 minutes, or until the orzo is bite-tender. Do this while occasionally stirring.
- Garnish with crumbled feta and chopped basil – serve.
- To freeze-dry the soup. First, spoon it onto the trays, and then spread it out to a thickness of approximately half an inch. Place the trays into the freeze dryer's rack.
- Put in the insulating pad, and close and secure the door. Push start.
- After it's done, extract the trays from the freeze dryer. Put it in a Mylar bag with an oxygen-absorbing packet, seal it, and label it with the date.

STRAWBERRY LEMONADE DEEP DISH PIE

Preparation time: 5 minutes
Cooking time: 10 minutes
Servings: 2

Ingredients:

- 2½ cups frozen strawberry slices (thawed)
- 1 (3.4 ounce) container instant lemon pudding mix
- 8 ounces whipped topping
- 1 (9") graham cracker crust

Directions:

- Combine the strawberries (along with any thawing juices) and the pudding mix. Set aside for 5 minutes. Fold in the whipped topping.
- Spoon the mixture into the graham cracker crust.
- To freeze-dry the dish. First, spoon it onto the tray, and then spread it out to a thickness of approximately half an inch. Place the tray into the freeze dryer's rack.
- Put in the insulating pad, and close and secure the door. Push start.
- After it's done, extract the tray from the freeze dryer. Put it in a Mylar bag with an oxygen-absorbing packet, seal it, and label it with the date.

APPLE CRISP

Preparation time: 5 minutes
Cooking time: 50 minutes
Servings: 2

Ingredients: Apples:

- 5 cups apples (cored, sliced)
- ¼ cup brown sugar
- ½ tbsp fresh lemon juice
- Pinch nutmeg
- ½ tsp cinnamon
- 2 tbsp flour
- Crisp:
- 4 cups brown sugar
- 4 cups flour
- 2 cups oats
- ½ tsp nutmeg
- 1 tsp cinnamon
- 2 cups salted butter (cubed)

Directions:

- ❖ First, prepare the apples. Toss the apples together with the brown sugar, lemon juice, nutmeg, cinnamon, and flour in a large bowl. Divide the mixture between 6 small disposable, freezer-safe aluminum trays.
- ❖ Next, using clean hands, combine the sugar, flour, oats, nutmeg, and cinnamon together in a bowl. Rub in the cubes of butter until you form a crumbly mixture. Scatter the mixture evenly over the apples.
- ❖ To freeze-dry the food. First, spoon it onto the tray, and then spread it out to a thickness of approximately half an inch. Place the tray into the freeze dryer rack.
- ❖ Put in the insulating pad, and close and secure the door. Push start.
- ❖ After it's done, extract the tray from the freeze dryer. Put it in a Mylar bag with an oxygen-absorbing packet, seal it, and label it with the date.

LEMON MERINGUE FREEZE

Preparation time: 5 minutes
Cooking time: 5 hours
Servings: 3

Ingredients:

- 1 (4½ ounce) package instant lemon pie filling
- 1 tbsp fresh lemon zest
- 3 ounces whipped topping
- 14 soft ladyfingers
- ½ cup fresh raspberries
- 1 tbsp lemon peel twists

Directions:

- ❖ Prepare the pie filling as per the package directions and pour into a bowl.
- ❖ Stir in the lemon zest and allow it to completely cool.
- ❖ Prepare the whipped dessert topping mix as directed on the package directions and stir gently into the pie filling.
- ❖ Cut a 2" piece from one end of each of the 14 ladyfingers and put to one side.
- ❖ Arrange the ladyfingers, rounded-side out, around the rim of a 9" springform pan. They need to be standing up around the edge.
- ❖ Use the trimmed pieces to cover the bottom of the pan.
- ❖ Spoon the pie filling into the pan and freeze until firm, for approximately 4 hours.
- ❖ Heat the main oven to 425 degrees F.
- ❖ Remove the rim of the springform pan.
- ❖ Next, prepare the meringue as directed on the pie filling package and spread evenly over the dessert.
- ❖ Bake until golden, for 5 minutes.
- ❖ Top with fresh raspberries and lemon peel twists.
- ❖ To freeze-dry the meal. First, spoon it onto the tray, and then spread it out to a thickness of approximately half an inch. Place the tray into the freeze dryer's rack.
- ❖ Put in the insulating pad, and close and secure the door. Push start.
- ❖ After it's done, extract the tray from the freeze dryer. Put it in a Mylar bag with an oxygen-absorbing packet, seal it, and label it with the date.

MAPLE MUFFINS

Preparation time: 5 minutes
Cooking time: 30 minutes
Servings: 2

Ingredients:

- 2 cups all-purpose flour
- 2 tsp baking powder
- ½ cup brown sugar
- ½ tsp salt
- ¾ cup whole milk
- ½ cup salted butter (melted)
- ½ cup pure maple syrup
- ¼ cup sour cream
- 1 large egg
- ½ tsp vanilla essence

Topping:

- 3 tbsp all-purpose flour
- 3 tbsp sugar
- 2 tbsp nuts (chopped)
- ½ tsp ground cinnamon
- 2 tbsp cold butter

Directions:

- ❖ Preheat the main oven to 400 degrees F.
- ❖ In a large mixing bowl, combine the flour with the baking powder, brown sugar, and salt.
- ❖ In a second bowl, combine the milk with the butter, maple syrup, sour cream, egg, and vanilla essence. Add to the dry ingredients, and stir until just moistened.
- ❖ Fill paper-lined muffin cups ⅔ full.
- ❖ For the topping, combine the flour with the sugar, chopped nuts and cinnamon; cut in the butter until a crumbly consistency and sprinkle over batter.
- ❖ Bake in the preheated oven for between 15-20 minutes.
- ❖ Set aside to cool for 5 minutes before removing from the muffin cups to a wire baking rack.
- ❖ Serve the muffins warm.
- ❖ To freeze-dry the maple muffins. First, spoon them onto the trays, and then spread it out to a thickness of approximately half an inch. Place the trays into the freeze dryer's rack.
- ❖ Put in the insulating pad, and close and secure the door. Push start.
- ❖ After it's done, extract the trays from the freeze dryer. Put it in a Mylar bag with an oxygen-absorbing packet, seal it, and label it with the date.

MINI WATERMELON AND LIME TARTS

Preparation time: 5 minutes
Cooking time: 2 hours
Servings: 6

Ingredients:

- 2 cups seedless watermelon (cubed)
- 2 tbsp honey
- 1 cup Greek yogurt
- 1 tbsp fresh lime juice
- 1½ tsp lime zest (grated)
- 2 tbsp slivered almonds (toasted)

Directions:

- ❖ Add the watermelon to a food processor and blitz to a smooth puree. Divide the mixture between 8 cupcake liners. Freeze for an hour.
- ❖ Combine the honey, yogurt, lime juice, and zest in a bowl. Spoon the mixture on top of the watermelon and sprinkle with toasted almonds. Return to the freezer for at least another hour.
- ❖ To freeze-dry the dish. First, spoon it onto the tray, and then spread it out to a thickness of approximately half an inch. Place the tray into the freeze dryer's rack.
- ❖ Put in the insulating pad, and close and secure the door. Push start.

- ❖ After it's done, extract the tray from the freeze dryer. Put it in a Mylar bag with an oxygen-absorbing packet, seal it, and label it with the date.

PEANUT BUTTER CHOC CHIP BANANA BREAD

Preparation time: 5 minutes
Cooking time: 1hour
Servings: 2

Ingredients:

- Nonstick spray
- 1 cup granulated sugar
- 2 cups all-purpose flour
- 1 tsp bicarb of soda
- 1 tsp baking powder
- 1 tsp pumpkin pie spice
- 1 tsp salt
- 2 large eggs (at room temperature)
- 4 ripe bananas (peeled, mashed)
- ¼ cup unsweetened applesauce
- ½ cup smooth peanut butter
- 2 tsp vanilla essence
- ¼ cup canola oil
- ⅔ cup semisweet choc chips

Directions:

- ❖ Preheat the main oven to 350 degrees F.
- ❖ Spritz three 4x3x2" loaf tins with nonstick spray.
- ❖ Combine the sugar, flour, bicarb of soda, baking powder, pie spice, and salt in a bowl.
- ❖ In a second bowl, beat together the eggs, banana, applesauce, peanut butter, vanilla essence, and canola oil.
- ❖ Fold the dry mixture into the wet until incorporated.
- ❖ Fold in the choc chips.
- ❖ Divide the batter between the three loaf tins. Bake in the oven for just over 45 minutes until golden. Allow to cool completely.
- ❖ To freeze-dry this recipe. First, put it onto the tray, and then spread it out to a thickness of approximately half an inch. Place the trays into the freeze dryer's rack.
- ❖ Put in the insulating pad, and close and secure the door. Push start.
- ❖ After it's done, extract the tray from the freeze dryer. Put it in a Mylar bag with an oxygen-absorbing packet, seal it, and label it with the date.

GARLIC LIME CHICKEN

Preparation time: 5 minutes
Cooking time: 4 hours
Servings: 4

Ingredients:

- 2½ pounds chicken breasts (trimmed, halved)
- ½ cup low sodium soy sauce
- ¼ cup freshly squeezed lime juice
- 1 tbsp Worcestershire sauce
- 2 tbsp garlic (peeled, minced)
- ½ dry mustard
- ½ tsp ground black pepper
- ¼ cup water

Directions:

- ❖ Add the chicken breasts, soy sauce, lime juice, Worcestershire sauce, garlic, mustard, black pepper and water to a large Ziplock bag, seal, and gently shake to combine.
- ❖ To freeze-dry the meal. First, spoon it onto the tray, and then spread it out to a thickness of approximately half an inch. Place the tray into the freeze dryer's rack.
- ❖ Put in the insulating pad, and close and secure the door. Push start.
- ❖ After it's done, extract the tray from the freeze dryer. Put it in a Mylar bag with an oxygen-absorbing packet, seal it, and label it with the date.

POLISH SAUSAGE AND PASTA CASSEROLE

Preparation time: 5 minutes
Cooking time: 1 hour
Servings: 2

Ingredients:

- 4 cups uncooked penne pasta
- 1½ pounds Polish smoked sausage (cut into ½" slices)
- 1 (16 ounce) jar sauerkraut (rinsed, well-drained)
- 2 (10¾ ounce) cans of condensed cream of mushroom soup, undiluted
- 1⅓ cups 2% milk
- 3 cups Swiss cheese (shredded, divided)
- 2 tbsp Dijon mustard
- 4 green onions (chopped)
- 4 garlic cloves (peeled, minced)

Directions:

- ❖ Preheat the main oven to 350 F.
- ❖ Cook the penne pasta according to the package directions; drain and transfer to a large mixing bowl.
- ❖ Stir in the slices of sausage, sauerkraut, cream of mushroom soup, milk, 2 cups of Swiss cheese, Dijon mustard, onions, and garlic.
- ❖ Spoon the mixture into 2 (8") square greased casserole dishes and sprinkle with the remaining 1 cup of cheese.
- ❖ Bake, uncovered, in the preheated oven until it is golden brown and bubbly, this will take between 45-50 minutes.

- ❖ To freeze-dry the Polish Sausage and Pasta Casserole. First, spoon them onto the trays, and then spread it out to a thickness of approximately half an inch. Place the trays into the freeze dryer's rack.
- ❖ Put in the insulating pad, and close and secure the door. Push start.
- ❖ After it's done, extract the trays from the freeze dryer. Put it in a Mylar bag with an oxygen-absorbing packet, seal it, and label it with the date.

ROSEMARY SHRIMP

Preparation time: 5 minutes
Cooking time: 45 minutes
Servings: 3

Ingredients:

- 6 tbsp freshly squeezed lemon juice
- 8 tbsp olive oil
- 2 tsp salt
- ½ tsp ground black pepper
- ½ tsp red pepper flakes
- 6 cloves of garlic (peeled, minced)
- 2 (6") sprigs of rosemary (stems discarded, finely chopped)
- 40 jumbo shrimp (peeled, deveined)
- Nonstick cooking spray
- Wedges of lemon

Directions:

- ❖ In a zip lock bag, combine the lemon juice, oil, salt, pepper, red pepper flakes, garlic, and rosemary.
- ❖ Add the shrimp to the bag, seal and gently shake to coat evenly.
- ❖ Transfer to the fridge to marinate for half an hour, while occasionally turning the bag.
- ❖ When you are ready to cook, run the zip lock bag under warm running water until the shrimp are thawed.
- ❖ Remove the shrimp from the bag and grill, for a couple of minutes on each side, until pink.
- ❖ Serve with wedges of lemon and enjoy.
- ❖ To freeze-dry the shrimps. First, put them onto the trays, and then spread it out to a thickness of approximately half an inch. Place the trays into the freeze dryer's rack.
- ❖ Put in the insulating pad, and close and secure the door. Push start.
- ❖ After it's done, extract the trays from the freeze dryer. Put it in a Mylar bag with an oxygen-absorbing packet, seal it, and label it with the date.

SHRIMP STIR FRY

Preparation time: 5 minutes
Cooking time: 25 minutes
Servings: 2

Ingredients:

- ⅓ cup soy sauce
- 1 tbsp brown sugar
- 1 tsp garlic (peeled, minced)
- ½ tsp ground ginger
- Pinch of crushed red pepper flakes
- 1-pound raw shrimp (peeled)
- 2 cups broccoli florets
- 1 red bell pepper (sliced)
- 1½ cups snow peas
- 1 cup carrots (trimmed, shredded)
- 1 tbsp cornstarch + 1 tbsp water (optional)

Directions:

- ❖ For the freezer: In freezer-safe, one-gallon Ziplock bag combine the soy sauce with the brown sugar, garlic, ginger, and red pepper flakes. Seal and gently shake to combine.
- ❖ Add the shrimp to the bottom of the Ziplock bag along with the broccoli florets, peppers, peas, and carrots. Re-seal the bag and gently squeezed to expel as much air as you can. Lay the bag flat in the freezer and freeze.
- ❖ When you are ready to serve, over moderate heat, heat a large frying pan or skillet and drizzle with oil.
- ❖ Add the stir-fry to the pan and cook until the veggies are tender and the shrimp are pink, this will take between 10-15 minutes.
- ❖ If the stir-fry needs thickening, combine the cornstarch with the water in a bowl, stir to create a slurry and stir into the pan, stir-frying for an addition 2-3 minutes, to allow the sauce to thicken.
- ❖ Remove the pan from the heat and serve at once with boiled rice, fried rice or noodles.
- ❖ To freeze-dry the dish. First, spoon it onto the trays, and then spread it out to a thickness of approximately half an inch. Place the trays into the freeze dryer's rack.
- ❖ Put in the insulating pad, and close and secure the door. Push start.
- ❖ After it's done, extract the trays from the freeze dryer. Put it in a Mylar bag with an oxygen-absorbing packet, seal it, and label it with the date.

SLOW COOKER PEPPER STEAK

Preparation time: 5 minutes
Cooking time: 6 hours
Servings: 4

Ingredients:

- 1 (3 pound) beef top round roast
- 1 large onion (peeled, halved, sliced)
- 1 large green pepper (cut into ½" strips)
- 1 large sweet red pepper (cut into ½" strips)
- 1 cup water
- 4 garlic cloves (peeled, minced)
- ⅓ cup cornstarch

- ½ cup reduced-sodium soy sauce
- 2 tsp sugar
- 2 tsp ground ginger
- 8 cups hot cooked brown rice

Directions:

- ❖ Add the roast beef, onion, green and red peppers to a slow cooker.
- ❖ Add the water along with the garlic and covered, cook for 6-8 hours on low, until the meat is bite-tender.
- ❖ Remove the meat to a chopping board.
- ❖ Transfer the veggies along with the cooking juices to a large pan and bring to boil.
- ❖ In a small-size bowl, combine the cornstarch with the soy sauce, sugar and ginger until silky smooth. Stir into the veggie mixture.
- ❖ Return to boil, while continually stirring and cook for 1-2 minutes, until thickened.
- ❖ Slice the beef and gently stir it into the sauce, until heated through.
- ❖ Serve and enjoy with rice.
- ❖ To freeze-dry the steaks. First, put them onto the trays, and then spread it out to a thickness of approximately half an inch. Place the trays into the freeze dryer's rack.
- ❖ Put in the insulating pad, and close and secure the door. Push start.
- ❖ After it's done, extract the trays from the freeze dryer. Put it in a Mylar bag with an oxygen-absorbing packet, seal it, and label it with the date.

SPEEDY FREEZER CHICKEN CURRY

Preparation time: 5 minutes
Cooking time: 45 minutes
Servings: 2

Ingredients:

- 2 pounds boneless skinless chicken breasts (rinsed, trimmed, cut into bite-size pieces)
- Salt and pepper
- ⅓ cup butter
- ⅔ cups onion (peeled, chopped)
- 1 tbsp + 1 tsp curry powder
- 2 tsp ginger (minced)
- 2 tsp garlic (minced)
- 2 tsp sugar
- 2 tsp chicken bouillon powder
- ⅔ tsp salt
- ⅓ cup all-purpose flour
- 1⅓ cups water
- 1⅓ cups milk
- 2 tsp freshly squeezed lemon juice

Directions:

- ❖ For the freezer: Lightly season the chicken with salt and pepper.

- ❖ Over moderate heat, in a large frying pan, cook the chicken for 10 minutes, until no pink remains. Remove from the heat and then set aside to cool.
- ❖ While the chicken is cooling, over moderate heat, in a large pan melt the butter.
- ❖ Add the onions and then cook while stirring until softened for approximately 5 minutes.
- ❖ Add the curry powder followed by the ginger, garlic, sugar, chicken bouillon powder, and salt, and cook while stirring for a couple of minutes.
- ❖ Add the flour and cook while stirring for 2 minutes, to create a paste-like consistency.
- ❖ A little at a time, add the water along with the milk and cook while continually stirring, until thickened.
- ❖ Whisk in the fresh lemon juice and allow the sauce to cool.
- ❖ Evenly spread the sauce over the chicken, serve.
- ❖ To freeze-dry the chicken curry. First, put it onto the tray, and then spread it out to a thickness of approximately half an inch. Place the tray into the freeze dryer's rack.
- ❖ Put in the insulating pad, and close and secure the door. Push start.
- ❖ After it's done, extract the tray from the freeze dryer. Put it in a Mylar bag with an oxygen-absorbing packet, seal it, and label it with the date.

SWEET N' SPICY ASIAN MEATBALLS

Preparation time: 5 minutes
Cooking time: 3 hours
Servings: 2

Ingredients:

- 1 egg (beaten)
- ½ medium onion (peeled, finely chopped)
- ⅓ cup sliced water chestnuts (diced)
- 3 tbsp fresh cilantro (minced)
- 1 jalapeno pepper (deseeded, finely chopped)
- 3 tbsp reduced-sodium soy sauce
- 4 garlic cloves (peeled, minced)
- 1 tbsp fresh ginger root (minced)
- ⅔ cup panko breadcrumbs
- 2 pounds ground pork

Sauce:

- 2 cups ready-made sweet and sour sauce
- ¼ cup BBQ sauce, of choice
- ¼ cup store-bought duck sauce
- 2 tbsp chicken broth
- 1 tbsp fresh cilantro (minced)
- 1 tbsp reduced-sodium soy sauce
- 2 garlic cloves (peeled, minced)
- 1½ tsp fresh gingerroot (minced)
- Green onions (thinly sliced)

Directions:

- ❖ Preheat the main oven to 375 degrees F.

- ❖ In a bowl, combine the first eight ingredients (egg, onion, chestnuts, cilantro, jalapeno pepper, soy sauce, garlic, and ginger root).
- ❖ Stir in the breadcrumbs and add the ground pork, mixing thoroughly but lightly.
- ❖ Shape the mixture into a 1¼" balls and arrange in a single layer on a greased rack set in a 15x10x1" baking pan and bake in the oven for 18-20 minutes, until gently browned.
- ❖ Transfer the meatballs to a slow cooker of 4-5 quart capacity.
- ❖ In a bowl, prepare the sauce, by mixing the sweet and sour sauce with the BBQ sauce, duck sauce, chicken broth, cilantro, soy sauce, garlic cloves, and the ginger root. Mix to combine and pour evenly over the meatballs.
- ❖ Cook on low, while covered for 3-4 hours until sufficiently cooked through.
- ❖ If cooking immediately, garnish with sliced green onions and serve.
- ❖ To freeze-dry the meatballs. First, put them onto the trays, and then spread it out to a thickness of approximately half an inch. Place the trays into the freeze dryer's rack.
- ❖ Put in the insulating pad, and close and secure the door. Push start.
- ❖ After it's done, extract the trays from the freeze dryer. Put it in a Mylar bag with an oxygen-absorbing packet, seal it, and label it with the date.

TUSCAN CHICKEN PASTA BAKE

Preparation time: 5 minutes
Cooking time: 55 minutes
Servings: 2

Ingredients:

- Nonstick spray
- 1 (13¼ ounce) package whole wheat penne pasta
- 1 (7 ounce) jar julienne-cut sun-dried tomatoes in oil (drained, oil reserved, patted dry)
- 1¼ pounds boneless skinless chicken breasts (cut into bite-sized pieces)
- 1 small onion (peeled, diced)
- 1 clove garlic (peeled, minced)
- 5 ounces fresh baby kale
- 3 ounces reduced-fat cream cheese
- 1 cup whole milk
- ½ cup Parmesan cheese (freshly grated)
- 1 cup Mozzarella cheese (shredded)

Directions:

- ❖ Spritz a 9x13" baking dish with nonstick baking spray. If enjoying immediately, rather than freezing, preheat the main oven to 350 degrees F.
- ❖ Bring a pan of salted water to boil and cook the penne until al dente. Drain.

- In the meantime, in a large deep frying pan, heat 1 tbsp of the reserved sun-dried tomatoes in oil and add the chicken along with the onions.
- Cook until the chicken is sufficiently cooked through and the onions translucent while occasionally stirring for approximately 5 minutes.
- Add the garlic and cook for 60 seconds, until fragrant.
- Add the kale along with the sun-dried tomatoes and while frequently stirring, cook until the kale is wilted.
- Add the cream cheese, milk, and grated Parmesan cheese, stirring well to incorporate. Cook until the cream cheese is entirely melted and combined.
- Add the drained penne pasta and gently stir to coat evenly.
- Transfer the mixture into the baking dish and top with shredded Mozzarella cheese.
- If immediately serving, place the dish in the preheated oven and cook for half an hour, until the cheese is entirely melted.
- To freeze-dry the chicken pasta dish. First, put it onto the trays, and then spread it out to a thickness of approximately half an inch. Place the trays into the freeze dryer's rack.
- Put in the insulating pad, and close and secure the door. Push start.
- After it's done, extract the trays from the freeze dryer. Put it in a Mylar bag with an oxygen-absorbing packet, seal it, and label it with the date.

CHICKEN CACCIATORE

Preparation time: 5 minutes
Cooking time: 1 hour
Servings: 5

Ingredients:

- 4 ounces chicken (chopped)
- ¼ cup all-purpose flour
- Salt and black pepper
- 2 tbsp olive oil
- 2 tbsp butter
- 1 large-size onion (peeled and chopped)
- 2 ribs of celery (sliced)
- 1 large-size green bell pepper (cut into strips)
- ½ pound fresh mushrooms (sliced)
- 2 (14 ounces) cans tomatoes (drained and chopped)
- 1 (6 ounces) can tomato paste
- 1 cup dry red wine
- 1 tsp dried thyme
- 1 tsp dried oregano
- 1 tsp dried rosemary (crushed)
- 1 tsp dried basil
- 3 cloves of garlic (peeled and minced)
- 1 tbsp sugar
- Pasta (cooked, hot, to serve)
- Parmesan cheese (freshly grated, to serve)

Directions:

- Lightly dust the pieces of chicken with flour and season with salt and black pepper.
- In a large-size skillet or frying pan, in oil and butter, brown the chicken on all sides over moderate-heat heat. Remove the chicken to a plate.
- In the same pan, while stirring, cook the onion along with the celery, pepper, and mushrooms for 5 minutes.
- Stir in the canned tomatoes followed by the tomato sauce, tomato paste, red wine, thyme, oregano, rosemary, basil, garlic, and sugar. Bring to boil, cover with a lid, then simmer for half an hour.
- Return the chicken to the pan, and cover with a lid. Next, simmer for 45-60 minutes, until the chicken is cooked through.
- Serve on a bed of pasta, garnished with freshly grated Parmesan cheese.
- To freeze-dry the chicken cacciatore. First, put them onto the trays, and then spread it out to a thickness of approximately half an inch. Place the trays into the freeze dryer's rack.
- Put in the insulating pad, and close and secure the door. Push start.
- After it's done, extract the trays from the freeze dryer. Put it in a Mylar bag with an oxygen-absorbing packet, seal it, and label it with the date.

CHICKEN POT PIE

Preparation time: 5 minutes
Cooking time: 1hour
Servings: 7

Ingredients:

- 2 cups potatoes (peeled and diced)
- 1¾ cups carrots (sliced)
- 1 cup butter (cubed)
- ⅔ cup onion (peeled and chopped)
- 1 cup all-purpose flour
- 1¾ tsp salt
- 1 tsp dried thyme
- ¾ tsp pepper
- 1½ cups whole milk
- 3 cups chicken stock
- 4 cups cooked chicken (cubed)
- 1 cup frozen peas
- 1 cup frozen corn kernels
- 4 sheets store-bought refrigerated pie crust

Directions:

- Add the potatoes along with the carrots to a large pan. Pour in sufficient water to cover and bring to boil. Turn the heat down and cook, while covered for 8-10 minutes, until tender but crisp. Drain.

- In a large frying pan, over moderate-high heat, heat the butter. Add the onion to the pan and cook while stirring until tender. Stir in the flour along with the salt, thyme, and pepper until incorporated.
- A little at a time, stir in the milk and chicken stock. Bring the mixture to boil, stirring continually, and cook for 3 minutes, until it thickens.
- Stir in the chicken followed by the peas, corn kernels, and the potato mixture. Take the pan off the heat.
- Unroll 2 sheets of pastry and use it to line 2 (9") pie plates. Trim, so the pastry is even with the rims of the dishes.
- Add the chicken mixture, unroll the remaining 2 sheets of pastry and place them over the filling. Trim, seal and flute the pastry edges. Then, make slits in the top of each pie to allow any steam to escape.
- Preheat your main oven to 425 degrees F. Next, bake in the oven for 35-40 minutes, until the pie crust browns. Allow the pies to stand for 15 minutes before slicing.
- To freeze-dry the meal. First, put it onto the trays, and then spread it out to a thickness of approximately half an inch. Place the trays into the freeze dryer's rack.
- Put in the insulating pad, and close and secure the door. Push start.
- After it's done, extract the trays from the freeze dryer. Put it in a Mylar bag with an oxygen-absorbing packet, seal it, and label it with the date.

SKILLET GARLIC CHICKEN PASTA

Preparation time: 5 minutes
Cooking time: 55 minutes
Servings: 8

Ingredients:

- 1 pound fresh chicken breast (cut into 1" pieces)
- 3 tbsp olive oil (divided)
- 1 tbsp butter
- 1 tsp Italian seasoning
- Salt and black pepper (to taste)
- ½ cup onion (peeled and chopped)
- 2 garlic cloves (peeled and minced)
- 2½ cups chicken broth
- 1 (14 ounces) can diced tomatoes (undrained)
- 2½ cup uncooked penne pasta
- ¼ tsp crushed red pepper flakes
- ½ cup half and half
- 1 cup mozzarella cheese (shredded)

Directions:

- Warm a large skillet over moderately-high heat. Next, add 1½ tbsp of olive oil and butter to the pan.

- When the butter is melted, add the chicken along with the Italian seasoning, salt, and black pepper. Cook until golden brown, for around 15 minutes.
- Remove the chicken from the pan and transfer to a plate. Set to one side.
- Turn the heat down to moderate, then add the remaining oil, followed by the onions. Cook the onions until translucent, for 5-6 minutes. Next, add the garlic and cook for 60 seconds.
- Pour the chicken broth, and add the diced tomatoes, uncooked pasta, red pepper flakes, and chicken set aside in Step 4. Stir well and bring to boil. Then, cover your pan with a lid and turn the heat down to low. Simmer for 15 minutes, until the pasta is bite-tender.
- Stir in the half and half. Then, allow to stand for approximately 10 minutes, until the sauce thickens. Serve and enjoy.
- To freeze-dry the garlic chicken pasta. First, put them onto the trays, and then spread it out to a thickness of approximately half an inch. Place the trays into the freeze dryer's rack.
- Put in the insulating pad, and close and secure the door. Push start.
- After it's done, extract the trays from the freeze dryer. Put it in a Mylar bag with an oxygen-absorbing packet, seal it, and label it with the date.

SLOW COOKER ITALIAN TURKEY AND SPINACH BEAN STEW

Preparation time: 5 minutes
Cooking time: 4 hours
Servings: 2

Ingredients:

- 2 pounds ground turkey
- 1 medium-size onion (peeled)
- 1 (14½ ounces) can great Northern beans (drained and rinsed)
- 2 celery ribs (diced)
- 3 carrots (diced)
- 6 cloves of garlic (peeled and minced)
- 16 ounces chicken stock
- 2 tbsp cooking sherry
- 1 (14½ ounces) can diced tomatoes
- 1 (6 ounces) can green chilies
- 2 tbsp tomato paste
- 8 ounces spinach (frozen and chopped)
- 2 tbsp Herbes de Provence
- 1 tbsp dried basil
- 2 tsp salt
- 1 tsp chili powder
- 1 bay leaf
- ¼ cup fresh parsley (minced, to garnish)

Directions:

- In a large frying pan over moderate-high heat, sauté the turkey cooking until no pink remains. Transfer to a bowl.
- Puree the onion and add it to the bowl containing the turkey followed by the Northern beans, celery, carrots, and garlic.
- Next to the bowl, add the chicken stock, sherry, tomatoes, green chilies, tomato paste, spinach, Herbes de Provence, basil, salt, chili powder, and bay leaf. Mix thoroughly to combine.
- Transfer the mixture to a slow cooker of 5-quart capacity. Cover and on low cook for 8-10 hours or on high for 4-6 hours.
- Garnish with parsley and serve.
- To freeze-dry the stew. First, put it onto the tray, and then spread it out to a thickness of approximately half an inch. Place the tray into the freeze dryer's rack.
- Put in the insulating pad, and close and secure the door. Push start.
- After it's done, extract the tray from the freeze dryer. Put it in a Mylar bag with an oxygen-absorbing packet, seal it, and label it with the date.

CHEESY HAM AND POTATO CASSEROLE

Preparation time: 5 minutes
Cooking time: 1 hour
Servings: 4

Ingredients:

- Butter (to grease)
- 2 cans (10¾ ounces) condensed cream of celery soup
- ½ cup water
- 2 cups sour cream
- ½ tsp black pepper
- 2½ cups deli ham (cubed)
- 16 ounces processed cheese (cubed)
- 2 (28 ounces) packages frozen hash brown potatoes

Directions:

- First, preheat the main oven to 375 degrees F. Grease two 2-quart baking dishes.
- In your large bowl, stir together the soup, water, sour cream, and black pepper.
- Stir the ham, cheese, and hash browns into the soup mixture, then divide the mixture evenly between the two prepared baking dishes.
- Next, cover the dishes with aluminum foil and bake in the oven for 40 minutes. Next, uncover and bake for another 10-15 minutes until bubbling.
- Allow the casseroles to stand for 10 minutes before serving.

- To freeze-dry the recipe. First, put it onto the tray, and then spread it out to a thickness of approximately half an inch. Place the tray into the freeze dryer's rack.
- Put in the insulating pad, and close and secure the door. Push start.
- After it's done, extract the tray from the freeze dryer. Put it in a Mylar bag with an oxygen-absorbing packet, seal it, and label it with the date.

CROCK POT BEEF FAJITAS

Preparation time: 5 minutes
Cooking time: 7 hours
Servings: 2

Ingredients:

- 1½ pounds beef chuck steak (cut into 4 pieces)
- 1 medium-size onion (peeled and diced)
- 1 red bell pepper (diced)
- 1 (15 ounces) can diced tomatoes (drained of juice)
- 1 cup beef broth
- 2 tsp garlic (minced)
- 12 ounces ground chorizo
- To serve (optional):
- Warm tortillas
- Freshly squeezed lime juice
- Cilantro (chopped)

Directions:

- In a bowl, combine the steak pieces with the onion, red bell pepper, tomatoes, beef broth, and garlic.
- In pinch-size amounts, add the ground chorizo to the mixture and stir gently to incorporate.
- Transfer to your crockpot and cook on low for 7 hours or high for 4-5 hours.
- To serve, either from fresh or frozen: Remove from the crockpot, shred the meat, removing and discarding any fat. Return the meat to the crop pot, Drain off any excess liquid, as necessary.
- Serve with warm tortillas, a squeeze of fresh lime juice and chopped cilantro.
- To freeze-dry the beef fajitas. First, put it onto the tray, and then spread it out to a thickness of approximately half an inch. Place the tray into the freeze dryer rack.
- Put in the insulating pad, and close and secure the door. Push start.
- After it's done, extract the tray from the freeze dryer. Put it in a Mylar bag with an oxygen-absorbing packet, seal it, and label it with the date.

PORK CASSOULET

Preparation time: 5 minutes
Cooking time: 45 minutes

Servings: 4

Ingredients:

- Nonstick cooking spray
- 1 pound pork tenderloin (cubed)
- 1 pound smoked kielbasa sausage (sliced)
- 1 yellow onion (peeled, then cut into wedges)
- 3 carrots (peeled and chopped)
- 4 cloves garlic (peeled and minced)
- 2 (14½ ounces) cans stewed tomatoes (chopped)
- 1 (14½ ounces) can chicken broth
- 3 tsp Herbes de Provence
- 1½ tsp garlic powder
- 1½ tsp dried basil
- ½ tsp dried oregano
- ¼ tsp black pepper
- 4 (15½ ounces) cans great Northern beans (drained, rinsed)
- ¾ cup dry white wine

Directions:

- ❖ Spritz a Dutch oven with nonstick cooking spray.
- ❖ Place the Dutch oven over moderately high heat, add the pork and sausage and sauté until browned. Drain away any fat from the pan.
- ❖ Next, add the onion and carrots, Fry for 3-4 minutes until softened. Add the garlic and fry for 60 more seconds.
- ❖ Pour in the tomatoes, chicken broth, Herbes de Provence, garlic powder, basil, oregano, and black pepper. Bring then the mixture to a boil before turning down to a simmer for 10 minutes.
- ❖ Add one of the cans of beans to a food processor along with a ¼ cup white wine and blitz to a puree. Transfer to the Dutch oven and stir until incorporated.
- ❖ Add the remaining white wine and canned beans to the cassoulet and stir to combine. Return the mixture to a boil. Lastly, reduce back down to a simmer, then cook for 10 minutes until the veggies and meat are tender.
- ❖ Serve.
- ❖ To freeze-dry the dish. First, put it onto the tray, and then spread it out to a thickness of approximately half an inch. Place the tray into the freeze dryer rack.
- ❖ Put in the insulating pad, and close and secure the door. Push start.
- ❖ After it's done, extract the tray from the freeze dryer. Put it in a Mylar bag with an oxygen-absorbing packet, seal it, and label it with the date.

SLOW-COOKED BRAZILIAN PORK AND BLACK BEAN STEW

Preparation time: 5 minutes
Cooking time: 7 hours
Servings: 2

Ingredients:

- 1½ cups dried black beans (rinsed)
- 1 pound country-style, boneless pork ribs
- 1 pound smoked kielbasa sausage (sliced)
- 1 smoked ham hock
- 12 ounces cooked chorizo (sliced)
- 3 cloves garlic (peeled and minced)
- 1 yellow onion (peeled, chopped)
- 2 bay leaves
- ¾ tsp salt
- ½ tsp black pepper
- 5 cups water

Directions:

- ❖ Soak the beans according to the packet instructions. Drain, rinse and discard the soaking water.
- ❖ Add the soaked beans to a slow cooker along with the pork ribs, sausage, ham hock, chorizo, garlic, onion, bay leaves, salt, and black pepper. Stir gently to combine.
- ❖ Pour in the water. Cover with the lid and cook for 7-9 hours on low heat until the meat is tender.
- ❖ Take the ham hock and pork ribs out of the slow cooker and allow to cool a little. Next, pick the meat from the bones, set the meat to one side, and discard the bones. Using 2 forks, shred the meat. Then, return to the slow cooker.
- ❖ 5. Discard the bay leaves and stir the stew before serving.
- ❖ To freeze-dry the stew. First, put it onto the tray, and then spread it out to a thickness of approximately half an inch. Place the tray into the freeze dryer rack.
- ❖ Put in the insulating pad, and close and secure the door. Push start.
- ❖ After it's done, extract the tray from the freeze dryer. Put it in a Mylar bag with an oxygen-absorbing packet, seal it, and label it with the date.

SWEET 'N SOUR PORK

Preparation time: 5 minutes
Cooking time: 25 minutes
Servings: 5

Ingredients:

- ½ cup unsweetened pineapple juice
- 1 tbsp cornstarch
- ½ cup BBQ sauce
- 1 cup whole-berry cranberry sauce
- 1 tbsp canola oil
- 1½ cups pork tenderloin (cubed)
- ½ tsp salt
- ¼ tsp black pepper
- ¾ cup canned pineapple tidbits
- 1 green bell pepper (seeded, sliced thinly)

Directions:

- In a bowl, stir together the pineapple juice and cornstarch until combined. Add the BBQ sauce and cranberry sauce and stir again. Set aside for a moment.
- Warm the oil in your skillet over moderately high heat, add the pork and sauté until browned all over, for approximately 3 minutes—season with salt and black pepper. Take the meat out of the skillet and keep warm.
- Add the pineapple and bell pepper to the skillet and fry for a couple of minutes. Pour in the set-aside sauce and stir to combine. Cook the mixture for 2-3 minutes until thickened.
- Return the pork to the skillet and cook until heated through. Serve.
- To freeze-dry the dish. First, put it onto the tray, and then spread it out to a thickness of approximately half an inch. Place the tray into the freeze dryer rack.
- Put in the insulating pad, and close and secure the door. Push start.
- After it's done, extract the tray from the freeze dryer. Put it in a Mylar bag with an oxygen-absorbing packet, seal it, and label it with the date.

CRAB CAKES

Preparation time: 5 minutes
Cooking time: 30 minutes
Servings: 2

Ingredients:

- 2 tbsp olive oil
- 2 tbsp celery (diced)
- 2 tbsp yellow onion (diced)
- 2 tbsp red bell pepper (diced)
- Salt and black pepper
- ½ cup mayonnaise
- 1 tsp Dijon mustard
- 1 tsp Worcestershire sauce
- 1 egg (lightly beaten)
- ½ tsp Old Bay seasoning
- 1 tsp dried parsley
- ½ tsp garlic powder
- 2 (6 ounces) cans crabmeat (drained)
- ½ cup + extra panko breadcrumbs
- 1 tbsp unsalted butter
- Lemon wedges (to serve)
- Salad (to serve)

Directions:

- Warm 1 tbsp of oil in a skillet over moderately high heat. Add the celery, onion, and red bell pepper, sauté for 2-3 minutes until softened. Season then to taste with salt and black pepper. Take off the heat and allow to cool.

- In your bowl, combine the mayonnaise, Worcestershire sauce, egg, Old Bay seasoning, parsley, and garlic powder. Stir in the sautéed veggies.
- Next, fold in the crabmeat and ½ cup breadcrumbs. Cover the bowl with plastic wrap and chill for half an hour.
- Form the mixture into 4 equally-sized patties.
- Add breadcrumbs to a shallow dish and dip each patty in the breadcrumbs to coat lightly.
- Melt together the remaining oil and butter in a pan over moderate heat. Add the patties to the pan and cook for 3-4 minutes on each side.
- Lastly, serve hot with lemon wedges on the side and salad.
- To freeze-dry the crab cakes. First, put them onto the trays, and then spread it out to a thickness of approximately half an inch. Place the trays into the freeze dryer's rack.
- Put in the insulating pad, and close and secure the door. Push start.
- After it's done, extract the trays from the freeze dryer. Put it in a Mylar bag with an oxygen-absorbing packet, seal it, and label it with the date.

FISH STICKS

Preparation time: 5 minutes
Cooking time: 20 minutes
Servings: 2

Ingredients:

- Avocado oil (to grease)
- 1 pound frozen cod filets (defrosted)
- 1 cup all-purpose flour
- 4 large-size eggs (beaten)
- 2½ cups seasoned panko breadcrumbs
- 1 tsp sea salt

Directions:

- First, preheat the main oven to 400 degrees F.
- Prepare 2 roasting pans. Place a wire cooking rack inside each pan. Lightly grease the racks with avocado oil.
- Partially defrost the fish, before slicing the fish into 24-30 (½" wide by 3" long) strips. Pat the strip dry with kitchen paper towels.
- Add the flour to a shallow bowl, and the beaten egg to a second shallow bowl and then the breadcrumbs to a third shallow bowl.
- In batches, dredge the fish sticks, first in the flour, second in the egg, and third in the breadcrumbs. Make sure that the sticks are evenly coated.
- Place the breaded fish stick on top of the wire racks. Season with salt.
- Bake the fish sticks in the oven for 8 minutes. Turn them over and bake on the other side for 6 minutes before transferring them to the broiler to brown for approximately 60 seconds. Serve hot.

- ❖ To freeze-dry the fish sticks. First, put them onto the trays, and then spread it out to a thickness of approximately half an inch. Place the trays into the freeze dryer's rack.
- ❖ Put in the insulating pad, and close and secure the door. Push start.
- ❖ After it's done, extract the trays from the freeze dryer. Put them in a Mylar bag with an oxygen-absorbing packet, seal it, and label it with the date.

MEDITERRANEAN SHRIMP

Preparation time: 5 minutes
Cooking time: 20 minutes
Servings: 5

Ingredients:

- ¼ cup olive oil
- 3 cloves garlic (peeled and minced)
- 3 tbsp fresh lemon juice
- ¼ tsp black pepper
- 1 tsp salt
- ½ tsp dried oregano
- ⅛ tsp red pepper flakes
- ½ tsp dried basil
- 1 pound large, fresh shrimp (peeled, then deveined)
- Small handful fresh parsley (chopped)
- 3 tbsp feta cheese (crumbled)
- Lemon wedges

Directions:

- ❖ In your bowl, combine the olive oil, minced garlic, lemon juice, black pepper, salt, oregano, red pepper flakes, and dried basil to create a marinade.
- ❖ Add the shrimp to the marinade, toss to combine, and chill for half an hour.
- ❖ Preheat your oven's broiler and cover a baking sheet with kitchen foil.
- ❖ Take the shrimp out of the marinade and arrange on the baking sheet. Place the shrimp under the broiler and cook for 2 minutes on each side or until cooked through.
- ❖ Serve the shrimp garnished with fresh parsley, crumbled feta cheese, and lemon wedges.
- ❖ To freeze-dry the shrimp. First, put it onto the tray, and then spread it out to a thickness of approximately half an inch. Place the tray into the freeze dryer rack.
- ❖ Put in the insulating pad, and close and secure the door. Push start.
- ❖ After it's done, extract the tray from the freeze dryer. Put it in a Mylar bag with an oxygen-absorbing packet, seal it, and label it with the date.

PECAN-CRUSTED SNAPPER

Preparation time: 5 minutes

Cooking time: 20 minutes
Servings: 2

Ingredients:

- ½ cup dried breadcrumbs
- ½ tsp salt
- 2 tbsp pecans (finely chopped)
- ¼ tsp black pepper
- ¼ tsp powdered garlic
- ½ tsp hot sauce
- ½ cup buttermilk
- 3 tbsp all-purpose flour
- 4 (6 ounces) snapper fillets
- 1 tbsp canola oil

Directions:

- ❖ In your shallow dish, combine the breadcrumbs, salt, pecans, black pepper, and garlic.
- ❖ To a second shallow dish, add hot sauce and buttermilk – stir to combine.
- ❖ Next, add the flour to a third shallow dish.
- ❖ Dredge each fish fillet in the flour firstly, then the buttermilk, and finally the breadcrumbs.
- ❖ Warm half of the oil in your skillet over moderately high heat. Add two pieces of the fish to the pan and sauté for 3 minutes on each side until cooked through.
- ❖ Repeat with the remaining oil and fish.
- ❖ To freeze-dry the dish. First, put it onto the tray, and then spread it out to a thickness of approximately half an inch. Place the tray into the freeze dryer rack.
- ❖ Put in the insulating pad, and close and secure the door. Push start.
- ❖ After it's done, extract the tray from the freeze dryer. Put it in a Mylar bag with an oxygen-absorbing packet, seal it, and label it with the date.

GREEK WHOLE GRAIN PASTA BAKE

Preparation time: 5 minutes
Cooking time: 45 minutes
Servings: 5

Ingredients:

- 3⅓ cups uncooked whole grain spiral pasta
- 1 (29 ounces) can tomato sauce
- 4 cups cooked chicken breast (cubed)
- 1 (14½ ounces) can diced tomatoes (drained)
- 1 (10 ounces) package frozen spinach, chopped (thawed)
- 5½ ounces sliced olives
- ¼ cup green pepper (chopped)
- ¼ cup red onion (peeled and thinly sliced)
- 1 tsp dried oregano
- 1 tsp dried basil
- Nonstick cooking spray
- 1 cup mozzarella cheese (shredded)

- ½ cup feta cheese (crumbled)
- Fresh oregano (chopped, to garnish)

Directions:

- ❖ Cook the pasta firstly according to the package instructions and until al dente, drain well.
- ❖ In a bowl, combine the drained pasta with the tomato sauce, cubed chicken, diced tomatoes, spinach, olives, green pepper, red onion, oregano, and basil.
- ❖ Spritz a 13x9" casserole with nonstick cooking spray.
- ❖ Transfer the pasta mixture to the prepared dish. Then, scatter the shredded cheese over the top and uncovered, bake at 400 degrees F, for 25-30 minutes, until heated through and the cheese melted.
- ❖ Season with chopped oregano and enjoy.
- ❖ To freeze-dry the pasta dish. First, put it onto the trays, and then spread it out to a thickness of approximately half an inch. Place the trays into the freeze dryer's rack.
- ❖ Put in the insulating pad, and close and secure the door. Push start.
- ❖ After it's done, extract the trays from the freeze dryer. Put it in a Mylar bag with an oxygen-absorbing packet, seal it, and label it with the date.

GREEN CHILI QUICHE

Preparation time: 5 minutes
Cooking time: 1hour
Servings: 2

Ingredients:

- 1 (9") prepared single crust pie shell
- 2 tbsp cornmeal
- 1 ½ cups Monterey Jack cheese (shredded)
- 1 cup Cheddar cheese (shredded)
- 1 (4 ounces) can chopped green chilies
- 3 large-size eggs
- ¾ cup sour cream
- 1 tbsp fresh cilantro (minced)
- 2-4 drops hot pepper sauce (as needed)

Directions:

- ❖ First, line the pie shell with a double layer of heavy-duty aluminum foil. Then, bake at 450 degrees F. for 8 minutes. Take the foil off, then bake for an additional 5 minutes. Set aside to cool on a wire baking rack and turn the heat down to 350 degrees F.
- ❖ Scatter the cornmeal over the crust.
- ❖ In a small-size bowl, combine the Monterey Jack cheese with the Cheddar cheese. Set ½ cup aside for the topping.
- ❖ Add the green chilies to the remaining cheese mixture, and sprinkle onto the crust.
- ❖ In a small-size bowl, whisk the eggs with the sour cream, cilantro, and hot sauce.

- ❖ Then, pour the mixture into the crust and scatter with the cheese mixture set aside in Step 3.
- ❖ Bake in the oven until springy to the touch, this will take 35-40 minutes. Allow to stand for 4-5 minutes before slicing.
- ❖ To freeze-dry the quiche dish. First, put it onto the tray, and then spread it out to a thickness of approximately half an inch. Place the tray into the freeze dryer rack.
- ❖ Put in the insulating pad, and close and secure the door. Push start.
- ❖ After it's done, extract the tray from the freeze dryer. Put it in a Mylar bag with an oxygen-absorbing packet, seal it, and label it with the date.

TOFU PINEAPPLE STIR FRY

Preparation time: 5 minutes
Cooking time: 30 minutes
Servings: 2

Ingredients:

Sauce:

- ¼ cup liquid aminos
- 3 garlic cloves (peeled and minced)
- 2 tbsp fresh ginger (peeled and grated)
- 2 tbsp pure maple syrup
- 2 tbsp unseasoned rice vinegar
- 2 tbsp fresh lime juice
- 2 tbsp avocado oil

Stir Fry:

- 2 tsp oil
- 1 (14 ounces) block tofu (cut into bite-size cubes)
- 1 green bell pepper (chopped)
- 1 red bell pepper (chopped)
- 2 cups frozen, canned or fresh pineapple chunks
- 1 cup green beans (chopped)
- ½ yellow onion (peeled and chopped)

Directions:

- ❖ In a bowl, combine the liquid aminos with the minced garlic, fresh ginger, maple syrup, rice vinegar, fresh lime juice, and avocado oil, whisk until incorporated. If making ahead to freeze rather than enjoying immediately, follow freezer instructions, otherwise continue with Steps 2-4.
- ❖ Add the oil to a pan and over moderate-high heat, cook the tofu until golden brown. This step will take 7-9 minutes in total, and you will need to stir every 1-2 minutes.
- ❖ Next, add the bell peppers, pineapple chunks, green beans, and yellow onion to a large frying pan and cook while stirring continually over moderate heat until tender, for 2-3 minutes.
- ❖ Add the sauce to the pan, stir to combine, heat through for 2-3 minutes, and serve.

- ❖ To freeze-dry the recipe. First, put it onto the trays, and then spread it out to a thickness of approximately half an inch. Place the tray into the freeze dryer rack.
- ❖ Put in the insulating pad, and close and secure the door. Push start.
- ❖ After it's done, extract the tray from the freeze dryer. Put it in a Mylar bag with an oxygen-absorbing packet, seal it, and label it with the date.

TOMATO AND BASIL SOUP

Preparation time: 5 minutes
Cooking time: 10 minutes
Servings: 2

Ingredients:

- ¼ cup tomato powder
- 1/3 cup instant dried milk powder
- 2 tbsp bouillon granules
- 1 tsp dried basil
- 1/8 tsp of garlic powder 1/8 Tsp onion powder
- 1/8 teaspoon freshly ground black pepper
- ¼ tsp salt
- 1¾ cups boiling water (divided)

Directions:

- ❖ Toss in the tomato powder, instant milk powder, bouillon powders, dried basil, garlic powder and onion powder.
- ❖ Mix the ingredients together by stirring or massaging them until they are well combined.
- ❖ Mix the ingredients in a 2+ cup mug or bowl. Stir in half the boiling water and mix well until it is all incorporated. Stir in the remaining boiling water.
- ❖ Cover with a towel and let it rest for between 8-10 minutes.
- ❖ To freeze-dry the soup. First, put it onto the tray, and then spread it out to a thickness of approximately half an inch. Place the tray into the freeze dryer rack.
- ❖ Put in the insulating pad, and close and secure the door. Push start.
- ❖ After it's done, extract the tray from the freeze dryer. Put it in a Mylar bag with an oxygen-absorbing packet, seal it, and label it with the date.

BANANA BREAD INSTANT OATMEAL

Preparation time: 5 minutes
Cooking time: 5 minutes
Servings: 4

Ingredients:

- ½ cup instant oatmeal
- 3 tbsp frozen-dried banana (chopped).
- ⅛ tsp vanilla bean
- 1 tbsp walnuts (chopped)
- 2 tsp sugar

- 3/4 cup milk (boiling).
- Walnuts (optional, chopped, to serve)

Directions:

- ❖ Combine the instant oatmeal, bananas, vanilla bean and walnuts in a Mason jar.
- ❖ The jar can be kept in a dry, cool place for up to 28 day.
- ❖ Pour the boiling water or milk over the oatmeal and stir it well. Mix well and let it sit for three minutes to rehydrate.
- ❖ Add extra chopped walnuts to your dish and enjoy.
- ❖ To freeze-dry the oatmeal. First, put them onto the trays, and then spread it out to a thickness of approximately half an inch. Place the trays into the freeze dryer's rack.
- ❖ Put in the insulating pad, and close and secure the door. Push start.
- ❖ After it's done, extract the trays from the freeze dryer. Put it in a Mylar bag with an oxygen-absorbing packet, seal it, and label it with the date.

BEEF 'N BEAN STEW IN A JAR

Preparation time: 5 minutes
Cooking time: 15 minutes
Servings: 2

Ingredients:

- 1 cup quick-cook black beans
- 1 cup freeze-dried diced beef
- 2 tbsp powdered beef bouillon
- 2 tbsp frozen minced onions
- 1 tsp granulated garlic
- 1 tsp thyme
- 2 tbsp tomato powder
- 1 cup dehydrated diced potatoes
- 1 cup freeze-dried mixed vegetables
- 1 tsp salt
- 6 cups water

Directions:

- ❖ In a clean 1-quart jar, layer the ingredients according to recipe. To settle the mixture, shake the jar gently.
- ❖ Place a canning lid over the jar. Seal it with a vacuum seal. Add a ring and tighten by hand, taking care to not overtighten.
- ❖ Label, date and store until required.
- ❖ Once you're ready to cook, take off the lid and discard.
- ❖ Transfer the contents of the jar to a large saucepan.
- ❖ Bring 6 cups water into the pot. Heat on medium to high heat until it boils.
- ❖ Reduce the heat and let it simmer for 20 minutes. Serve and enjoy.
- ❖ To freeze-dry the stew. First, put it onto the trays, and then spread it out to a thickness of

approximately half an inch. Place the trays into the freeze dryer's rack.

❖ Put in the insulating pad, and close and secure the door. Push start.

❖ After it's done, extract the trays from the freeze dryer. Put it in a Mylar bag with an oxygen-absorbing packet, seal it, and label it with the date.

BREAKFAST SCRAMBLE WITH SPINACH AND SUN-DRIED PEPPERS

Preparation time: 5 minutes
Cooking time: 10 minutes
Servings: 4

Ingredients:

- ¾ cup whole egg crystals
- 1/2 teaspoon powdered garlic powder
- ½ tbsp salt
- 1/2 tsp ground black pepper
- 1/2 cup sun-dried tomatoes (chopped).
- ½ cup dehydrated spinach
- 1¼ cups water
- 1 tbsp olive oil

Directions:

❖ At home, combine the whole egg crystals with the garlic powder and salt. Add the water outside your home to the Ziplock bag. Mix the ingredients together with a fork until they are well combined. Allow the spinach to rest for three minutes before putting it on the plate.

❖ Heat the oil in a saucepan or pot on low heat. Mix the egg-spinach and pepper mixtures together and use a spoon to scramble the eggs.

❖ Serve and enjoy.

❖ To freeze-dry the dish. First, put it onto the tray, and then spread it out to a thickness of approximately half an inch. Place the tray into the freeze dryer rack.

❖ Put in the insulating pad, and close and secure the door. Push start.

❖ After it's done, extract the tray from the freeze dryer. Put it in a Mylar bag with an oxygen-absorbing packet, seal it, and label it with the date.

BACKPACKER'S CHOCOLATE AND BERRY BARK

Preparation time: 5 minutes
Cooking time: 25 minutes
Servings: 5

Ingredients:

- 1 pound semi-sweet or dark chocolate (chopped)
- 1 cup freeze-dried strawberries (divided)
- 1 cup crisp rice cereal

- ½ cup mini white chocolate chips

Directions:

❖ Using parchment paper, line a cookie sheet and put it aside.

❖ In a suitable bowl, microwave your choice of chocolate on high in 25-second increments, stirring between increments until melted and smooth. Using a wooden spoon, fold in ½ cup of the freeze-dried strawberries, along with the rice cereal until all of the cereal is coated.

❖ With a spatula, spread the mixture as thinly as possible onto the prepared cookie sheet.

❖ Before the melted chocolate starts to harden, and while working very quickly, scatter over the remaining strawberries and mini white chocolate chips. Press down gently to adhere.

❖ To freeze-dry the Backpacker's Chocolate and Berry Bark. First, put them onto the trays, and then spread it out to a thickness of approximately half an inch. Place the trays into the freeze dryer's rack.

❖ Put in the insulating pad, and close and secure the door. Push start.

❖ After it's done, extract the trays from the freeze dryer. Put it in a Mylar bag with an oxygen-absorbing packet, seal it, and label it with the date.

CHOCOLATE-COVERED STRAWBERRY TRAIL MIX

Preparation time: 5 minutes
Cooking time: 15 minutes
Servings: 2

Ingredients:

- ¾ cup roasted almonds
- ¾ cup roasted cashews
- ¾ cup roasted sunflower seeds
- 1 cup freeze-dried strawberries
- ⅔ cup dark chocolate chunks

Directions:

❖ In a large bowl, combine the almonds with cashews, sunflower seeds, freeze-dried strawberries, and dark chocolate chunks.

❖ Transfer the mixture to a large Ziplock bag.

❖ To freeze-dry the dish. First, put it onto the trays, and then spread it out to a thickness of approximately half an inch. Place the trays into the freeze dryer's rack.

❖ Put in the insulating pad, and close and secure the door. Push start.

❖ After it's done, extract the trays from the freeze dryer. Put it in a Mylar bag with an oxygen-absorbing packet, seal it, and label it with the date.

MOCHA PEANUT BUTTER AND BANANA SMOOTHIE

Preparation time: 5 minutes
Cooking time: 5 minutes
Servings: 2

Ingredients:

- ⅓ cup egg white protein powder
- 2 tsp freeze-dried espresso instant coffee
- ¼ cup freeze-dried bananas (ground)
- 1 individual sachet peanut butter
- 12 ounces water (divided)
- 1 individual sachet powdered hot chocolate mix

Directions:

- ❖ While at home, combine the egg white protein powder with the coffee and ground bananas in a Ziplock bag. Shake the bag gently to distribute evenly.
- ❖ Outside your home, gently massage the peanut butter packet until softened. Pour 6 ounces of water into a sports bottle with a secure screw-top lid.
- ❖ Add the contents from the Ziplock bag along with the hot chocolate mix and coffee to the sports bottle.
- ❖ Screw on the lid and vigorously shake the sports bottle until the smoothie is lump-free, for 35-45 seconds,
- ❖ Add the remaining water to the bottle.
- ❖ Shake the bottle vigorously once more to combine and blend.
- ❖ To freeze-dry the smoothie. First, put the smoothie onto the tray, and then spread it out to a thickness of approximately half an inch. Place the tray into the freeze dryer rack.
- ❖ Put in the insulating pad, and close and secure the door. Push start.
- ❖ After it's done, extract the tray from the freeze dryer. Put it in a Mylar bag with an oxygen-absorbing packet, seal it, and label it with the date.

WHITE CHOCOLATE PEACH AND STRAWBERRY TRAIL MIX

Preparation time: 5 minutes
Cooking time: 4 minutes
Servings: 2

Ingredients:

- ½ cup freeze-dried peaches (broken into bite-size pieces) ½ cup freeze-dried strawberries (broken into bite-size pieces) ¼ cup white chocolate chips
- ½ cup granola
- ¼ cup pretzels (broken into bite-size pieces)
- ¼ cup roasted peanuts

Directions:

- ❖ In a bowl, combine the peaches with the strawberries, white chocolate chips, granola, pretzels, and roasted peanuts.
- ❖ Transfer the trail mix to a large Ziplock bag and enjoy.
- ❖ To freeze-dry the dish. First, put the dish onto the tray, and then spread it out to a thickness of approximately half an inch. Place the tray into the freeze dryer rack.
- ❖ Put in the insulating pad, and close and secure the door. Push start.
- ❖ After it's done, extract the tray from the freeze dryer. Put it in a Mylar bag with an oxygen-absorbing packet, seal it, and label it with the date.

YOGURT TRAIL MIX

Preparation time: 5 minutes
Cooking time: 5 minutes
Servings: 4

Ingredients:

- 2 cups freeze-dried, flavor of choice yogurt bites
- 1 cup almonds or peanuts
- ½ cup hulled sunflower seeds
- ½ cup freeze-dried cherries
- 1 cup freeze-dried strawberry slices

Directions:

- ❖ In a bowl, combine the yogurt bites with the nuts, sunflower seeds, freeze-dried cherries, and strawberry slices.
- ❖ Transfer the mixture to individual Ziplock bags.
- ❖ To freeze-dry the yogurt trail mix. First, put the recipe onto the tray, and then spread it out to a thickness of approximately half an inch. Place the tray into the freeze dryer rack.
- ❖ Put in the insulating pad, and close and secure the door. Push start.
- ❖ After it's done, extract the tray from the freeze dryer. Put it in a Mylar bag with an oxygen-absorbing packet, seal it, and label it with the date.

LASAGNA

Preparation time: 5 minutes
Cooking time: 50 minutes
Servings: 2

Ingredients:

- 18 lasagna noodles
- 3 pounds ground beef
- 3 (26 ounce) jars spaghetti sauce
- 2 large eggs (lightly beaten)
- 1½ pounds ricotta cheese
- 1 tbsp dried parsley flakes
- 6 cups part-skim mozzarella cheese (shredded, divided)
- 1 tsp salt

- ½ tsp freshly ground black pepper
- 1 cup Parmesan cheese (freshly grated)

Directions:
- ❖ Cook the noodles according to the package directions.
- ❖ In the meantime, in a Dutch oven, cook the beef over moderate heat until no pink remains and drain.
- ❖ Stir in the spaghetti sauce to combine and set aside. In a large mixing bowl, combine the eggs with the ricotta cheese followed by the parsley, 4½ cups of shredded mozzarella cheese, salt, and black pepper.
- ❖ Drain the pasta.
- ❖ Evenly spread 1 cup of meat sauce into each of 2 (13x9") greased casserole dishes.
- ❖ Layer each with three noodles followed by 1 cup ricotta mixture and 1½ cups of meat sauce. Repeat the layers twice. Top with grated Parmesan cheese and the remaining mozzarella.
- ❖ Cover the casserole dish and freeze one lasagna for up to 3 months.
- ❖ Cover and bake the remaining lasagna at 375 degrees F for 45 minutes. Uncover, and bake for an additional 10 minutes or until bubbling. Set aside to stand for several minutes before serving.
- ❖ To freeze-dry the lasagna. First, put the lasagna onto the tray, and then spread it out to a thickness of approximately half an inch. Place the tray into the freeze dryer rack.
- ❖ Put in the insulating pad, and close and secure the door. Push start.
- ❖ After it's done, extract the tray from the freeze dryer. Put it in a Mylar bag with an oxygen-absorbing packet, seal it, and label it with the date.

BAKED POTATO, CHEESE, AND ONION SOUP

Preparation time: 5 minutes
Cooking time: 6 hours
Servings: 7

Ingredients:
- 5 pounds baking potatoes (cut into ½" cubes)
- 1 large onion (peeled, chopped)
- ¼ cup butter
- 4 garlic cloves (peeled, minced)
- 1 tsp salt
- ½ tsp pepper
- 3 (14½ ounce) cans chicken broth
- 1 cup mature Cheddar cheese (shredded)
- 1 cup half-and-half cream
- 3 tbsp fresh chives (minced)
- Toppings (optional):
- Cheddar cheese (shredded)
- Sour cream
- Cooked bacon (crumbled)

Directions:
- ❖ Add the first seven ingredients to a slow cooker of 6-quart capacity (potatoes, onion, butter, garlic, salt, pepper, and chicken broth).
- ❖ Cover and cook on low for 6-8 hours, until the potatoes, are fork tender.
- ❖ Slightly mash the potatoes to thicken the soup.
- ❖ Add the shredded Cheddar along with the half and half cream, and chives and heat through, stirring until combined.
- ❖ Serve with your favorite toppings.
- ❖ To freeze-dry the soup. First, put the soup onto the trays, and then spread it out to a thickness of approximately half an inch. Place the trays into the freeze dryer rack.
- ❖ Put in the insulating pad, and close and secure the door. Push start.
- ❖ After it's done, extract the trays from the freeze dryer. Put it in a Mylar bag with an oxygen-absorbing packet, seal it, and label it with the date.

CHEATS CHICKEN POT PIE

Preparation time: 5 minutes
Cooking time: 1 hour
Servings: 2

Ingredients:
- 2 cups cooked chicken (shredded)
- 1 (16 ounce) bag frozen hash browns
- 12 ounces frozen carrot and pea mix
- ¼ cup onion (peeled, diced small)
- 2½ cups gravy
- Salt and black pepper
- 4 frozen ready-made double pie crusts in foil trays (thawed)

Directions:
- ❖ Preheat the main oven to 350 degrees F.
- ❖ In a bowl, combine the shredded chicken with the hash browns, veggie mix, onion, and gravy.
- ❖ Season with salt and pepper.
- ❖ Spoon the chicken filling into the bottom crusts and evenly spread.
- ❖ Take the top crust and place it on top of the filling. Spread it to fit and pinch the crusts together to seal.
- ❖ Make a few slash cuts on the top of each pie, to allow the steam to escape.
- ❖ To freeze-dry this recipe. First, put the it onto the trays, and then spread it out to a thickness of approximately half an inch. Place the trays into the freeze dryer rack.
- ❖ Put in the insulating pad, and close and secure the door. Push start.
- ❖ After it's done, extract the trays from the freeze dryer. Put it in a Mylar bag with an oxygen-absorbing packet, seal it, and label it with the date.

CHICKEN BURRITO CASSEROLE

Preparation time: 5 minutes
Cooking time: 3 hours
Servings: 8

Ingredients:
- 6 tbsp butter
- 1 large onion (peeled, chopped)
- ¼ cup green pepper (chopped)
- ½ cup all-purpose flour
- 3 cups chicken broth
- 1 (10 ounce) can diced tomatoes and green chiles (undrained)
- 1 tsp ground cumin
- 1 tsp chili powder
- ½ tsp garlic powder
- ½ tsp salt
- 2 tbsp jalapeno pepper (chopped)
- 1 (15 ounces) can chili with beans
- 1 (8 ounce) package cream cheese (cut into cubes)
- 8 cups rotisserie chicken (cut into cubes)
- 24 (6") flour tortillas (warm)
- 6 cups s Colby-Monterey Jack cheese (shredded)
- Salsa, store-bought (to serve)

Directions:
- ❖ Over moderate-high heat, in a Dutch oven heat the butter. Add the onion followed by the green pepper and cook while stirring until fork tender.
- ❖ Stir in the flour until incorporated, and gradually stir in the chicken broth. Bring to boil and while stirring cook for an additional 2 minutes.
- ❖ Turn the heat down, and stir in the tomatoes, cumin, chili powder, garlic powder, salt, and jalapeno pepper — Cook for 5 minutes.
- ❖ Add the can of chili along with the cream cheese and stir until entirely melted. Stir in the chicken.
- ❖ Spoon approximately ½ cup of the filling across the middle of each of the tortillas. Scatter ¼ cup Colby-Monterey Jack cheese.
- ❖ Fold the bottom and sides of the tortilla over the filling and carefully roll. Repeat the process until all 24 tortillas are assembled.
- ❖ Transfer each of the filled tortillas in 2 (13x9") lightly greased casserole dishes.
- ❖ To freeze-dry the chicken burrito casserole. First, put the casserole dish onto the freeze dryer trays, and then spread it out to a thickness of approximately half an inch. Place the trays into the freeze dryer rack.
- ❖ Put in the insulating pad, and close and secure the door. Push start.
- ❖ After it's done, extract the trays from the freeze dryer. Put it in a Mylar bag with an oxygen-absorbing packet, seal it, and label it with the date.

BROWN RICE WITH CORN AND CHICKEN

Preparation time: 5 minutes
Cooking time: 10 minutes
Servings: 2

Ingredients:
- ⅔ cup instant brown rice
- 1 tsp chia seeds
- 1/3 cup frozen chopped chicken
- ½ cup freeze-dried corn
- 1/4 cup frozen chopped tomatoes
- 1/4 teaspoon minced dried jalapeno
- 1 tbsp freeze-dried onions
- 1 1/2 tsp powdered Chicken flavor base
- 1½ tsp chili powder
- ¼ tsp cumin
- 1/4 teaspoon dried Mexican oregano
- ½ tsp freeze-dried cilantro ¼ tsp garlic powder
- 1/8 tsp ground black pepper
- 1/4 teaspoon salt (or more according to your taste)
- 1½ cups water

Directions:
- ❖ Mix the brown rice, chia seed, chicken, tomatoes, jalapeno and onions in a Ziplock bag. Add chili powder, cumin.
- ❖ Bring the water to boil outside your home.
- ❖ Place the water in the bag and place it on a plate or bowl. Let the mixture soak in the bag for between 8-10 minutes. After 3-4 minutes, flip the bag upside-down to allow the ingredients to spread evenly.
- ❖ To freeze-dry the rice dish. First, put the rice recipe onto the freeze dryer trays, and then spread it out to a thickness of approximately half an inch. Place the trays into the freeze dryer rack.
- ❖ Put in the insulating pad, and close and secure the door. Push start.
- ❖ After it's done, extract the trays from the freeze dryer. Put it in a Mylar bag with an oxygen-absorbing packet, seal it, and label it with the date. Take the bag out, open it and share.

CHICKEN ALFREDO WITH PINE NUTS

Preparation time: 5 minutes
Cooking time: 15 minutes
Servings: 5

Ingredients:
- 1 cup angel hair pasta (broken into pieces) 1 tsp chia seeds
- 1/4 cup frozen chopped chicken
- 1/4 cup toasted pine nuts
- 1/4 cup frozen chopped mushrooms
- 1 1/2 tsp powdered Chicken flavor base

- 3 Tbsp dry, canned refrigerated, and grated Parmesan Cheese
- 2 tbsp powdered milk
- 2 tbsp cornstarch
- 2 tsp freeze-dried Italian herb blend ¼ tsp garlic powder
- 1/8 teaspoon freshly ground black pepper
- 1/4 teaspoon salt (to taste).
- 1¼ cups water

Directions:
- ❖ When you are at home, add the pasta, chia seeds and freeze-dried chopped chicken to a 1 quart Ziplock bag.
- ❖ Cook in the bag outside your home. Bring the water to boil. The boiling water should be poured into the Ziplock bag. Allow the contents to soak for about 8 minutes. After that, turn the bag around to mix the ingredients evenly.
- ❖ Enjoy the contents of the Ziplock bag.
- ❖ Alternatively, you can transfer the contents of the Ziplock bag into a large bowl or mug that is microwave-safe.
- ❖ Place the water in a bowl or mug and heat it in the microwave until it boils.
- ❖ Cover the container and let it rest for at least 4-6 minutes. Stir and allow Alfredo to rest for about a minute before you enjoy.
- ❖ To freeze-dry the chicken alfredo. First, put the dish onto the freeze dryer trays, and then spread it out to a thickness of approximately half an inch. Place the trays into the freeze dryer rack.
- ❖ Put in the insulating pad, and close and secure the door. Push start.
- ❖ After it's done, extract the trays from the freeze dryer. Put it in a Mylar bag with an oxygen-absorbing packet, seal it, and label it with the date.

RASPBERRY MARSHMALLOW CRÈME PIE

Preparation time: 5 minutes
Cooking time: 10 minutes
Servings: 4

Ingredients:
- 7 ounces marshmallow crème
- 8 ounces full-fat cream cheese (at room temperature)
- 2 cups raspberry sherbet (softened)
- 2½ cups whipped topping
- 1 (9") graham cracker crust

Directions:
- ❖ Beat together the marshmallow crème and cream cheese until fluffy.
- ❖ Stir in the sherbet, then fold in the whipped topping until incorporated.
- ❖ Spoon the mixture into the pie crust.

- ❖ To freeze-dry the marshmallows. First, put the marshmallows recipe onto the freeze dryer trays, and then spread it out to a thickness of approximately half an inch. Place the trays into the freeze dryer rack.
- ❖ Put in the insulating pad, and close and secure the door. Push start.
- ❖ After it's done, extract the trays from the freeze dryer. Put it in a Mylar bag with an oxygen-absorbing packet, seal it, and label it with the date.

SALTED CARAMEL BLONDIES

Preparation time: 5 minutes
Cooking time: 35 minutes
Servings: 2

Ingredients:
- Nonstick spray
- 1 cup brown sugar
- ½ cup unsalted butter (at room temperature)
- 1 egg
- ¼ tsp salt
- 1 cup all-purpose flour
- 2 tsp vanilla essence
- ¼ cup salted caramel sauce

Directions:
- ❖ Preheat the main oven to 350 degrees F. Spritz an 8" square baking tin with nonstick spray.
- ❖ Cream together the sugar and butter until super fluffy and light. Beat in the egg, followed by the salt, flour, and vanilla.
- ❖ Spoon the mixture into the baking tin.
- ❖ Drop blobs of salted caramel on top of the batter and swirl into the mixture using a toothpick or knife.
- ❖ Place in the oven and bake for just over 20 minutes until golden.
- ❖ To freeze-dry the caramel blondies. First, put the dish onto the freeze dryer trays, and then spread it out to a thickness of approximately half an inch. Place the trays into the freeze dryer rack.
- ❖ Put in the insulating pad, and close and secure the door. Push start.
- ❖ After it's done, extract the trays from the freeze dryer. Put it in a Mylar bag with an oxygen-absorbing packet, seal it, and label it with the date.

ZINGY GINGER LEMON LAYER 'CAKE'

Preparation time: 5 minutes
Cooking time: 8 hours
Servings: 5

Ingredients:
- 2 tsp lemon zest (grated)
- 8 ounces full-fat cream cheese (at room temperature)
- 10 ounces lemon curd

- 2 cups heavy whipping cream
- 10½ ounces thin ginger cookies
- 2 tbsp crystallized ginger (chopped)

Directions:

- ❖ Beat the lemon zest into the cream cheese until fluffy.
- ❖ Next, beat in the lemon curd.
- ❖ Beat in the cream gradually, until the mixture can hold soft peaks.
- ❖ Layer 9 ginger cookies in the base of an 8" square dish and spread over ⅔ of a cup of the cream cheese mixture. Repeat these layers 6 more times.
- ❖ Scatter over the chopped crystallized ginger. Chill overnight until firm.
- ❖ To freeze-dry the cake. First, put the dish onto the freeze dryer trays, and then slice the cake and spread it out to a thickness of approximately half an inch. Place the trays into the freeze dryer rack.
- ❖ Put in the insulating pad, and close and secure the door. Push start.
- ❖ After it's done, extract the trays from the freeze dryer. Put it in a Mylar bag with an oxygen-absorbing packet, seal it, and label it with the date

CONCLUSION

Thank you for taking the time to read this book. Almost any food can be freeze-dried, though some perform better than others. The meat you intend to freeze-dry should be cut up into smaller chunks to be more suitable for this method, as smaller-sized food will fare better. Coffee, soups, and other liquids fare well after freeze-drying as well. Most of the instant coffees we consume daily to keep us awake, and alert are either freeze-dried or spray-dried. Freeze-dried fruits and vegetables are becoming more popular in stores as healthier alternatives to dehydrated foods.

A freeze-drying machine is costly. One machine will cost you between $2000 and $4000. On the bright side, if you only freeze-dry a small amount of food each year, you don't need to spend that much.

A deep freezer is more efficient and will speed up the process, as a standard freezer will take weeks to complete. Neither method works well with meat, which is difficult to store.

Before freezing food, make sure it is clean and dry. Remove any dirt or moisture from the items, and cut all food into uniform chunks to ensure consistency. Bread, cakes, and other yeast-based products should not be frozen because they will change color when reconstituted.

The best time to freeze-dry food is when it is cold, and you have cooled it off. If you're making a complete meal, freeze-dry it as soon as you're done cooking it. Then, when re-condensing, you'll need to test the results with a thermometer.

Good luck and have fun!

BOOK 7

SMOKING & SALT CURING COOKBOOK FOR PREPPERS

1000 Days of Recipes to Preserve Meat and Fish for Survival

INTRODUCTION

Prepping means being prepared for any disaster that may occur in the future. It is the process of actively preparing for any disaster or emergency. Natural disasters, such as earthquakes and floods, can occur as well as man-made disasters, such as terrorism. Our preparation gives us three major advantages when a disaster strikes.

When a disaster strikes, people rush to markets and hardware stores searching for provisions, fixtures, tools, medical supplies, etc. You may forget what you require due to your fragile state of mind during a disaster, and the items you need may have already been sold by the time you return to the stores. Thus, prepping gives us the advantage of having a head start on others.

If you already have a lot of supplies and the necessary medicines, items, and provisions, you probably don't need to worry about getting more supplies. Also, if disaster strikes, you will have a handy kit with all the necessary items, making it easier to flee during such events. As a result, having everything under control increases your chances of survival. Furthermore, you will only have to worry about minor details when you prepare rather than searching for supplies.

Another issue with disasters is that you may have to survive without technology or electricity. You can meet these unforeseen events by having a handy survival kit and being well prepared. It will also lessen your reliance on emergency services.

Another advantage of prepping is that you will have to live without modern conveniences on which we humans are inherently dependent. We have become overly reliant on technology and power in recent years. We also take them for granted, assuming that there will never be a time when we will need them. Thus, prepping will assist us in overcoming such dependency and difficulties when a disaster strikes.

You must understand the fundamentals of prepping and ask yourself why you must prepare for any situation. Modern-day preppers attempt to prepare for a specific time when life becomes difficult. They intend to be self-sufficient and independent enough to face any challenge, no matter how difficult. These challenges could take the form of almost anything or everything, and they all fall under the SHTF umbrella. It could be as simple as a harsh winter, an earthquake, or a pandemic. Everything that interferes with your usual way of life is a challenge for you. Every prepper takes the initiative to prepare for all risks unique to them or their location.

Prepping is the process by which preppers adapt to be capable of dealing with almost anything that violates the peace around them. The approach promotes anticipating and planning for potential risk factors and the necessary needs to overcome them. As a result, this is the best way to mitigate the adverse effects of a disaster or emergency that the SHTF situation may cause for your livelihood. Prepping promotes the idea that 'Change' is a constant in life. Everyone who considers caring for their families in a disaster without relying on government assistance is a prepper. All governments launch counter-measures to natural disasters and pandemics to keep people safe in the modern era. They are also preparing on a large scale rather than focusing on a single individual.

Prepping is the process of preparing for survival without the use of complex infrastructure. It is the action that promotes being ready to face life before, during, and after an apocalyptic event. You may have heard most of the time during natural disaster alerts when people raid grocery and essential stores right before storms, tsunamis, and other such events. However, preppers plan for such common problems far in advance. They have the idea and consideration to have water, food, first aid, and other supplies that one might require due to the inaccessibility of grocery stores for the next few days or weeks. Preppers risk stockpiling pantry items, bottled waters, battery lamps, candles, first-aid kits, antibiotics, generic medications, and other similar items. The most fundamental level of prepping is gathering all the items required for a camping or outdoor trip.

An important consideration is how you will obtain the items you require. Food, water, fuel, and shelter are all included. If you live in an area where growing your food will be difficult or impossible due to the climate, consider moving to a more suitable location if you are passionate about farming. Many people have gardens for growing food, but they do not live in climates that allow them to garden all year. This means that if you rely on your garden for everything, the same winter freeze that kills it could also kill you. Learning how to preserve food by canning or smoking will be critical if this is the case. If you live in an area where hunting is permitted, learning how to hunt and gut a deer will provide you with a backup plan if necessary.

Getting enough food and clean water can be difficult when you have to rely on yourself for everything. A first-aid kit, essential medicines, and a first-aid class will come in handy here. These should be addressed as soon as possible to ensure you understand how to treat injuries following an accident or other event. Many classes on first-aid are available through the Boy Scouts, churches, and other organizations. If having the supplies isn't enough to pique your interest in learning these skills, consider how much it will cost you to keep going to the doctor when there isn't anyone else for miles.

In this book, you will learn the fundamentals of smoking and salt curing for preppers. Our goal is to teach you the fundamentals of smoking. Once you've mastered the fundamentals, you can progress to more complex techniques and recipes. We've included tips on improving your smoking skills, whether cooking your first brisket, learning how to use an injection marinade, or creating the perfect candied salmon or smoked chicken. Let's get started!

CHAPTER 1

UNDERSTANDING SMOKING AND SALT CURING

SMOKING MEAT

Smoking is the process of flavoring, cooking, or preserving food by exposing it to smoke produced by burning or smoldering plant materials such as wood, mainly hardwood wood. Food smoking is practiced both commercially and at home. The meats are hung or placed on racks in an enclosed area, preventing smoke from escaping and penetrating the foods. Steam pipes are sometimes used in commercial smoking to supplement the wood fire.

Because it is antimicrobial and antioxidant, smoke is used to preserve foods. Smoking is most likely the oldest method of food preservation, emerging shortly after the discovery of fire. Because of the use of chemical preservatives, smoking as a preservative has declined in popularity, but it is regaining popularity because it is considered natural. The most commonly smoked foods are meat and fish, but cheeses, nuts, vegetables, and beverages such as tea and whisky are also smoked. In Scandinavia, smoking fish is popular, whereas ham is famous in Europe and the United States.

Smoking evolved from ancient traditions, beginning as a method of preserving meats and fish for the long winters and eventually becoming a popular outdoor activity and a staple of our modern-day patio culture. Cooking with smoke has recently become something of a craze. Smokers and grills are more widely available than ever before, and many supermarkets stock wood pellets, chunks, planks, and almost anything else you might need to add smoke to your cooking.

Smoking is fundamentally similar to roasting or baking in many ways. You cook in an enclosed, heated chamber, either quickly at a high temperature or slowly at a low temperature. If you imagine this as a cooking process in your oven, all you need to learn is how to add smoke. That is the subject of this book.

To properly add smoke, you'll need the right kind of wood. There are numerous wood "flavors" to choose from, ranging from heavy and robust to light and sweet and everything in between. Consider the cooking equipment next. You can use strategies to produce a good dose of smoke, whether you own a large smoking rig or a small gas grill. Once you've mastered a few fundamentals, which we'll go over in this chapter, you'll be able to smoke the perfect barbecue brisket, holiday turkey, or weeknight salmon fillet, as well as delicious appetizers and side dishes to round out the meal.

Smoking is a preservation method that extends the shelf life of a product while also improving its flavor profile. It flavors, cooks, and preserves food by exposing it to a consistent smoke. Smoke is produced when plant material, such as wood or hardwood is burned. While it is primarily a commercial process, it can be done at home with the proper equipment.

The smoke required to cook food is extremely precise. Fortunately, achieving it is not difficult, but you must be prepared. Because smoke can be powerful, it must flow properly around the food. Even if you're cooking low and slow, it should be generated by hot, fast combustion. This is what produces the much-desired thin blue smoke.

Dark gray or black smoke will impart a bitter, tongue-numbing flavor to your food. Slowly billowing white smoke can cause a stale aroma from your cooker. Worse, both of these can indicate creosote buildup. This thick, tar-like substance is caused by smoke that lingers too long and is tainted with resins, lighter fluid, or charcoal additives.

The following is how smoking meat works: You cook at a much lower temperature than you would grill a steak, and the smoke slowly absorbs into the meat. This "low and slow" process infuses maximum flavor while gently breaking down and melting the intramuscular fat, collagen, and tough tissues to produce a uniquely tender, succulent, smoky, and savory bite. It's not something you can rush. Each roast or cut of meat has a different internal temperature at which it goes from tough to tender. Generally, this smoking temperature can be achieved by cooking with an external indirect heat source ranging from 225°F to 250°F, and occasionally even 275°F. An accurate thermometer is always helpful, but don't worry about the temporary temperature swings when adding wood chips or fuel.

When you go slowly, a few things happen. First, the tissues degrade into juiciness. Bark eventually forms on the outside of the meat. The combination of smoke, protein, and seasonings should produce a firm, deep, dark brown color. Not entirely black, but close. The color is caused by a chemical reaction on the meat's surface. In the following pages, we'll go over the smoke ring and the burning sugar.

Finally, with enough time and smoke, you'll be able to tenderize the meat fibers. With a bite and an easy chew, they should gently break apart. When you marinate meats or bite into filet mignon, you expect this level of tenderness. The difference is that cuts like filet mignon remain tender at lower (rare) internal temperatures of 125°F to 130°F. In contrast, traditional low-and slow-smoked meats achieve pull-apart tenderness only when topping internal temperatures over 190°F (considered an insult to prime steaks).

SMOKING METHODS

Hot and cold smoking are both popular. Hot smoking occurs when food is directly exposed to smoke in controlled environments. Smoked foods can be cooked or reheated as needed. These foods can also be eaten right away without further preparation. The temperature range for hot smoking is typically between 125 and 180°F. This temperature is considered normal for food. 180°F is the ideal temperature for most meats. If the ingredients are exposed to heat and smoke, they can be eaten immediately. Foods retain moisture and texture when heated to this temperature. When a smoky flavor is added to food, it can cause it to dry out. Foods can lose moisture if the temperature rises above this level and fats begin to dry. Smoking is frequently used with other preservation methods, such as drying or curing. Salt-cured foods can be smoked to extend their shelf life.

The next method of smoking is cold smoking. This smoking technique is more of a flavor enhancer than a cooking technique. It's frequently used to season chicken breasts, pork chops, scallops, steaks, and salmon. This is done at temperatures ranging from 68 to 90°F. This temperature is maintained to ensure moisture retention. It is not intended for food storage. It is simply used to give food a smoky flavor. Cold-smoked foods should not be consumed immediately. They must instead be dried before being cold-smoked. Curing removes moisture from meats, preventing bacteria from growing. Cold smoking meat after it has been cured in any other way is possible.

BENEFITS OF SMOKING MEAT

Smoke is thought to have antimicrobial and antioxidant properties. This means that any pathogens on the surface of the meat are destroyed, as are their chances of resurfacing. Smoking, on the other hand, cannot be used as a stand-alone preservation technique. The issue is that the smoke compound only adheres to the outer surface of the food and does not penetrate the meat or food you are attempting to preserve. As a result, smoke's antioxidant and antimicrobial properties are limited to the meat's outer surfaces. This is why smoking must be used with other preservation methods such as salt curing or drying.

When wood is burned, the smoke contains phenol, and other phenolic compounds thought to be natural antioxidants. Oxidation is the process by which the structure of molecules changes as a result of oxygen exposure. Rancidity is a common example of food damage caused by oxidation. When food is exposed to the elements for an extended period, it spoils. As a result, the beneficial compounds in wood smoke slow the rancidification of fats found in meat, fish, and even poultry. This, in conjunction with antimicrobial agents such as formaldehyde, acetic acid, and a variety of other beneficial organic acids, lowers the pH of smoke. The pH of smoke is typically around 2.5. Pathogens struggle to survive in this environment due to the low pH.

Smoking not only extends the shelf life of food but also improves the flavor profile. Smoked meats are delectable! Once smoked and preserved, the meats can be stored at the proper temperature for up to a year! This allows you to access the necessary ingredients whenever you want to cook easily. This makes the meat more flavorful and appetizing. The color of the meat changes as well when it is smoked. The meats appear to be shinier and redder. This simply adds to their allure.

MEAT SMOKING TIPS

Always Cook Meat Slowly

When you taste authentic barbecue for yourself, you will quickly realize that it is not made by smothering your meat in barbecue sauce. The secret to authentic barbecue is slow cooking your meat for several hours over low heat. This is how most authentic barbecued meat stays moist and tender, and it is something you should keep in mind when smoking your meat.

Always Begin Early

When it comes to smoking meat, one of the best ways to ensure that your meat has a ton of flavor is to start prepping early. It is best to begin preparing your meat while it is still raw if you want it to absorb all of the smoky flavors as soon as possible. This is the time to get your meat into the smoker as soon as possible. Remember that the longer your meat sits out, the more dried it will become.

Keep the Air Flowing At All Times

The most important thing you can do while your meat is smoking is to keep it well ventilated throughout the cooking process. You should keep the vents of your grill or smoker open while your meat is smoking. This will assist in drawing smoke from your charcoal or woodchips and causing it to swirl around your food while properly exiting the top.

Use a Pan of Water to Control the Temperature Inside Your Smoker

When the temperature inside your smoker fluctuates dramatically, it can cause your meat to become too tight or dry. The best way to prevent this is to place a pan filled with water inside your smoker. This pan of water will help to stabilize the temperature inside your smoker and even add some humidity, keeping your meat moist and tender.

Never Go Overboard

Overdoing it is one of the most common mistakes that new smokers make. They frequently add far too many woodchips to their smoker or overseason it. When it comes to smoking, the general rule is that you should only smoke your meat for half the time it takes to cook. If you follow these steps, your meat will taste delicious every time.

Keep in Mind that Black Smoke is a Bad Thing

You may notice a few puffs of white smoke escaping your smoker while smoking your meat. White smoke is a good sign because it means your meat is being layered with that addictive smoky flavor you crave. This is a bad sign if you start noticing black smoke coming out of your smoker. This can be caused by several factors, such as your smoker not receiving adequate ventilation or your food is cooked directly over the fire. The general rule of thumb is always to aim for your smoker's white smoke. Avoid inhaling black smoke.

Never Leave Your Smoker Unattended

While smoking meat requires many hours of your time, this does not mean you should ever leave your smoker unattended during this time. You want to ensure a safe cooking environment, so check the temperature of your smoker every hour or two to ensure that it isn't reaching dangerous levels.

Don't Look At Your Food While It's Cooking

One thing you might have to fight yourself against is peeking at your food while it cooks. You should remember that opening your grill or smoker loses heat and adds time to the cooking process. That said, never peek at your food to see how it's doing.

Open your grill or smoker only when you need to add more woodchips, tend to the fire inside, add a water pan, or check the doneness of your meat as it approaches the end of its cooking time.

Check that Your "Bark" Darkens Evenly

The special glisten with a dark brown crust we all love and wish for is a sign of authentic barbecued and smoked meat. This is referred to as the "bark" of your meat and is the hallmark of good smoking. Before you remove your meat from the smoker at the end of its cooking time, make sure the "bark" on the surface is the perfect shade of mahogany brown to ensure it tastes like a little slice of heaven.

Always Season Your Meat to Perfection

Every flavor should play a role in the overall taste, which is one of the critical ingredients of any perfect smoked recipe. You want to avoid having one flavor that overpowers the others and instead strives for the ideal balance of all of your spices.

SALT CURING

Salt curing produces and preserves meats such as bacon, ham, sausage, chorizo, and even corned beef. Salt is the foundation for preventing bacteria and keeping meats fresher for longer without using a refrigerator.

Curing is essentially a salt-preserving technique for meat. Salt aids in their death and prevents this process. When pathogens consume and metabolize meat, the meat's texture, color, and flavor change. These are all indicators of food spoilage.

So, how exactly does salt aid in food preservation? Through a process known as osmosis, salt removes all of the moisture or water present within the meat cells. Osmosis has two positive effects. The first effect is that it dries the meat, and the second effect is that it kills all pathogens. It's important to remember that salt does not refer to regular table salt in this context. Instead, it refers to a mixture of salt, salt cures, and a small amount of sugar.

Bacon, ham, and corned beef are the most common salt-cured meats. Other salt-cured meats include pancetta, liverwurst, summer sausage, salami, and chorizo. Even if salt-curing meats take several weeks, the flavor it produces is worth the wait. During curing, various enzymes in the meat undergo chemical changes that contribute to the meat's flavor. Aside from that, the salt used in curing enhances the natural flavor. This, combined with sugar, herbs, and spices, further balances and elevates the flavors. When salted meat is smoked later, it develops a fantastic and well-rounded flavor profile. Salted meats have not been cooked. Some salted meats are further dried to ensure they are safe to eat.

It works because salt kills any bacteria already present in the meat. It also draws moisture from it, which inhibits the growth of bacteria. It's the perfect one-two punch for long-term meat preservation.

Salt curing, on the other hand, is not simply coating a steak in table salt and leaving it on the counter until dinnertime. It's not a creative or interesting way to use table salt. Instead, salt curing combines regular salt, salt cures, and sugar to keep everything together. Balance is crucial when it comes to salt curing!

Salt, like sugar, draws water out of food and inhibits bacterial growth. At a high level, it may destroy the cells of microscopic organisms, though the food is logically unappealing by this point.

CURING METHODS

There are three methods for curing meat with salt. There are three methods for salt curing meats: dry curing, wet curing, and injecting. For at-home curing, wet curing is the best option. We will go over these options and how they work.

Dry Curing

Remember the different curing methods we discussed in the previous section? The most common is dry curing.

When dry curing, plenty of curing powder should be applied. Rub the meat in the curing mixture before placing it in a container. Place the meat in a refrigerator or other cold area that can keep a temperature of 36-40°F. The most important aspects of curing meat are temperature and humidity control, so pay close attention to them.

Wet Curing

Wet curing is the most effective method for curing meat in small quantities. This is especially useful if you intend to re-cook the cured meat. You'll need to make a brine solution and immerse the meat. The brine aids in the removal of excess moisture and the creation of an ideal balance that prevents pathogen growth.

This method makes it simple to adjust the amount of salt used. This ensures that the salt is evenly distributed throughout the meat and that there are no salt pockets.

Place the meat in the refrigerator or freezer once you've finished curing it. You must keep the meat submerged in the brine at all times and turn it every few days to ensure even exposure to the brine. The meat should not be left out in the open. Keeping the meat in a separate area is best to avoid cross-contamination.

Injecting

As the name implies, you will inject salty brine into your meat using a syringe. It can be difficult to distribute the salty brine evenly utilizing this method, especially if the equipment is not professional. This is not a recommended do-it-yourself solution. This technique may result in salt pockets in the meat.

A lot goes into salt curing meats; it isn't the easiest thing in the world. Measuring, judging weight, and being cautious is all essential. Curing powders are safe and effective in small amounts.

Salt-cured meats are still popular today, not only for their convenience but also for their distinct flavor. If you understand how curing works, you can make cured meats like bacon, sausage, ham, and corned beef at home.

The most apparent advantage of salt curing is that it extends the shelf life of ingredients. For example, if the meats are properly cured and then dried or smoked, their shelf life is extended by a few months. Cured meats can be kept at the proper temperature for nearly a year if stored properly. This is an excellent method for preserving meats, poultry, fish, and even game meats.

Another benefit of salt curing is that it kills any pathogens in the meat. The salt dries out the meat and absorbs any remaining moisture. Pathogens are automatically killed when this occurs. Pathogens that cause disease become unwelcome in the meat.

Salting can also improve the flavor and texture of certain meats. After the meats have been cured, they can be cooked in various ways. Bacon, for example, tastes different from a regular strip of pork belly, doesn't it? This is due to the curing process it goes through.

TYPES OF SALTS TO USE

Numerous curing salt options are available, and the evidence is frequently contradictory. Previously, regular salt was used to cure meat, but saltpeter was added to the curing mixture in the 1600s. The common name for sodium nitrate or potassium nitrate is saltpeter. Salt is primarily used to preserve food. Saltpeter, on the other hand, does not directly preserve the food.

Certain bacteria cannot be killed by salt alone. As a result, saltpeter is added to guard against them. Bacteria in food consume the nitrates in saltpeter, producing nitrites in the process. Following this, another reaction occurs, converting the nitrites to nitric oxide. Nitric oxide begins to form bonds with various proteins found in meat. This turns the meat pink and reduces the possibility of oxidation. Nitric oxide preserves the meat while killing Botulism spores and other harmful bacteria. When using saltpeter, it is always used in conjunction with salt. Saltpeter is not a salt substitute.

This brings us to what is commonly referred to as pink salt or Prague powder. It is another name for saltpeter, which is used to cure meat. Pink salt is so named because it contains a food coloring that prevents consumers from mistaking it for regular salt. The pink color of the cured meat caused by salt-curing is unrelated to the red dye used in the cure. Remember that the activation of nitric oxide is what gives the meat its pink color. Pink salts come in two varieties: Prague powder #1 and Prague powder #2. Pink salt #1 and pink salt #2 are their other names. The former comprises 93% common table salt, and the remainder is sodium nitrite. When cooking meat, poultry, or fish after curing, use Prague powder #1. Pink salt #2, on the other hand, contains 4% sodium nitrate, 6.25% sodium nitrite, and the rest is table salt. This is a dry cure for meats, such as prosciutto, which will not be cooked further.

Aside from that, Morton Tender Quick is used in some recipes. It contains salt, sodium nitrite, sugar, and sodium nitrate. It is not pink as its counterparts are. If you use it at home, keep it separate from regular table salt. Most beginners make the mistake of believing that all curing salts are the same. Curing salts are not interchangeable, so please avoid this error. Follow the instructions if a curing recipe calls for a specific curing salt. Try not to change it. The salts are selected based on the preservation process.

Now that you've learned about the various types of curing salts used for food preservation, it's time to address some common concerns about curing salts. Curing salts are extremely toxic, contrary to popular belief. Curing salts are toxic only in large and excessive amounts. Curing salts should not be consumed directly. You should not inhale it or rub it in your eyes. It should be kept out of the reach of children. Don't be concerned because home curing recipes do not require such large amounts of salt. Furthermore, it does not endanger your health because you are not constantly exposed to it.

Another common concern about nitrites is their link to increased cancer risk. Natural foods contain nitrates. They are more common than you might think. For example, a single serving of spinach contains more nitrites than a serving of salami.

The only thing to be concerned about when curing meats is the risk of botulism. Aside from that, there's nothing else to be worried about. Botulism risk is reduced when the curing recipe is followed correctly, and the required salting and smoking temperatures are maintained.

Curing salts are not the only option. The only reason to use curing salts is to remove all Botulism spores from the meat. You can cure with regular salt, but there are a few things to remember. The presence of iodine in regular or table salt is a significant concern. Table salt is always iodized, and iodine can give the cured meat an odd flavor. Table salt's anti-clumping active ingredients make the dry cure lumpy. If you use it to make a brine, it may contain sediments. Stick to the recipe and use non-iodized salt when curing the meat with regular salt.

If you're using regular salt, consider the size of the salt granules. This can impact the amount of salt used in a recipe. For example, a cup of kosher salt weighs about 5-8 ounces, whereas one cup of table salt weighs about 10 ounces. So, one cup of table salt differs from one cup of kosher salt. When curing meats at home, a weighing scale is an efficient way to measure the ingredients.

Choose celery juice if you want a natural source of nitrate, as these can be found in celery juice. Celery juice causes a reaction similar to saltpeter during the curing process. This, however, is not a substitute for the results obtained with saltpeter.

CHAPTER 2

SMOKERS AND OTHER MUST-HAVE TOOLS

Cooking has been overlooked as a necessary survival skill in the age of convenience and technology. Fresh-grown produce and local meats are more readily available than ever, but the question remains about storing them without canning or smoking correctly. Will you know how to start a fire if you get lost in the wilderness?

To start a fire, you'll need three things:

- **Tinder:** A small, dry, flammable substance used to catch a spark and ignite a fire.
- **Kindling:** A slightly larger but flammable material that catches the tinder's flame and spreads it until it becomes a bonfire. Dead twigs and branches the size of your thumb make excellent kindling.
- **Fuel:** A larger material, usually hardwood or deadfall, is used to keep the fire going once it's started.

You'll need matches or another heat source, such as flint and steel, to start a fire. If you're using matches, keep them in a tight, waterproof container to ensure longevity. Tease apart a piece of cattail fibers until they are fine and fluffy to make a matchstick. Then, using your fingers, roll the fibers into a tight bundle, careful not to crush them. Roll a thin strand of dry grass around the center of the bundle and secure it with another piece of grass. When you have enough, strike your heat source along the side of the bundle, and it should light instantly.

Once you have a flame, carefully add kindling. Smaller pieces of wood will catch more easily than larger ones, so start by placing your kindling around the edges of the fire. When you have a nice medium-sized flame, add larger wood pieces.

We must control the fire when using charcoal. This entails closing the lid and adjusting the vents so that the grill maintains the desired temperature. When you open the lid, you let out heat and oxygen. As a result, the temperature drops, jumps, and then stabilizes. Don't freak out. This is normal; low and slow cooking has been practiced for decades.

Begin with a large fire when cooking with charcoal. You want a lot of charcoal burning, and once the coals are cleanly burning, close the vents and the grill lid to reach your desired temperature. If you plan to cook for more than 6 to 8 hours, you may need to add more fuel. In this case, light more charcoal with a charcoal chimney and add it to the grill when the first charcoal has burned to one-third of its original size. Adding more fuel early in the cooking process is always preferable rather than later.

When burning wood for smoke, you want clean and consistent combustion. You don't want a smoldering, steamy smoke with little aroma. As a result, do not soak your wood chips and chunks. That has been the advice for a generation, but it has resulted in poor smoke production.

Whatever wood you choose, it must be dry. It should be carefully stored to keep it dry. Even in moderately humid environments, dry wood will absorb moisture from the air, leading to mold growth and bad smoke. So, until you're ready to use it, keep your smoking wood in an airtight container.

The first thing you'll need to start smoking meat at home is the smokers themselves. Smokers come in various sizes and shapes; you can buy them commercially or make your own out of barrels, as Nonno did. Smoking is essentially the process of hanging or placing meat on a rack with a smoldering pile of slow-burning wood beneath it. An electric griddle or a small metal bucket filled with charcoal and terracotta pots can be used to make your smoker. You can even smoke meats on your grill if you know what you're doing.

SALT CURING EQUIPMENT

You will need basic equipment, regardless of whether you are dry curing or smoking meats. Here are a few things to get the most out of salt curing.

Grinder

A grinder is essential if you plan on making your own cured sausages. Consider the shape of most salt-cured meats... Isn't it ground meat that's been processed, seasoned, and then cured? You'll have difficulty producing cured sausages if you rely on your butcher to do all your grinding.

Instead, purchasing a meat grinder will save you time and trouble in the long run and provide a much better final product. Aside from your curing chamber, a meat grinder may be your most expensive purchase. These range from $50-60 to hundreds of dollars.

At the very least, your cutting blades should be stainless steel. These will last much longer and cut through frozen or semi-frozen meat the most easily. They are also the simplest to clean and sanitize, which is extremely useful when working with raw meat.

There are vital points to remember if you're looking for a separate stuffer.

One consideration is capacity; if you plan on making 10-20 pounds of sausage or processing most of a deer, boar, or elk, you'll need a larger stuffer. It will make your life much easier because you won't have to reload every 3-4 pounds until you've stuffed it all.

Thermometer

A good, easy-to-use thermometer is essential when smoking meats, in addition to everything else mentioned above! A long cord and a clear digital readout are essential for finding something you can easily read without opening the smoker. You don't need those fancy Bluetooth ones you can control with your phone, though they are convenient.

Curing and Smoking Ingredients

Aside from keeping Instacure in your kitchen, you can keep a few other items in your pantry or kitchen to help you produce the best final products.

In my opinion, high-quality spices are essential. Don't season your game meat with a generic branded spice blend, especially if you're curing it. Starting with a new, high-quality product will produce the best-finished product.

Like a quality spice, a quality herb is essential when using a recipe that calls for herbs. Fresh is always preferable to dry, and if you have a small area with adequate sunlight, such as a porch or windowsill, you can probably grow your own.

The most common spice is ground pepper, which comes in several varieties: black, white, and green. The fruits of the future spice grow on pepper vines and, when ripe, take on their distinctive color. Right before cooking, ground pepper is thought to be the most aromatic.

Smokers

Smokers made of wood or fire are the most basic and have been used for centuries. These will provide a richer, woodier flavor. However, because you are dealing with naked fire, it will require constant tending and attention - definitely not for beginners, as mastering temperature control with these smokers will take longer.

Making use of charcoal is another old way of smoking meat. It will give your meat a different flavor when compared to wood smokers. It's not inferior to wood smoke - it's simply different and ultimately depends on a person's preferences. And like fire, it will be hard to maintain the temperature with these smokers and need constant tending - and fanning for those old-school charcoal smokers. It's not recommended for beginners.

Refrigerator for Storage

A refrigerator or cool place is an essential thing when curing meats. The critical aspect of curing is temperature regulation. Incorrect temperature can lead to pathogens breeding in your meats if you aren't careful. The final product is not suitable for consumption. Curing and storing meats should be kept at 40°F. Anything higher than that, and you run the risk of getting pathogens. You will need a fridge, freezer, or other cold place to keep the meat at this temperature as long as it is cured.

WHAT KIND OF SMOKER SHOULD YOU USE?

You can choose between gas, electric, and charcoal smokers based on your needs and preferences.

Charcoal smokers produce the best smoky flavor, but they can be challenging to control at first.

Gas and electric smokers are simple to use and regulate the temperature; they also cook meat slightly faster. The smoky flavor may not be as authentic as if charcoal were used. If you go with gas, ensure your gas bottle is full enough to last the duration of your smoking session.

After some practice, move on to chicken or turkey, keeping in mind that the meat is leaner and can become tough, so choose a whole bird and smoke for a shorter time to avoid this. If you want to try seafood, go for a robust, oily fish like salmon.

SELECTING THE WOOD

If you want good smoking results, pay special attention to the wood you use. Yes, the type of wood is important here. Different types of wood tend to pair with different meat flavors and would need to complement the meat flavor. Let's take a look at some of the most common smoking woods.

Apple wood has a fruity, sweet flavor. It's mild and goes great with poultry, ham, and fish. Alder is another commonly used smoking wood. Alder has a delicate flavor profile and natural sweetness that complements the flavor of pork, fish, poultry, and other light meats. Hickory is the best way to add some hearty smokiness to red meats and ribs. This is the most commonly used word in barbecues. The pungent and strong aroma of hickory perfectly complements the hardness of red meats. This brings us to another popular wood, oak. Oak is ideal for smoking large cuts of meat for extended periods. It has a pleasant smoky flavor that is not overpowering. This is an excellent choice of wood for short brisket or game meats. Mesquite is another popular material, but it can be overwhelming. Mesquite should be used in the same way that peppers are. When combined with other woods, it is ideal for short-term use.

Maple has a light and sweet flavor that complements ham and poultry. However, use caution when using maple because it can darken the color of meat. Maple, like mesquite, is combined with other woods such as oak and apple. Use pecan sparingly because it has a strong fruity flavor. It also burns cooler than other woods, making it ideal for smoking larger cuts of meat. Add some cherry wood to any meat to improve its color. It goes great with pork and beef.

If in doubt, go with oak or alder. These are the most secure options for smoking meats.

Different types of wood complement various types of meat. For example, lighter and sweeter woods like apple and cherry would pair better when smoking poultry and fish because they can absorb more flavor from the smoke. Whereas heavier, stronger-smelling woods like walnut and mesquite pair well with beef and pork, which require more time for the smoke to impart flavor.

You must now decide on the size and shape of the wood you will use. The largest is the wood chunks. Most commercial smokers use larger chunks of wood because they last longer and can smoke the meat for hours or days. Wood chips are smaller and have a shorter lifespan than wood chunks.

If you want, you can soak the wood as well. Although it is not required, dry wood burns much faster than wet wood. If you soak the wood, properly drain it before putting it in the smoker. This will increase the burn time as well as the smoldering time. Larger sizes, such as chunks, require an hour of soak time, whereas chips require only 30 minutes. Another option is to soak the wood in beer or juice. This will give the smoked meat an extra kick of flavor. Mix some dried herbs and spices with the wood to add even more complex flavors. To control the smoke, adjust the moisture and oxygen levels inside your smoker. Moisture in the wood causes it to burn longer and produce more smoke. More oxygen inside the smoker means larger flames consuming fuel and wood faster.

You need to choose your wood carefully because the wood you will use greatly affects the meat's flavor and taste. Here are a few options for you:

- **Maple:** Maple has a smoky and sweet taste and goes well with pork or poultry
- **Alder:** Alder is sweet and light. Perfect for poultry and fish.
- **Apple:** Apple has a mild and sweet flavor. Goes well with pork, fish, and poultry.
- **Oak:** Oak is great for slow cooking. Ideal for game, pork, beef, and lamb.
- **Mesquite:** Mesquite has a smoky flavor and is extremely strong. Goes well with pork or beef.
- **Hickory:** Has a smoky and strong flavor. Goes well with beef and lamb.
- **Cherry:** Has a mild and sweet flavor. Great for pork, beef, and turkey.

In general, there are essentially three different types of charcoal. All of them are porous residues of black color made of carbon and ashes. However, the following are a little distinguishable due to their specific features.

- **BBQ Briquettes:** These are the ones that are made from a fine blend of charcoal and char.
- **Charcoal Briquettes:** These are created by compressing charcoal and are made from sawdust or wood products.
- **Lump Charcoal:** These are made directly from hardwood and are the most premium quality charcoals. They are entirely natural and are free from any form of additive.

CHAPTER 3

SELECTING THE MEAT

We need to talk about the best meats for smoking. Essentially, any meat can benefit from the deeper flavor that smoking provides. However, larger cuts will perform better in the smoker, especially if they have an excellent marbling of fat on and in them. Slow smoking causes the fats to melt slowly, giving the meat that desired fall-off-the-bone texture.

Here are some cuts that will be good for smoking:

- Pork roast
- Pork shoulder
- Pork butt
- Whole poultry (chicken or turkey)
- Ribs
- Beef brisket Prime rib

Consider jerky, smoked salmon, or smoked potato casserole. Consider the s'mores you made over a campfire. We've got you covered for all of this and more. So many classic foods enjoyed for generations have had a touch of smoke, and we now have the equipment, wood, and know-how to do it properly.

Before even considering smoking, you should figure out what ingredients you want to use. Smoking can be used on various foods, including poultry and other types of meat. What is the significance of taking the cut of meat into account? The time it takes to smoke depends on how thick the cut is.

The most popular smoking cuts are all motion muscles. Spareribs from the loin, belly, beef brisket and ribs are among the most popular cuts of meat for smoking.

Fatty cuts are preferable for smoking. The meat has fat will absorb the delicious smoky flavors better. When smoking meat, choose cuts high in fat and connective tissue. Fattier cuts of meat keep it moist and tender. The fat melts and coats the meat in juices. This improves the flavor and makes it easier to incorporate the smokiness into the meat.

While reading the various chapters on food preservation in this book, remember that smoking is the final step in the preservation process. Before being smoked, the ingredients, whether fish, poultry, meat, or game, are salt-cured.

Everything from poultry and various types of meat to fish can be smoked. Why is the cut of meat significant in this case? The time required for smoking will vary depending on the thickness of the cut. The most common smoking cuts include all of the motion muscles. Spareribs from the belly, loin, beef brisket, and ribs, for example, are the most popular meat cuts for smoking.

It is always preferable to smoke fatty cuts. The fat aids in the absorption of the delicious smoky flavors of the meat. So, when selecting meat to smoke, look for cuts with a lot of fat and connective tissue. Choosing fattier cuts of meat keeps it tender and moist. When the fat begins to melt, it coats the meat in its juices. This enhances the flavor profile while easily incorporating smokiness into the selected meat.

CHAPTER 4

RECIPES

SMOKED TROUT WITH ORANGE & BASIL

Preparation and Cooking time: 4 hours and 30 minutes
Servings: 4

Ingredients:

- 1 Orange zest, grated
- 6 lbs. (2.7kg) ground trout
- ½ c. fresh oregano
- ½ c. Kosher salt
- Apple wood chips

Directions:

- ❖ Butterfly the fish and remove the insides.
- ❖ Mix oregano with orange zest in a dish.
- ❖ Apply salt to the trout on both sides.
- ❖ Sprinkle oregano on the inside of the fish and refrigerate overnight.
- ❖ The next morning, wash off the salt on the trout and refrigerate for a day.
- ❖ Place the trout on a preheated smoker for 3-4 hours and serve.

KELP-CURED BLUE MACKEREL WITH FENNEL SALAD

Preparation and Cooking time: 3-8 hours
Servings: 2

Ingredients:

- 2 whole blue mackerel, headless, remove pin bones, gutted, made into 2 fillets
- ½ c. rice wine vinegar
- ½ tsp. brine from a jar of preserved lemons
- ½ tbsp. finely chopped chives
- 3 tbsp. broken pomelo segments
- ½ tbsp. fine salt
- 2 sheets of dried kelp (kombu)
- Extra-virgin olive oil, to drizzle
- Microgreens like red garnets, shallots, etc.

For Dressing:

- 1 tbsp. Mirin
- ¼ tsp. finely chopped red Asian shallots
- 2 tbsp. Soy sauce
- ¼ tsp. Finely grated ginger
- ½ tsp. Finely grated lemon zest

For Salad:

- 1 young fennel bulb shaved
- 1 tbsp. fresh lemon juice
- Salt to taste
- Freshly ground black pepper to taste
- ¾ tbsp. Extra-virgin olive oil

Directions:

- ❖ With the flesh side facing up, lay the fish fillets on a tray. Sprinkle it with salt. Keep in the refrigerator for 30 minutes.

- ❖ Add rice wine vinegar into a bowl. Dip the fish fillets in the vinegar one at a time and keep them on a plate—brush the remaining vinegar over the kelp sheets.
- ❖ Brush lemon juice on the flesh side of mackerel and keep each on a piece of kelp, with the flesh side touching the kelp.
- ❖ Cover mackerel with the remaining two pieces of kelp and place them on a tray. Keep the tray covered with cling wrap in the refrigerator for 3 – 8 hours, depending on how much time you have on hand.
- ❖ To make the dressing: Whisk together mirin, shallots, soy sauce, ginger, and lemon zest in a bowl. Cover and set aside a couple of hours for the flavors to fuse.
- ❖ Sprinkle salt and pepper over the fennel. Drizzle lemon juice and olive oil over the fennel and toss well. Spread over a serving platter.
- ❖ Discard the skin from the mackerel and cut it into thin slices across the grain.
- ❖ Place mackerel slices over the fennel—drizzle dressing over the fennel and mackerel.
- ❖ Sprinkle chives, pommel, and microgreens over the salad. Trickle some extra-virgin olive oil on top and serve.

TASTY AND EASY SMOKED TURKEY

Preparation and Cooking time: 3 hours and 30 minutes
Servings: 4

Ingredients:

- 1 (12 lbs.) entire turkey, defrosted if solidified, neck and giblets expelled
- ¾ c. salt
- ¾ glass unsalted spread softened

Directions:

- ❖ Place turkey in a cooking dish. Rub salt all over and inside the turkey. Let sit for 60 minutes.
- ❖ Preheat smoker to 250°F (120°C). If your smoker is outfitted with a water dish, fill it.
- ❖ Wash salt off the turkey and pat dry with paper towels. Come back to the cooking dish and treat with liquefied better. Spread with aluminum foil and place in smoker.

- ❖ Cook for around 3 hours; expel aluminum foil. Keep on cooking, revealed until a moment read thermometer embedded into the thickest part of the turkey thigh peruses 165°F (74°C), 3 to 3 ½ hours.
- ❖ Expel turkey from the smoker and tent with aluminum foil. Allow it to rest in a warm region before cutting, 45 minutes to an hour.

MARINATED AND SMOKED VENISON TENDERLOIN

Preparation and Cooking time: 8-12 hours
Servings: 4

Ingredients:

- 4 venison tenderloins (6 – 8 oz. each) remove silver skins
- ½ c. extra-virgin olive oil
- 2 tsp. brown or Dijon mustard
- 1 small onion, diced
- 2 tsp. dried rosemary
- 2 tsp. cracked black pepper
- ⅔ c. dry red wine
- 2 tbsp. soy sauce or tamari
- 2 tsp. honey or maple syrup
- 4 cloves of garlic, minced
- 2 tsp. sea salt

Directions:

- ❖ In a bowl, combine olive oil, mustard, onion, rosemary, pepper, red wine, soy sauce, honey, garlic, and sea salt.
- ❖ Take 2 – 3 large Ziploc bags and put the tenderloins in them. Drizzle the marinade over the tenderloins. Seal the bags after removing extra air from the bags.
- ❖ With the bag sealed, massage the meat so that the meat is coated with the marinade. Keep the bags in a dish and chill for 8 – 12 hours.
- ❖ About 20 minutes before starting the smoker, remove the meat from the refrigerator.
- ❖ Take a grill rack from the smoker and place it over paper towels.
- ❖ Set up your smoker and preheat it to 250°F. Keep the top vent open. Place the venison on the rack and discard the marinade. Place the rack in the smoker and smoke the venison until the internal temperature of the meat in the thickest part shows between 140°F - 150°F on an instant-read thermometer or meat thermometer, depending on how you like it cooked. Add wood chunks or wood chips as and when required. (Follow the manufacturer's instructions on how to use the wood chips). See that the temperature of the smoker is maintained between 240°F and 225°F. It should be cooked for 2 – 2 ½ hours.

- ❖ Once cooked, place the venison on your cutting board. Cover loosely with foil.
- ❖ After about 20 – 25 minutes, cut into thin slices and serve with a side dish of your choice.

SPICY SMOKED TROUT

Preparation and Cooking time: 3 hours and 30 minutes
Servings: About 10

Ingredients:

- 6 lbs. trout
- ½ c. white sugar
- ½ c. brown sugar
- 1 tbsp. kosher salt
- 1 tbsp. smoked paprika
- 1 tbsp. ground ginger powder
- 4 garlic cloves, minced
- 1 tbsp. chili powder
- 1 tbsp. onion powder
- 1 tsp. cumin
- 1 tsp. mustard powder
- 1 tbsp. Dried oregano, powdered
- ½ tsp. cayenne pepper
- 1 tbsp. dried basil
- 1 tsp. ground black pepper
- Wood chips or chunks

Directions:

- ❖ Mix brown sugar with paprika, white sugar, kosher salt, smoked paprika, garlic powder, ginger powder, mustard powder, cumin, cayenne pepper, black pepper, and oregano in a large bowl.
- ❖ Marinate the fish with the above mixture on the inside and outside.
- ❖ Refrigerate the marinated fish for about 3-4 hours or overnight.
- ❖ Soak the wood chips for about an hour and preheat the smoker.
- ❖ Smoke the fish for 2-3 hours until flaky and serve.

PERFECTLY SMOKED SALMON

Preparation and Cooking time: 4 hours and 30 minutes
Servings: 8

Ingredients:

- 5 lbs. (2.2kgs) salmon
- ⅓ c. Diamond Crystal Kosher salt
- 1 qt. cool water
- ½ c. maple syrup
- 1 c. brown sugar
- Maple wood chips

Directions:

- ❖ Prepare the brine by mixing water, Kosher salt, maple syrup, and brown sugar.

- Cover the fish with the brine and put it in a zip lock bag. Refrigerate overnight.
- Remove the salmon the next morning, pat it dry, and leave it in a cool and dry place to form the pellicle.
- Put fish in the smoker and gradually increase the temperature (120°F, 50°C for about 2 hours, 140°F, 60°C for about one more hour, and finally 175°F, 80°C for the last hour).
- Ensure basting the fish every hour with the maple syrup.
- Serve as per individual preferences.

SMOKED PORK LOIN WITH RASPBERRY CHIPOTLE GLAZE

Preparation and Cooking time: 2 hours and 10 minutes
Servings: 4

Ingredients:

- 1 jar raspberry jam, seedless (10 oz.)
- 1 pork loin (4 lbs.) white silver skin trimmed
- 3 tbsp. Spice rub, dry for pork
- 1 bottle (5 oz.) Tabasco chipotle hot pepper sauce
- Extra-virgin olive oil, as needed

Directions:

- Preheat your outdoor smoker or stovetop to approximately 230°F in advance.
- Coat the entire loin lightly with olive oil. Liberally sprinkle the rub on the loin, preferably on all sides.
- Arrange the pork in a smoker & smoke for an hour or two until a meat thermometer reflects an internal temperature of pork as 150°F. Remove the pork from the smoker & lightly wrap them in aluminum foil.
- In the meantime, preheat your broiler.
- Place the jam in a bowl, preferably medium-sized & stir in approximately ⅓ of the chipotle sauce; mix well. Feel free to add more chipotle sauce until you get your desired level of heat & taste.
- Unwrap the pork & cover them with the glaze. Place the pork on a preheated broiler pan & broil for three minutes until the glaze starts bubbling. Slice the pork against the grain. Serve & enjoy.

THE ORIGINAL JUICE AND SUCCULENT ALABAMA PULLED PIG PORK

Preparation and Cooking time: 12 Hours and 10 Minutes
Servings: 8

Ingredients:

- 2 c. soy sauce
- 1 c. Worcestershire sauce
- 1 c. cranberry grape juice
- 1 c. teriyaki sauce
- 1 tbsp. of hot pepper sauce
- 2 tbsp. of steak sauce
- 1 c. light brown sugar
- ½ tsp. of ground black pepper
- 2 lbs. flank steak cut up into ¼-inch slices
- 4 c. wood chips

Directions:

- Take a non-reactive saucepan and add cider, salt, vinegar, brown sugar, cayenne pepper, black pepper, and butter
- Bring the mix to a boil over medium-high heat
- Add in water and return the mix to a boil
- Keep saucing the pork with the mixture before smoking
- Place your pork butt on a slow smoker using apple wood chips
- Smoke it for about 6-10 hours. Make sure to keep basting it with the sauce every hour or so
- After the first smoking is done, take an aluminum foil and wrap up the meat forming a watertight seal
- Place the meat in the center of your foil and bring the edges to the top, cupping up the meat complete
- Pour one cup of sauce over the meat and tight it up
- Place the package back into your smoker and smoke for two hours until the meat easily pulls off from the bone
- Once done, remove it from the smoker and pull off the pork, discarding the gristle and fat
- Place the meat chunks in a pan and pour one cup of sauce for every four pounds of meat
- Heat until simmering and serve immediately!

OREGANO PECAN RUB SMOKED LAMB LEG WITH YOGURT MARINADE

Preparation and Cooking time: 5 Hours and 10 Minutes
Servings: 10
Ingredients for 10 Servings:

- 5-lb. (2.3-kg.) Lamb leg

For the Marinade:

- 3 c. Greek yogurt

- 2 tbsp. Ground cumin
- 2 tsp. Ground coriander
- ½ tsp. Ground turmeric
- ¼ tsp. Allspice
- 2 tsp. Kosher salt
- 1 tsp. Black pepper

For the Rub:

- 1 c. Roasted pecans
- 1 c. Chopped fresh oregano
- 1 c. Chopped thyme leaves
- 3 tbsp. Minced garlic
- ½ c. Brown sugar
- 2 tbsp. Smoked paprika
- 1 tsp. Pepper
- 1 tsp. Grated lemon zest
- 1 tsp. Kosher salt
- ½ c. Vegetable oil

For the Water Pan:

- 2 c. Water

For the Heat:

- Oak wood chunks

Directions:

- ❖ Season the yogurt with cumin, coriander, turmeric, allspice, kosher salt, and black pepper. Mix well.
- ❖ Add the lamb leg to the yogurt mixture and marinate it for at least four hours. Store it in the fridge to keep the lamb leg fresh.
- ❖ In the meantime, place the roasted pecans in a food processor and process until becoming crumble.
- ❖ Mix the pecan crumbles with oregano, thyme, minced garlic, brown sugar, smoked paprika, pepper, grated lemon zest, and salt.
- ❖ Pour vegetable oil into the dry spice mixture and stir until becoming a paste.
- ❖ Take the marinated lamb leg out of the fridge and coat it with pecan paste. Set aside.
- ❖ Prepare the smoked grill and fill it with fuel.
- ❖ Add wood chunks to the smoker grill and start the fire. Set the smoked grill for indirect heat.
- ❖ Place a disposable aluminum pan in the smoker grill and pour water into it.
- ❖ Set the temperature of the smoker grill to 225°F (107°C) and wait until it reaches the desired temperature.
- ❖ Place the seasoned lamb leg in the smoker grill and smoke it for five hours.
- ❖ Check the smoked lamb leg and once the internal temperature reaches 135°F (57°C), remove it from the smoker grill.
- ❖ Place the smoked lamb leg on a serving dish and serve.
- ❖ Enjoy!

AROMATIC CLOVES SMOKED LAMB RIBS TENDER WITH PINEAPPLE MARINADE

Preparation and Cooking time: 5 hours and 10 minutes
Servings: 10
Ingredients for 10 Servings:

- 6-lb. (2.7-kg.) Lamb ribs

For the Marinade:

- 3 c. Pineapple juice
- ½ c. Pineapple preserves
- 1 c. Ginger beer
- 2 tbsp. Worcestershire sauce
- ½ c. Brown sugar
- 2 tbsp. Minced garlic
- 2 tbsp. Kosher salt

For the Glaze:

- ½ c. Maple syrup
- 2 tbsp. Olive oil
- 2 tbsp. Fish sauce
- 2 tbsp. Soy sauce
- ½ tsp. Chili powder
- ½ tsp. Grated lemon zest
- A pinch of Ground clove
- ½ tsp. Pepper

For the Water Pan:

- 2 c. Water

For the Heat:

- Oak wood chunks

Directions:

- ❖ Combine pineapple juice with pineapple preserves and ginger beer. Stir until incorporated.
- ❖ Season the pineapple mixture with Worcestershire sauce, brown sugar, minced garlic, and salt. Mix well.
- ❖ Add the lamb ribs to the pineapple mixture and make sure that the lamb ribs are entirely coated with the pineapple mixture.
- ❖ Marinate the lamb ribs for at least six hours or overnight and store the ribs in the fridge to keep the lamb ribs fresh.
- ❖ The next day, remove the marinated lamb ribs from the fridge and thaw them at room temperature.
- ❖ Prepare the smoked grill and fill it with fuel.
- ❖ Add wood chunks to the smoker grill and start the fire. Set the smoked grill for indirect heat.
- ❖ Place a disposable aluminum pan in the smoker grill and pour water into it.
- ❖ Set the temperature of the smoker grill to 225°F (107°C) and wait until it reaches the desired temperature.

- Once the smoke is ready, place the marinated lamb ribs in the smoker grill and smoke the ribs for approximately five hours.
- In the meantime, combine maple syrup with olive oil, fish sauce, and soy sauce.
- Add chili powder, grated lemon zest, ground cloves, and pepper. Stir until dissolved.
- After 3 hours of smoking, baste the glaze mixture over the smoked lamb ribs and repeat it once every thirty minutes.
- Regularly check the smoked lamb ribs and once the internal temperature reaches 135°F (57°C), remove the smoked ribs from the smoker grill.
- Lightly baste the remaining glaze mixture over the smoked lamb ribs and wrap the ribs with aluminum foil. Let the ribs rest for approximately 25 to 30 minutes.
- Unwrap the smoked lamb ribs and transfer them to a serving dish.
- Serve and enjoy.

GOURMET SMOKEHOUSE BEEF JERKY

Preparation and Cooking time: 12 hours and 10 minutes
Servings: 6

Ingredients:

- 2 c. soy sauce
- 1 c. Worcestershire sauce
- 1 c. cranberry grape juice
- 1 c. teriyaki sauce
- 1 tbsp. of hot pepper sauce
- 2 tbsp. of steak sauce
- 1 c. light brown sugar
- ½ tsp. of ground black pepper
- 2 lbs. flank steak cut up into ¼-inch slices
- 4 c. wood chips

Directions:

- Take a bowl and whisk in the soy sauce, cranberry grape juice, Worcestershire sauce, teriyaki sauce, steak sauce, hot sauce, brown sugar, and black pepper
- Mix them well and pour the mix into a re-sealable bag
- Add the flank steak to the bag and coat it well with the marinade
- Squeeze out any excess air and seal it up
- Let it refrigerate for about 8-10 hours
- Remove the flank steak from the marinade and wipe off any excess
- Place the steak onto the wire racks of your smoker, then place the racks into the smoker
- Smoke for about 6-8 hours and keep adding pans of wood chips (1 pan every hour) until perfectly done!
- Serve!

TIPSY MAPLE GLAZED SMOKED BACON

Preparation and Cooking time: 15 hours and 20 minutes
Servings: 8

Ingredients:

- 1 ½ gal. of water
- 2 tbsp. sodium nitrate
- 1 c. sugar-based curing mix
- 2 c. coarse salt
- 1 c. brown sugar
- 1 14 lb. whole pork belly
- Maple, apple, or cherry woods

Directions:

- Take a large-sized kettle and add water, sodium nitrate, brown sugar, curing salt, and maple syrup
- Bring the whole mix to a boil over high heat and cook it for about 15 minutes until everything dissolves perfectly
- Pour the bring into a 5-gallon plastic bucket and let it cool to room temperature for about 8 hours
- Cut the pork belly against the grain into about 4-6 slabs (keeping the skin on) so that you can fit them in your smoker
- Place them into your brine bucket and weight them down so that they are fully submerged
- Cove r them up and let them refrigerate for seven days
- When you are ready to smoke, remove the pork from the brine and rinse them well under cold water
- Allow the pieces to stand under the fan for about 1-3 hours until the skin is dry and glossy
- Smoke the belly slabs at a temperature of 110°F for about 8-12 hours
- Remove the rinds and slice up to serve!

HONEY DRIZZLED CITRUS SMOKE TURKEY

Preparation and Cooking time: 12 hours and 10 minutes
Servings: 7

Ingredients:

- 1 gal. hot water
- 1 lb. kosher salt
- 2 qt. vegetable broth
- 8 oz. jars of honey
- 1 c. orange juice
- 7 lbs. bag of ice cubes
- 15 lbs. whole turkey with giblets and neck removed
- ¼ c. vegetable oil
- 1 tsp. poultry seasoning
- 1 granny smith apple, cored and cut up into large chunks
- 1 celery stalk, cut up into small chunks
- 1 small-sized onion, cut up into chunks
- 1 quartered orange

Directions:

- ❖ Take a 54-quart cooler and add kosher salt and hot water. Mix them well until everything dissolves.
- ❖ Add vegetable broth, orange juice, and honey. Pour ice cubes into the mix and add the turkey to your brine, keeping the breast side up.
- ❖ Lock up your cooler's lid and let it marinate overnight for 12 hours. Make sure that the bring temperature stays under 40°F.
- ❖ Remove the turkey from the brine and discard the brine. Dry the turkey using a kitchen towel.
- ❖ Take a bowl and mix vegetable oil and poultry seasoning. Rub the turkey with the mixture. Place apple, onion, celery, and orange pieces inside the turkey cavity.
- ❖ Preheat your smoker to a temperature of 400°F and add one cup of hickory wood chips. Set your turkey onto your smoker and insert a probe into the thickest part of your turkey breast.
- ❖ Set the probe for 160°F. Smoke the turkey for 2 hours until the skin is golden brown.
- ❖ Cover the breast, wings, and legs using aluminum foil and keep smoking it for 2-3 hours until the probe thermometer reads 160°F.
- ❖ Make sure to keep adding some hickory chips to your heat box occasionally. Remove the vegetables and fruit from your Turkey's cavity and cover it with aluminum foil.
- ❖ Let it rest for one hour and carve it up!

SMOKED SALMON FILLETS WITH WHISKEY

Preparation and Cooking time: 12 hours
Servings: 3

Ingredients:

- 1 salmon fillet
- 1½ c. Bourbon whiskey
- 1 qt. distilled water
- 4 tsp. non-iodized salt
- ½ c. brown sugar
- 1 tsp. fresh ground black pepper
- 1 tsp. garlic powder
- Wood chips as per choice

Directions:

- ❖ Prepare the brine with whiskey, brown sugar, salt, garlic powder, and black pepper.
- ❖ Cover the fish with the brine and put it in a zip lock bag. Refrigerate overnight.
- ❖ Remove the salmon the next morning, pat it dry, and leave it in a cool and dry place to form the pellicle.
- ❖ Preheat the smoker and cook for 10 to 12 hours between 100°F (40°C) to 150°F (65°C).
- ❖ Ensure to change the wood chips at least three times before the dish is finally prepared (i.e., every 4 hours).

TASTY SMOKED BEEF FILETS

Preparation and Cooking time: 1 hour and 30 minutes
Servings: 5

Ingredients:

- 4 lbs. hamburger filets
- 2 tbsp. olive oil
- 4 garlic cloves, squashed
- Fit salt
- Ground pepper

Directions:

- ❖ Preheat smoker to 225°F.
- ❖ Season meat with garlic cloves, salt, and pepper. Heat olive oil in an expansive griddle. Burn/cocoa

meat on all sides. This will seal in juices before smoking.

- ❖ Wrap every filet in aluminum foil, leaving the highest points of each revealed. Sprinkle somewhat olive oil on top of every filet.
- ❖ Place foil-wrapped filets in the smoker and cook for roughly 1 to ½ hours for medium-uncommon. The cook's reality of the situation will eventually become obvious in the thickness of the filet. Consider a longer cooking time for medium and well-done. Deliberately screen the inner temperature of the meat.

DELICIOUS SMOKED MEATLOAF

Preparation and Cooking time: 3 hours and 30 minutes
Servings: 2

Ingredients:

- 1 (8 oz.) jug stout salsa
- 4 eggs
- 1 onion, sliced
- ¼ c. grill sauce
- ¼ glass mustard
- ¼ glass ketchup
- ¼ c. Parmesan cheddar
- 2 tbsp. sriracha sauce
- 2 tbsp. soy sauce
- 2 tbsp. malt vinegar
- 1 (1.25 oz.) parcel of meatloaf flavoring blend
- 1 tbsp. salt
- 1 tbsp. garlic powder
- 1 tbsp. ground dark pepper
- 5 lbs. ground hamburger, broken into little pieces
- 2 lbs. frankfurter, broken into little chunks
- 1 c. bread crumbs, or more as required

For the Topping:

- 2 tbsp. grill coating
- 2 tbsp. grill sauce
- 2 tbsp. mustard
- 2 tbsp. ketchup
- 1 tsp. Worcestershire sauce

Directions:

- ❖ Blend salsa, eggs, onion, ¼ cup grill sauce, ¼ glass mustard, ¼ cup ketchup, Parmesan cheddar, sriracha sauce, soy sauce, malt vinegar, meatloaf flavoring blend, salt, garlic powder, and dark pepper together in an extensive dish. Mix hamburger and frankfurter into a salsa blend all together. Add enough bread crumbs to unite the meatloaf blend.
- ❖ Line a container with plastic wrap. Pack meatloaf blend into the container. Chill until set, 3 to 4 hours.
- ❖ Preheat the smoker to 250°F (121°C) as the maker's bearings indicate.

- ❖ Line a wire rack with aluminum foil. Position in a cake cup lined with aluminum foil. Use plastic wrap to lift the meatloaf onto the readied wire rack.
- ❖ Smoke meatloaf until there is no more pink on the inside (around three hours).
- ❖ Join grill coat, two tablespoons of grill sauce, mustard, ketchup, and Worcestershire sauce in a little bowl. Treat meatloaf with ingredients.
- ❖ Keep smoking until a moment read thermometer embedded into the inside peruses 185°F (85°C), 1 to 2 hours more.

SMOKED BRISKET

Preparation and Cooking time: 7 hours and 30 minutes
Servings: 2

Ingredients:

- 5 lbs. hamburger brisket, trimmed of fat
- 3 tbsp. mustard, or as required
- 2 tbsp. brisket rub

Directions:

- ❖ Coat meat brisket with mustard. Spread with brisket rub. Let marinate in the refrigerator for 8 hours to overnight.
- ❖ Expel brisket from the fridge and keep it at room temperature.
- ❖ Preheat a smoker to 220°F (104°C).
- ❖ Place hamburger brisket in the smoker and smoke until penetrated with a blade and a moment read thermometer embedded into the middle peruses 190°F (88°C), 6 ¼ to 7 ½ hours.
- ❖ Wrap brisket with aluminum foil and let rest

BURNT ENDS SMOKED PORK SHOULDER WITH CHILI AND CAYENNE RUB

Preparation and Cooking time: 6 hours and 10 minutes
Servings: 10
Ingredients for 10 Servings:

- 4-lbs. (1.8-kg.) Pork shoulder

For the Rub:

- ¾ c. Brown sugar

- ½ c. Smoked paprika
- 1 tbsp. Chili powder
- ½ tsp. Cayenne pepper
- 1 ½ tbsp. Garlic powder
- 1 tbsp. Onion powder
- 1 tsp. Black pepper
- 1 tsp. Kosher salt

For the Glaze:

- ¼ c. Apple juice
- ¼ c. Apple jelly
- 3 tbsp. Apple cider vinegar
- 1 tbsp. Hot sauce
- ¾ c. Ketchup
- 2 tsp. Worcestershire sauce
- 1 tsp. Lemon juice
- 1 tbsp. Honey
- 2 tbsp. Brown sugar

For the Water Pan:

- 2 c. Apple juice

For the Heat:

- Apple wood chunks

Directions:

- ❖ Combine the rub ingredients.
- ❖ Place brown sugar, smoked paprika, chili powder, cayenne pepper, garlic powder, onion powder, black pepper, and salt in a container. Stir well.
- ❖ Score the pork shoulder several times and rub it with the spice mixture. Let it rest for approximately two hours.
- ❖ After two hours, prepare the smoked grill and fill it with fuel.
- ❖ Add wood chunks to the smoker grill and start the fire. Set the smoked grill for indirect heat.
- ❖ Place a disposable aluminum pan in the smoker grill and pour apple juice into it.
- ❖ Set the temperature of the smoker grill to 225°F (107°C) and wait until it reaches the desired temperature.
- ❖ Arrange the seasoned pork shoulder in the smoker grill and smoke it for 5 hours.
- ❖ In the meantime, combine apple juice with apple jelly, apple cider vinegar, hot sauce, ketchup, Worcestershire sauce, lemon juice, honey, and sugar. Stir until incorporated and set it aside.
- ❖ After five hours of smoking, baste the glaze mixture over the smoked pork shoulder and repeat it once every fifteen minutes.
- ❖ Check the smoked pork shoulder and once the internal temperature reaches 170°F (77°C), remove it from the smoker grill.
- ❖ Quickly baste the remaining glaze mixture over the smoked pork shoulder and serve.
- ❖ Enjoy!

MAPLE COLA MARINATED SMOKED PORK TENDERLOIN WITH MUSTARD GLAZE

Preparation and Cooking time: 5 hours and 10 minutes
Servings: 10
Ingredients for 10 Servings:

- 4-lbs. (1.8-kg.) Pork tenderloin

For the Marinade:

- ½ c. Maple syrup
- ¼ c. Soy sauce
- ½ c. Orange juice
- 2 c. Coca-Cola
- ¼ c. Dry sherry
- ¼ c. Chopped scallions
- 1 tsp. Grated ginger
- 2 tbsp. Minced garlic
- 1 tbsp. Kosher salt

For the Glaze:

- 1 c. Ketchup
- ¼ c. Water
- 3 tbsp. Yellow mustard
- ½ c. Brown sugar
- ½ tsp. Chili powder

For the Water Pan:

- 2 c. Apple juice

For the Heat:

- Apple wood chunks

Directions:

- ❖ Mix the maple syrup with soy sauce, orange juice, Coca-Cola, and dry sherry. Stir until incorporated.
- ❖ Season the mixture with scallion, ginger, garlic, and salt. Mix well.
- ❖ Add the pork tenderloin to the spice mixture and squeeze until the pork tenderloin is coated with the spice mixture.
- ❖ Marinate the pork tenderloin overnight and store it in the fridge to keep the pork tenderloin fresh.
- ❖ The next day, prepare the smoked grill and fill it with fuel.
- ❖ Add wood chunks to the smoker grill and start the fire. Set the smoked grill for indirect heat.
- ❖ Place a disposable aluminum pan in the smoker grill and pour apple juice into it.
- ❖ Set the temperature of the smoker grill to 225°F (107°C) and wait until it reaches the desired temperature.
- ❖ Arrange the seasoned pork shoulder in the smoker grill and smoke it for five hours.
- ❖ In the meantime, pour ketchup and water into a saucepan and bring it to a simmer.
- ❖ Add brown sugar, mustard, and chili powder to the saucepan. Stir until dissolved.

- ❖ Remove the glaze mixture from heat and let it cool.
- ❖ Check the smoked pork tenderloin and once the internal temperature reaches 160°F (71°C), remove it from the smoker grill.
- ❖ Quickly baste the glaze mixture over the smoked pork tenderloin as thick as possible and wrap it with aluminum foil. Let it rest for approximately 30 minutes.
- ❖ Unwrap the smoked pork tenderloin and transfer it to a serving dish.
- ❖ Serve and enjoy!

TASTY SMOKED TURKEY

Preparation and Cooking time: 5 hours and 30 minutes
Servings: 2

Ingredients:

Infusion Marinade:

- Margarine
- 12 oz. squeezed apple
- 1 tbsp. Eagle Rub All Purpose Seasoning
- 1 tbsp. paprika
- 1 tbsp. fine ground dark pepper
- 1 tbsp. salt
- 1 tbsp. garlic powder
- 1 tbsp. onion powder
- 1 tbsp. dry yellow mustard
- 1 tsp. cayenne pepper

Directions:

- ❖ Ensure your entire turkey or entire bone in the bosom is defrosted and washed. Remember to take out the giblet pack and neck from within the turkey. Presently make your marinade: Melt the margarine on the stove in a medium size pan.
- ❖ Include the apple and the greater part of the remaining ingredients. Blend it extremely well on low for around three minutes. The night you plan to cook your turkey, you infuse everything over with the marinade. I jump at the chance to just set my turkey in a vast foil skillet that will even now fit in my smoker while I infuse it. Ensure you mix up the marinade every time you fill your injector.
- ❖ You don't need to utilize the greater part of your marinade. It relies on how huge your turkey is. Presently rub the whole outside of the turkey with a light layer of olive oil. Cover the entire turkey with a layer of Eagle Rub. I likewise hurl some Eagle Rub inside the hole of the turkey. I then return the turkey to the cooler and let it marinate throughout the night.
- ❖ On the off chance that you don't have time for this, it is alright. Set up your smoker for circuitous warmth at 300°F. I utilize a blend of apple and pecan for the smoke on fowls. They will deliver a mellow, fruitier smoke taste. Cooking it in the foil skillet makes scarcely any wreckage, and it is

anything but difficult to expel from your smoker when it is done cooking.

- ❖ I cook the turkey for 12 to 15 minutes for each pound and like the bosom meat to get up to 175°F. When it is done, I take it out and cover it with a huge bit of overwhelming obligation foil. I let it set for 30 minutes before cutting. After cutting, I get a kick out of the chance to season the pieces with the juice in the container.

SMOKED GLAZED SPARE RIBS

Preparation and Cooking time: 4 hours and 20 minutes
Servings: 4

Ingredients:

- 1 tbsp. roasted Garlic pepper seasoning, preferably Irvine Spices
- 2 sides of pork spare ribs (approximately 3 lbs. each)
- 1 tsp. garlic powder
- ½ c. honey
- 1 tsp. onion powder
- ½ c. brown sugar
- 1 tsp. lemon pepper
- 2 tsp. salt

Directions:

- ❖ Rinse the spare ribs under cold running tap water & place them on paper towels; pat them dry. Combine the Garlic Pepper Seasoning with lemon pepper, onion powder, salt, and garlic powder in a small-sized bowl and prepare a rub. Rub the mixture over the spare ribs, preferably the entire surface.
- ❖ Preheat your smoker as per the directions provided by the manufacturer and try maintaining a temperature between 255 to 300°F (over indirect heat). Smoke the coated meat until cooked through.
- ❖ Combine brown sugar with honey in a small-sized bowl at the end of the smoking time & spread the mixture on the spare ribs.

SANDWICH WITH SMOKED MEAT & GOUDA

Preparation and Cooking time: 1 hour and 30 minutes
Servings: 2

Ingredients:

- 15 mL (1 tbsp.) olive oil
- 2 cuts of Portobello mushroom
- 1 approx. 15-cm part of Les Trois Moulins Traditional Baguette, cut in 2 (the long way)
- 15 mL (1 tbsp.) Our Compliments Old Fashioned Whole Grain Dijon Prepared Mustard
- 125 g smoked meat (eye of round), daintily cut
- 80 mL (⅓ container) ground Gouda cheddar
- 30 mL (2 tbsp.) fragmented almonds

Directions:

- ❖ Heat the oil in a skillet on medium-high.
- ❖ Chestnut the mushrooms for one minute on every side and put them aside.
- ❖ Spread the mustard on the baguette parts. Organize the cuts of smoked meat and portobello mushroom on every baguette half and top with the ground cheddar. Sprinkle the almond bits on top.
- ❖ Cook for around three minutes or until the cheddar turns brilliant cocoa.
- ❖ Present with a serving of mixed greens.

TASTY SMOKED HAM

Preparation and Cooking time: 4 hours and 30 minutes
Servings: 3

Ingredients:

- 1 winding cut cured ham
- Falcon Rub All Purpose Seasoning
- Sweet Honey Mustard
- 2 measures of cocoa sugar
- Pineapple juice
- 2 tbsp. nectar
- Heavy duty foil
- Foil container

Directions:

- ❖ Get a cured winding cut bone-in ham at the market. These hams are generally sugar cured, and hickory smoked. They are, as of now, completely cooked. We are "twofold smoking" them and conveying them up to temp for serving.
- ❖ If you smoke a new ham that is uncured (these are not normally in most markets), they often wind up posing a flavor like pulled pork. Along these lines, ensure you get one that is now cured and thoroughly cooked for this formula. I like Hormel Cure 81 winding cut bone in hams.

- ❖ There are various other incredible brands out there. I like purchasing a few of these during Christmas when they are at a bargain and stop them. Take your defrosted ham out of the bundle and place the chop side in a foil container. Rub an even layer of sweet nectar mustard everywhere throughout the ham.
- ❖ Shake on Eagle Rub All Purpose Seasoning everywhere throughout the ham. It will adhere to the mustard. Sprinkle a liberal measure of cocoa sugar everywhere throughout the ham, moreover. Pour 1/some water into the skillet. This makes steam and keeps the ham damp. Set up your smoker backhanded at 230°F.
- ❖ I like pecan, oak, apple, cherry, or mesquite. Place your ham in the foil container in your smoker for 4 hours. After 4 hours, brush or splash the ham with around 1/some pineapple juice. Leave the juice that is as of now in the container. Spread with substantial obligation thwart and set back in the smoker at 230°F for another 2 hours.
- ❖ After 2 hours, bring your ham inside and empty the greater part of the juice of the container. Bring the ham out with a substantial spatula and deplete or scoop the juice. This juice will be too Smokey to use for treating the ham or whatever else. Place the ham back in the dish or another if you need it. Consolidate some cocoa sugar and 2 tbsp nectar in a pan, and gradually include some pineapple juice until you make a thick coating while cooking over medium-low warmth. Try not to permit it to bubble.
- ❖ This will just take around 15 minutes. Set your stove to 425°F. I then brush the coating everywhere throughout the ham. Heat the ham at 425°F for 10 minutes. The coating will start to air pocket and transform into a chewy treat-like coating. Take out the ham and permit it to rest for around 10 minutes (a pleasant time to take pictures of it!). Take the ham out of the skillet, lay it on its side, and the winding cuts will tumble off

SMOKED TUNA FILLETS WITH CHAMPAGNE

Preparation and Cooking time: 3 hours
Servings: 4

Ingredients:

- 12-15 lbs. (5.4-6.8kgs) tuna fillets, sliced into ½-inch pieces
- 2 c. water
- 2 c. champagne of choice
- 2 tbsp. white Worcestershire sauce
- 2 bottles of teriyaki glaze
- Juice of 1 lemon
- 1 tbsp. Red hot pepper sauce
- 2 c. brown sugar

- 1 tbsp. Lime zest
- 2 tbsp. black pepper
- 1 tbsp. onion salt
- 1 tbsp. white pepper
- 1 tbsp. garlic salt
- 1 tsp. red pepper
- Wood chunks of choice

Directions:

- ❖ Pre-soak the wood chunks for about an hour
- ❖ Preheat the smoker on medium heat settings and fill the pan with champagne and water
- ❖ Prepare a wet mixture of teriyaki glaze, red hot pepper sauce, lime zest, lemon juice, and Worcestershire sauce
- ❖ Slice the fillets into half-inch pieces
- ❖ Prepare a dry mixture of red, white, black pepper, garlic, and onion salt
- ❖ Place the fillets on the wet mixture and later coat the fillets with the dry mixture
- ❖ Put the fillets on the smoker and smoke for complete 2 hours (moist) or 3 hours (dry)
- ❖ Add water and champagne to the pan if required

HONEY SMOKED TUNA STEAKS

Preparation and Cooking time: 6 hours and 30 minutes
Servings: 6

Ingredients:

- 4 tuna steaks, about an inch thick
- 3/8 c. kosher salt
- 1 c. sugar
- ¼ tsp. garlic
- 1 tsp. black pepper
- 1 c. honey
- ¼ tsp. Prague powder
- 1 gal. water
- Cherry wood chips

Directions:

- ❖ In water, prepare a brine of salt, sugar, Prague powder, garlic, pepper, and honey.
- ❖ Immerse tuna steaks in the brine and refrigerate overnight.
- ❖ Preheat the smoker to 140°F (60°C).
- ❖ Remove the steaks from the brine, dry them and place them on the smoker.
- ❖ Smoke for three hours, flip over and smoke for another three hours to achieve a dry, flaky texture.

SMOKEY YELLOW TUNA DIP

Preparation and Cooking time: Approximately 2 hours
Servings: 8

Ingredients:

- 2.5 lbs. (1.1kgs) yellowfin tuna, cut into steaks

- ½ c. Kosher salt
- Warm water (for covering fillets)
- ½ c. mayonnaise
- ¼ c. soy sauce, reduced sodium
- ⅓ c. diced red onion,
- 8 oz. (226g) whipping cream cheese
- 1 tbsp. lime juice
- ¼ c. chopped Chervil
- ½ tsp. black pepper
- 2 minced garlic cloves
- ½ tbsp. hot sauce
- Wood chips of choice

Directions:

- ❖ Dissolve kosher salt in the water to prepare the brine.
- ❖ Immerse the steaks in the brine and refrigerate overnight.
- ❖ Rinses the steaks with cold water and dry them.
- ❖ Brush the steaks with soy sauce on both sides.
- ❖ Preheat the smoker to 250°F (120°C) and smoke the steaks for about an hour.
- ❖ Prepare a mixture of mayonnaise and whipping cheese.
- ❖ Chop garlic, onions, and chervils and add them to the cheese and mayonnaise mixture.
- ❖ Add lime juice, hot sauce, salt, and pepper to the mixture and mix them well.
- ❖ Dip the smoked steaks into the above-prepared mixture and refrigerate for 30 minutes.
- ❖ Serve with pita or toasted bread.

WILD GAME BACKSTRAP

Preparation and Cooking time: 4 hours and 30 minutes
Servings: 2

Ingredients:

- 2 lbs. elk or deer backstrap or tenderloin
- ¾ c. butter
- 3 sprigs rosemary
- 4 cloves of garlic, sliced
- Coarse salt to taste
- Ground black pepper to taste
- 2 tbsp. Olive oil or as much as needed

Directions:

- Brush olive oil lightly all over the backstrap. Sprinkle salt and pepper over it.
- Set up your smoker and preheat it to 225°F. Place the meat in the smoker and smoke for 1 – 2 hours. Add wood chunks or wood chips as and when required. (Follow the manufacturer's instructions on how to use the wood chips). See that the temperature of the smoker is maintained between 200°F and 225°F.
- Cook until the internal temperature of the meat in the thickest part shows 100°F on an instant-read thermometer or meat thermometer.
- Remove the meat from the smoker.
- Meanwhile, make garlic herb butter: Combine ½ cup butter, half the garlic, and two sprigs of rosemary in a small pot.
- Place the pot over low flame, let the butter melt, and cook for 3 to 4 minutes.
- Turn off the heat and set it aside.
- Place a cast-iron skillet over medium flame. Add ¼ cup butter, remaining garlic, and rosemary, and let the butter melt.
- Place backstrap in the pan and cook the meat until you have a crust on the meat. Use the butter from the same pan to baste while cooking. Cook until the internal temperature of the meat in the thickest part shows 125°F on an instant-read thermometer or meat thermometer.
- Take the meat from the pan and place it on your cutting board. When it cools a bit, cut into about ¼-inch thick slices.
- Spread the garlic herb butter over the meat. Sprinkle salt on top and serve.

SUGAR CURED FERAL HOG

Preparation and Cooking time: 6 hours and 30 minutes
Servings: 2

Ingredients:

- 4 – 6 lbs. ham
- 1 c. sugar
- 1 c. sea salt or kosher salt
- 12 – 16 c. cold water

For Basting:

- ½ jar Texas Gourmet's Mandarin orange Serrano jelly
- 1 ½ tsp. finely chopped rosemary leaves
- ¼ c. olive oil
- 1 ½ tbsp. Soy sauce
- ½ tbsp. ground ginger
- 3 oz. Crown Royal whiskey
- 2 tbsp. honey
- ¼ c. butter
- 1 tbsp. ground black pepper
- 3 cloves of garlic, peeled, minced

Directions:

- For curing: Combine sugar, salt, and cold water in a container and stir until sugar and salt dissolve completely.
- Place the ham in a Ziploc bag or food-grade plastic bag. Take your turkey injector and inject 2 – 3 full injectors of the solution into the ham at different places and adjacent to the bone.
- Pour the remaining solution into the bag. Remove air from the bag and seal it up tightly.
- Keep the bag in the refrigerator for 24 – 48 hours, depending on your time.
- Take the ham from the solution and rinse it well under cold running water. Pat dry with paper towels.
- To make basting mixture: Combine jelly, rosemary leaves, oil, soy sauce, ginger, whiskey, butter, pepper, and garlic in a bowl.
- Start up your smoker and preheat it to 275°F. Place the ham in the smoker and smoke the ham roast until the internal temperature of the meat in the thickest part shows about 160°F on an instant-read thermometer or meat thermometer. The approximate timing is about 45 minutes of smoking per pound of meat. Add wood chunks or wood chips as and when required. (Follow the manufacturer's instructions on how to use the wood chips). See to it that the smoker's temperature is maintained between 250°F and 275°F.
- As the ham is smoked, you must baste it as well. Baste with the basting mixture every 45 minutes. Turn the ham after every 1-½ hour.
- Once cooked, remove ham from the smoker and place it on your cutting board. Cover it loosely with foil. Let it rest for 45 minutes.
- Slice and serve with the remaining basting mixture.

CAROLINA AMAZING STYLE RIBS

Preparation and Cooking time: 4 hours
Servings: 3

Ingredients:

- ½ c. cocoa sugar
- ⅓ glass crisp lemon juice
- ¼ c. white vinegar
- ¼ glass apple juice vinegar

- 1 tbsp. Worcestershire sauce
- ¼ c. molasses
- 2 mugs mustard
- 2 tsp. dried minced garlic
- 2 tsp. salt
- 1 tsp. ground dark pepper
- 1 tsp. Red pepper drops
- ½ tsp. White pepper
- ¼ tsp. cayenne pepper
- 2 racks of pork spareribs
- ½ c. grill flavoring, or to taste

Directions:

❖ Whisk together the cocoa sugar, lemon juice, white vinegar, juice vinegar, Worcestershire sauce, molasses, and mustard in a medium dish. Season with granulated garlic, salt, pepper, red pepper pieces, white pepper, and cayenne pepper, and blend well. Put aside.

❖ Preheat an outside flame broil or smoker to 225-250°F (110-120°C).

❖ Rub ribs with grill flavoring, place them in the smoker or flame broil and cover. Cook for 4 hours, or until exceptionally delicate. The meat will be effectively isolated from the bone. Treat ribs with mustard sauce generously amid the last 30 minutes. Heat the remaining sauce to a bubble and serve as an afterthought.

SMOKED LEGS OF SUCKLING PIG

Preparation and Cooking time: 16 hours and 10 minutes
Servings: 4

Ingredients:

- 2 hind quarters suckling pig, approximately 6 lbs. each
- ½ c. molasses
- 1 tbsp. Five-spice powder
- Water, to cover
- 1 c. black tea leaves
- ¼ c. Chinese black vinegar
- 1 tbsp. ginger powder
- ½ c. dark soy sauce
- 1 c. rice
- 3 c. sugar
- 1 c. salt

For Garlic-Bacon Grits:

- ¼ c. scallions, sliced
- 6 bacon slices
- 1 jalapeno, minced
- 4 c. chicken stock
- 1 white onion, medium & minced
- 12 garlic cloves, sliced thinly
- 1 c. grits
- Salt and black pepper, to taste

For Cassia Apple Chutney:

- 1 large yellow onion, ½-inch dice
- 2 tbsp. butter
- 1 c. apple juice
- ½ tbsp. cinnamon or cassia powder
- 8 Fuji apples, peeled & ½" dice
- ½ c. chopped chives, for garnish
- 1 tbsp. ginger, minced
- 1 ¼ c. sambal
- White pepper & salt, to taste

Directions:

❖ Place the legs in brine (salt, sugar & water mixture) overnight. Using a large bamboo basket, prepare your steamer & cover.

❖ Mix the molasses with vinegar, soy, five-spice powder & ginger in a large-sized bowl. Coat the legs with the glaze & Place them in the steamer.

❖ Steam for a few hours on low steam; don't forget to check the water level and brush the meat with more glaze occasionally.

❖ The meat is ready when you can easily penetrate the pork using a knife. Pull off the steamer basket with the pork, rub the glaze again & set aside.

❖ Remove water from the wok, wipe it dry & line it with aluminum foil.

❖ Add the rice, sugar, and tea; mix well. Heat the wok over medium heat settings & watch for smoke.

❖ When starts smoking, decrease the heat settings to low & place the basket again on the wok.

❖ Using wet kitchen towels between the basket and wok; seal.

❖ Smoke for 10 minutes on low heat settings. Turn on the wok over high heat settings for half a minute & then turn it off. It would continue to smoke & let stand for half an hour.

❖ Just deep fry the pork.

For Cassia Apple Chutney:

❖ Over medium heat settings in a large saucepan, melt a tbsp. of butter & sauté the onions and ginger for 3 to 4 minutes, until soft.

❖ Add apples and cassia; cook for a couple of more minutes & season to taste. Add in the juice & let simmer until reduced by half. Whisk in the leftover butter & check the amount of seasoning.

❖ Place the grits in the middle on a large platter & surround them with apples. Place pig over the top & garnish with chives.

❖ Serve on the side of sambal & enjoy.

For Garlic-Bacon Grits:

❖ Over medium heat settings in a large skillet, cook the bacon until crisp for several minutes.

❖ Place the cooked bacon on paper towels & drain; when cool, chop into pieces, preferably ⅛." Pour the bacon fat off & reserve. Add garlic, onions, and jalapeno in the same skillet, brown & season for 5 to 6 minutes.

❖ Add the stock & let it boil. Slowly sprinkle the grits; Whisk until evenly incorporated. Cover & let simmer until all of the liquid is absorbed, for 12 minutes, preferably over extremely low heat settings. Check for seasoning & feel free to add back the scallions and bacon.

❖ Serve hot & enjoy.

CONCLUSION

Thank you for reading this book. Smoking meat, poultry, and fish is not a new concept. Our forefathers were able to preserve fish and other games to extend their shelf life. The most common methods of food preservation are salt curing and smoking. Almost any meat, from fresh fish and game to processed meats, can be smoked or cured. Once you're at ease with it, the sky's the limit. Learn how to salt cure and smoke meat, fish, and other foods!

Now that you have the necessary tools and knowledge, what are you waiting for? It's time to gather your supplies, gather your ingredients, and get started on something amazing. All you need right now is patience. You'll get the hang of it with practice and patience.

After you've mastered the theory, you can begin to explore the delectable recipes included in this book. These recipes are simple to understand and execute. All that remains after selecting a recipe is to gather the ingredients. You're done if you follow these simple steps!

Have a good time, good luck, and happy smoking!